UNCERTAIN PROGRAMMING

UNCERTAIN PROGRAMMING

BAODING LIU

A Wiley-Interscience Publication
JOHN WILEY & SONS, INC.
New York • Chichester • Weinheim • Brisbane • Singapore • Toronto

This text is printed on acid-free paper. ♾

Published simultaneously in Canada.

For ordering and customer service, call 1-800-CALL-WILEY.

Library of Congress Cataloging in Publication Data:

Liu, Baoding.
Uncertain programming / Baoding Liu.
p. cm.
"A Wiley-Interscience publication."
Includes bibliographical references.
ISBN 0-471-35994-7 (cloth : alk. paper)
1. Computer programming. 2. Decision support systems. 3. Soft computing. I. Title.
QA76.6.L577 2000
005.1—dc21 99-28988
CIP

Printed in the United States of America
10 9 8 7 6 5 4 3 2 1

Contents

Preface

Two well-known measures of uncertainty are probability and possibility—the former may be measured by repetitions of experiments and the latter is employed to measure subjective belief in a fuzzy set—which lead to two subtopics of mathematical programming known as stochastic programming and fuzzy programming. Stochastic programming offers a means of dealing with optimization problems with stochastic parameters, while fuzzy programming provides a powerful tool of handling optimization problems for fuzzy decision systems. From the viewpoint of optimization theory, there is no difference between randomness and fuzziness except for the arithmetical operations on them. This fact provides the motivation to develop a unifying principle of stochastic programming and fuzzy programming.

Furthermore, real-life management decisions are usually made in uncertain (random, fuzzy, fuzzy random, gray, etc.) environments. How do we model decision problems under these circumstances? How do we solve these models? The main purpose of the book is just to lay a foundation for optimization theory in generally uncertain environments. Here we name such a theory *uncertain programming*.

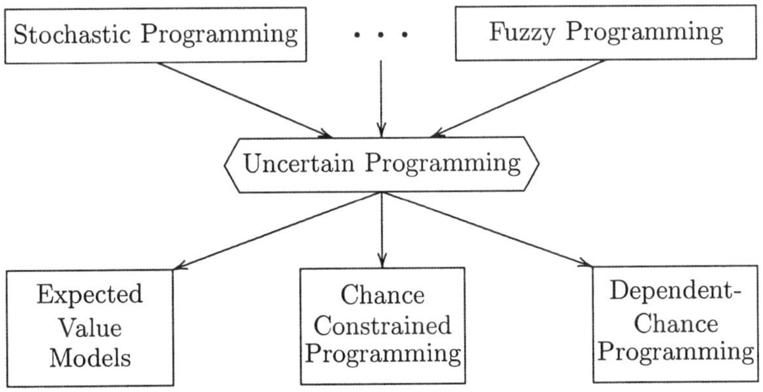

The concept of systems has been widely used in the areas of management, engineering, economics, industry, ecology, computers, and so on. Especially, complex decision systems are usually multidimensional, multifaceted, multifunctional, and treated with multiple criteria in uncertain environments. With the requirement of considering randomness, three broad classes of techniques of stochastic programming have been developed to suit the different purposes of management. The first method dealing with stochastic parameters in stochastic programming is the widely used *expected value model*, which optimizes the expected objective functions subject to some expected constraints. The second, *chance-constrained programming*, was pioneered by Charnes and Cooper as a means of handling randomness by specifying a confidence level at which it is desired that the stochastic constraint holds. The third way, *dependent-chance programming*, is related to optimizing some chance functions of events in an uncertain environment. In deterministic mathematical programming as well as expected value models and chance-constrained programming, the feasible set is essentially assumed to be deterministic after the real problem is modeled. That is, an optimal solution is always given regardless of whether it can be performed in practice. However, the given solution may be impossible to perform if the realization of uncertain parameters is unfavorable. Thus the dependent-chance programming model never assumes that the feasible set is deterministic. In fact, the feasible set of dependent-chance programming is described by the so-called uncertain environment. This special feature of dependent-chance programming is very different from the other existing stochastic programming techniques.

Following the idea of chance-constrained programming with stochastic parameters, in a fuzzy decision system we may assume that the fuzzy constraints will hold with at least possibility α. Thus we have a spectrum of fuzzy chance-constrained programming models. Analogously, following the idea of dependent-chance programming in stochastic environments, a series of dependent-chance programming models has also been constructed in fuzzy environments.

With the development of more effective computers and artificial intelligence, many new complex optimization problems can be processed by digital computers. Perhaps the computer resource can only deal with small-sized problems today. However, it is reasonable to believe that the computation ability should be greatly enhanced tomorrow. This provides a turning point in solving more complex decision problems, thus offering more abundant modeling theory. For example, the objective and constraint functions are allowed to be nonlinear, the stochastic/fuzzy parameters have more general density/membership functions, the structures of models are assumed to be more complicated, and so on. The intelligent computing techniques (genetic algorithm, artificial neural network, simulated annealing, parallel computation, etc.) not only solve uncertain programming models but also bring about a great advance in uncertain programming theory.

This book will introduce a spectrum of uncertain programming models such as expected value model, chance-constrained programming, and dependent-chance programming. Stochastic/fuzzy simulation-based genetic algorithms are designed for solving general uncertain programming models that are generally unable to be processed by traditional methods. Although this type of computing method is a slow and costly way to find the optimal solutions, it is indeed a powerful and easy-to-use tool in complex uncertain decision systems. Some real and potential applications are also presented to illustrate the modeling idea of uncertain programming.

This book consists of thirteen chapters. Chapter 1 offers a brief introduction to the basic concepts of mathematical programming, such as linear programming, nonlinear programming, multiobjective programming, goal programming, integer programming, multilevel programming, and dynamic programming, and moves toward uncertain programming. Chapter 2 provides a genetic algorithm for optimization problems (single-objective, multiobjective, and goal programming) and illustrates its effectiveness by some numerical examples. Chapter 3 lists various methods of generating random numbers and introduces the technique of stochastic simulations and fuzzy simulations. Chapter 4 covers some basic results of expected value models. Chapter 5 deals with chance-constrained programming with stochastic parameters. Chapter 6 illustrates the applications of chance-constrained programming models. Chapter 7 discusses dependent-chance programming in stochastic environments. Chapter 8 models stochastic decision systems by dependent-chance programming. Chapter 9 extends chance-constrained programming from stochastic to fuzzy cases. Chapter 10 extends dependent-chance programming from stochastic to fuzzy environments. Traditionally, mathematical programming models produce crisp decision vectors such that some objectives achieve the optimal values. However, for practical purposes, sometimes we should provide a fuzzy decision rather than a crisp one. Thus Chapter 11 constructs the theoretical framework of fuzzy programming with fuzzy rather than crisp decisions. We also mention that the chance-constrained programming models for fuzzy decision systems, discussed in Chapters 9 and 11, are essentially types of maximax models (optimistic models), which maximize the maximum possible return. As opposed to the maximax models, Chapter 12 introduces a spectrum of minimax chance-constrained programming models that will select the alternative that provides the best of the worst possible return. We conclude the book with Chapter 13, in which the uncertain programming theory is sketched and some further research problems appearing in this area are also posed.

It is assumed that readers are familiar with the basic concepts of mathematical programming, probability theory, and fuzzy set theory, as well as elementary knowledge of computer program. In order to make the book more readable, some background topics that will be useful in reading the book are also presented. The book reflects the most recent developments and emphasizes modeling ideas, evolutionary computations, and applications of uncertain programming, rather than mathematical theorems and proofs. This volume is suitable for researchers, engineers, and students in the field of operations research, management science, information science, system science, computer science, and engineering.

A special acknowledgment is due to Professor Chi-fa Ku for introducing me to the research area and for his constant encouragement. A number of my co-researchers contributed valuable insights and information, particularly K. Iwamura, M. Gen, T. Odanaka, A.O. Esogbue, and R. Zhao. I am also indebted to the National Natural Science Foundation of China for supporting much of the research work. Finally I express my deep gratitude to the editorial staff of Wiley for their wonderful cooperation and helpful comments.

Baoding Liu

Beijing, China
February 1999

To My Wife Jinlan

Chapter 1

Introduction to Mathematical Programming

As one of the most widely used techniques in operations research, *mathematical programming* is defined as a means of minimizing or maximizing a quantity (sometimes multiple quantities), known as *objective function*, subject to a set of constraints represented by mathematical relationships such as equations and inequalities. Some well-known subtopics of mathematical programming are linear programming, nonlinear programming, multiobjective programming, goal programming, integer programming, multilevel programming, dynamic programming, stochastic programming, and fuzzy programming.

It is impossible to cover in a single chapter every concept of mathematical programming. This chapter introduces only the basic concepts and techniques of mathematical programming such that readers gain an understanding of them throughout the book.

1.1 Linear Programming

As one of the most important tools of optimization, *linear programming* is specified by a linear function which is to be maximized (or minimized) subject to a set of linear constraints. The standard form of linear programming may be written as follows:

$$\begin{cases} \max\ c_1x_1 + c_2x_2 + \cdots + c_nx_n \\ \text{subject to:} \\ \qquad a_{11}x_1 + a_{12}x_2 + \cdots + a_{1n}x_n = b_1 \\ \qquad a_{21}x_1 + a_{22}x_2 + \cdots + a_{2n}x_n = b_2 \\ \qquad\quad \cdots \\ \qquad a_{m1}x_1 + a_{m2}x_2 + \cdots + a_{mn}x_n = b_m \\ \qquad x_i \geq 0, \quad i = 1, 2, \cdots, n \end{cases} \tag{1.1}$$

which is also represented in the following matrix form,

$$\begin{cases} \max\ C^T\boldsymbol{x} \\ \text{subject to:} \\ \qquad A\boldsymbol{x} = B \\ \qquad \boldsymbol{x} \geq 0 \end{cases} \tag{1.2}$$

where $C = (c_1, c_2, \cdots, c_n)^T$, $\boldsymbol{x} = (x_1, x_2, \cdots, x_n)^T$, $A = (a_{ij})_{m\times n}$ and $B = (b_1, b_2, \cdots, b_m)^T$. In the standard linear programming (1.2), all of the decision variables x_i, $i = 1, 2, \cdots, n$ are assumed nonnegative. This property is true for almost all real-world problems. If it is not so, for example, the variable x_i is unrestricted in sign, we may replace it by $x_i' - x_i''$, where x_i' and x_i'' are two new variables with $x_i' \geq 0$ and $x_i'' \geq 0$. Thus, the linear programming can be converted into an equivalent one with nonnegative variables. In many real problems, some constraints involve inequality signs $\leq$ or $\geq$. Each inequality can be made an equation by adding a nonnegative variable to a $\leq$ constraint, or subtracting a nonnegative variable from a $\geq$ constraint. The new variables added to the constraints are called *slack variables.* The original variables are called *structural.*

A solution $\boldsymbol{x}$ is *feasible* to linear programming (1.2) if it satisfies that $A\boldsymbol{x} = B$ and $\boldsymbol{x} \geq 0$. The collection of all feasible solutions is called the *feasible set.* A feasible solution $\boldsymbol{x}^*$ is called an *optimal solution* to the linear programming (1.2) if $C^T\boldsymbol{x} \leq C^T\boldsymbol{x}^*$ for all feasible solutions $\boldsymbol{x}$.

It is known that a subset S of n-dimensional Euclidean space $\Re^n$ is called *convex* if the line segment joining any two points of S is also in S, i.e., S is convex if and only if the convex combination $\lambda\boldsymbol{x}_1 + (1-\lambda)\boldsymbol{x}_2 \in S$ for any $\boldsymbol{x}_1, \boldsymbol{x}_2 \in S$ and $0 \leq \lambda \leq 1$. Let $\boldsymbol{x}_1$ and $\boldsymbol{x}_2$ be any two feasible solutions to (1.2) and $0 \leq \lambda \leq 1$, then we have

$$\begin{cases} A(\lambda\boldsymbol{x}_1 + (1-\lambda)\boldsymbol{x}_2) = \lambda A\boldsymbol{x}_1 + (1-\lambda)A\boldsymbol{x}_2 = \lambda B + (1-\lambda)B = B \\ \lambda\boldsymbol{x}_1 + (1-\lambda)\boldsymbol{x}_2 \geq \lambda 0 + (1-\lambda)0 = 0 \end{cases}$$

which means that $\lambda \boldsymbol{x}_1 + (1-\lambda)\boldsymbol{x}_2$ is also feasible. Hence the feasible set of linear programming is always convex.

A point $\boldsymbol{x}$ is called an *extreme point* of convex set S if $\boldsymbol{x} \in S$ and $\boldsymbol{x}$ cannot be expressed as a convex combination of two points in S. It has been shown that the optimal solution to linear programming (1.2) corresponds to an extreme point of its feasible set provided that the feasible set S is bounded. This fact is the basis of the *simplex algorithm*, which was developed by Dantzig [29] as a very efficient method for solving linear programming. Roughly speaking, the simplex method examines only the extreme points of the feasible set, rather than all feasible points. At first, the simplex method selects an extreme point as the initial point. The successive extreme point is selected so as to improve the objective function value. The procedure is repeated until no improvement in objective function value can be made. The last extreme point is the optimal solution. In order to solve large-scale or special-structural linear programming problems, some advanced techniques have been developed, such as the *revised simplex method*, the *dual simplex method*, the *primal-dual algorithm*, *Wolfe-Dantzig decomposition*, and *Karmarkar's interior-point algorithm*. For detailed expositions, the interested reader may consult the textbooks and papers dealing with linear programming.

1.2 Nonlinear Programming

There are many real decision problems that should be modeled by nonlinear programming in which we have to incorporate nonlinear terms in either the objective function or the constraints. The general form of nonlinear programming is written as follows,

$$\begin{cases} \min\ f(\boldsymbol{x}) \\ \text{subject to:} \\ \qquad g_j(\boldsymbol{x}) \le 0, \quad j = 1, 2, \cdots, p \end{cases} \tag{1.3}$$

which minimizes (or maximizes) a real-valued function of a number of real variables subject to a number of constraints. If there is no constraint in the nonlinear programming (1.3), then we call it *unconstrained programming*. If the functions $f(\boldsymbol{x})$ and $g_j(\boldsymbol{x})$, $j = 1, 2, \cdots, p$ are all convex, then the nonlinear programming is called *convex programming*. If $f(\boldsymbol{x})$ can be expressed as $f(\boldsymbol{x}) = f_1(x_1) + f_2(x_2) + \cdots + f_n(x_n)$, then the nonlinear programming is said to be *separable programming*. If the function $f(\boldsymbol{x})$ is quadratic and $g_j(\boldsymbol{x}), j = 1, 2, \cdots, p$ are all linear, then the nonlinear programming is said to be *quadratic programming*. The nonlinear programming is said to be *geometric programming* if the functions $f(\boldsymbol{x})$ and $g_j(\boldsymbol{x})$, $j = 1, 2, \cdots, p$ are of the form $\sum_j a_j \prod_{i=1}^n x_i^{b_{ij}}$ with $a_j > 0$ for all indexes j.

In the nonlinear programming (1.3), the vector $\boldsymbol{x} = (x_1, x_2, \cdots, x_n)$ is called a *decision vector*, which is composed of n real variables $x_1, x_2, \cdots, x_n$ called the *decision components.* The function f of decision vector $\boldsymbol{x}$ is called the *objective function.* The set of constraints, $g_j(\boldsymbol{x}) \leq 0$, $j = 1, 2, \cdots, p$, is called the *constraint set.* The set defined by

$$S = \left\{\boldsymbol{x} \in \Re^n \mid g_j(\boldsymbol{x}) \leq 0,\ j = 1, 2, \cdots, p\right\} \tag{1.4}$$

is called the *feasible set.* A solution satisfying that $\boldsymbol{x} \in S$ is called a *feasible solution.* The problem of nonlinear programming is related to finding a solution $\boldsymbol{x}^* \in S$ such that

$$f(\boldsymbol{x}^*) \leq f(\boldsymbol{x}), \quad \forall \boldsymbol{x} \in S. \tag{1.5}$$

The solution $\boldsymbol{x}^*$ is called the *optimal solution*, and in this case the *minimal solution.* The objective value $f(\boldsymbol{x}^*)$ is called the *optimum.*

The maximization problem represented by

$$\begin{cases} \max\ f(\boldsymbol{x}) \\ \text{subject to:} \\ \qquad g_j(\boldsymbol{x}) \leq 0, \quad j = 1, 2, \cdots, p \end{cases} \tag{1.6}$$

can be solved by multiplying its objective function by -1 and solving a minimization problem under the same constraints. Sometimes, the constraint set is composed not only of inequalities but also equations, for example,

$$\begin{cases} g_j(\boldsymbol{x}) \leq 0, \quad j = 1, 2, \cdots, p \\ h_k(\boldsymbol{x}) = 0, \quad k = 1, 2, \cdots, q. \end{cases}$$

It is clear that q equality constraints imply that we can eliminate q variables in the nonlinear programming by replacing them by the representations of the remaining variables, because we are usually able to solve the system of equations $h_k(\boldsymbol{x}) = 0$, $k = 1, 2, \cdots, q$ such that q variables are represented by others. So in this book, we employ (1.3) as the standard form of single-objective nonlinear programming.

A large number of classical optimization methods had been developed to treat special-structural nonlinear programming models based on the mathematical theory concerned with analyzing the structure of problems. One of the outstanding modern contributions to this theory was known as the Kuhn-Tucker conditions. In order to introduce them, let us give some definitions. An inequality constraint $g_j(\boldsymbol{x}) \leq 0$ is said to be active at a point $\boldsymbol{x}^*$ if $g_j(\boldsymbol{x}^*) = 0$. A point $\boldsymbol{x}^*$ satisfying $g_j(\boldsymbol{x}^*) \leq 0$ is said to be regular if the gradient vectors $\nabla g_j(\boldsymbol{x})$ of all active constraints are linearly independent. Let $\boldsymbol{x}^*$ be a regular point of the constraints of the nonlinear programming

(1.3) and assume that all the functions $f(\boldsymbol{x})$ and $g_j(\boldsymbol{x}), j = 1, 2, \cdots, p$ are differentiable. If $\boldsymbol{x}^*$ is a local minimal solution, then there exist Lagrange multipliers $\lambda_j, j = 1, 2, \cdots, p$ such that the following Kuhn-Tucker conditions hold,

$$\begin{cases} \nabla f(\boldsymbol{x}^*) + \sum_{j=1}^{p} \lambda_j \nabla g_j(\boldsymbol{x}^*) = 0 \\ \lambda_j g_j(\boldsymbol{x}^*) = 0, \quad j = 1, 2, \cdots, p \\ \lambda_j \geq 0, \quad j = 1, 2, \cdots, p. \end{cases} \tag{1.7}$$

If all the functions $f(\boldsymbol{x})$ and $g_j(\boldsymbol{x}), j = 1, 2, \cdots, p$ are convex and differentiable, and the point $\boldsymbol{x}^*$ satisfies the Kuhn-Tucker conditions (1.7), then it has been proved that the point $\boldsymbol{x}^*$ is a global minimal solution of the problem (1.3).

Now we consider an unconstrained optimization which is confronted solely with minimizing a real-valued function with domain $\Re^n$. In practice, the first or second derivatives of the function are often difficult or impossible to compute and hence classical methods are usually unsuitable. Whether derivatives are available or not, the usual strategy is first to select a point in $\Re^n$ which is thought to be the most likely place where the minimum exists. If there is no information available on which to base such a selection, a point is chosen at random. From this first point an attempt is made to construct a sequence of points, each of which yields an improved objective function value over its predecessor. The next point to be added to the sequence is chosen by analyzing the behavior of the function at the previous points. This construction continues until some termination criterion is met. Methods based upon this strategy are called *ascent methods*, which can be classified as *direct methods*, *gradient methods*, and *Hessian methods* according to the information about the behavior of objective function f. Direct methods require only that the function can be evaluated at each point. Gradient methods require the evaluation of first derivatives of f. Hessian methods require the evaluation of second derivatives. The known direct methods are pattern search, one-at-a-time search, the method of Rosenbrock, the method of Powell, the method of Brent, the method of Stewart, and so on. Gradient partan, conjugate directions, and conjugate gradients are known as gradient methods. The Hessian methods include the method of Newton and Raphson and the variable metric method. In fact, there is no superior method for all problems. The efficiency of a method is very much dependent upon the objective function.

The method of feasible directions, the gradient projection method, as well as the penalty function method and linear approximation are employed for solving constrained optimization.

The other active methods to optimization problems are the so-called intelligent computing techniques such as *genetic algorithms*, *neural networks*, and *simulated annealing*. Especially, the genetic algorithms will be discussed in detail in Chapter 2, and applied throughout this book.

1.3 Multiobjective Programming

Nonlinear programming is related to maximizing (or minimizing) a single-objective real-valued function subject to a number of constraints. However, it has been increasingly recognized that many real-world decision making problems involve multiple, noncommensurable, and conflicting objectives which should be considered simultaneously. As an extension of the single-objective case, *multiobjective programming* is defined as a means of optimizing multiple different objective functions subject to a number of constraints, i.e.,

$$\begin{cases} \max\ [f_1(\boldsymbol{x}), f_2(\boldsymbol{x}), \cdots, f_m(\boldsymbol{x})] \\ \text{subject to:} \\ \qquad g_j(\boldsymbol{x}) \le 0, \quad j = 1, 2, \cdots, p \end{cases} \tag{1.8}$$

where $\boldsymbol{x} = (x_1, x_2, \cdots, x_n)$ is an n-dimensional decision vector, $f_i(\boldsymbol{x})$ are objective functions, $i = 1, 2, \cdots, m$, and $g_j(\boldsymbol{x}) \le 0$ are system constraints, $j = 1, 2, \cdots, p$.

When the objectives are in conflict, there is no optimal solution that simultaneously maximizes all the objective functions. For this case, we employ a concept of *efficient solution*, which means that it is impossible to improve any one objective without sacrificing on one or more of the other objectives. The mathematical definition is stated as: a feasible solution $\boldsymbol{x}^*$ is called to be efficient if there is no $\boldsymbol{x} \in S$ such that

$$f_i(\boldsymbol{x}) \ge f_i(\boldsymbol{x}^*), \quad i = 1, 2, \cdots, m$$

and $f_j(\boldsymbol{x}) > f_j(\boldsymbol{x}^*)$ for at least one index j. The set of all efficient solutions in the continuous case is known as the efficient frontier. An efficient solution is also known as a *nondominated solution*, *noninferior solution*, or *Pareto solution*. For detailed expositions, interested readers may consult books such as Steuer [136].

If the decision maker has a real-valued *preference function* aggregating the m objective functions, then we may maximize the aggregating preference function subject to the same set of constraints. This model is referred to as a *compromise model* whose solution is called a *compromise solution*.

The first well-known compromise model is set up by weighting the objective functions, i.e.,

$$\begin{cases} \max \sum_{i=1}^{m} \lambda_i f_i(\boldsymbol{x}) \\ \text{subject to:} \\ \qquad g_j(\boldsymbol{x}) \le 0, \; j = 1, 2, \cdots, p \end{cases} \tag{1.9}$$

where the weights $\lambda_1, \lambda_2, \cdots, \lambda_m$ are nonnegative numbers with $\lambda_1 + \lambda_2 + \cdots + \lambda_m = 1$.

The second way is related to minimizing the *distance function* from a solution $(f_1(\boldsymbol{x}), f_2(\boldsymbol{x}), \cdots, f_m(\boldsymbol{x}))$ to an ideal vector $(f_1^*, f_2^*, \cdots, f_m^*)$ where f_i^* are the optimal values of the ith objective functions without considering other objectives, $i = 1, 2, \cdots, m$, respectively, i.e.,

$$\begin{cases} \min \left(\sum_{i=1}^{m} \lambda_i \| f_i(\boldsymbol{x}) - f_i^* \|^k \right)^{\frac{1}{k}} \\ \text{subject to:} \\ \qquad g_j(\boldsymbol{x}) \le 0, \; j = 1, 2, \cdots, p \end{cases} \tag{1.10}$$

where k is a given number with $1 \le k < \infty$ and $\lambda_1, \lambda_2, \cdots, \lambda_m$ are coefficients of convex combination, for example, $\lambda_i \equiv 1/m$ for all i.

By the third way a compromise solution can be found via an *interactive approach* consisting of a sequence of decision phases and computation phases. Various interactive approaches have been developed and are classified as *feasible region reduction*, *weighting vector space reduction*, *criterion cone contraction*, and *linear search* methods.

1.4 Goal Programming

The concept of goal programming was developed by Charnes and Cooper [22] and subsequently studied by many researchers. Goal programming can be regarded as a special compromise model for multiobjective optimization and has been applied in a wide variety of real-world problems. In multiobjective decision-making problems, we assume that the decision-maker is able to assign a target level for each goal and the key idea is to minimize the deviations (positive, negative, or both) from the target level. In the real-world situation, the goals are achievable only at the expense of other goals and these goals are usually incompatible. Therefore, there is a need to establish a hierarchy of importance among these incompatible goals so as to satisfy as many goals as possible in the order specified. In order to balance the multiple conflicting objectives, some real management problems may be modeled by goal programming according to the target levels and priority structure set by the decision-maker. The general form of goal programming is written as follows,

$$\left\{\begin{array}{l}\min \sum_{j=1}^{l} P_j \sum_{i=1}^{m}(u_{ij}d_i^+ + v_{ij}d_i^-) \\ \text{subject to:} \\ \qquad f_i(\boldsymbol{x}) + d_i^- - d_i^+ = b_i, \quad i = 1, 2, \cdots, m \\ \qquad g_j(\boldsymbol{x}) \le 0, \qquad\qquad\qquad j = 1, 2, \cdots, p \\ \qquad d_i^-, d_i^+ \ge 0, \qquad\qquad\quad i = 1, 2, \cdots, m \end{array}\right. \tag{1.11}$$

where

P_j = the preemptive priority factor which expresses the relative importance of various goals, $P_j \gg P_{j+1}$, for all j,

u_{ij} = weighting factor corresponding to positive deviation for goal i with priority j assigned,

v_{ij} = weighting factor corresponding to negative deviation for goal i with priority j assigned,

d_i^+ = positive deviation from the target of goal i, defined as

$$d_i^+ = \begin{cases} f_i(\boldsymbol{x}) - b_i, & f_i(\boldsymbol{x}) > b_i \\ 0, & f_i(\boldsymbol{x}) \le b_i, \end{cases} \tag{1.12}$$

d_i^- = negative deviation from the target of goal i, defined as

$$d_i^- = \begin{cases} 0, & f_i(\boldsymbol{x}) \ge b_i \\ b_i - f_i(\boldsymbol{x}), & f_i(\boldsymbol{x}) < b_i, \end{cases} \tag{1.13}$$

$\boldsymbol{x}$ = n-dimensional decision vector,
f_i = a function in goal constraints,
g_j = a function in system constraints,
b_i = the target value according to goal i,
l = number of priorities,
m = number of goal constraints,
p = number of system constraints.

Sometimes, the goal programming model (1.11) is written as follows,

$$\left\{\begin{array}{l}\text{lexmin} \left\{\sum_{i=1}^{m}(u_{i1}d_i^+ + v_{i1}d_i^-), \cdots, \sum_{i=1}^{m}(u_{il}d_i^+ + v_{il}d_i^-)\right\} \\ \text{subject to:} \\ \qquad f_i(\boldsymbol{x}) + d_i^- - d_i^+ = b_i, \quad i = 1, 2, \cdots, m \\ \qquad g_j(\boldsymbol{x}) \le 0, \qquad\qquad\qquad j = 1, 2, \cdots, p \\ \qquad d_i^-, d_i^+ \ge 0, \qquad\qquad\quad i = 1, 2, \cdots, m \end{array}\right. \tag{1.14}$$

where lexmin represents lexicographically minimizing the objective vector.

Linear goal programming can be successfully solved by the simplex goal method. The approaches of nonlinear goal programming are summarized by Saber and Ravindran [125] and the efficiency of these approaches varies. They are classified as follows:

(a) Simplex-based approach, such as the separable programming technique, method of approximation programming [62], quadratic goal programming technique. The main idea lies in converting the nonlinear goal programming into a set of approximation linear goal programming problems which can be handled by the simplex goal method;

(b) Direct search approach, such as the modified pattern search method [59][62], the modified pattern/gradient search algorithm [27]. In this approach, the given nonlinear goal programming problem is translated into a set of single-objective nonlinear programming problems, and then the nonlinear programming problems are solved by the well-discussed direct search methods for single-objective nonlinear programming;

(c) Gradient-based approach [84][125], which utilizes the gradient of constraints to identify a feasible direction and then solves the goal programming based on the feasible direction method;

(d) Interactive approach [143][110][37], which can yield a satisfactory solution in a relatively few iterations since the decision-maker is involved in the solution process; and

(e) Genetic algorithms [51], which can deal with complex nonlinear goal programming models but have to spend more CPU time.

1.5 Integer Programming

Integer programming is a special mathematical programming in which all of the variables are assumed to be only integer values. When there are not only integer variables but also conventional continuous variables, we call it *mixed integer programming.* Thus we have the following subtopics,

- (Mixed) integer linear programming
- (Mixed) integer nonlinear programming
- (Mixed) integer multiobjective programming
- (Mixed) integer goal programming

and so on. If all the variables are assumed either 0 or 1, then the problem is termed a *zero-one programming*.

Although integer programming can be solved by an *exhaustive enumeration* theoretically, it is impractical to solve realistically sized integer programming problems.

The most successful algorithm so far found to solve integer linear programming is called *branch-and-bound enumeration* developed by Balas [3] and Dakin [28]. Branch-and-bound enumeration first solves the associated linear programming. If the problem is shown to be infeasible, then the original problem is also infeasible and the problem has no solution. If an integer solution is found, then it is the optimal solution of the original problem. If the solution is fractional, it will be numbered as node 1 (a waiting node). In the waiting node, there must be a variable, say x, with fractional value. This variable is known as a *branching variable*. Then we may impose either $x \le \lfloor x \rfloor$ or $x \ge \lfloor x \rfloor + 1$ on the current linear programming problem, where $\lfloor x \rfloor$ represents the integer part of x. The two possibilities of choice give two *branching directions* that make two new problems. We will solve the two new problems separately by the above process. The whole procedure terminates when there exist no more waiting nodes. The best one among the integer solutions found is the optimal integer solution. If no integer solution has been found, the original problem is proved infeasible.

The other technique to integer linear programming is the *cutting plane method* developed by Gomory [53]. Cutting plane methods can be applied to general mixed integer linear programming. They usually start by solving an integer linear programming as if it were a linear programming by relaxing the integrality conditions. If the solution of the associated linear programming is integer, then it is just the optimal integer solution of the original integer programming. Otherwise extra constraints (i.e., cutting planes) are systematically added to the problem and a new problem is formulated. A new solution is obtained by solving the further constrained problem. Repeat the above-mentioned process until an integer solution is found or the problem is shown to be infeasible.

While a linear programming involving ten thousand variables can almost certainly be solved in a reasonable amount of time by using digital computers, a similar situation does not hold for integer programming. In fact, we have no one good algorithm for solving integer programming. Different algorithms prove better with different types of problems, often by exploiting the special structure of problems.

The original branch-and-bound enumeration is not suitable to solve nonlinear integer programming because the validity of the branching rules is tied with the assumption of linearity. A modified version proposed by Dakin [28] makes the branching rule independent of the linearity condition. In addition, Taha [137] presented an intelligent enumeration for solving nonlinear integer programming problems.

1.6 Multilevel Programming

Multilevel programming offers a means of studying decentralized decision systems in which we assume that the leader and followers may have their own decision variables and objective functions, and the leader can only influence the reactions of followers through his own decision variables, while the followers have full authority to decide how to optimize their own objective functions in view of the decisions of the leader and other followers.

We now assume that in a decentralized two-level decision system there are one leader and m followers. Let $\boldsymbol{x}$ and $\boldsymbol{y}_i$ be the control vectors of the leader and the ith followers, $i = 1, 2, \cdots, m$, respectively. We also assume that the objective functions of the leader and ith followers are $F(\boldsymbol{x}, \boldsymbol{y}_1, \cdots, \boldsymbol{y}_m)$ and $f_i(\boldsymbol{x}, \boldsymbol{y}_1, \cdots, \boldsymbol{y}_m)$, $i = 1, 2, \cdots, m$, respectively.

In addition, let S be the feasible set of control vector $\boldsymbol{x}$ of the leader, defined by

$$S = \left\{\boldsymbol{x} \mid G(\boldsymbol{x}) \le 0\right\} \tag{1.15}$$

where G is a vector-valued function of decision vector $\boldsymbol{x}$ and 0 is a vector with zero components. Then for each decision $\boldsymbol{x}$ chosen by the leader, the feasible set Y of control array $(\boldsymbol{y}_1, \boldsymbol{y}_2, \cdots, \boldsymbol{y}_m)$ of followers should be dependent on $\boldsymbol{x}$, and generally represented by

$$Y(\boldsymbol{x}) = \left\{(\boldsymbol{y}_1, \boldsymbol{y}_2, \cdots, \boldsymbol{y}_m) \mid g(\boldsymbol{x}, \boldsymbol{y}_1, \boldsymbol{y}_2, \cdots, \boldsymbol{y}_m) \le 0\right\} \tag{1.16}$$

where g is a vector-valued function not only of $\boldsymbol{x}$ but also of $\boldsymbol{y}_1, \boldsymbol{y}_2, \cdots, \boldsymbol{y}_m$.

Assume that the leader first chooses his control vector $\boldsymbol{x} \in S$, and the followers determine their control array $(\boldsymbol{y}_1, \boldsymbol{y}_2, \cdots, \boldsymbol{y}_m) \in Y(\boldsymbol{x})$ after that. Then a general bilevel programming has the following form,

$$\left\{\begin{array}{l} \max F(\boldsymbol{x}, \boldsymbol{y}_1, \boldsymbol{y}_2, \cdots, \boldsymbol{y}_m) \\ \text{subject to:} \\ \qquad G(\boldsymbol{x}) \le 0 \\ \qquad \text{where each } \boldsymbol{y}_i (i = 1, 2, \cdots, m) \text{ solves} \\ \qquad \left\{\begin{array}{l} \max\limits_{\boldsymbol{y}_i} f_i(\boldsymbol{x}, \boldsymbol{y}_1, \boldsymbol{y}_2, \cdots, \boldsymbol{y}_m) \\ \text{subject to:} \\ \qquad g(\boldsymbol{x}, \boldsymbol{y}_1, \boldsymbol{y}_2, \cdots, \boldsymbol{y}_m) \le 0. \end{array}\right. \end{array}\right. \tag{1.17}$$

A *Nash equilibrium* of followers is defined as the array $(\boldsymbol{y}_1^*, \boldsymbol{y}_2^*, \cdots, \boldsymbol{y}_m^*) \in Y(\boldsymbol{x})$ with respect to $\boldsymbol{x}$ such that

$$f_i(\boldsymbol{x}, \boldsymbol{y}_1^*, \cdots, \boldsymbol{y}_{i-1}^*, \boldsymbol{y}_i, \boldsymbol{y}_{i+1}^*, \cdots, \boldsymbol{y}_m^*) \le f_i(\boldsymbol{x}, \boldsymbol{y}_1^*, \cdots, \boldsymbol{y}_{i-1}^*, \boldsymbol{y}_i^*, \boldsymbol{y}_{i+1}^*, \cdots, \boldsymbol{y}_m^*)$$

for any $(\boldsymbol{y}_1^*, \cdots, \boldsymbol{y}_{i-1}^*, \boldsymbol{y}_i, \boldsymbol{y}_{i+1}^*, \cdots, \boldsymbol{y}_m^*) \in Y(\boldsymbol{x})$ and $i = 1, 2, \cdots, m$.

Let $\boldsymbol{x}^*$ be a feasible control vector of the leader and $(\boldsymbol{y}_1^*, \boldsymbol{y}_2^*, \cdots, \boldsymbol{y}_m^*)$ be a Nash equilibrium of followers with respect to $\boldsymbol{x}^*$. We call the array $(\boldsymbol{x}^*, \boldsymbol{y}_1^*, \boldsymbol{y}_2^*, \cdots, \boldsymbol{y}_m^*)$ a *Stackelberg-Nash equilibrium* to the bilevel programming (1.17) if and only if,

$$F(\overline{\boldsymbol{x}}, \overline{\boldsymbol{y}}_1, \overline{\boldsymbol{y}}_2, \cdots, \overline{\boldsymbol{y}}_m) \le F(\boldsymbol{x}^*, \boldsymbol{y}_1^*, \boldsymbol{y}_2^*, \cdots, \boldsymbol{y}_m^*) \tag{1.18}$$

for any $\overline{\boldsymbol{x}} \in S$ and the Nash equilibrium $(\overline{\boldsymbol{y}}_1, \overline{\boldsymbol{y}}_2, \cdots, \overline{\boldsymbol{y}}_m)$ with respect to $\overline{\boldsymbol{x}}$.

Ben-Ayed and Blair [10] showed that multilevel programming is an NP-hard problem via the well-known Knapsack Problem. In order to solve multilevel programming, a lot of numerical algorithms have been developed, for example, implicit enumeration scheme (Candler and Townsley [18]), the kth best algorithm (Bialas and Karwan [13]), parametric complementary pivot algorithm (Bialas and Karwan [13]), one-dimensional grid search algorithm (Bard [4][6]), branch-and-bound algorithm (Bard and Moore [5]), the steepest-descent direction (Savard and Gauvin [127]), and genetic algorithm (Liu [93]).

1.7 Dynamic Programming

Let us denote a multistage decision process by $[\boldsymbol{a}, T(\boldsymbol{a}, \boldsymbol{x})]$, where $\boldsymbol{a}$ is called *state*, $T(\boldsymbol{a}, \boldsymbol{x})$ is called a *transformation*, and $\boldsymbol{x}$ is called *decision vector*. It is clear that the transformation function depends on the state $\boldsymbol{a}$ and decision vector $\boldsymbol{x}$. We suppose that we have sufficient influence over the process so that at each stage we can choose a decision vector $\boldsymbol{x}$ from the allowable set S. Let $\boldsymbol{x}_i$ be the choice at the ith stage, then we have the following sequence,

$$\begin{aligned} \boldsymbol{a}_1 &= \boldsymbol{a}_0, \qquad \text{(an initial state)} \\ \boldsymbol{a}_n &= T(\boldsymbol{a}_{n-1}, \boldsymbol{x}_{n-1}), \quad n = 2, 3, \cdots. \end{aligned}$$

We shall be concerned with processes in which the decision vectors $\boldsymbol{x}_i$'s are chosen so as to optimize a prescribed real-valued function of the state and decision vectors,

$$R(\boldsymbol{a}_1, \boldsymbol{a}_2, \cdots; \boldsymbol{x}_1, \boldsymbol{x}_2, \cdots)$$

which is called the *criterion function*, or *return function*. A decision is called *optimal* if it optimizes the criterion function.

In view of the general nature of the criterion function R, the decisions $\boldsymbol{x}_n$'s are dependent upon the current state of the system as well as the past and future states and decisions. However, there are some criterion functions which have some special structures so that we can focus our attention solely upon the past history and current state of the process in searching the values of $\boldsymbol{x}_n$'s. With this assumption, we can represent the decision vector $\boldsymbol{x}_n$ at the stage n by the following form,

$$\boldsymbol{x}_n = \boldsymbol{x}_n(\boldsymbol{a}_1, \boldsymbol{a}_2, \cdots, \boldsymbol{a}_n; \boldsymbol{x}_1, \boldsymbol{x}_2, \cdots, \boldsymbol{x}_{n-1}) \tag{1.19}$$

which is called the *policy function.* Sometimes, we may have a simpler form of policy function, for example,

$$\boldsymbol{x}_n = \boldsymbol{x}_n(\boldsymbol{a}_n), \tag{1.20}$$

i.e., a function of the current state.

Let us henceforth suppose that we are dealing with multistage decision processes whose formulation permits us to restrict our examination of policies to those which are dependent only on the current states. In this special but extremely important case, the optimal policy is characterized by Bellman's principle of optimality: *An optimal policy has the property that whatever the initial state and initial decision are, the remaining decision must constitute an optimal policy with regard to the state resulting from the first decision.*

Consider a problem of maximizing the following special-structured function

$$R(\boldsymbol{a}_1, \boldsymbol{a}_2, \cdots, \boldsymbol{a}_N; \boldsymbol{x}_1, \boldsymbol{x}_2, \cdots, \boldsymbol{x}_N) = \sum_{n=1}^{N} g_n(\boldsymbol{a}_n, \boldsymbol{x}_n). \tag{1.21}$$

To dispose quickly of the problem of existence of an actual maximum point (rather than, say, a supremum), we can either restrict $\boldsymbol{a}$ and $\boldsymbol{x}$ on finite sets of values, or impose reasonable constraints of continuity on the functions $g_n(\boldsymbol{a}_n, \boldsymbol{x}_n)$. Now let $f_n(\boldsymbol{a})$ be the maximum values of criterion function R, starting in state $\boldsymbol{a}$ at the stage n, $n = 1, 2, \cdots, N$, respectively. Then by Bellman's principle of optimality, we have

$$\left\{ \begin{array}{rcl} f_N(\boldsymbol{a}) & = & \max\limits_{\boldsymbol{x}} g_N(\boldsymbol{a}, \boldsymbol{x}) \\ f_n(\boldsymbol{a}) & = & \max\limits_{\boldsymbol{x}} \left\{ g_n(\boldsymbol{a}, \boldsymbol{x}) + f_{n+1}(T(\boldsymbol{a}, \boldsymbol{x})) \right\} \\ n & \le & N-1. \end{array} \right. \tag{1.22}$$

We notice that,

$$\max_{\boldsymbol{x}_1, \boldsymbol{x}_2, \cdots, \boldsymbol{x}_N} R(\boldsymbol{a}_1, \boldsymbol{a}_2, \cdots, \boldsymbol{a}_N; \boldsymbol{x}_1, \boldsymbol{x}_2, \cdots, \boldsymbol{x}_N) = f_1(\boldsymbol{a}_0). \tag{1.23}$$

The system of equations (1.22) is called *dynamic programming* by Bellman [8].

In order to obtain the optimal solutions in reasonable time for real practical problems, we should develop effectively computational algorithms for dynamic programming. In recent years, there has been an increased effort to design more effective algorithms for dynamic programming. To explore the general dynamic programming algorithms, readers may consult the book by Bertsekas and Tsitsiklis [12] in which numerous different ways to solve dynamic programming problems have been suggested.

1.8 Toward Uncertain Programming

At first we consider a classical transportation problem which is related to determining a minimum-cost transportation plan for a single commodity from n sources S_i $(i = 1, 2, \cdots, n)$ to m destinations D_j $(j = 1, 2, \cdots, m)$.

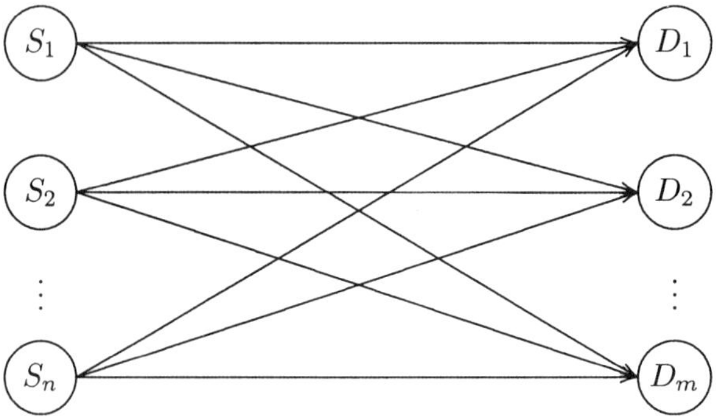

Figure 1.1: A Transportation Network

We assume that a_i are the amounts of commodity available at the source i, and b_j are the amounts of commodity demanded at the destination j, $i = 1, 2, \cdots, n$, $j = 1, 2, \cdots, m$, respectively.

Let decision variables x_{ij} be the amounts with unit transportation costs c_{ij} shipped from source S_i to destination D_j, $i = 1, 2, \cdots, n$, $j = 1, 2, \cdots, m$, respectively. Then the total transportation cost is $\sum_{i=1}^{n}\sum_{j=1}^{m} c_{ij}x_{ij}$.

On the one hand, the total shipments from each source cannot exceed its amount available. Thus we have the constraints $\sum_{j=1}^{m} x_{ij} \le a_i$, $i = 1, 2, \cdots, n$. On the other hand, the total shipments to each destination should satisfy its demand. Thus we have the other constraints $\sum_{i=1}^{n} x_{ij} \ge b_j$, $j = 1, 2, \cdots, m$.

Hence the above-mentioned transportation problem may be formulated as the following linear programming,

$$\begin{cases} \min \sum_{i=1}^{n} \sum_{j=1}^{m} c_{ij} x_{ij} \\ \text{subject to:} \\ \qquad \sum_{j=1}^{m} x_{ij} \le a_i, \quad i = 1, 2, \cdots, n \\ \qquad \sum_{i=1}^{n} x_{ij} \ge b_j, \quad j = 1, 2, \cdots, m \\ \qquad x_{ij} \ge 0, \quad i = 1, 2, \cdots, n, \quad j = 1, 2, \cdots, m. \end{cases} \tag{1.24}$$

If the parameters a_i, b_j and c_{ij} $(i = 1, 2, \cdots, n, j = 1, 2, \cdots, m)$ are all given deterministically, then the linear programming model (1.24) is well-defined and may be solved by the simplex method. However, if some of these parameters are stated as random or fuzzy numbers, then the model (1.24) is not defined mathematically because the meanings of min as well as of the constraints are not clear at all.

More generally, real-life management decisions are usually made in uncertain environments, for example, stochastic environments and fuzzy environments. In order to deal with the optimization problems with stochastic/fuzzy factors, stochastic programming and fuzzy programming have been greatly developed.

Complex decision systems are usually multidimensional, multifaceted, multifunctional, and multicriteria, and include stochastic or fuzzy factors. With the requirement of considering randomness, appropriate formulations of stochastic programming have been developed to suit the different purposes of management. The first method dealing with stochastic parameters in stochastic programming is the so-called *expected value models*, which optimize the expected objective functions subject to some expected constraints. The second, *chance-constrained programming*, was pioneered by Charnes and Cooper [21] as a means of handling uncertainty by specifying a confidence level at which it is desired that the stochastic constraint holds. Chance-constrained programming models can be converted into deterministic equivalents for some special cases, and then solved by some solution procedures of deterministic mathematical programming. However, it is almost impossible to do this for complex chance-constrained programming models. In order to overcome this dilemma, Iwamura and Liu [63] proposed a stochastic simulation-based genetic algorithm for solving general chance-constrained programming as well as chance-constrained multiobjective programming and chance-constrained goal programming, in which the stochastic simulation is employed to check the feasibility of solutions and to handle the objective functions. Sometimes a complex stochastic decision system undertakes multiple tasks called events, and the decision-maker wishes to maximize the chance functions which are defined as the probabilities of satisfying these events. In order to model this type of problem, Liu[88] provided a theoretical framework of the third type of stochastic programming, called *dependent-chance programming*. Dependent-chance multiobjective programming and dependent-chance goal programming have also been presented.

Roughly speaking, dependent-chance programming is related to maximizing some chance functions of events in an uncertain environment. In deterministic mathematical programming as well as expected value models and chance-constrained programming, the feasible set is essentially assumed to be deterministic after the real problem is modeled. That is, an optimal solution is always given regardless of whether it can be performed in practice. However, the given solution may be impossible to perform if the realization of uncertain parameter is unfavorable. Thus the dependent-chance programming model never assumes that the feasible set is deterministic. In fact, the feasible set of dependent-chance programming is described by a so-called *uncertain environment*. Although a deterministic solution is given by the dependent-chance programming model, this solution needs to be performed as far as possible. This special feature of dependent-chance programming is very different from the other existing stochastic programming techniques. However, such problems do exist in the real world. Some real and potential applications of dependent-chance programming have been presented by Liu and Ku [85], Liu [86] and Liu and Iwamura [89]. A stochastic simulation-based genetic algorithm for solving dependent-chance programming models has also been designed.

In addition, fuzzy mathematical programming offers a powerful means of handling optimization problems with fuzzy parameters. Fuzzy programming has been used in different ways in the past. A detailed survey on fuzzy optimization has also been made by Luhandjula [105]. Following the idea of chance-constrained programming with stochastic parameters, in a fuzzy decision system we assume that the fuzzy constraints will hold with at least possibility α, called a confidence level. Then we may construct the fuzzy version of chance-constrained programming. Several papers (see Luhandjula [103][104], Yazenin [150], etc.) had considered fuzzy linear programming or fuzzy multiobjective linear programming problems and proposed a series of ideas of translating the original chance constraints into crisp equivalents via possibility theory provided by Zadeh [153]. However, with the development of more effective computers and intelligent computing techniques, many new complex optimization problems can be processed by digital computers. This enables Liu and Iwamura [90][91] and Liu [95] to construct a generally theoretical framework of nonlinear chance-constrained programming as well as chance-constrained multiobjective programming and chance-constrained goal programming with fuzzy coefficients. A fuzzy simulation-based genetic algorithm was also presented to solve general chance-constrained programming models. Following the idea of dependent-chance programming in stochastic environments, Liu [99] provided a theory of dependent-chance programming as well as dependent-chance multiobjective programming and dependent-chance goal programming in fuzzy environments. A fuzzy simulation-based genetic algorithm for solving dependent-chance programming models was also designed.

Traditionally, mathematical programming models produce crisp decision vectors such that some objectives achieve the optimal values. However, for practical purposes, we should provide a fuzzy decision rather than a crisp one. Bouchon-Meunier et al. [15] surveyed various approaches to maximizing a real-valued function over a fuzzy set. Buckley and Hayashi [17] presented a fuzzy genetic algorithm for maximizing a real-valued function by selecting an optimal fuzzy set and applying it to fuzzy optimization, fuzzy maximum flow problem, fuzzy regression, and tuning a fuzzy controller. More generally, Liu and Iwamura [101] provided a spectrum of chance-constrained programming as well as chance-constrained multiobjective programming and chance-constrained goal programming with fuzzy decisions, while Liu [100] constructed the framework of dependent-chance programming and dependent-chance multiobjective programming as well as dependent-chance goal programming with fuzzy decisions. The fuzzy simulation-based genetic algorithm has also been revised for solving these fuzzy programming models with fuzzy decisions.

Since we would like to provide a unifying principle of stochastic programming and fuzzy programming, this book uses the term *uncertain programming* to represent mathematical programming with uncertain factors (randomness, fuzziness, fuzzy randomness, grayness, etc.). The main purpose of the book is to lay a theoretical foundation for uncertain programming.

Chapter 2

Genetic Algorithms

Genetic algorithms are a stochastic search method for optimization problems based on the mechanics of natural selection and natural genetics (i.e., the principle of evolution—survival of the fittest). Genetic algorithms have demonstrated considerable success in providing good solutions to many complex optimization problems and received more and more attentions during the past three decades. When the objective functions to be optimized in the optimization problems are multimodal or the search spaces are particularly irregular, algorithms need to be highly robust in order to avoid getting stuck at a local optimal solution. The advantage of genetic algorithms is just to obtain the global optimal solution fairly. In addition, genetic algorithms do not require the specific mathematical analysis of optimization problems, which makes genetic algorithms themselves easily coded and employed by users who are not necessarily good at mathematics and algorithms.

One of the important technical terms in genetic algorithms is *chromosome*, which is usually a string of symbols or numbers. A chromosome is a coding of a solution of an optimization problem, not necessarily the solution itself. Genetic algorithms start with an initial set of random-generated chromosomes called a *population*. The number of individuals in the population is a predetermined integer and is called *population size*. All chromosomes are evaluated by the so-called *evaluation function*, which is some measure of *fitness*. A new population will be formed by a *selection process* using some *sampling mechanism* based on the fitness values. The cycle from one population to the next one is called a *generation*. In each new generation, all chromosomes will be updated by genetic operators—*crossover* and *mutation*. The revised chromosomes are also called *offspring*. The selection process selects chromosomes to form a new population and the genetic system enters a new generation. After performing the genetic system a given number of cycles, we decode the best chromosome into a solution which is regarded as the optimal solution of the optimization problem.

Genetic algorithms (evolution programs, evolution strategies, and genetic programming) have been well-documented in the literature, such as in Holland [58], Goldberg [52], Michalewicz [111], Fogel [45], Koza [79][80], Bäck [2], and Mitchell [113], and applied to a wide variety of problems, such as optimal control problems, transportation problems, traveling salesman problems, drawing graphs, scheduling, group technology, facility layout and location, statistics, and pattern recognition.

The aim of this chapter is not to present a detailed survey on genetic algorithms. In fact, this chapter only attempts to introduce an effective genetic algorithm for complex optimization problems in which we do not assume any convexity of feasible set or unimodality and differentiability of objective function. Moreover, we design this algorithm for solving not only single-objective optimization but also multiobjective programming and goal programming. Finally, we illustrate the effectiveness of genetic algorithms by some numerical examples.

2.1 Optimization Problems

The genetic algorithms will be designed for solving the following single-objective programming and multiobjective programming as well as goal programming models.

The general form of single-objective mathematical programming is written as follows,

$$\begin{cases} \max\ f(\boldsymbol{x}) \\ \text{subject to:} \\ \qquad g_j(\boldsymbol{x}) \le 0, \quad j = 1, 2, \cdots, p \end{cases} \tag{2.1}$$

which maximizes (sometimes minimizes) a real-valued function of a number of real variables subject to a number of constraints, where $\boldsymbol{x} = (x_1, x_2, \cdots, x_n)$ is an n-dimensional decision vector, $f(\boldsymbol{x})$ and $g_j(\boldsymbol{x})$, $j = 1, 2, \cdots, p$ are general real-valued functions.

Multiobjective programming is defined as a means of optimizing m different objective functions subject to a number of constraints, i.e.,

$$\begin{cases} \max\ [f_1(\boldsymbol{x}), f_2(\boldsymbol{x}), \cdots, f_m(\boldsymbol{x})] \\ \text{subject to:} \\ \qquad g_j(\boldsymbol{x}) \le 0, \quad j = 1, 2, \cdots, p \end{cases} \tag{2.2}$$

where $f_i(\boldsymbol{x})$, $i = 1, 2, \cdots, m$ and $g_j(\boldsymbol{x})$, $j = 1, 2, \cdots, p$ are general real-valued functions of decision vector $\boldsymbol{x} = (x_1, x_2, \cdots, x_n)$.

A typical nonlinear goal programming is written in the following form according to the target levels and priority structure set by the decision-maker,

$$\begin{cases} \min \sum_{j=1}^{l} P_j \sum_{i=1}^{m} (u_{ij} d_i^+ + v_{ij} d_i^-) \\ \text{subject to:} \\ \qquad f_i(\boldsymbol{x}) + d_i^- - d_i^+ = b_i, \quad i = 1, 2, \cdots, m \\ \qquad g_j(\boldsymbol{x}) \le 0, \qquad\qquad\quad j = 1, 2, \cdots, p \\ \qquad d_i^-, d_i^+ \ge 0, \qquad\qquad\quad i = 1, 2, \cdots, m \end{cases} \tag{2.3}$$

where P_j = the preemptive priority factor which expresses the relative importance of various goals, $P_j \gg P_{j+1}$, for all j, u_{ij} = weighting factor corresponding to positive deviation for goal i with priority j assigned, v_{ij} = weighting factor corresponding to negative deviation for goal i with priority j assigned, d_i^+ = positive deviation from the target of goal i, d_i^- = negative deviation from the target of goal i, $\boldsymbol{x}$ = n-dimensional decision vector, f_i = a function in goal constraints, g_j = a function in real constraints, b_i = the target value according to goal i, l = number of priorities, m = number of goal constraints, and p = number of real constraints.

In the above-mentioned three types of mathematical programming models, there is no equality constraint. In fact, as we will discuss later, all potential equality constraints can be eliminated. We also mention that there is no unimodality assumption on objective functions or convexity assumption on feasible sets.

2.2 Representation Structure

There are many ways to represent a solution of optimization problems. Binary vector and floating vector are two popular representation structures.

We can use a binary vector as a chromosome to represent a real value of a decision variable, where the length of the vector depends on the required precision. The necessity for binary coding has received considerable criticism.

An alternative approach to represent a solution is the floating point implementation in which each chromosome vector is coded as a vector of floating numbers, of the same length as the solution vector. Here we use a vector $V = (x_1, x_2, \cdots, x_n)$ as a chromosome to represent a solution $\boldsymbol{x} = (x_1, x_2, \cdots, x_n)$ of the optimization problem, where n is the dimension.

2.3 Handling Constraints

The main idea of handling constraints lies in (i) an elimination of the equalities in the set of constraints, and (ii) careful design of special genetic operators which guarantee to keep all chromosomes within the feasible solution set.

In the mathematical programming models, if there are some equality constraints, for example, $h_k(\boldsymbol{x}) = 0$, $k = 1, 2, \cdots, q$, we should eliminate the q equality constraints by replacing q variables of them by the representations of the remaining variables, where the representations are obtained by solving the system of equalities in the constraints. To ensure that the chromosomes are feasible, we should check all of the new chromosomes generated by genetic operators. The detailed techniques will be stated later. We suggest that a function is designed for each optimization problem, the output value 1 means that the chromosome is feasible, 0 infeasible. For example, we can make a subfunction to the constraints $g_j(\boldsymbol{x}) \leq 0$, $j = 1, 2, \cdots, p$ as follows,

for $j = 1$ *to* p *do*
  if $(g_j(\boldsymbol{x}) > 0)$ *return 0;*
endfor
return 1.

We strongly suggest that the program designer should pay more attention to the *hidden constraints*, which indicate that some points cannot be an optimal solution even when they are indeed feasible. For example, the feasible set of mathematical programming model

$$\max_{x \in \Re} \exp\left[-x^2\right]$$

is the whole line $\Re$. However, we can believe that the optimal solution is on $[-5, +5]$ by some mathematical analysis. Hence we should add one constraint

$$-5 \leq x \leq 5$$

to reduce the search space of the computer program. Such a hidden constraint is not very difficult to find, especially in real management problems. You can speed up the evolution process of your problem if you follow this suggestion: *Reduce the search space as much as possible by adding hidden constraints.* Therefore, do not detest the mathematical analysis or experience of your problem.

Finally, we should employ some constraint-handling methods in order to save the time spent on infeasible chromosomes. For example, we may convert the infeasible chromosomes into feasible ones when infeasible chromosomes are generated by genetic operators. However, these methods are generally problem-dependent. Therefore we should carefully design the initialization process and genetic operators for each given optimization problem.

2.4 Initialization Process

We define an integer *pop_size* as the number of chromosomes and initialize *pop_size* chromosomes randomly. Usually, it is difficult for complex optimization problems to produce feasible chromosomes explicitly. Thus we employ one of the following two ways as the initialization process, depending on what type of information the decision-maker can present.

The first case is that the decision-maker can determine an interior point, denoted by V_0, in the constraint set. This is very possible for real decision problems. Now let M be an appropriate large positive number which ensures that all the genetic operators are probabilistically complete for the feasible solutions. Certainly, the choice of M is problem dependent. The *pop_size* chromosomes will be produced in the following way. We randomly select a direction $\mathbf{d}$ in $\Re^n$ and define a chromosome V as $V_0 + M \cdot \mathbf{d}$ if it is feasible for the inequality constraints. Otherwise, we set M as a random number between 0 and M until $V_0 + M \cdot \mathbf{d}$ is feasible. We mention that a feasible solution for the inequality constraints can be found in finite times by taking a new random number M since V_0 is an interior point. Repeat this process *pop_size* times and produce *pop_size* initial feasible chromosomes $V_1, V_2, \cdots, V_{pop\_size}$.

The second case is that the decision-maker can predetermine a region which contains the optimal solution (not necessarily the whole feasible set). Such a region is also problem dependent. At any rate, the decision-maker can provide such a region, only it may be a bit too large. Usually, this region will be designed to have a nice sharp, for example, n-dimensional hypercube, because the computer can easily sample points from a hypercube. We generate a random point from the hypercube and check the feasibility of this point. If it is feasible, then it will be accepted as a chromosome. If not, then we regenerate a point from the hypercube randomly until a feasible one is obtained. We can make *pop_size* initial feasible chromosomes $V_1, V_2, \cdots, V_{pop\_size}$ by repeating the above process *pop_size* times.

2.5 Evaluation Function

Evaluation function, denoted by $eval(V)$, is to assign a probability of reproduction to each chromosome V so that its likelihood of being selected is proportional to its fitness relative to the other chromosomes in the population. That is, the chromosomes with higher fitness will have more chance to produce offspring by using *roulette wheel selection.*

Let $V_1, V_2, \cdots, V_{pop\_size}$ be the *pop_size* chromosomes at the current generation. One well-known evaluation function is based on allocation of reproductive trials according to rank rather than actual objective values. No matter what type of mathematical programming (single-objective, multiobjective, or goal programming) it is, it is reasonable to assume that the decision-maker can give an order relationship among the *pop_size* chromosomes $V_1, V_2, \cdots, V_{pop\_size}$ such that the *pop_size* chromosomes can be rearranged from good to bad (i.e., the better the chromosome is, the smaller the ordinal number it has). For example, for a single-objective maximizing problem, a chromosome with larger objective value is better; for a multiobjective programming model, we may define a preference function to evaluate the chromosomes; for a goal programming model, we have the following order relationship for the chromosomes: for any two chromosomes, if the higher-priority objectives are equal, then, in the current priority level, the one with minimal objective value is better, and if two different chromosomes have the same objective values at every level, then we are indifferent between them. We will later illustrate this issue with some numerical examples.

Now let a parameter $a \in (0,1)$ in the genetic system be given. We can define the so-called *rank-based evaluation function* as follows,

$$eval(V_i) = a(1-a)^{i-1}, \qquad i = 1, 2, \cdots, pop\_size. \tag{2.4}$$

We mention that $i = 1$ means the best individual, $i = pop\_size$ the worst individual.

The second evaluation function is designed by introducing a scaling mechanism based on the actual objectives. Let $f_1, f_2, \cdots, f_{pop\_size}$ denote the original fitness (i.e., the objectives) of chromosomes $V_1, V_2, \cdots, V_{pop\_size}$, respectively. Usually, the original fitness proportionate-reproduction scheme frequently causes two significant difficulties: premature convergence termination at early generations, and stalling at late generations. To overcome these two problems, Goldberg [52] suggested a linear-fitness scaling scheme,

$$f_i' = af_i + b, \qquad i = 1, 2, \cdots, pop\_size \tag{2.5}$$

where f_i' are the new fitness values, $i = 1, 2, \cdots, pop\_size$. Parameters a and b are normally selected so that the average fitness is mapped to itself and the best fitness is increased by a designed multiple of the average fitness. For this case, the evaluation function is defined by

$$eval(V_i) = f_i' / \sum_{j=1}^{pop\_size} f_j', \qquad i = 1, 2, \cdots, pop\_size. \tag{2.6}$$

However, this mechanism assumes that the user has knowledge of the characteristics of the function so that the parameters a and b are designed reasonably.

Gen, Liu and Ida [49] presented a type of evaluation function which is between a rank-based evaluation function and a linear-fitness scaling scheme. We define three preference parameters p_1, p_0, and p_2 $(0 < p_1 < p_0 < p_2 < 1)$, which can determine three critical numbers u_1, u_0, and u_2 (taken from the set of objective values of the *pop_size* chromosomes) such that there are $(p_1 \cdot \textit{pop\_size})$, $(p_0 \cdot \textit{pop\_size})$, and $(p_2 \cdot \textit{pop\_size})$ chromosomes whose objective values are less than u_1, u_0, and u_2, respectively, in the set of the *pop_size* chromosomes in the current iteration.

For the maximizing problem, the original fitness u_1 maps to $e^{-1} \approx 0.37$, the original fitness u_0 maps to 1, and the original fitness u_2 maps to $2 - e^{-1} \approx 1.63$. Then the relationship between the original fitness u and the exponential fitness u' is

$$u' = \begin{cases} \exp\left[-\dfrac{u-u_0}{u_1-u_0}\right], & u < u_0 \\ 2 - \exp\left[-\dfrac{u-u_0}{u_2-u_0}\right], & u \geq u_0 \end{cases} \tag{2.7}$$

which is shown in Figure 2.1.

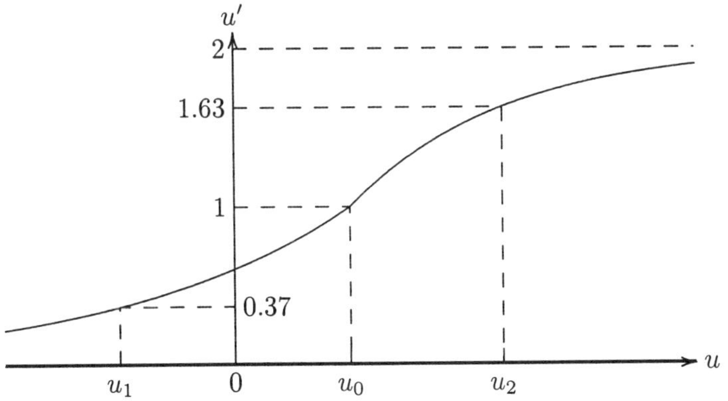

Figure 2.1: Exponential Fitness for Maximizing Problem

Thus we can define the evaluation function as follows,

$$eval(V_i) = u'_i / \sum_{j=1}^{pop\_size} u'_j, \qquad i = 1, 2, \cdots, pop\_size \tag{2.8}$$

where u_i' is the exponential fitness of chromosome V_i, $i = 1, 2, \cdots, pop\_size$, respectively.

2.6 Selection Process

The selection process is based on spinning the roulette wheel *pop_size* times. Each time we select a single chromosome for a new population. The roulette wheel is a fitness-proportional selection. No matter what type of evaluation function is employed, the selection process is always stated as follows:

Step 1. Calculate the cumulative probability q_i for each chromosome V_i,

$$\begin{cases} q_0 = 0, \\ q_i = \sum_{j=1}^{i} eval(V_j), \quad i = 1, 2, \cdots, pop\_size. \end{cases} \tag{2.9}$$

Step 2. Generate a randomly real number r in $(0, q_{pop\_size}]$.

Step 3. Select the ith chromosome V_i $(1 \le i \le pop\_size)$ such that $q_{i-1} < r \le q_i$.

Step 4. Repeat the second and third steps *pop_size* times and obtain *pop_size* copies of chromosomes.

Please note that in the above-mentioned process we do not require the condition $q_{pop\_size} = 1$. In fact, if we want, we can divide all q_i's, $i = 1, 2, \cdots, pop\_size$, by q_{pop_size} such that $q_{pop\_size} = 1$ and the new probabilities are also proportional to the fitnesses. However, it does not exert any influence on the genetic process.

2.7 Crossover Operation

We define a parameter P_c of a genetic system as the probability of crossover. This probability gives us the expected number $P_c \cdot pop\_size$ of chromosomes which undergo the crossover operation.

In order to determine the parents for crossover operation, let us do the following process repeatedly from $i = 1$ to *pop_size*: generating a randomly real number r from the interval $[0, 1]$, the chromosome V_i is selected as a parent if $r < P_c$.

We denote the selected parents by $V_1', V_2', V_3', \cdots$ and divide them into the following pairs:

$$(V_1', V_2'), \quad (V_3', V_4'), \quad (V_5', V_6'), \quad \cdots.$$

Let us illustrate the crossover operator on each pair by (V_1', V_2'). At first, we generate a random number c from the open interval $(0, 1)$, then the crossover operator on V_1' and V_2' will produce two children X and Y as follows:

$$X = c \cdot V_1' + (1 - c) \cdot V_2', \qquad Y = (1 - c) \cdot V_1' + c \cdot V_2'. \tag{2.10}$$

If the feasible set is convex, this arithmetical crossover operation ensures that both children are feasible if both parents are. However, in many cases, the feasible set is not necessarily convex, nor is it hard to verify the convexity. Thus we must check the feasibility of each child. If both children are feasible, then we replace the parents by them. If not, we keep the feasible one if it exists, and then redo the crossover operator by regenerating the random number c until two feasible children are obtained or a given number of cycles is finished. In this case, we only replace the parents by the feasible children.

2.8 Mutation Operation

We define a parameter P_m of a genetic system as the probability of mutation. This probability gives us the expected number of $P_m \cdot$ *pop_size* of chromosomes which undergo the mutation operations.

Similar to the process of selecting parents for crossover operation, we repeat the following steps from $i = 1$ to *pop_size*: generating a randomly real number r from the interval $[0, 1]$, the chromosome V_i is selected as a parent for mutation if $r < P_m$.

For each selected parent, denoted by $V = (x_1, x_2, \cdots, x_n)$, we mutate it in the following way. Let M be an appropriate large positive number defined in the section Initialization Process. We choose a mutation direction $\mathbf{d}$ in $\Re^n$ randomly. If $V + M \cdot \mathbf{d}$ is not feasible for the constraints, then we set M as a random number between 0 and M until it is feasible. If the above process cannot find a feasible solution in a predetermined number of iterations, then we set $M = 0$. Anyway, we replace the parent V by its child

$$X = V + M \cdot \mathbf{d}. \tag{2.11}$$

2.9 Genetic Algorithm Procedure

Following selection, crossover, and mutation, the new population is ready for its next evaluation. The genetic algorithm will terminate after a given number of cyclic repetitions of the above steps or a suitable solution has been found. We now summarize the genetic algorithms for optimization problems as follows.

Step 0. *Input parameters pop_size, a, P_c and P_m.*

Step 1. *Initialize pop_size chromosomes.*

Step 2. *Update the chromosomes by crossover and mutation operations.*

Step 3. *Calculate the objective values for all chromosomes.*

Step 4. *Compute the fitness of each chromosome according to the objective values.*

Step 5. *Select the chromosomes by spinning the roulette wheel.*

Step 6. *Repeat the second to fifth steps a given number of cycles.*

Step 7. *Report the best chromosome as the optimal solution.*

It is known that the best chromosome does not necessarily appear in the last generation. Thus we have to keep the best one from the beginning. If we find a better one in the new population, then we replace the old one with it. This chromosome will be reported as the optimal solution after finishing the evolution.

2.10 Genetic Algorithms versus Ascent Methods

Recall that ascent methods are the general name of direct methods, gradient methods, and Hessian methods. The ascent methods are first to choose an initial point which is thought to be the most likely place where the optimal solution exists. Then they find a new point from the initial one by analyzing the behavior of the objective function. This process continues from the new point until some termination criterion is met. In order to understand genetic algorithms, now let us compare ascent methods and genetic algorithms.

Ascent methods are a deterministic search process which produces a deterministic sequence of points usually converging to an optimal solution (sometimes locally). Genetic algorithms are a stochastic search process which produces a stochastic sequence of populations usually including a satisfactory solution. In general, the primary distinction points between the two types of methods are as follows.

(i) Ascent methods have only one initial point which is usually given by the decision-maker; genetic algorithms have multiple initial points which are usually random generated.

(ii) Ascent methods search a new point from the previous one by analyzing the behavior of objective function; genetic algorithms randomly change the chromosomes in the current population by genetic operators (i.e., crossover and mutation), and select them to the next population by some sampling mechanism.

For the same optimization problem, genetic algorithms usually spend more CPU time than ascent methods. However, genetic algorithms can deal with more complicated optimization problems that cannot be solved by ascent methods.

2.11 Numerical Examples

The computer code for genetic algorithms has been written in C language. Here we give some numerical examples which are all performed on a personal computer with the following parameters: the population size is 30, the probability of crossover is 0.2, the probability of mutation is 0.5, and the parameter a in the rank-based evaluation function is 0.05. Genetic algorithms are often criticized due to the setting of these parameters. Fortunately, genetic algorithms are very robust in parameter setting.

Example 1: Single-Objective Programming

Let us consider an example which is related to maximizing a function over a nonconvex set, i.e.,

$$\begin{cases} \max\ f(\boldsymbol{x}) = \dfrac{x_1^2 x_2 x_3^2}{2x_1^3 x_3^2 + 3x_1^2 x_2^2 + 2x_2^2 x_3^3 + x_1^3 x_2^2 x_3^2} \\ \text{subject to:} \\ \qquad x_1^2 + x_2^2 + x_3^2 \ge 1 \\ \qquad x_1^2 + x_2^2 + x_3^2 \le 4 \\ \qquad x_1, x_2, x_3 > 0 \end{cases} \tag{2.12}$$

which has a known optimum $f(\boldsymbol{x}) = 0.1537$, and the feasible set is shown by Figure 2.2 in which the shaded part represents the cross section of the feasible set at $x_3 = 0$. It is clear from the figure that the feasible set is nonconvex.

In order to solve this problem by genetic algorithms, let us code each solution by a chromosome $V = (x_1, x_2, x_3)$. Then the subfunction of checking the feasibility of the chromosome $V = (x_1, x_2, x_3)$ may be written as follows,

If $(x_1 \le 0 || x_2 \le 0 || x_3 \le 0)$ *return 0;*
If $(x_1^2 + x_2^2 + x_3^2 < 1)$ *return 0;*
If $(x_1^2 + x_2^2 + x_3^2 > 4)$ *return 0;*
Return 1;

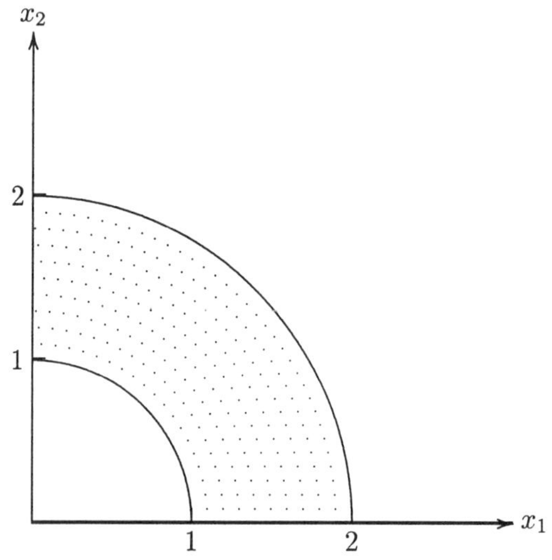

Figure 2.2: Cross Section of Feasible Set at $x_3 = 0$

where 0 represents *infeasible*, 1 *feasible*. It is easy to know that the feasible set is contained in the following hypercube

$$\Omega = \left\{(x_1, x_2, x_3) \,\middle|\, 0 \le x_1 \le 2,\ 0 \le x_2 \le 2,\ 0 \le x_3 \le 2\right\}$$

which is simple for the computer because we can easily sample points from it. For example, we can take

$$x_1 = \mathcal{U}(0,2), \quad x_2 = \mathcal{U}(0,2), \quad x_3 = \mathcal{U}(0,2) \tag{2.13}$$

where the function $\mathcal{U}(a, b)$ generates uniformly distributed variables on the interval $[a, b]$ and will be discussed in detail in Chapter 3. If this chromosome is infeasible, then we reject it and regenerate one by (2.13). If the generated chromosome is feasible, then we accept it as one in the population. After finite times, we can obtain 30 feasible chromosomes listed as follows,

$$
\begin{array}{rlrl}
V_1 &= (0.3903, 0.6723, 1.2507) & V_2 &= (0.9167, 0.2930, 0.3297) \\
V_3 &= (0.2373, 0.1267, 1.7370) & V_4 &= (0.8523, 0.9683, 1.4477) \\
V_5 &= (0.1280, 0.8337, 1.1807) & V_6 &= (0.3283, 0.6830, 1.8263) \\
V_7 &= (1.1223, 0.6363, 1.2303) & V_8 &= (0.5020, 0.8447, 1.0840) \\
V_9 &= (0.0490, 1.7077, 0.2813) & V_{10} &= (0.5643, 0.5450, 1.6913) \\
V_{11} &= (1.1430, 0.6000, 0.3623) & V_{12} &= (1.6243, 1.0153, 0.5573) \\
V_{13} &= (0.7953, 1.3563, 1.1223) & V_{14} &= (0.1240, 1.7903, 0.5593) \\
V_{15} &= (1.2320, 0.0733, 0.9930) & V_{16} &= (1.4473, 1.3397, 0.2947) \\
V_{17} &= (0.3960, 0.6173, 1.2623) & V_{18} &= (0.5420, 0.4000, 1.6593) \\
V_{19} &= (0.1517, 1.0047, 0.5590) & V_{20} &= (1.2550, 1.2957, 0.6413) \\
V_{21} &= (0.1313, 0.8217, 1.4523) & V_{22} &= (0.2383, 1.2930, 0.3637) \\
V_{23} &= (1.3047, 0.4163, 0.4673) & V_{24} &= (1.7893, 0.5220, 0.4343) \\
V_{25} &= (1.1910, 0.1460, 0.5890) & V_{26} &= (0.6023, 1.3187, 0.3897) \\
V_{27} &= (0.9907, 0.8447, 0.9030) & V_{28} &= (0.7467, 1.2017, 1.0873) \\
V_{29} &= (0.9263, 1.5153, 0.0503) & V_{30} &= (0.0823, 0.1867, 1.1217)
\end{array}
$$

A direct computation obtains the original fitness values (i.e., the objective values), which are shown as follows,

$$
\begin{array}{lll}
f(V_1) = 0.0727 & f(V_2) = 0.0674 & f(V_3) = 0.0854 \\
f(V_4) = 0.1277 & f(V_5) = 0.0082 & f(V_6) = 0.0401 \\
f(V_7) = 0.1482 & f(V_8) = 0.0906 & f(V_9) = 0.0022 \\
f(V_{10}) = 0.1144 & f(V_{11}) = 0.0539 & f(V_{12}) = 0.0663 \\
f(V_{13}) = 0.0971 & f(V_{14}) = 0.0068 & f(V_{15}) = 0.0294 \\
f(V_{16}) = 0.0197 & f(V_{17}) = 0.0792 & f(V_{18}) = 0.1269 \\
f(V_{19}) = 0.0170 & f(V_{20}) = 0.0711 & f(V_{21}) = 0.0071 \\
f(V_{22}) = 0.0215 & f(V_{23}) = 0.0784 & f(V_{24}) = 0.0616 \\
f(V_{25}) = 0.0560 & f(V_{26}) = 0.0327 & f(V_{27}) = 0.1275 \\
f(V_{28}) = 0.1013 & f(V_{29}) = 0.0006 & f(V_{30}) = 0.0158
\end{array}
$$

It is clear that the chromosome V_7 is the best one and the chromosome V_{29} is the worst. Notice that we must keep the best chromosome V_7 in this iteration, written as V_0. If we find a new chromosome which is better than V_0 in the remaining iterations, then we replace V_0 by the new one. According to the objectives of chromosomes, we can rearrange these chromosomes from good to bad as follows,

$$
\begin{array}{ll}
V_1' = (1.1223, 0.6363, 1.2303)(V_7) & V_2' = (0.8523, 0.9683, 1.4477)(V_4) \\
V_3' = (0.9907, 0.8447, 0.9030)(V_{27}) & V_4' = (0.5420, 0.4000, 1.6593)(V_{18}) \\
V_5' = (0.5643, 0.5450, 1.6913)(V_{10}) & V_6' = (0.7467, 1.2017, 1.0873)(V_{28}) \\
V_7' = (0.7953, 1.3563, 1.1223)(V_{13}) & V_8' = (0.5020, 0.8447, 1.0840)(V_8) \\
V_9' = (0.2373, 0.1267, 1.7370)(V_3) & V_{10}' = (0.3960, 0.6173, 1.2623)(V_{17}) \\
V_{11}' = (1.3047, 0.4163, 0.4673)(V_{23}) & V_{12}' = (0.3903, 0.6723, 1.2507)(V_1) \\
V_{13}' = (1.2550, 1.2957, 0.6413)(V_{20}) & V_{14}' = (0.9167, 0.2930, 0.3297)(V_2) \\
V_{15}' = (1.6243, 1.0153, 0.5573)(V_{12}) & V_{16}' = (1.7893, 0.5220, 0.4343)(V_{24}) \\
V_{17}' = (1.1910, 0.1460, 0.5890)(V_{25}) & V_{18}' = (1.1430, 0.6000, 0.3623)(V_{11}) \\
V_{19}' = (0.3283, 0.6830, 1.8263)(V_6) & V_{20}' = (0.6023, 1.3187, 0.3897)(V_{26}) \\
V_{21}' = (1.2320, 0.0733, 0.9930)(V_{15}) & V_{22}' = (0.2383, 1.2930, 0.3637)(V_{22}) \\
V_{23}' = (1.4473, 1.3397, 0.2947)(V_{16}) & V_{24}' = (0.1517, 1.0047, 0.5590)(V_{19}) \\
V_{25}' = (0.0823, 0.1867, 1.1217)(V_{30}) & V_{26}' = (0.1280, 0.8337, 1.1807)(V_5) \\
V_{27}' = (0.1313, 0.8217, 1.4523)(V_{21}) & V_{28}' = (0.1240, 1.7903, 0.5593)(V_{14}) \\
V_{29}' = (0.0490, 1.7077, 0.2813)(V_9) & V_{30}' = (0.9263, 1.5153, 0.0503)(V_{29})
\end{array}
$$

By the rank-based evaluation function (2.4), it follows from $a = 0.05$ that

$$eval(V_i') = 0.05 \cdot (1 - 0.05)^{i-1}, \quad i = 1, 2, \cdots, 30.$$

Hence we have

$$
\begin{array}{lllll}
q_1 = 0.0500 & q_2 = 0.0975 & q_3 = 0.1426 & q_4 = 0.1855 & q_5 = 0.2262 \\
q_6 = 0.2649 & q_7 = 0.3017 & q_8 = 0.3366 & q_9 = 0.3698 & q_{10} = 0.4013 \\
q_{11} = 0.4312 & q_{12} = 0.4596 & q_{13} = 0.4867 & q_{14} = 0.5123 & q_{15} = 0.5367 \\
q_{16} = 0.5599 & q_{17} = 0.5819 & q_{18} = 0.6028 & q_{19} = 0.6226 & q_{20} = 0.6415 \\
q_{21} = 0.6594 & q_{22} = 0.6765 & q_{23} = 0.6926 & q_{24} = 0.7080 & q_{25} = 0.7226 \\
q_{26} = 0.7365 & q_{27} = 0.7497 & q_{28} = 0.7622 & q_{29} = 0.7741 & q_{30} = 0.7854
\end{array}
$$

Now we are ready to spin the roulette wheel 30 times. The first random number on $(0, q_{30}] = (0, 0.7854]$ generated by the computer is 0.0328, which is larger than $q_0 = 0$ and smaller than $q_1 = 0.0500$. Thus the chromosome $V_1'(V_7)$ is selected for the new population. The second random number is 0.1284, which is larger than $q_2 = 0.0975$ and smaller than $q_3 = 0.1426$. Thus the chromosome $V_3'(V_{27})$ is selected. Repeating this process 30 times, we obtain the new population listed as follows,

$$
\begin{array}{ll}
V_1'' = (1.1223, 0.6363, 1.2303) & V_2'' = (0.9907, 0.8447, 0.9030) \\
V_3'' = (0.7467, 1.2017, 1.0873) & V_4'' = (1.1223, 0.6363, 1.2303) \\
V_5'' = (0.9167, 0.2930, 0.3297) & V_6'' = (0.5420, 0.4000, 1.6593) \\
V_7'' = (0.9167, 0.2930, 0.3297) & V_8'' = (0.8523, 0.9683, 1.4477) \\
V_9'' = (1.3047, 0.4163, 0.4673) & V_{10}'' = (0.9263, 1.5153, 0.0503) \\
V_{11}'' = (0.0823, 0.1867, 1.1217) & V_{12}'' = (0.5020, 0.8447, 1.0840) \\
V_{13}'' = (0.9263, 1.5153, 0.0503) & V_{14}'' = (0.9263, 1.5153, 0.0503) \\
V_{15}'' = (0.3960, 0.6173, 1.2623) & V_{16}'' = (1.7893, 0.5220, 0.4343) \\
V_{17}'' = (0.8523, 0.9683, 1.4477) & V_{18}'' = (0.9263, 1.5153, 0.0503) \\
V_{19}'' = (0.6023, 1.3187, 0.3897) & V_{20}'' = (0.1313, 0.8217, 1.4523) \\
V_{21}'' = (0.9263, 1.5153, 0.0503) & V_{22}'' = (1.3047, 0.4163, 0.4673) \\
V_{23}'' = (1.1223, 0.6363, 1.2303) & V_{24}'' = (1.6243, 1.0153, 0.5573) \\
V_{25}'' = (1.1910, 0.1460, 0.5890) & V_{26}'' = (0.9907, 0.8447, 0.9030) \\
V_{27}'' = (0.1517, 1.0047, 0.5590) & V_{28}'' = (1.1223, 0.6363, 1.2303) \\
V_{29}'' = (0.0490, 1.7077, 0.2813) & V_{30}'' = (1.6243, 1.0153, 0.5573)
\end{array}
$$

This population is ready to be updated by genetic operators—crossover and mutation. The probability of crossover $P_c = 20\%$ gives us the expected number 6 of chromosomes which undergo the crossover operation. The first random number on $[0, 1]$ generated by computer is 0.6437, which is larger than $P_c = 0.20$. Thus the first chromosome V_1'' is not selected. The second random number is 0.1256, which is smaller than $P_c = 0.20$. Thus the second chromosome V_2'' is selected as a parent for crossover. Repeating this process 30 times, 10 chromosomes are selected and listed as follows,

$$V_2'', V_3'', V_4'', V_6'', V_{12}'', V_{13}'', V_{15}'', V_{16}'', V_{19}'', V_{28}''$$

which may be randomly grouped into the following pairs,

$$(V_{16}'', V_{19}''), (V_3'', V_6''), (V_{15}'', V_2''), (V_4'', V_{12}''), (V_{13}'', V_{28}'').$$

We mention that the number of selected chromosomes is even, hence we can pair them easily. If the number of selected chromosomes is odd, we may remove one from the selected chromosomes. The crossover operation on each pair is performed by (2.10) and we obtain the following new version of the population,

$$
\begin{array}{ll}
V_1''' = (1.1223, 0.6363, 1.2303) & V_2''' = (0.5631, 0.6812, 1.1614) \\
V_3''' = (0.6068, 0.6540, 1.4781) & V_4''' = (1.0155, 0.6722, 1.2051) \\
V_5''' = (0.9167, 0.2930, 0.3297) & V_6''' = (0.6818, 0.9477, 1.2685) \\
V_7''' = (0.9167, 0.2930, 0.3297) & V_8''' = (0.8523, 0.9683, 1.4477) \\
V_9''' = (1.3047, 0.4163, 0.4673) & V_{10}''' = (0.9263, 1.5153, 0.0503) \\
V_{11}''' = (0.0823, 0.1867, 1.1217) & V_{12}''' = (0.6088, 0.8088, 1.1092) \\
V_{13}''' = (0.9810, 1.2702, 0.3794) & V_{14}''' = (0.9263, 1.5153, 0.0503) \\
V_{15}''' = (0.8236, 0.7808, 1.0040) & V_{16}''' = (1.6400, 0.6222, 0.4287) \\
V_{17}''' = (0.8523, 0.9683, 1.4477) & V_{18}''' = (0.9263, 1.5153, 0.0503) \\
V_{19}''' = (0.7517, 1.2184, 0.3953) & V_{20}''' = (0.1313, 0.8217, 1.4523) \\
V_{21}''' = (0.9263, 1.5153, 0.0503) & V_{22}''' = (1.3047, 0.4163, 0.4673) \\
V_{23}''' = (1.1223, 0.6363, 1.2303) & V_{24}''' = (1.6243, 1.0153, 0.5573) \\
V_{25}''' = (1.1910, 0.1460, 0.5890) & V_{26}''' = (0.9907, 0.8447, 0.9030) \\
V_{27}''' = (0.1517, 1.0047, 0.5590) & V_{28}''' = (1.0677, 0.8814, 0.9013) \\
V_{29}''' = (0.0490, 1.7077, 0.2813) & V_{30}''' = (1.6243, 1.0153, 0.5573)
\end{array}
$$

Similar to the selecting process of crossover, a run of the computer program selects the following 17 chromosomes as parents for mutation,

$$
\begin{array}{c}
V_1''', V_3''', V_4''', V_7''', V_9''', V_{10}''', V_{13}''', V_{14}''', V_{15}''', \\
V_{16}''', V_{17}''', V_{18}''', V_{19}''', V_{21}''', V_{22}''', V_{23}''', V_{24}'''.
\end{array}
$$

Let us generate a random direction $\mathbf{d} = (0.1130, -0.8072, 0.1279)$ in $\Re^3$ and mutate the chromosome V_1''' in this direction. If the large positive number M is 10, then we have to check the feasibility of

$$V_1''' + M \cdot \mathbf{d} = (2.2523, -7.4357, 2.5093).$$

It is proven infeasible. Thus we have to generate a random number between 0 and M and set it to M, for example, $M = 0.2345$. The checking subfunction shows that

$$V_1''' + M \cdot \mathbf{d} = (1.1488, 0.4470, 1.2333)$$

is feasible. Thus we replace the chromosome $V_1''' = (1.1223, 0.6363, 1.2303)$ by $(1.1488, 0.4470, 1.2333)$. After finishing the mutation operation, the population is as follows,

$$
\begin{array}{ll}
V_1'''' = (1.1488, 0.4470, 1.2333) & V_2'''' = (0.5631, 0.6812, 1.1614) \\
V_3'''' = (0.1701, 0.6540, 1.4550) & V_4'''' = (0.9978, 0.6722, 1.2077) \\
V_5'''' = (0.9167, 0.2930, 0.3297) & V_6'''' = (0.6818, 0.9477, 1.2685) \\
V_7'''' = (0.9811, 0.2930, 0.1346) & V_8'''' = (0.8523, 0.9683, 1.4477) \\
V_9'''' = (1.3047, 0.4163, 0.4285) & V_{10}'''' = (0.8192, 1.5153, 0.0503) \\
V_{11}'''' = (0.0823, 0.1867, 1.1217) & V_{12}'''' = (0.6088, 0.8088, 1.1092) \\
V_{13}'''' = (0.9810, 1.2702, 0.6591) & V_{14}'''' = (0.1878, 1.5153, 0.0503) \\
V_{15}'''' = (0.8236, 0.7808, 0.7472) & V_{16}'''' = (1.7911, 0.6222, 0.3176) \\
V_{17}'''' = (0.6160, 0.9683, 1.4477) & V_{18}'''' = (1.0359, 1.5153, 0.0503) \\
V_{19}'''' = (0.7517, 1.2268, 0.3953) & V_{20}'''' = (0.1313, 0.8217, 1.4523) \\
V_{21}'''' = (0.9263, 1.7268, 0.3645) & V_{22}'''' = (1.2524, 0.4163, 0.4673) \\
V_{23}'''' = (1.1223, 0.6363, 1.2303) & V_{24}'''' = (1.6243, 0.8745, 0.5573) \\
V_{25}'''' = (1.1910, 0.1460, 0.5890) & V_{26}'''' = (0.9907, 0.8447, 0.9030) \\
V_{27}'''' = (0.1517, 1.0047, 0.5590) & V_{28}'''' = (1.0677, 0.8814, 0.9013) \\
V_{29}'''' = (0.0490, 1.7077, 0.2813) & V_{30}'''' = (1.6243, 1.0153, 0.5573)
\end{array}
$$

Up to now we have finished one generation. After performing the computer program with 150 generations, we obtain the best solution

$$\boldsymbol{x}^* = (0.8597, 0.5273, 1.3245)$$

with optimum $f(\boldsymbol{x}^*) = 0.1537$, which is very close to the known optimum. The CPU time for this program is 4.1 seconds and the process of evolution is shown in Figure 2.3.

Example 2: Goal Programming

Here we consider the following complex nonlinear goal programming model,

$$
\left\{
\begin{array}{l}
\text{lexmin } \{d_1^-, d_2^-, d_3^+, d_4^- + d_4^+\} \\
\text{subject to:} \\
\qquad \sum_{i=1}^{5} x_i \sin(i\pi \cdot x_i) + d_1^- - d_1^+ = 18 \\
\qquad \sum_{i=1}^{4} x_i \sin(i\pi \cdot x_i) + d_2^- - d_2^+ = 15 \\
\qquad \sum_{i=1}^{3} x_i \sin(i\pi \cdot x_i) + d_3^- - d_3^+ = 10 \\
\qquad \sum_{i=1}^{2} x_i \sin(i\pi \cdot x_i) + d_4^- - d_4^+ = 0 \\
\qquad x_1^2 + x_2^2 + x_3^2 + x_4^2 + x_5^2 \le 100.
\end{array}
\right.
$$

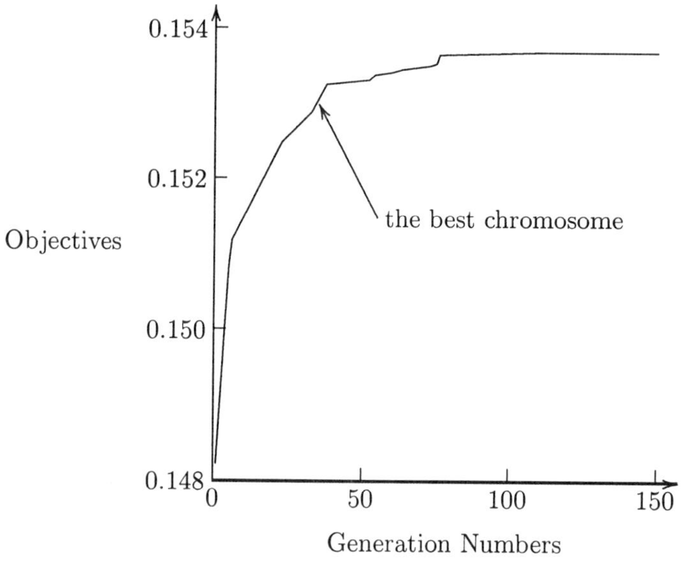

Figure 2.3: Process of Evolution for Example 1

We mention that this example is quite complex because the functions are multimodal and highly nonlinear. Thus the traditional methods can do nothing about such a nonlinear goal programming. However, genetic algorithms are proven effective for this example.

The general objective function of goal programming is

$$\sum_{j=1}^{l} P_j \sum_{i=1}^{m} (u_{ij} d_i^+ + v_{ij} d_i^-)$$

where P_j is the preemptive priority factor which expresses the relative importance of various goals, $P_j \gg P_{j+1}$, for all j, but it is not suitable for the objective function to be as an evaluation function because we have only the information $P_j \gg P_{j+1}$ on the priority factors. In fact, we have the following order relationship for the chromosomes: for any two chromosomes, if the higher-priority objectives are equal, then, in the current priority level, the one with minimal objective value is better. This relationship is an order on the feasible set and can rearrange these chromosomes in order. If two different chromosomes have the same objective value, then we are indifferent between them and rearrange them randomly.

The evolution process of goal programming is very similar to that of single-objective programming except for the fact that we have to rearrange the chromosomes in each population by the above-mentioned order relationship.

A run of genetic algorithm with 6000 generations shows that the best solution of Example 2 is

$$\boldsymbol{x} = (2.2710, 1.4520, -6.8352, 6.1263, 2.9016)$$

which satisfies the first three goals, but the last objective is 2.1397. Although we do not know the exact global solution of this problem, the result obtained by genetic algorithm is satisfactory because we did not find any better result by a series of experiments. The CPU time spent for the genetic algorithm with 6000 generations is 68.8 seconds on a personal computer. The result of the evolution process is shown in Figure 2.4.

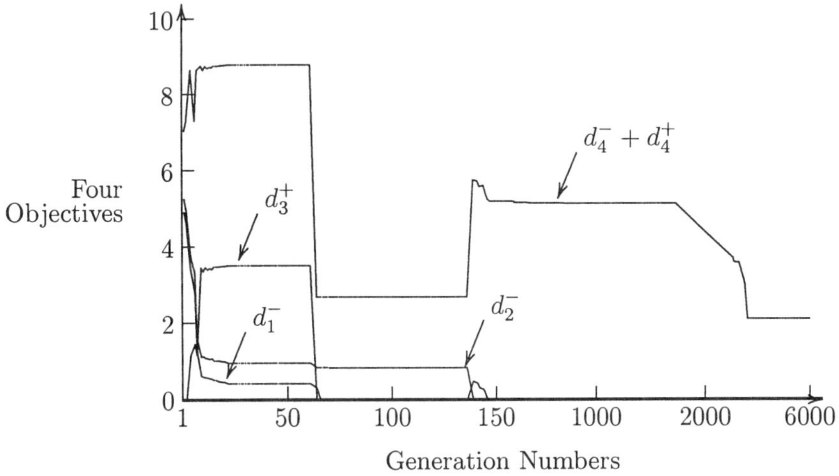

Figure 2.4: Evolution Process of Example 2

Example 3: Multiobjective Programming

Although all efficient solutions to a multiobjective programming might be of some interest, there is no point in reporting all potential efficient solutions. The purpose of solving a multiobjective optimization is to perform the solution in practice. In addition, it is impossible to perform multiple solutions at the same time. Therefore, one and only one satisfactory solution should be finally produced by a computation system in which there may be an interactive procedure between the decision-maker and the computer.

No matter how many objectives one problem has, it is reasonable to assume that the decision-maker can evaluate any given two potential solutions. In other words, the decision-maker can point out the better one. If not, then either one of the two solutions is considered acceptable for the decision-maker.

There are some known methods for evaluating the potential solutions. The first one is the *weighted-sum* method, in which m objective functions f_i, $i = 1, 2, \cdots, m$ are combined into one as

$$f(\boldsymbol{x}) = \lambda_1 f_1(\boldsymbol{x}) + \lambda_2 f_2(\boldsymbol{x}) + \cdots + \lambda_m f_m(\boldsymbol{x})$$

where $\lambda_1, \lambda_2, \cdots, \lambda_m$ are weighting factors with $0 \le \lambda_i \le 1$, $i = 1, 2, \cdots, m$, and $\lambda_1 + \lambda_2 + \cdots + \lambda_m = 1$. The second one is the *distance function method*, which combines m objective functions into one based on a target vector $(f_1^0, f_2^0, \cdots, f_m^0)$, i.e.,

$$f(\boldsymbol{x}) = \left(\sum_{i=1}^{m} |f_i(\boldsymbol{x}) - f_i^0|^{\lambda} \right)^{\frac{1}{\lambda}}$$

where λ is a positive parameter.

Any sequence of potential solutions to a multiobjective optimization can be rearranged from good to bad by any one of the above-mentioned methods.

Now let us consider a biobjective optimization on a nonconvex set,

$$\begin{cases} \max\ f_1(\boldsymbol{x}) = x_1^2 + x_2^2 \\ \max\ f_2(\boldsymbol{x}) = x_3/(1 + x_1 + x_2) \\ \text{subject to:} \\ \qquad x_1^2 + x_2^2 + x_3^2 \ge 1 \\ \qquad x_1^2 + x_2^2 + x_3^2 \le 4 \\ \qquad x_1, x_2, x_3 > 0. \end{cases} \tag{2.14}$$

If we employ the weighted-sum method to rearrange the chromosomes, for example, we assign 0.4 and 0.6 as the weighting factors to the objective functions $f_1(\boldsymbol{x})$ and $f_2(\boldsymbol{x})$, respectively. Then a run of the genetic algorithm with 2000 generations shows that the optimal solution is $\boldsymbol{x}^* = (0.0000, 1.9837, 0.2545)$, whose objective values are

$$f_1(\boldsymbol{x}^*) = 3.9352, \qquad f_2(\boldsymbol{x}^*) = 0.0853.$$

The CPU time spent for this computer program is 32.4 seconds.

Example 4: Bilevel Programming

For the bilevel programming,

$$\begin{cases} \max F(\boldsymbol{x}, \boldsymbol{y}_1, \boldsymbol{y}_2, \cdots, \boldsymbol{y}_m) \\ \text{subject to:} \\ \quad G(\boldsymbol{x}) \le 0 \\ \quad \text{where each } \boldsymbol{y}_i (i = 1, 2, \cdots, m) \text{ solves} \\ \quad \begin{cases} \max\limits_{\boldsymbol{y}_i} f_i(\boldsymbol{x}, \boldsymbol{y}_1, \boldsymbol{y}_2, \cdots, \boldsymbol{y}_m) \\ \text{subject to:} \\ \quad g(\boldsymbol{x}, \boldsymbol{y}_1, \boldsymbol{y}_2, \cdots, \boldsymbol{y}_m) \le 0, \end{cases} \end{cases} \tag{2.15}$$

we define symbols

$$\boldsymbol{y}_{-i} = (\boldsymbol{y}_1, \cdots, \boldsymbol{y}_{i-1}, \boldsymbol{y}_{i+1}, \cdots, \boldsymbol{y}_m), \quad i = 1, 2, \cdots, m. \tag{2.16}$$

For any decision $\boldsymbol{x}$ revealed by the leader, if the ith follower knows the strategies $\boldsymbol{y}_{-i}$ of other followers, then the optimal reaction of the ith follower is represented by a mapping $\boldsymbol{y}_i = r_i(\boldsymbol{y}_{-i})$, which should solve the subproblem

$$\begin{cases} \max\limits_{\boldsymbol{y}_i} f_i(\boldsymbol{x}, \boldsymbol{y}_1, \boldsymbol{y}_2, \cdots, \boldsymbol{y}_m) \\ \text{subject to:} \\ \quad g(\boldsymbol{x}, \boldsymbol{y}_1, \boldsymbol{y}_2, \cdots, \boldsymbol{y}_m) \le 0. \end{cases} \tag{2.17}$$

In order to search for the Stackelberg-Nash equilibrium to a bilevel programming by genetic algorithms, at first we should compute the Nash equilibrium with respect to any decision revealed by the leader. It is clear that the Nash equilibrium of the m followers will be the solution $(\boldsymbol{y}_1, \boldsymbol{y}_2, \cdots, \boldsymbol{y}_m)$ of the system of equations

$$\boldsymbol{y}_i = r_i(\boldsymbol{y}_{-i}), \quad i = 1, 2, \cdots, m. \tag{2.18}$$

In other words, we should find a fixed point of the vector-valued function $(r_1, r_2, \cdots, r_m)$. In order to solve the system of equations (2.18), we should design some efficient algorithms. The argument breaks down into three cases.

Case I. If we have explicit expressions of all functions r_i, $i = 1, 2, \cdots, m$, then we might get an analytic solution to the system (2.18). Unfortunately, it is almost impossible to do this in practice.

Case II. In many cases, no analytic solution of (2.18) can be obtained. Thus the system (2.18) might be solved by some iterative method that generates a sequence of points $\boldsymbol{y}^k = (\boldsymbol{y}_1^k, \boldsymbol{y}_2^k, \cdots, \boldsymbol{y}_m^k)$, $k = 0, 1, 2, \cdots$ via the iteration formula

$$\boldsymbol{y}_i^{k+1} = r_i(\boldsymbol{y}_{-i}^k), \quad i = 1, 2, \cdots, m \tag{2.19}$$

where $\boldsymbol{y}_{-i}^k = (\boldsymbol{y}_1^k, \cdots, \boldsymbol{y}_{i-1}^k, \boldsymbol{y}_{i+1}^k, \cdots, \boldsymbol{y}_m^k)$. However, generally speaking, it is not easy to verify the conditions on the convergence of the iterative method for practical problems. When we solve some given problem on a computer, we might employ the iterative method. If we indeed find a solution, then the problem is solved. Otherwise, we have to try other methods.

Case III. If the iterative method fails to find a fixed point, we may employ a genetic algorithm to solve the following minimization problem,

$$\begin{cases} \min R(\boldsymbol{y}_1, \boldsymbol{y}_2, \cdots, \boldsymbol{y}_m) = \sum_{i=1}^{m} \|\boldsymbol{y}_i - r_i(\boldsymbol{y}_{-i})\| \\ \text{subject to:} \\ \qquad g(\boldsymbol{x}, \boldsymbol{y}_1, \boldsymbol{y}_2, \cdots, \boldsymbol{y}_m) \le 0. \end{cases} \tag{2.20}$$

If an array $(\boldsymbol{y}_1^*, \boldsymbol{y}_2^*, \cdots, \boldsymbol{y}_m^*)$ satisfies that $R(\boldsymbol{y}_1^*, \boldsymbol{y}_2^*, \cdots, \boldsymbol{y}_m^*) = 0$, then $\boldsymbol{y}_i^* = r_i(\boldsymbol{y}_{-i}^*)$, $i = 1, 2, \cdots, m$ and $(\boldsymbol{y}_1^*, \boldsymbol{y}_2^*, \cdots, \boldsymbol{y}_m^*)$ must be a solution of (2.18). That is, if the minimizing solution $(\boldsymbol{y}_1^*, \boldsymbol{y}_2^*, \cdots, \boldsymbol{y}_m^*)$ of the minimization problem (2.20) is such that the objective value $R(\boldsymbol{y}_1^*, \boldsymbol{y}_2^*, \cdots, \boldsymbol{y}_m^*)$ is zero, then $(\boldsymbol{y}_1^*, \boldsymbol{y}_2^*, \cdots, \boldsymbol{y}_m^*)$ is a solution of (2.18). Otherwise, the system of equations (2.18) might be considered inconsistent. In other words, there is no Nash equilibrium of followers in the given bilevel programming. Although this method can deal with general problems, it is a slow way to find a Nash equilibrium.

After obtaining the Nash equilibrium for each given control vector of the leader by an iterative method or a genetic algorithm, we may directly compute the objective value of the leader for each given control vector according to the Nash equilibrium. That is, we may compute the fitness for any chromosome. Hence we may employ the genetic algorithm to search for the optimal solution—Stackelberg-Nash equilibrium.

Now we consider a bilevel programming with three followers in which the leader has a control vector $\boldsymbol{x} = (x_1, x_2, x_3)$ and the three followers have control vectors $\boldsymbol{y}_i = (y_{i1}, y_{i2})$, $i = 1, 2, 3$,

$$
\begin{cases}
\max F(\boldsymbol{x}, \boldsymbol{y}_1, \boldsymbol{y}_2) = y_{11}y_{12}\sin x_1 + y_{21}y_{22}\sin x_2 + y_{31}y_{32}\sin x_3 \\
\text{subject to:} \\
\qquad x_1 + x_2 + x_3 \le 10,\ x_1 \ge 0,\ x_2 \ge 0,\ x_3 \ge 0 \\
\qquad \begin{cases} \max f_1(\boldsymbol{y}_1) = y_{11}\sin y_{12} + y_{12}\sin y_{11} \\ \text{subject to:} \\ \qquad y_{11} + y_{12} \le x_1,\ y_{11} \ge 0,\ y_{12} \ge 0 \end{cases} \\
\qquad \begin{cases} \max f_2(\boldsymbol{y}_2) = y_{21}\sin y_{22} + y_{22}\sin y_{21} \\ \text{subject to:} \\ \qquad y_{21} + y_{22} \le x_2,\ y_{21} \ge 0,\ y_{22} \ge 0 \end{cases} \\
\qquad \begin{cases} \max f_3(\boldsymbol{y}_3) = y_{31}\sin y_{32} + y_{32}\sin y_{31} \\ \text{subject to:} \\ \qquad y_{31} + y_{32} \le x_3,\ y_{31} \ge 0,\ y_{32} \ge 0. \end{cases}
\end{cases}
$$

For this bilevel programming model, the traditional methods cannot work because of the complexity and multimodality of objective functions of each player. For each optimization problem of leader and followers, we have to employ genetic algorithms to search for the best solutions. A run of the genetic algorithm with 300 generations shows that the Stackelberg-Nash equilibrium is

$$
\begin{aligned}
&\boldsymbol{x}^* = (1.946, 8.054, 0.000), \\
&\boldsymbol{y}_1^* = (0.973, 0.973), \quad \boldsymbol{y}_2^* = (1.315, 6.793), \quad \boldsymbol{y}_3^* = (0.000, 0.000)
\end{aligned}
$$

with optimal objective values

$$
\begin{aligned}
&F(\boldsymbol{x}^*, \boldsymbol{y}_1^*, \boldsymbol{y}_2^*, \boldsymbol{y}_3^*) = 9.566, \\
&f_1(\boldsymbol{y}_1^*) = 1.609, \quad f_2(\boldsymbol{y}_2^*) = 7.099, \quad f_3(\boldsymbol{y}_3^*) = 0.000.
\end{aligned}
$$

The total CPU time spent for this example is about 36 minutes.

We notice that the optimal solution of the follower is not unique. For example, an optimal solution of the second follower is $\boldsymbol{y}_2^* = (1.315, 6.739)$. By the symmetry of the control variables y_{21} and y_{22}, the vector $\boldsymbol{y}_2^{*\prime} = (6.739, 1.315)$ is also an optimal solution. Fortunately, the leader is indifferent between the two solutions. From the symmetry of the followers, we know that the Stackelberg-Nash equilibrium is also not unique. For example, we have also the following Stackelberg-Nash equilibrium

$$
\begin{aligned}
&\boldsymbol{x}^* = (8.054, 1.946, 0.000), \\
&\boldsymbol{y}_1^* = (1.315, 6.793), \quad \boldsymbol{y}_2^* = (0.973, 0.973), \quad \boldsymbol{y}_3^* = (0.000, 0.000).
\end{aligned}
$$

If the objective function of the leader is replaced by

$$F(\boldsymbol{x}, \boldsymbol{y}_1, \boldsymbol{y}_2, \boldsymbol{y}_3) = y_{11}y_{12}\sin x_1 + 2y_{21}y_{22}\sin x_2 + 3y_{31}y_{32}\sin x_3,$$

then a run of genetic algorithm with 300 generations shows that the Stackelberg-Nash equilibrium is

$$\begin{aligned}
&\boldsymbol{x}^* = (0.000, 1.936, 8.064),\\
&\boldsymbol{y}_1^* = (0.000, 0.000), \quad \boldsymbol{y}_2^* = (0.968, 0.968), \quad \boldsymbol{y}_3^* = (1.317, 6.747)
\end{aligned}$$

with optimal objective values

$$\begin{aligned}
&F(\boldsymbol{x}^*, \boldsymbol{y}_1^*, \boldsymbol{y}_2^*, \boldsymbol{y}_3^*) = 27.822,\\
&f_1(\boldsymbol{y}_1^*) = 0.000, \quad f_2(\boldsymbol{y}_2^*) = 1.595, \quad f_3(\boldsymbol{y}_3^*) = 7.120.
\end{aligned}$$

Although the Nash equilibrium is not unique, the optimal control vector $\boldsymbol{x}^*$ of the leader is unique.

Let us now consider a bilevel programming with three followers in which there is information exchange among the three followers. Assume that the leader has a control vector $\boldsymbol{x} = (x_1, x_2)$ and the three followers have control vectors $\boldsymbol{y}_i = (y_{i1}, y_{i2})$, $i = 1, 2, 3$, respectively. The bilevel programming is formulated as follows,

$$\begin{cases}
\min F(\boldsymbol{x}, \boldsymbol{y}_1, \boldsymbol{y}_2, \boldsymbol{y}_3) = \dfrac{3(y_{11}+y_{12})^2 + 5(y_{21}+y_{22})^2 + 10(y_{31}+y_{32})^2}{2x_1^2 + x_2^2 + 3x_1x_2}\\
\text{subject to:}\\
\qquad x_1 + 2x_2 \le 10,\ x_1 > 0,\ x_2 > 0\\
\qquad \begin{cases}
\min f_1(\boldsymbol{y}_1) = y_{11}^2 + y_{12}^2\\
\text{subject to:}\\
\qquad y_{11} + y_{21} + y_{31} \ge x_1\\
\qquad y_{12} + y_{22} + y_{32} \ge x_2\\
\qquad y_{11} \ge 1,\ y_{12} \ge 2
\end{cases}\\
\qquad \begin{cases}
\min f_2(\boldsymbol{y}_2) = y_{21} + y_{22} + y_{11}/y_{21} + y_{12}/y_{22}\\
\text{subject to:}\\
\qquad y_{21} > 0,\ y_{22} > 0
\end{cases}\\
\qquad \begin{cases}
\min f_3(\boldsymbol{y}_3) = (y_{31} - y_{21})^2/y_{31} + (y_{32} - y_{22})^2/y_{32}\\
\text{subject to:}\\
\qquad 2y_{31} + 3y_{32} = 5\\
\qquad y_{31} > 0,\ y_{32} > 0.
\end{cases}
\end{cases}$$

For this bilevel programming model, each subproblem of followers is a parametric optimization which can be solved by any existing means of mathematical programming when the parameters are given. However, in order to obtain the Nash equilibrium of followers, we might employ the iterative method. Fortunately, for this problem, all iterative processes converge to the Nash equilibrium. A run of the genetic algorithm with 300 generations shows that the Stackelberg-Nash equilibrium of the bilevel programming is

$$\begin{aligned} &\boldsymbol{x}^* = (5.768,\ 2.116), \\ &\boldsymbol{y}_1^* = (2.885,\ 2.000), \quad \boldsymbol{y}_2^* = (1.699,\ 1.414), \quad \boldsymbol{y}_3^* = (1.183, 0.878) \end{aligned}$$

with optimal value

$$\begin{aligned} &F(\boldsymbol{x}^*, \boldsymbol{y}_1^*, \boldsymbol{y}_2^*, \boldsymbol{y}_3^*) = 1.510, \\ &f_1(\boldsymbol{y}_1^*) = 12.323, \quad f_2(\boldsymbol{y}_2^*) = 6.225, \quad f_3(\boldsymbol{y}_3^*) = 0.835. \end{aligned}$$

The total CPU time spent for the evolution process is about 9 minutes.

Although the genetic algorithm is a slow and costly way to find optimal solutions and can deal only with small-scale problems, it indeed provides a powerful means of obtaining the Stackelberg-Nash equilibrium of complicated bilevel programming.

Chapter 3

Stochastic Simulation and Fuzzy Simulation

Simulation has long been an important tool in system analysis and operations research. Although simulation is an imprecise technique which provides only statistical estimates rather than exact results and is also a slow and costly way to study problems, it is indeed a power tool dealing with complex problems without analytic techniques.

Stochastic simulation is defined as a technique of performing sampling experiments on the models of not only stochastic but also deterministic systems. It is heavily based on sampling random variables from probability distributions. Stochastic simulation is also referred to as *Monte Carlo simulation.*

Fuzzy simulation is developed by Liu and Iwamura [90][91] and defined as a technique of performing sampling experiments on the models of fuzzy systems. Many numerical experiments show that the technique of fuzzy simulation indeed works very well for handling fuzzy constraints and estimating the possibility of fuzzy systems.

In this chapter we are concerned with the techniques of stochastic simulation and fuzzy simulation, which will be the basis of computer algorithms for solving uncertain programming models throughout the book. The emphasis in this chapter is mainly on the random number generation, basic fuzzy set theory, and the techniques of stochastic simulation and fuzzy simulation.

3.1 Random Number Generation

The basis of stochastic simulation is random number generation. Generally, let x be a random variable with cumulative probability distribution $F(\cdot)$. Since $F(\cdot)$ is a nondecreasing function, the inverse function $F^{-1}(\cdot)$ is defined on $[0,1]$. Assume that u is a uniformly distributed variable on the interval $[0,1]$. Then we have

$$\Pr\left\{F^{-1}(u) \le y\right\} = \Pr\left\{u \le F(y)\right\} = F(y) \tag{3.1}$$

which proves that the variable

$$x = F^{-1}(u) \tag{3.2}$$

has a cumulative distribution function $F(\cdot)$. In order to get a random variable x with cumulative distribution $F(\cdot)$, we can produce a uniformly distributed variable u from the interval $[0,1]$, and x is assigned to be $F^{-1}(u)$. The above process is called the *inverse transform method.*

But for the main known distributions, instead of using the inverse transform method, we have direct generating processes. This section summarizes some computer methods for generating random numbers from the main known distributions: uniform distribution, Bernoulli distribution, binomial distribution, Cauchy distribution, empirical distribution, exponential distribution, Erlang distribution, gamma distribution, beta distribution, Weibull distribution, geometrical distribution, negative binomial distribution, logistic distribution, normal distribution, χ^2 distribution, F distribution, Student's t distribution, lognormal distribution, multinormal distribution, Poisson distribution, triangular distribution, and uniform distribution in a complex region. The generating tree for these random numbers is shown in Figure 3.1. For detailed expositions, interested readers may consult Fishman [42], Law and Kelton [82], Bratley et al. [16], Rubinstein [123], and so on.

Uniform Distribution: $\mathcal{U}(a,b)$

A random variable x has a uniform distribution if its probability density function is defined as:

$$f(x) = \begin{cases} \dfrac{1}{b-a}, & a \le x \le b \\ 0, & \text{otherwise} \end{cases} \tag{3.3}$$

denoted by $\mathcal{U}(a,b)$, where a and b are given real numbers with $a < b$. We need to pay more attention to the uniform distribution because it is the basic technique for generating other random numbers. In fact, we produce

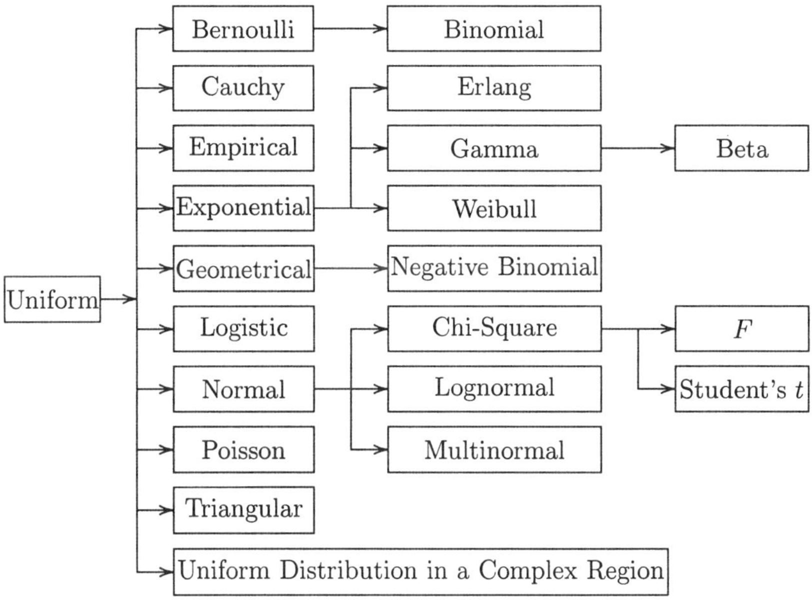

Figure 3.1: Generating Tree for Random Numbers

it on a digital computer by a deterministic sequence called *pseudorandom numbers*. The deterministic sequence is regarded as random numbers because the numbers generated by this sequence are uniformly distributed and stochastically independent. The proof of this fact is of independent interest, and readers may consult the relevant literature.

The most commonly used method for generating uniformly distributed numbers is called the *congruential method*, which is based on a fundamental congruence relationship expressed as

$$x_{i+1} = ax_i + c \pmod{m}, \quad i = 1, 2, \cdots, n-1 \tag{3.4}$$

where the multiplier a, the increment c, and the modulus m are nonnegative integers, and n is the length of the pseudorandom number sequence. Thus, any initial value x_1 (also called the *seed*, and $0 \le x_1 < m$) yields a sequence $\{x_1, x_2, \cdots, x_n\}$ by (3.4). The uniformly distributed numbers on $[0,1]$ can be obtained by

$$u_i = \frac{x_i}{m-1}, \quad i = 1, 2, \cdots, n. \tag{3.5}$$

Equivalently, the uniformly distributed numbers on an interval $[a, b]$ are obtained by

$$u_i = a + \frac{x_i}{m-1}(b-a), \quad i = 1, 2, \cdots, n. \tag{3.6}$$

We have seen that a sequence of pseudorandom numbers produced by a congruential generator is completely defined by the numbers x_1, a, c, and m. In order to obtain a satisfactory statistical result, it is suggested that we should design them carefully, for example, we may choose $a = 2^7 + 1$, $c = 1$, and $m = 2^{35}$. Fortunately, the subfunction of generating pseudorandom numbers has been provided by the C library for any type of computer.

There are two subfunctions in the C library to produce pseudorandom numbers. The first one is

#include ⟨stdlib.h⟩
int rand(void)

which produces a pseudorandom integer between 0 and RAND_MAX, where RAND_MAX is defined in stdlib.h as $2^{15} - 1$, while the second is

#include ⟨stdlib.h⟩
int random(int num)

which produces a pseudorandom integer between 0 and $num - 1$. Thus a randomly real number on an interval $[a, b]$ can be produced as follows,

u = random(num); // num, an integer, for example, 10000
$u = u/(num - 1)$;
Return $a + u(b - a)$.

Bernoulli Distribution: $\mathcal{BE}(p)$

A random variable x has a Bernoulli distribution with parameter p ($0 < p < 1$) if its probability mass function is defined as:

$$f(x) = \begin{cases} p, & x = 1 \\ 1 - p, & x = 0, \end{cases} \tag{3.7}$$

denoted by $\mathcal{BE}(p)$.

Generate μ from $\mathcal{U}(0, 1)$;
If $\mu \le p$, then return 1
Else return 0.

Binomial Distribution: $\mathcal{BN}(n, p)$

A random variable x has a binomial distribution if its probability mass function is defined as:

$$f(x) = \frac{n!}{(n-x)!x!} p^x (1-p)^{n-x}, \quad x = 0, 1, 2, \cdots, n, \tag{3.8}$$

denoted by $\mathcal{BN}(n,p)$, where n is a positive integer and p is a number between 0 and 1. It represents the number of successes in n independent trials, each with probability p of success.

Generate $y_1, y_2, \cdots, y_n$ *from* $\mathcal{BE}(p)$;
Return $y_1 + y_2 + \cdots + y_n$.

Cauchy Distribution: $\mathcal{C}(\alpha, \beta)$

A random variable x has a Cauchy distribution if its probability density function is defined as:

$$f(x) = \frac{\beta}{\pi\left[\beta^2 + (x-\alpha)^2\right]}, \quad \alpha > 0,\ \beta > 0,\ -\infty < x < \infty \tag{3.9}$$

denoted by $\mathcal{C}(\alpha, \beta)$. It can be generated in the following way.

Generate u *from* $\mathcal{U}(0,1)$;
$x = \alpha - \beta / \tan(\pi u)$;
Return x.

Empirical Distribution

Let $a_1, a_2, \cdots, a_n$ be n observations with $a_1 \le a_2 \le \cdots \le a_n$. By empirical distribution we mean the function

$$F(x) = \begin{cases} 0, & x < a_1 \\ \dfrac{i-1}{n-1} + \dfrac{x - a_i}{(n-1)(a_{i+1} - a_i)}, & \begin{array}{l} a_i \le x \le a_{i+1} \\ 1 \le i \le n-1 \end{array} \\ 1, & a_n \le x. \end{cases} \tag{3.10}$$

A random variable with empirical distribution $F(x)$ can be generated as follows.

Generate μ *from* $\mathcal{U}(0,1)$;
Let i *be the integer part of* $(n-1)\mu + 1$;
Return $a_i + [(n-1)\mu - i + 1](a_{i+1} - a_i)$.

Exponential Distribution: $\mathcal{EXP}(\beta)$

A random variable x has an exponential distribution if its probability density function is defined as:

$$f(x) = \begin{cases} \dfrac{1}{\beta} e^{-x/\beta}, & 0 \le x < \infty,\ \beta > 0 \\ 0, & \text{otherwise} \end{cases} \tag{3.11}$$

denoted by $\mathcal{EXP}(\beta)$, whose mean, variance, and mode are β, β^2, and 0, respectively. It can be generated in the following way.

Generate u *from* $\mathcal{U}(0,1)$;
Return $-\beta\ln(u)$.

Erlang Distribution: $\mathcal{ER}(k,\beta)$

A random variable x has an Erlang distribution with k degrees of freedom and mean β, denoted by $\mathcal{ER}(k,\beta)$, if it is the sum of k exponentially distributed variables each with mean β/k.

Generate $y_1, y_2, \cdots, y_k$ *from* $\mathcal{EXP}(\beta/k)$;
Rcturn $y_1 + y_2 + \cdots + y_k$.

Gamma Distribution: $\mathcal{G}(\alpha,\beta)$

A random variable x has a gamma distribution if its probability density function is defined as:

$$f(x) = \begin{cases} \dfrac{x^{\alpha-1}e^{-x/\beta}}{\beta^\alpha\Gamma(\alpha)}, & 0 \le x < \infty,\ \alpha > 0,\ \beta > 0 \\ 0, & \text{otherwise} \end{cases} \tag{3.12}$$

denoted by $\mathcal{G}(\alpha,\beta)$ whose mean and variance are $\alpha\beta$ and $\alpha\beta^2$, respectively. Note that $\mathcal{G}(1,\beta)$ is just $\mathcal{EXP}(\beta)$. When α is integer, we can generate a gamma distributed variable as follows.

$x = 0$;
Repeat
    Generate v *from* $\mathcal{EXP}(1)$;
    $x = x + v$;
    $\alpha = \alpha - 1$;
Until($\alpha = 1$)
Return (βx).

Beta Distribution: $\mathcal{B}(\alpha,\beta)$

A random variable x has a beta distribution if its probability density function is defined as:

$$f(x) = \frac{\Gamma(\alpha+\beta)}{\Gamma(\alpha)\Gamma(\beta)}x^{\alpha-1}(1-x)^{\beta-1}, \quad \alpha > 0,\ \beta > 0,\ 0 \le x \le 1 \tag{3.13}$$

denoted by $\mathcal{B}(\alpha,\beta)$. When α and β are integer, the generating process is shown below.

Generate y_1 *from* $\mathcal{G}(\alpha,1)$;
Generate y_2 *from* $\mathcal{G}(\beta,1)$;
$x = y_1/(y_1 + y_2)$;
Return x.

Weibull Distribution: $\mathcal{W}(\alpha, \beta)$

A random variable x more general than the exponential, yet frequently applied in statistical theory of reliability, has a Weibull distribution if its probability density function is defined as:

$$f(x) = \begin{cases} \dfrac{\alpha}{\beta^\alpha} x^{\alpha-1} e^{-(x/\beta)^\alpha}, & 0 \le x < \infty,\ \alpha > 0,\ \beta > 0 \\ 0, & \text{otherwise} \end{cases} \tag{3.14}$$

denoted by $\mathcal{W}(\alpha, \beta)$. It can be generated as follows.

Generate v *from* $\mathcal{EXP}(1)$;
$x = \beta v^{1/\alpha}$;
Return x.

Geometric Distribution: $\mathcal{GE}(p)$

A random variable x has a geometric distribution with parameter $p(0 < p < 1)$ if its probability mass function is defined as:

$$f(x) = \begin{cases} p(1-p)^x, & x = 0, 1, 2, \cdots \\ 0, & \text{otherwise} \end{cases} \tag{3.15}$$

denoted by $\mathcal{GE}(p)$.

Generate r *from* $\mathcal{U}(0, 1)$;
Return the integer part of $\ln r / \ln(1-p)$.

Negative Binomial Distribution: $\mathcal{NB}(k, p)$

A random variable x has a negative binomial distribution with parameter k and p ($k = 1, 2, \cdots$ and $0 < p < 1$) if it is the sum of k independent geometric variables each with parameter p, denoted by $\mathcal{NB}(k, p)$.

Generate $y_i, i = 1, 2, \cdots, k$ *from* $\mathcal{GE}(p)$;
Return $y_1 + y_2 + \cdots + y_k$.

Logistic Distribution: $\mathcal{L}(a, b)$

A random variable x has a logistic distribution if its probability density function is defined as:

$$f(x) = \frac{\exp\left[-(x-a)/b\right]}{b\left\{1 + \exp\left[-(x-a)/b\right]\right\}^2} \tag{3.16}$$

whose mean, variance, and mode are a, $(b\pi)^2/3$, and a, respectively, denoted by $\mathcal{L}(a, b)$.

Generate μ *from* $\mathcal{U}(0, 1)$;
Return $a - b\ln(1/\mu - 1)$.

Normal Distribution: $\mathcal{N}(\mu, \sigma^2)$

A random variable x has a normal distribution if its probability density function is defined as:

$$f(x) = \frac{1}{\sigma\sqrt{2\pi}} \exp\left[-\frac{(x-\mu)^2}{2\sigma^2}\right], \qquad -\infty < x < +\infty \tag{3.17}$$

denoted by $\mathcal{N}(\mu, \sigma^2)$, where μ is the mean and σ^2 is the variance.

Generate μ_1 *from* $\mathcal{U}(0,1)$;
Generate μ_2 *from* $\mathcal{U}(0,1)$;
$z = [-2\ln(\mu_1)]^{\frac{1}{2}} \sin(2\pi\mu_2)$;
$x = \mu + \sigma z$;
Return x.

Chi-Square Distribution: $\mathcal{X}^2(k)$

Let $z_1, z_2, \cdots, z_k$ be from $\mathcal{N}(0,1)$. Then the variable

$$y = \sum_{i=1}^{k} z_i^2 \tag{3.18}$$

has a Chi-Square distribution with k degrees of freedom and is denoted by $\mathcal{X}^2(k)$. Its probability density function is

$$f(x) = \frac{x^{(k/2)-1} \exp[-x/2]}{\Gamma(k/2)\, 2^{k/2}}, \qquad x \ge 0 \tag{3.19}$$

whose mean and variance are k and $2k$, respectively. The generating process is as follows.

Generate $z_i, i = 1, 2, \cdots, k$, *from* $\mathcal{N}(0,1)$;
Return $z_1^2 + z_2^2 + \cdots + z_k^2$.

F Distribution: $\mathcal{F}(k_1, k_2)$

Let y_1 be from $\mathcal{X}^2(k_1)$, y_2 from $\mathcal{X}^2(k_2)$. Then

$$x = \frac{y_1/k_1}{y_2/k_2} \tag{3.20}$$

has an F distribution with k_1 and k_2 degrees of freedom and is denoted by $\mathcal{F}(k_1, k_2)$.

Generate y_1 *from* $\mathcal{X}^2(k_1)$;
Generate y_2 *from* $\mathcal{X}^2(k_2)$;
$x = \frac{y_1/k_1}{y_2/k_2}$;
Return x.

Student's t Distribution: $\mathcal{S}(k)$

Let z be from $\mathcal{N}(0,1)$, y from $\mathcal{X}^2(k)$. Then the variable

$$x = \frac{z}{\sqrt{y/k}} \tag{3.21}$$

has a Student's t distribution with k degrees of freedom and is denoted by $\mathcal{S}(k)$.

Generate z from $\mathcal{N}(0,1)$;
Generate y from $\mathcal{X}^2(k)$;
$x = z/\sqrt{y/k}$;
Return x.

Lognormal Distribution: $\mathcal{LOGN}(\mu,\sigma^2)$

Let x be from $\mathcal{N}(\mu,\sigma^2)$. Then the variable $y = \exp[x]$ has a lognormal distribution with probability density function

$$f(y) = \begin{cases} \dfrac{1}{\sqrt{2\pi}\sigma y}\exp\left[-\dfrac{(\ln(y)-\mu)^2}{2\sigma^2}\right], & 0 \le y < \infty \\ 0, & \text{otherwise} \end{cases} \tag{3.22}$$

denoted by $\mathcal{LOGN}(\mu,\sigma^2)$, whose mean and variance are $\exp[\mu+\sigma^2/2]$ and $[\exp(\sigma^2)-1]\exp[2\mu+\sigma^2]$, respectively. It can be generated by the following steps.

Generate z from $\mathcal{N}(0,1)$;
$x = u + \sigma z$;
Return $\exp[x]$.

Multinormal Distribution: $\mathcal{N}(\mu,\Sigma)$

An n-dimensional random vector $\boldsymbol{x} = (x_1, x_2, \cdots, x_n)$ has a multinormal distribution if its probability density function is defined as:

$$f(\boldsymbol{x}) = \frac{1}{(2\pi)^{\frac{n}{2}} \mid \Sigma \mid^{\frac{1}{2}}} \exp\left[-\frac{1}{2}(\boldsymbol{x}-\mu)'\Sigma^{-1}(\boldsymbol{x}-\mu)\right] \tag{3.23}$$

where Σ is a real positive definite symmetric matrix. Notice that the inverse Σ^{-1} exists and is also positive definite.

Generate an upper triangular matrix C such that $\Sigma = CC'$;
Generate $\mu_1, \mu_2, \cdots, \mu_n$ from $\mathcal{N}(0,1)$;
$x_k = \mu_k + \sum_{i=1}^{k} c_{ki}\mu_i$, $(k = 1, 2, \cdots, n)$;
Return $\boldsymbol{x} = (x_1, x_2, \cdots, x_n)$.

Triangular Distribution: $\mathcal{T}(a,b,m)$

A random variable x has a triangular distribution if its probability density function is defined as:

$$f(x) = \begin{cases} \dfrac{2(x-a)}{(b-a)(m-a)}, & a < x \le m, \\ \dfrac{2(b-x)}{(b-a)(b-m)}, & m < x \le b, \\ 0, & \text{otherwise} \end{cases} \tag{3.24}$$

denoted by $\mathcal{T}(a,b,m)$, where $a < m < b$.

$c = (m-a)/(b-a)$;
Generate u *from* $\mathcal{U}(0,1)$;
If $u < c$ *then* $y = \sqrt{cu}$;
Else $y = 1 - \sqrt{(1-c)(1-u)}$;
Return $a + (b-a)y$.

Poisson Distribution: $\mathcal{P}(\lambda)$

A random variable x has a Poisson distribution with mean $\lambda (\lambda > 0)$ if its probability mass function is defined as:

$$f(x) = \begin{cases} \dfrac{\lambda^x e^{-\lambda}}{x!}, & x = 0, 1, 2, \cdots \\ 0, & \text{otherwise} \end{cases} \tag{3.25}$$

denoted by $\mathcal{P}(\lambda)$, whose mean and variance are both λ.

$x = 0$;
$b = 1$;
mark:
Generate u *from* $\mathcal{U}(0,1)$;
$b = bu$;
If $b \ge e^{-\lambda}$, *then* $x = x + 1$ *and goto mark*;
Return x.

Uniform Distribution in Complex Region

It is interesting to generate a uniformly distributed vector in a complex region S in an n-dimensional Euclidean space $\Re^n$, where S may be understood as a feasible set of mathematical programming.

First we should determine a simple region Ω containing S. For example, an n-dimensional hypercube

$$\Omega = \left\{(x_1, x_2, \cdots, x_n) \in \Re^n \;\middle|\; a_i \le x_i \le b_i,\ i = 1, 2, \cdots, n\right\}$$

is a good candidate because it is easy for a computer to sample a random vector uniformly distributed on the hypercube Ω. In fact, if x_i are uniformly distributed variables on $[a_i, b_i]$, $i = 1, 2, \cdots, n$, respectively, then $(x_1, x_2, \cdots, x_n)$ is a uniformly distributed vector on the hypercube Ω. An acceptance-rejection method will accept or reject the generated vector, depending on whether it is inside or outside the region S.

Given a hypercube Ω containing S;
Repeat
  Generate x_i from $\mathcal{U}(a_i, b_i)$, $i = 1, 2, \cdots, n$, respectively;
  Set $\boldsymbol{x} = (x_1, x_2, \cdots, x_n)$;
Until($\boldsymbol{x} \in S$)
Return $\boldsymbol{x}$.

3.2 Stochastic Simulations

Stochastic simulation has been applied to integration, linear algebra, optimization, probability estimation, and so on. Here we give some numerical examples to illustrate the technique of stochastic simulations.

Example 1: In stochastic optimization problems, a multiple stochastic integral usually needs to be calculated. Let us consider the problem of estimating the multiple stochastic integral

$$\theta = \int_{\Re^n} g(\boldsymbol{\xi}) d\Phi(\boldsymbol{\xi}) \tag{3.26}$$

where $g(\boldsymbol{\xi})$ is an integrable function and $\Phi(\boldsymbol{\xi})$ is a joint or separate distribution function of random vector $\boldsymbol{\xi}$. Since θ is the expected value of the stochastic variable $g(\boldsymbol{\xi})$ (roughly speaking, $g(\boldsymbol{\xi})$ has the same probability distribution with $\boldsymbol{\xi}$), we can estimate the integral θ by

$$\theta = \frac{1}{N} \sum_{i=1}^{N} g(\boldsymbol{\xi}_i) \tag{3.27}$$

where $\boldsymbol{\xi}_1, \boldsymbol{\xi}_2, \cdots, \boldsymbol{\xi}_N$ are a sequence of random vectors generated from the distribution function $\Phi(\boldsymbol{\xi})$. In contrast to the classical method of multiple integral by iteration, the number of sampling points required to obtain a given degree of accuracy is independent of the number of dimensions, which makes the stochastic simulation very attractive for large numbers of dimensions.

Example 2: Let us consider an unconstrained optimization problem formulated as

$$\max_{\boldsymbol{x}\in\Re^n} f(\boldsymbol{x}). \tag{3.28}$$

Recall that the gradient is the direction of greatest slope of the function at any point. Gradient methods for seeking a maximum for f involve evaluating the gradient at an initial point, moving along the gradient direction for a calculable distance, and repeating this process until the maximum is found. In this case the gradient methods generate a new point $\boldsymbol{x}_{i+1}$ in the following way,

$$\boldsymbol{x}_{i+1} = \boldsymbol{x}_i + a_i \nabla f(\boldsymbol{x}_i), \quad a_i > 0 \tag{3.29}$$

where

$$\nabla f(\boldsymbol{x}) = \left(\frac{\partial f(\boldsymbol{x})}{\partial x_1}, \frac{\partial f(\boldsymbol{x})}{\partial x_2}, \cdots, \frac{\partial f(\boldsymbol{x})}{\partial x_n}\right)$$

is the gradient of $f(\boldsymbol{x})$, $\partial f(\boldsymbol{x})/\partial x_j$, $j = 1, 2, \cdots, n$, are the partial derivatives, and a_i is the ith step size.

It is well-known that this algorithm always converges to the local maxima, especially when the function $f(\boldsymbol{x})$ is multimodal. For this case, the designed algorithms need to be highly robust in order to avoid getting stuck at local maxima. To do so, one way is to replace (3.29) by a random formula as follows,

$$\boldsymbol{x}_{i+1} = \boldsymbol{x}_i + \frac{a_i}{2b_i}\left[f(\boldsymbol{x}_i + b_i \cdot \boldsymbol{d}_i) - f(\boldsymbol{x}_i - b_i \cdot \boldsymbol{d}_i)\right] \cdot \boldsymbol{d}_i, \quad a_i, b_i > 0 \tag{3.30}$$

where the random vector $\boldsymbol{d}_i$ is generated at the ith iteration and uniformly distributed on the n-dimensional unit sphere.

This method is called *stochastic simulation method*, in particular *random search algorithm*.

Example 3: Here we want to estimate the following probability of an event defined by a system of inequalities

$$\theta = \Pr\left\{g_j(\boldsymbol{\xi}) \le 0, \; j = 1, 2, \cdots, k\right\} \tag{3.31}$$

where $\boldsymbol{\xi}$ is a stochastic vector with probability distribution $\Phi(\boldsymbol{\xi})$, and $g_j(\boldsymbol{\xi})$ are real-valued functions, $j = 1, 2, \cdots, k$. We can generate N independent random vectors $\boldsymbol{\xi}_i$, $i = 1, 2, \cdots, N$, from the probability distribution $\Phi(\boldsymbol{\xi})$. Let N' be the number of occasions on which

$$g_j(\boldsymbol{\xi}_i) \le 0, \quad j = 1, 2, \cdots, k$$

for $i = 1, 2, \cdots, N$ (i.e., the number of random vectors satisfying the system of inequalities). Then by the law of large numbers, θ can be estimated by

$$\theta = \frac{N'}{N}. \tag{3.32}$$

For example, we consider the following problem,

$$\theta = \Pr\left\{\xi_1 + \xi_2^2 \geq 3,\ \xi_3 + \xi_4^2 \leq 9\right\} \tag{3.33}$$

where ξ_1 is a uniformly distributed variable $\mathcal{U}(2, 5)$, ξ_2 is an exponentially distributed variable $\mathcal{EXP}(3)$, and ξ_3 and ξ_4 are normally distributed variables $\mathcal{N}(3, 2)$ and $\mathcal{N}(1, 1)$, respectively. The result of stochastic simulation is shown in Figure 3.2, in which the straight line represents the known probability 0.85 and the curve represents the probabilities obtained by different numbers of cycles in simulation.

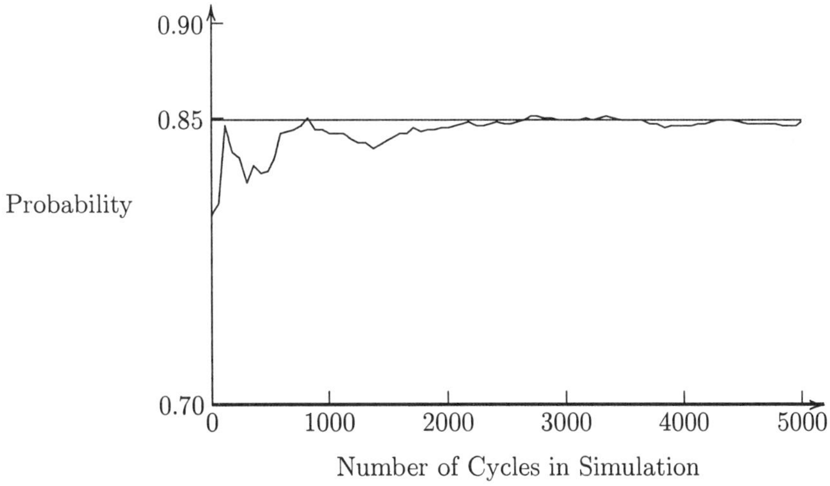

Figure 3.2: Stochastic Simulation for Example 3

From Figure 3.2, we see that the relative error of the results obtained by performing over 1000 cycles is less than 1%. Thus the stochastic simulation is effective for this type of problem.

Example 4: Now let us consider the problem

$$\Pr\left\{f(\boldsymbol{\xi}) \geq \overline{f}\right\} \geq \alpha \tag{3.34}$$

in which $\boldsymbol{\xi}$ is a random vector with probability distribution $\Phi(\boldsymbol{\xi})$, and α is a predetermined level between 0 and 1. We should find the maximal value of $\overline{f}$ such that the inequality (3.34) holds. For this problem, we may produce N independent random vectors $\boldsymbol{\xi}_i$, $i = 1, 2, \cdots, N$, from the probability distribution $\Phi(\boldsymbol{\xi})$. Then we get a sequence of $\{f_1, f_2, \cdots, f_N\}$ with $f_i = f(\boldsymbol{\xi}_i)$ for $i = 1, 2, \cdots, N$, respectively. We take N' as the integer part of αN, then by the law of large numbers, the N'th greatest element in $\{f_1, f_2, \cdots, f_N\}$ is regarded as the estimation of $\overline{f}$.

For example, we now want to obtain the maximal $\overline{f}$ such that

$$\Pr\left\{\xi_1 + \xi_2^2 + \xi_3^3 \geq \overline{f}\right\} \geq 0.8$$

where ξ_1 is a uniformly distributed variable $\mathcal{U}(1,3)$, ξ_2 is an exponentially distributed variable $\mathcal{EXP}(1)$, and ξ_3 is a normally distributed variable $\mathcal{N}(2,1)$. A run of stochastic simulation with 1000 cycles shows that the maximal value of $\overline{f}$ is 4.988.

3.3 Fuzzy Set Theory

Since its introduction in 1965 by Zadeh [151], fuzzy set theory has been well developed and applied in a wide variety of real problems. This section will list the technical terms and results of fuzzy set theory that are used in this book.

Let us first introduce the concept of *fuzzy sets* initiated by Zadeh [151]:

Definition 3.1 *Let X denote a universal set. Then a fuzzy subset A of X is defined by its membership function*

$$\mu_A: \quad X \to [0,1] \tag{3.35}$$

which assigns to each element $x \in X$ a real number $\mu_A(x)$ in the interval $[0,1]$, where the value of $\mu_A(x)$ at x represents the grade of membership of x in A. Thus, the nearer the value of $\mu_A(x)$ is unity, the higher the grade of membership of x in A.

That is, a fuzzy set A is defined as a set of ordered pairs,

$$A = \left\{(x, \mu_A(x)) \mid x \in X\right\}. \tag{3.36}$$

This definition can be generalized if the closed interval $[0,1]$ is replaced by a more general lattice with maximal and minimal elements.

Now let $A, B \subset X$ be two fuzzy sets with membership functions $\mu_A(x)$ and $\mu_B(x)$, respectively. We say A is a subset of B, denoted by $A \subset B$, if and only if

$$\mu_A(x) \leq \mu_B(x), \quad \forall x \in X. \tag{3.37}$$

This definition yields that A is equal to B, denoted by $A = B$, if and only if

$$\mu_A(x) = \mu_B(x), \quad \forall x \in X. \tag{3.38}$$

The *complement* $\bar{A}$ of a fuzzy set A is also a fuzzy set defined as

$$\mu_{\bar{A}}(x) = 1 - \mu_A(x), \quad \forall x \in X. \tag{3.39}$$

The *union* of two fuzzy sets A and B is a fuzzy set with membership function

$$\mu_{A \cup B}(x) = \max\left(\mu_A(x), \mu_B(x)\right) = \mu_A(x) \vee \mu_B(x), \quad \forall x \in X \tag{3.40}$$

and the intersection is also a fuzzy set with membership function

$$\mu_{A \cap B}(x) = \min\left(\mu_A(x), \mu_B(x)\right) = \mu_A(x) \wedge \mu_B(x), \quad \forall x \in X. \tag{3.41}$$

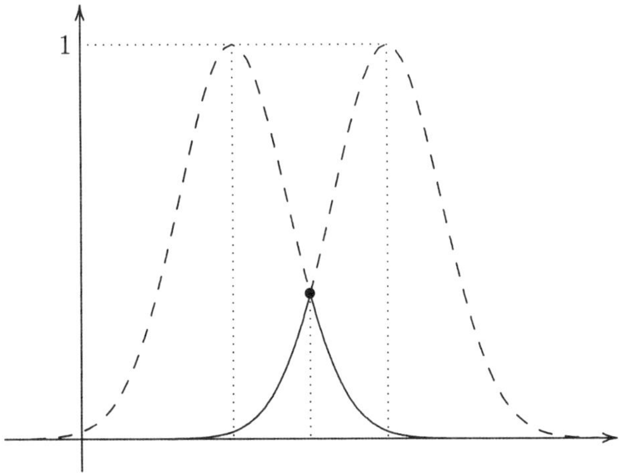

Figure 3.3: Intersection and Union of Two Fuzzy Sets Represented by Solid and Dashed Curves, Respectively

Definition 3.2 *The set of elements that belong to the fuzzy set A at least to the degree of membership α is called the α-level set, denoted by*

$$A_\alpha = \left\{x \in X \mid \mu_A(x) \geq \alpha\right\}. \tag{3.42}$$

Especially, we call a *fuzzy number* (or *fuzzy quantity*) any fuzzy subset $\tilde{a}$ of the real line $\Re$ with a membership function $\mu_{\tilde{a}}\colon \Re \to [0, 1]$. Let $\tilde{a}$ and $\tilde{b}$ be two fuzzy numbers with membership functions $\mu_{\tilde{a}}$ and $\mu_{\tilde{b}}$, respectively.

Based on the concepts and techniques of possibility theory proposed by Zadeh [153], the possibility of $\tilde{a} \le \tilde{b}$ is defined as follows (Dubois and Prade [35][36]),

$$\text{Pos}\{\tilde{a} \le \tilde{b}\} = \sup\left\{\min(\mu_{\tilde{a}}(x), \mu_{\tilde{b}}(y)) \mid x, y \in \Re, x \le y\right\}, \tag{3.43}$$

where the abbreviation Pos represents possibility. This means that the possibility of $\tilde{a} \le \tilde{b}$ is the greatest possibility that there exists at least one pair of values $x, y \in \Re$ such that $x \le y$, and the values of $\tilde{a}$ and $\tilde{b}$ are x and y, respectively. Analogously, the possibility of $\tilde{a} < \tilde{b}$ is defined by

$$\text{Pos}\{\tilde{a} < \tilde{b}\} = \sup\left\{\min(\mu_{\tilde{a}}(x), \mu_{\tilde{b}}(y)) \mid x, y \in \Re, x < y\right\}. \tag{3.44}$$

The possibility of $\tilde{a} = \tilde{b}$ is defined by

$$\text{Pos}\{\tilde{a} = \tilde{b}\} = \sup\left\{\min(\mu_{\tilde{a}}(x), \mu_{\tilde{b}}(x)) \mid x \in \Re\right\}. \tag{3.45}$$

In particular, when $\tilde{b}$ is a crisp number b, we have

$$\begin{cases} \text{Pos}\{\tilde{a} \le b\} = \sup\left\{\mu_{\tilde{a}}(x) \mid x \in \Re, x \le b\right\} \\ \text{Pos}\{\tilde{a} < b\} = \sup\left\{\mu_{\tilde{a}}(x) \mid x \in \Re, x < b\right\} \\ \text{Pos}\{\tilde{a} = b\} = \mu_{\tilde{a}}(b). \end{cases} \tag{3.46}$$

Let f: $\Re \times \Re \to \Re$ be a binary operation over real numbers. Then it can be extended to the operation over the set of fuzzy numbers. If we denote for the fuzzy numbers $\tilde{a}, \tilde{b}$ the number $\tilde{c} = f(\tilde{a}, \tilde{b})$, then the membership function $\mu_{\tilde{c}}$ is derived from the membership functions $\mu_{\tilde{a}}$ and $\mu_{\tilde{b}}$ by

$$\mu_{\tilde{c}}(z) = \sup\left\{\min(\mu_{\tilde{a}}(x), \mu_{\tilde{b}}(y)) \mid x, y \in \Re, z = f(x, y)\right\} \tag{3.47}$$

for any $z \in \Re$. That is, the possibility that the fuzzy number $\tilde{c} = f(\tilde{a}, \tilde{b})$ achieves value $z \in \Re$ is as great as the most possible combination of real numbers x, y such that $z = f(x, y)$, where the values of $\tilde{a}$ and $\tilde{b}$ are x and y, respectively.

Generally speaking, let $f : \Re^n \to \Re$ be a real-valued function over the n-dimensional Euclidean space. If we denote for fuzzy numbers $\tilde{a}_1, \tilde{a}_2, \cdots, \tilde{a}_n$ the fuzzy number $\tilde{c} = f(\tilde{a}_1, \tilde{a}_2, \cdots, \tilde{a}_n)$, then the membership function $\mu_{\tilde{c}}$ is derived from the membership functions $\mu_{\tilde{a}_1}, \mu_{\tilde{a}_2}, \cdots, \mu_{\tilde{a}_n}$ by

$$\mu_{\tilde{c}}(z) = \sup\left\{\min_{1 \le i \le n} \mu_{\tilde{a}_i}(x_i) \;\middle|\; \begin{array}{c} x_i \in \Re, i = 1, 2, \cdots, n \\ z = f(x_1, x_2, \cdots, x_n) \end{array}\right\}. \tag{3.48}$$

Thus the possibility of $f(\tilde{a}_1, \tilde{a}_2, \cdots, \tilde{a}_n) \le b$ should be defined by

$$\text{Pos}\left\{f(\tilde{a}_1, \tilde{a}_2, \cdots, \tilde{a}_n) \le b\right\} = \sup\left\{\mu_{\tilde{c}}(z) \mid z \in \Re, z \le b\right\} \tag{3.49}$$

where the membership function $\mu_{\tilde{c}}$ is defined by (3.48). In other words, the possibility of $f(\tilde{a}_1, \tilde{a}_2, \cdots, \tilde{a}_n) \le b$ is given by

$$\begin{aligned} &\text{Pos}\left\{f(\tilde{a}_1, \tilde{a}_2, \cdots, \tilde{a}_n) \le b\right\} \\ =\; &\sup\left\{ \min_{1\le i\le n} \mu_{\tilde{a}_i}(x_i) \;\middle|\; \begin{array}{c} x_i \in \Re, i = 1, 2, \cdots, n \\ f(x_1, x_2, \cdots, x_n) \le b \end{array} \right\}. \end{aligned} \tag{3.50}$$

More generally, assume that $f_j : \Re^n \to \Re$ are real-valued functions over the n-dimensional Euclidean space, $j = 1, 2, \cdots, m$. Then the possibility of a system of inequalities

$$f_j(\tilde{a}_1, \tilde{a}_2, \cdots, \tilde{a}_n) \le b_j, \quad j = 1, 2, \cdots, m, \tag{3.51}$$

where $b_j, j = 1, 2, \cdots, m$ are crisp numbers, should be defined as

$$\begin{aligned} &\text{Pos}\left\{f_j(\tilde{a}_1, \tilde{a}_2, \cdots, \tilde{a}_n) \le b_j,\ j = 1, 2, \cdots, m\right\} \\ =\; &\sup_{x_1, x_2, \cdots, x_n}\left\{ \min_{1\le i\le n} \mu_{\tilde{a}_i}(x_i) \;\middle|\; \begin{array}{r} f_j(x_1, x_2, \cdots, x_n) \le b_j \\ j = 1, 2, \cdots, m \end{array} \right\}. \end{aligned} \tag{3.52}$$

This means that the possibility of the system of inequalities is as great as the most possible vector $(x_1, x_2, \cdots, x_n) \in \Re^n$ at which the system of inequalities is met, and the values of $\tilde{a}_i$ are x_i, $i = 1, 2, \cdots, n$, respectively. Analogously, we have

$$\begin{aligned} &\text{Pos}\left\{f_j(\tilde{a}_1, \tilde{a}_2, \cdots, \tilde{a}_n) < b_j,\ j = 1, 2, \cdots, m\right\} \\ =\; &\sup_{x_1, x_2, \cdots, x_n}\left\{ \min_{1\le i\le n} \mu_{\tilde{a}_i}(x_i) \;\middle|\; \begin{array}{r} f_j(x_1, x_2, \cdots, x_n) < b_j \\ j = 1, 2, \cdots, m \end{array} \right\} \end{aligned} \tag{3.53}$$

and

$$\begin{aligned} &\text{Pos}\left\{f_j(\tilde{a}_1, \tilde{a}_2, \cdots, \tilde{a}_n) = b_j,\ j = 1, 2, \cdots, m\right\} \\ =\; &\sup_{x_1, x_2, \cdots, x_n}\left\{ \min_{1\le i\le n} \mu_{\tilde{a}_i}(x_i) \;\middle|\; \begin{array}{r} f_j(x_1, x_2, \cdots, x_n) = b_j \\ j = 1, 2, \cdots, m \end{array} \right\} \end{aligned} \tag{3.54}$$

as well as the analogous form of mixed system of inequalities and equations.

Now let us illustrate the above results by *trapezoidal fuzzy numbers*, which are fuzzy quantities fully determined by quadruples (r_1, r_2, r_3, r_4) of crisp numbers such that $r_1 < r_2 \le r_3 < r_4$, whose membership functions can be denoted by

$$\mu(x) = \begin{cases} \dfrac{x - r_1}{r_2 - r_1}, & r_1 \le x \le r_2 \\ 1, & r_2 \le x \le r_3 \\ \dfrac{x - r_4}{r_3 - r_4}, & r_3 \le x \le r_4 \\ 0, & \text{otherwise.} \end{cases} \tag{3.55}$$

We mention that the trapezoidal fuzzy number is a *triangular fuzzy number* if $r_2 = r_3$, denoted by a triple (r_1, r_2, r_4). Now let us consider two trapezoidal fuzzy numbers $\tilde{r} = (r_1, r_2, r_3, r_4)$ and $\tilde{b} = (b_1, b_2, b_3, b_4)$, as shown in Figure 3.4.

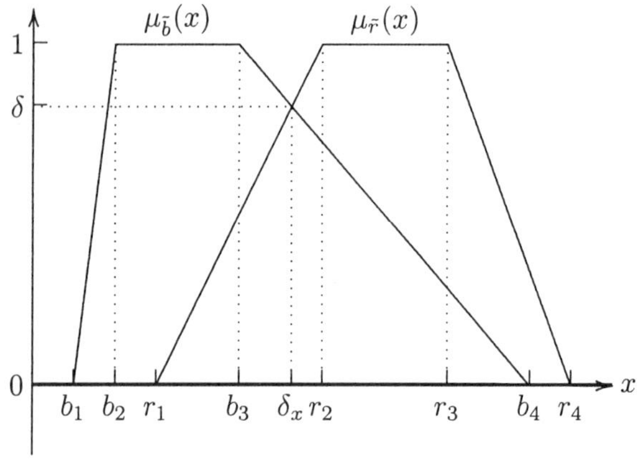

Figure 3.4: Two Trapezoidal Fuzzy Numbers $\tilde{r}$ and $\tilde{b}$

If $r_2 \le b_3$, then we have

$$\begin{aligned} \text{Pos}\left\{\tilde{r} \le \tilde{b}\right\} &= \sup\left\{\min\left\{\mu_{\tilde{r}}(x), \mu_{\tilde{b}}(y)\right\} \mid x \le y\right\} \\ &\ge \min\left\{\mu_{\tilde{r}}(r_2), \mu_{\tilde{b}}(b_3)\right\} \\ &= \min\{1, 1\} = 1, \end{aligned}$$

which implies that $\text{Pos}\{\tilde{r} \le \tilde{b}\} = 1$. If $r_2 > b_3$ and $r_1 \le b_4$, then the supremum is achieved at the point of intersection δ_x of the two membership functions $\mu_{\tilde{r}}(x)$ and $\mu_{\tilde{b}}(x)$. A simple computation shows that

$$\text{Pos}\left\{\tilde{r} \le \tilde{b}\right\} = \delta = \frac{b_4 - r_1}{(b_4 - b_3) + (r_2 - r_1)}$$

and

$$\delta_x = r_1 + (r_2 - r_1)\delta.$$

If $r_1 > b_4$, then for any $x < y$, at least one of the equalities

$$\mu_{\tilde{r}}(x) = 0, \qquad \mu_{\tilde{b}}(y) = 0$$

holds. Thus we have $\text{Pos}\{\tilde{r} \le \tilde{b}\} = 0$. Now we summarize the above results as

$$\text{Pos}\left\{\tilde{r} \le \tilde{b}\right\} = \begin{cases} 1, & r_2 \le b_3 \\ \delta, & r_2 \ge b_3,\ r_1 \le b_4 \\ 0, & r_1 \ge b_4. \end{cases} \tag{3.56}$$

Especially, when $\tilde{b}$ is a crisp number 0, then we have

$$\text{Pos}\left\{\tilde{r} \le 0\right\} = \begin{cases} 1, & r_2 \le 0 \\ \delta, & r_1 \le 0 \le r_2 \\ 0, & r_1 \ge 0 \end{cases} \tag{3.57}$$

where

$$\delta = \frac{r_1}{r_1 - r_2}. \tag{3.58}$$

We now turn our attention to proving the following lemma.

Lemma 3.1 *Assume that the trapezoidal fuzzy number* $\tilde{r} = (r_1, r_2, r_3, r_4)$. *Then for any given confidence level* α *with* $0 \le \alpha \le 1$, $\text{Pos}\{\tilde{r} \le 0\} \ge \alpha$ *if and only if* $(1-\alpha)r_1 + \alpha r_2 \le 0$.

Proof. If $\text{Pos}\{\tilde{r} \le 0\} \ge \alpha$, then we have either $r_2 \le 0$ or $r_1/(r_1 - r_2) \ge \alpha$. If $r_2 \le 0$, then $r_1 < r_2 \le 0$, so that $(1-\alpha)r_1 + \alpha r_2 \le 0$. If $r_1/(r_1 - r_2) \ge \alpha$, then $r_1 \le \alpha(r_1 - r_2)$ by the fact that $r_1 < r_2$. Hence we have $(1-\alpha)r_1 + \alpha r_2 \le 0$ for any cases.

If $(1-\alpha)r_1 + \alpha r_2 \le 0$, the argument breaks down into two cases. When $r_2 \le 0$, we have $\text{Pos}\{\tilde{r} \le 0\} = 1$, which implies that $\text{Pos}\{\tilde{r} \le 0\} \ge \alpha$. When $r_2 > 0$, we have $r_1 - r_2 < 0$, which can rearrange $(1-\alpha)r_1 + \alpha r_2 \le 0$ as $r_1/(r_1 - r_2) \ge \alpha$, i.e., $\text{Pos}\{\tilde{r} \le 0\} \ge \alpha$. The lemma is proved.

From the binary operation (3.47), we can obtain the sum of trapezoidal fuzzy numbers $\tilde{a} = (a_1, a_2, a_3, a_4)$ and $\tilde{b} = (b_1, b_2, b_3, b_4)$ as

$$\begin{aligned}\mu_{\tilde{a}+\tilde{b}}(z) &= \sup\left\{\min\left\{\mu_{\tilde{a}}(x), \mu_{\tilde{b}}(y)\right\} \mid z = x + y\right\} \\ &= \begin{cases} \dfrac{z-(a_1+b_1)}{(a_2+b_2)-(a_1+b_1)}, & a_1+b_1 \le z \le a_2+b_2 \\ 1, & a_2+b_2 \le z \le a_3+b_3 \\ \dfrac{z-(a_4+b_4)}{(a_3+b_3)-(a_4+b_4)}, & a_3+b_3 \le z \le a_4+b_4 \\ 0, & \text{otherwise.} \end{cases}\end{aligned}$$

That is, the sum of two trapezoidal fuzzy numbers is also a trapezoidal fuzzy number, and

$$\tilde{a} + \tilde{b} = (a_1 + b_1, a_2 + b_2, a_3 + b_3, a_4 + b_4). \tag{3.59}$$

Next we consider the product of a trapezoidal fuzzy number and a scalar number λ. We have

$$\mu_{\lambda \cdot \tilde{a}}(z) = \sup\left\{\mu_{\tilde{a}}(x) \mid z = \lambda x\right\}$$

which yields that

$$\lambda \cdot \tilde{a} = \begin{cases} (\lambda a_1, \lambda a_2, \lambda a_3, \lambda a_4), & \lambda \ge 0 \\ (\lambda a_4, \lambda a_3, \lambda a_2, \lambda a_1), & \lambda < 0. \end{cases} \tag{3.60}$$

That is, the product of a trapezoidal fuzzy number and a scalar number is also a trapezoidal fuzzy number. Thus a weighted sum of trapezoidal fuzzy numbers is also a trapezoidal fuzzy number. For example, we assume that $\tilde{a}_i$ are trapezoidal fuzzy numbers $(a_{i1}, a_{i2}, a_{i3}, a_{i4})$, and λ_i are scalar numbers, $i = 1, 2, \cdots, n$, respectively. If we define

$$\lambda_i^+ = \begin{cases} \lambda_i, & \text{if } \lambda_i \ge 0 \\ 0, & \text{otherwise,} \end{cases} \qquad \lambda_i^- = \begin{cases} 0, & \text{if } \lambda_i \ge 0 \\ -\lambda_i, & \text{otherwise} \end{cases}$$

for $i = 1, 2, \cdots, n$, then λ_i^+ and λ_i^- are all nonnegative and satisfy that $\lambda_i = \lambda_i^+ - \lambda_i^-$. By the sum and product operations of trapezoidal fuzzy numbers, we can obtain

$$\tilde{a} = \sum_{i=1}^{n} \lambda_i \cdot \tilde{a}_i = \begin{pmatrix} \sum_{i=1}^{n} \left(\lambda_i^+ a_{i1} - \lambda_i^- a_{i4}\right) \\ \sum_{i=1}^{n} \left(\lambda_i^+ a_{i2} - \lambda_i^- a_{i3}\right) \\ \sum_{i=1}^{n} \left(\lambda_i^+ a_{i3} - \lambda_i^- a_{i2}\right) \\ \sum_{i=1}^{n} \left(\lambda_i^+ a_{i4} - \lambda_i^- a_{i1}\right) \end{pmatrix}^T .$$

3.4 Fuzzy Simulations

For the fuzzy optimization problems, Liu and Iwamura [90][91] presented fuzzy simulations to check the possibility inequalities like

$$\text{Pos}\left\{g_i(\boldsymbol{\xi}) \le 0,\ i = 1, 2, \cdots, k\right\} \ge \alpha$$

and to compute the possibility

$$G = \text{Pos}\left\{g_i(\boldsymbol{\xi}) \le 0,\ i = 1, 2, \cdots, k\right\}$$

as well as to find the maximal value f such that

$$\text{Pos}\left\{g(\boldsymbol{\xi}) \ge f\right\} \ge \alpha$$

where $\boldsymbol{\xi}$ is a fuzzy vector with a known membership function $\mu(\cdot)$. In this section, we will introduce the fuzzy simulation technique to deal with this type of problem in fuzzy systems. Let us discuss this for the following cases.

Case I. Checking $\text{Pos}\left\{g_i(\boldsymbol{\xi}) \le 0, i = 1, 2, \cdots, k\right\} \ge \alpha$

From the definition of operations over fuzzy numbers, we say

$$\text{Pos}\left\{g_i(\boldsymbol{\xi}) \le 0, i = 1, 2, \cdots, k\right\} \ge \alpha$$

if and only if there is a crisp vector $\boldsymbol{\xi}^0$ such that

$$g_i(\boldsymbol{\xi}^0) \le 0, \quad i = 1, 2, \cdots, k$$

and $\mu(\boldsymbol{\xi}^0) \ge \alpha$. In order to check the inequality by computers, we can generate a crisp vector $\boldsymbol{\xi}^0$ uniformly from the fuzzy vector $\boldsymbol{\xi}$ such that $\mu(\boldsymbol{\xi}^0) \ge \alpha$ (i.e., the α-level set of fuzzy vector $\boldsymbol{\xi}$). If the α-level set of the fuzzy vector is too complex to determine, we can sample a vector $\boldsymbol{\xi}^0$ from a hypercube Ω

containing the α-level set and then accept or reject it, depending on whether $\mu(\boldsymbol{\xi}^0) \geq \alpha$ or not. If the vector $\boldsymbol{\xi}^0$ satisfies that $g_i(\boldsymbol{\xi}^0) \leq 0, i = 1, 2, \cdots, k$, then we can believe that the inequality $\text{Pos}\{g_i(\boldsymbol{\xi}) \leq 0, i = 1, 2, \cdots, k\} \geq \alpha$ holds. If not, we will regenerate a crisp vector $\boldsymbol{\xi}^0$ from the fuzzy vector $\boldsymbol{\xi}$ in the same way and check the constraints again. After a given number N of cycles, if there is no feasible vector $\boldsymbol{\xi}^0$ generated, then we say that the inequality $\text{Pos}\{g_i(\boldsymbol{\xi}) \leq 0, i = 1, 2, \cdots, k\} \geq \alpha$ does not hold. Now we summarize the above process as follows.

Step 1. Generate $\boldsymbol{\xi}^0$ uniformly from the α-level set of fuzzy vector $\boldsymbol{\xi}$.
Step 2. If $g_i(\boldsymbol{\xi}^0) \leq 0, i = 1, 2, \cdots, k$, return YES.
Step 3. Repeat the first and second steps N times.
Step 4. Return NO.

Case II. Computing $G = \text{Pos}\{g_i(\boldsymbol{\xi}) \leq 0, i = 1, 2, \cdots, k\}$

At first we set $G = 0$. Next we generate a crisp vector $\boldsymbol{\xi}^0$ from the fuzzy vector $\boldsymbol{\xi}$. In practice, we are not interested in the decision vectors with too low possibility. Thus we can predetermine a level, say α_0. Then we generate the crisp vector $\boldsymbol{\xi}^0$ uniformly from the α_0-level set of fuzzy vector $\boldsymbol{\xi}$. If this set is not easy for a computer to describe, we can give a larger region, for example, a hypercube Ω containing all potential interesting samples. Certainly, the smaller the region, the more effective the fuzzy simulation. If $g_i(\boldsymbol{\xi}^0) \leq 0, i = 1, 2, \cdots, k$ and $G < \mu(\boldsymbol{\xi}^0)$, then we set $G = \mu(\boldsymbol{\xi}^0)$. Repeat this process N times. The value G is regarded as an estimation of the possibility. We now summarize it as follows.

Step 1. Set $G = 0$.
Step 2. Generate $\boldsymbol{\xi}^0$ uniformly from the α_0-level set of fuzzy vector $\boldsymbol{\xi}$.
Step 3. If $g_i(\boldsymbol{\xi}^0) \leq 0, i = 1, 2, \cdots, k$ and $G < \mu(\boldsymbol{\xi}^0)$, then we set

$$G = \mu(\boldsymbol{\xi}^0).$$

Step 4. Repeat the second and third steps N times.
Step 5. Return G.

Case III. Handling $\text{Pos}\{g(\boldsymbol{\xi}) \geq f\} \geq \beta$

For fuzzy constraints like

$$\text{Pos}\{g(\boldsymbol{\xi}) \geq f\} \geq \beta, \tag{3.61}$$

we should find the maximal f such that the inequality (3.61) holds. First we set $f = -\infty$. Then we generate a crisp vector $\boldsymbol{\xi}^0$ uniformly from the fuzzy vector $\boldsymbol{\xi}$ such that $\mu(\boldsymbol{\xi}^0) \geq \beta$ (i.e., the β-level set of fuzzy vector $\boldsymbol{\xi}$). We set $f = g(\boldsymbol{\xi}^0)$ provided that $f < g(\boldsymbol{\xi}^0)$. Repeat this process N times.

The value f is regarded as the estimation. We summarize this process as follows.

Step 1. Set $f = -\infty$.
Step 2. Generate $\boldsymbol{\xi}^0$ uniformly from the β-level set of fuzzy vector $\boldsymbol{\xi}$.
Step 3. If $f < g(\boldsymbol{\xi}^0)$, then we set $f = g(\boldsymbol{\xi}^0)$.
Step 4. Repeat the second and third steps N times.
Step 5. Return f.

Case IV. Handling $\text{Pos}\{g(\boldsymbol{\xi}) \le f\} \ge \beta$

For fuzzy constraints like

$$\text{Pos}\{g(\boldsymbol{\xi}) \le f\} \ge \beta, \tag{3.62}$$

we should find the minimal f such that the inequality (3.62) holds. First we set $f = +\infty$. Then we generate a crisp vector $\boldsymbol{\xi}^0$ uniformly from the fuzzy vector $\boldsymbol{\xi}$ such that $\mu(\boldsymbol{\xi}^0) \ge \beta$ (i.e., the β-level set of fuzzy vector $\boldsymbol{\xi}$). We set $f = g(\boldsymbol{\xi}^0)$ provided that $f > g(\boldsymbol{\xi}^0)$. Repeat this process N times. The value f is regarded as the estimation. We summarize it as follows.

Step 1. Set $f = +\infty$.
Step 2. Generate $\boldsymbol{\xi}^0$ uniformly from the β-level set of fuzzy vector $\boldsymbol{\xi}$.
Step 3. If $f > g(\boldsymbol{\xi}^0)$, then we set $f = g(\boldsymbol{\xi}^0)$.
Step 4. Repeat the second and third steps N times.
Step 5. Return f.

In order to illustrate the fuzzy simulation, let us consider some numerical examples.

Example 1: Now we focus our attention on two fuzzy numbers $\tilde{r}$ and $\tilde{b}$ with membership functions

$$\mu_{\tilde{r}}(\xi) = \exp\left[-(\xi - 2)^2\right]$$

and

$$\mu_{\tilde{b}}(\xi) = \exp\left[-(\xi - 1)^2\right],$$

respectively. These two fuzzy numbers are also shown in Figure 3.5.

The known possibility of $\tilde{r} \le \tilde{b}$ is $\text{Pos}\{\tilde{r} \le \tilde{b}\} = \exp(-0.5^2) = 0.778$. Let us search for it by the technique of fuzzy simulation. At first, we take the interval $[0, 3]$ as a hypercube containing the α-level set for both fuzzy numbers $\tilde{r}$ and $\tilde{b}$, by the fact that we are not interested in the points out of that range because of too low possibility. Now we generate two crisp numbers r and b uniformly on $[0, 3]$. If $r > b$, then we exchange their values such that $r \le b$. We set $p = \min\left\{\mu_{\tilde{r}}(r), \mu_{\tilde{b}}(b)\right\}$. Next we generate two new crisp numbers r and b uniformly on $[0, 3]$ and exchange their values

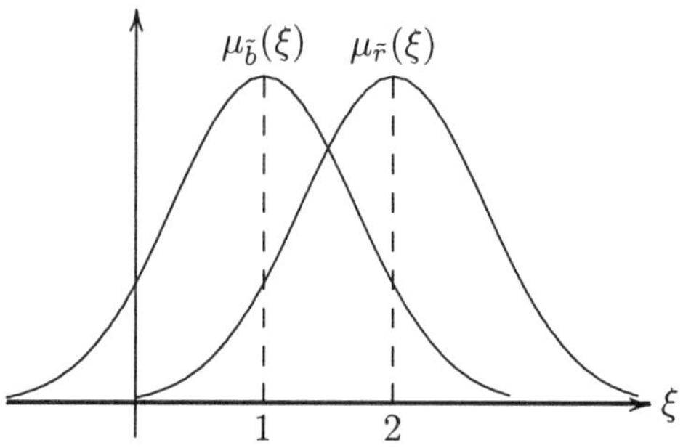

Figure 3.5: Two Fuzzy Numbers with Exponential Membership Functions

if $r > b$. If $p < \min\{\mu_{\tilde{r}}(r), \mu_{\tilde{b}}(b)\}$, then we set $p = \min\{\mu_{\tilde{r}}(r), \mu_{\tilde{b}}(b)\}$. Repeat the above process by generating new crisp numbers r and b until a given number of cycles is finished. Finally, we report the value of p as the possibility $\text{Pos}\{\tilde{r} \le \tilde{b}\}$.

A run of fuzzy simulation with 3000 cycles shows that the possibility is 0.760, which is close enough to the correct value 0.778 since the relative error is 2%. We should mention that the determination of membership functions as well as the desired confidence level are not *precise*, too. The result of the fuzzy simulation for Example 1 is shown in Figure 3.6.

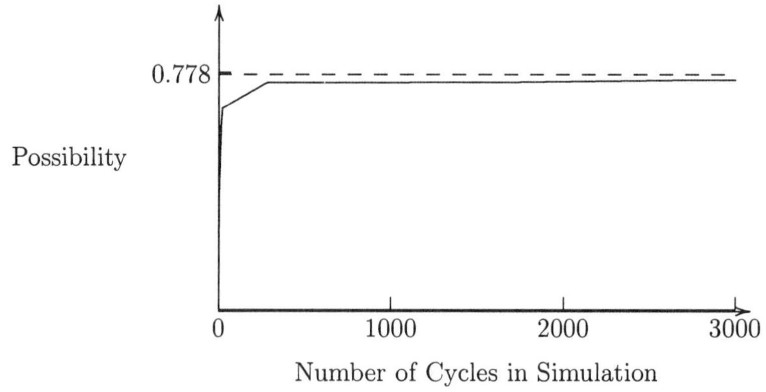

Figure 3.6: Fuzzy Simulation for Example 1

Example 2: Let us consider a complex numerical example, which is to calculate the possibility

$$\text{Pos}\left\{\tilde{a}^2 + \tilde{b} \cdot \tilde{c} - \tilde{d}^{-1} \geq 4\right\}$$

where $\tilde{a}$ and $\tilde{b}$ are fuzzy numbers with membership functions

$$\mu_{\tilde{a}}(\xi) = \exp\left[-\xi^2\right], \qquad \mu_{\tilde{b}}(\xi) = \exp\left[-|\xi - 2|\right]$$

respectively, $\tilde{c}$ is a trapezoidal fuzzy number $(-1, 1, 2, 3)$, and $\tilde{d}$ is a triangular fuzzy number $(1, 2, 3)$. We take the hypercubes containing the α-level sets of $\tilde{a}, \tilde{b}, \tilde{c}$, and $\tilde{d}$ as $\mathcal{A} = [-1, 1]$, $\mathcal{B} = [1, 3]$, $\mathcal{C} = [-1, 3]$, and $\mathcal{D} = [1, 3]$, respectively. We generate four crisp numbers a, b, c, d uniformly from $\mathcal{A}, \mathcal{B}, \mathcal{C}, \mathcal{D}$, respectively. If $a^2 + b \cdot c - d^{-1} \geq 4$, then we set $p = \min\left\{\mu_{\tilde{a}}(a), \mu_{\tilde{b}}(b), \mu_{\tilde{c}}(c), \mu_{\tilde{d}}(d)\right\}$; otherwise we set $p = 0$. We regenerate a, b, c, d uniformly from $\mathcal{A}, \mathcal{B}, \mathcal{C}, \mathcal{D}$, respectively. If $a^2 + b \cdot c - d^{-1} \geq 4$ and $p < \min\left\{\mu_{\tilde{a}}(a), \mu_{\tilde{b}}(b), \mu_{\tilde{c}}(c), \mu_{\tilde{d}}(d)\right\}$, then we set

$$p = \min\left\{\mu_{\tilde{a}}(a), \mu_{\tilde{b}}(b), \mu_{\tilde{c}}(c), \mu_{\tilde{d}}(d)\right\}.$$

Repeat the above process until a given number of cycles is finished. The value of p is regarded as the possibility $\text{Pos}\{\tilde{a}^2 + \tilde{b} \cdot \tilde{c} - \tilde{d}^{-1} \geq 4\}$.

We perform the computer program with 5000 cycles and obtain that

$$\text{Pos}\left\{\tilde{a}^2 + \tilde{b} \cdot \tilde{c} - \tilde{d}^{-1} \geq 4\right\} = 0.874$$

which is also close to the correct possibility 0.908 and the relative error is not larger than 3%.

Example 3: Now assume that $\tilde{a}$ is a triangular fuzzy number $(1, 2, 3)$, and $\tilde{b}$ and $\tilde{c}$ are fuzzy numbers with membership functions

$$\mu_{\tilde{b}}(x) = \frac{1}{1 + (x - 3)^2}, \qquad \mu_{\tilde{c}}(x) = \exp\left[-(x - 5)^2\right],$$

respectively. We want to determine the maximal value of f such that

$$\text{Pos}\left\{\tilde{a} + (\tilde{b} - \tilde{c})^2 \geq f\right\} \geq 0.8.$$

The known maximal value of f is 11.035. A fuzzy simulation with 1000 cycles obtains a solution whose relative error is less than 2%.

Chapter 4

Expected Value Models

One popular method of stochastic programming is the so-called *expected value models*, which optimize some expected objective functions subject to some expected constraints, for example, minimizing expected cost, maximizing expected profit, and so forth.

Now let us recall the well-known newsboy problem in which a boy operating a news stall has to determine the number x of newspapers to order in advance from the publisher at a cost of c\$/newspaper every day. It is known that the selling price is a\$/newspaper. However, if the newspapers are not sold at the end of the day, then the newspapers have a small value of b\$/newspaper at the recycling center. Assume that the demand for newspapers is denoted by ξ in a day, then the number of newspapers at the end of the day is clearly $x - \xi$ if $x > \xi$, or 0 if $x \le \xi$. Thus the profit of the newsboy should be

$$f(x, \xi) = \begin{cases} (a-c)x, & x \le \xi \\ (b-c)x + (a-b)\xi, & x > \xi. \end{cases} \tag{4.1}$$

In practice, the demand ξ for newspapers is usually a stochastic variable, so is the profit function $f(x, \xi)$. Since we cannot predict how profitable the decision of ordering x newspapers will actually be, a natural idea is to employ the expected profit, shown as follows,

$$E[f(x,\xi)] = \int_0^x [(b-c)x + (a-b)\xi]\phi(\xi)d\xi + \int_x^{+\infty} (a-c)x\phi(\xi)d\xi \tag{4.2}$$

where E denotes the expectation operator and $\phi(\xi)$ is the probability density function of demand ξ. The newsboy problem is related to determining the optimal integer number x of newspapers such that the expected profit

$E[f(x, \xi)]$ achieves the maximal value. This is a typical example of expected value models.

In this chapter, we will provide a spectrum of expected value single-objective programming and expected value multiobjective programming as well as expected value goal programming models. We also discuss some properties of expected value models and introduce stochastic programming with recourse. In order to solve these models, a stochastic simulation-based genetic algorithm is designed and illustrated by some numerical examples.

4.1 Expectation Operator

Suppose that a t-dimensional random vector $\boldsymbol{\xi}$ has a probability density function $\phi(\boldsymbol{\xi})$. Then the expectation of $\boldsymbol{\xi}$ is defined by

$$E[\boldsymbol{\xi}] = \int_{\Re^t} \boldsymbol{\xi}\phi(\boldsymbol{\xi})d\boldsymbol{\xi}. \tag{4.3}$$

Note that the terms expectation, expected value, and mean can be used interchangeably.

Now let f be a (real- or vector-valued) function defined on $\Re^t$. Then $f(\boldsymbol{\xi})$ is also a stochastic vector. It has been shown that the expectation $E[f(\boldsymbol{\xi})]$ can be calculated directly by

$$E[f(\boldsymbol{\xi})] = \int_{\Re^t} f(\boldsymbol{\xi})\phi(\boldsymbol{\xi})d\boldsymbol{\xi}. \tag{4.4}$$

We know the following basic properties of expectations. If $\boldsymbol{\eta} = a\boldsymbol{\xi} + b$, where a and b are constants, then we have

$$E[\boldsymbol{\eta}] = aE[\boldsymbol{\xi}] + b. \tag{4.5}$$

More generally, let $\boldsymbol{\xi}_1, \boldsymbol{\xi}_2, \cdots, \boldsymbol{\xi}_n$ be n random vectors such that each expectation $E[\boldsymbol{\xi}_i]$ exists $(i = 1, 2, \cdots, n)$. Then we have

$$E[\boldsymbol{\xi}_1 + \boldsymbol{\xi}_2 + \cdots + \boldsymbol{\xi}_n] = E[\boldsymbol{\xi}_1] + E[\boldsymbol{\xi}_2] + \cdots + E[\boldsymbol{\xi}_n]. \tag{4.6}$$

If the random vectors $\boldsymbol{\xi}_1, \boldsymbol{\xi}_2, \cdots, \boldsymbol{\xi}_n$ are independent, then we also have

$$E[\boldsymbol{\xi}_1 \cdot \boldsymbol{\xi}_2 \cdots \boldsymbol{\xi}_n] = E[\boldsymbol{\xi}_1] \cdot E[\boldsymbol{\xi}_2] \cdots E[\boldsymbol{\xi}_n]. \tag{4.7}$$

4.2 General Formulations

The general form of expected value single-objective programming model is formulated as follows,

$$\begin{cases} \max\ E[f(\boldsymbol{x}, \boldsymbol{\xi})] \\ \text{subject to:} \\ \qquad E[g_j(\boldsymbol{x}, \boldsymbol{\xi})] \le 0, \quad j = 1, 2, \cdots, p \\ \qquad E[h_k(\boldsymbol{x}, \boldsymbol{\xi})] = 0, \quad k = 1, 2, \cdots, q \end{cases} \tag{4.8}$$

where $\boldsymbol{x}$ is an n-dimensional decision vector, $\boldsymbol{\xi}$ is a t-dimensional stochastic vector with a separate or joint probability density function $\phi(\boldsymbol{\xi})$, $f(\boldsymbol{x}, \boldsymbol{\xi})$ is the return function, $g_j(\boldsymbol{x}, \boldsymbol{\xi})$ and $h_k(\boldsymbol{x}, \boldsymbol{\xi})$ are stochastic constraint functions for $j = 1, 2, \cdots, p$, $k = 1, 2, \cdots, q$, and E denotes the expectation operator. Thus we have

$$\begin{aligned} E[f(\boldsymbol{x}, \boldsymbol{\xi})] &= \int_{\Re^t} f(\boldsymbol{x}, \boldsymbol{\xi})\phi(\boldsymbol{\xi})d\boldsymbol{\xi}, \\ E[g_j(\boldsymbol{x}, \boldsymbol{\xi})] &= \int_{\Re^t} g_j(\boldsymbol{x}, \boldsymbol{\xi})\phi(\boldsymbol{\xi})d\boldsymbol{\xi}, \quad j = 1, 2, \cdots, p, \\ E[h_k(\boldsymbol{x}, \boldsymbol{\xi})] &= \int_{\Re^t} h_k(\boldsymbol{x}, \boldsymbol{\xi})\phi(\boldsymbol{\xi})d\boldsymbol{\xi}, \quad k = 1, 2, \cdots, q. \end{aligned} \tag{4.9}$$

If the stochastic vector $\boldsymbol{\xi}$ has a discrete distribution having mass θ_i at $\boldsymbol{\xi}_i$ for $i \in I$, where I is an index set, then we have

$$\begin{aligned} E[f(\boldsymbol{x}, \boldsymbol{\xi})] &= \sum_{i \in I} \theta_i f(\boldsymbol{x}, \boldsymbol{\xi}_i), \\ E[g_j(\boldsymbol{x}, \boldsymbol{\xi})] &= \sum_{i \in I} \theta_i g_j(\boldsymbol{x}, \boldsymbol{\xi}_i), \quad j = 1, 2, \cdots, p, \\ E[h_k(\boldsymbol{x}, \boldsymbol{\xi})] &= \sum_{i \in I} \theta_i h_k(\boldsymbol{x}, \boldsymbol{\xi}_i), \quad k = 1, 2, \cdots, q. \end{aligned} \tag{4.10}$$

Thus, a solution $\boldsymbol{x}$ is feasible if and only if $E[g_j(\boldsymbol{x}, \boldsymbol{\xi})] \le 0$, $j = 1, 2, \cdots, p$ and $E[h_k(\boldsymbol{x}, \boldsymbol{\xi})] = 0$, $k = 1, 2, \cdots, q$. A feasible solution $\boldsymbol{x}^*$ is an optimal solution to the expected value model (4.8) if $E[f(\boldsymbol{x}^*, \boldsymbol{\xi})] \ge E[f(\boldsymbol{x}, \boldsymbol{\xi})]$ for any feasible solution $\boldsymbol{x}$.

As an extension of single-objective programming models, expected value multiobjective programming models have the following general form:

$$\begin{cases} \max \left[E[f_1(\boldsymbol{x},\boldsymbol{\xi})], E[f_2(\boldsymbol{x},\boldsymbol{\xi})], \cdots, E[f_m(\boldsymbol{x},\boldsymbol{\xi})]\right] \\ \text{subject to:} \\ \qquad E[g_j(\boldsymbol{x},\boldsymbol{\xi})] \le 0, \quad j = 1, 2, \cdots, p \\ \qquad E[h_k(\boldsymbol{x},\boldsymbol{\xi})] = 0, \quad k = 1, 2, \cdots, q \end{cases} \tag{4.11}$$

where $f_i(\boldsymbol{x},\boldsymbol{\xi})$ are return functions for $i = 1, 2, \cdots, m$.

We can also formulate a stochastic decision system as an expected value goal programming model according to the priority structure and target levels set by the decision-maker:

$$\begin{cases} \min \sum_{j=1}^{l} P_j \sum_{i=1}^{m} (u_{ij} d_i^+ + v_{ij} d_i^-) \\ \text{subject to:} \\ \qquad E[f_i(\boldsymbol{x},\boldsymbol{\xi})] + d_i^- - d_i^+ = b_i, \quad i = 1, 2, \cdots, m \\ \qquad E[g_j(\boldsymbol{x},\boldsymbol{\xi})] \le 0, \qquad\qquad\qquad j = 1, 2, \cdots, p \\ \qquad E[h_k(\boldsymbol{x},\boldsymbol{\xi})] = 0, \qquad\qquad\qquad k = 1, 2, \cdots, q \end{cases} \tag{4.12}$$

where

P_j = the preemptive priority factor which expresses the relative importance of various goals, $P_j \gg P_{j+1}$, for all j,

u_{ij} = weighting factor corresponding to positive deviation for goal i with priority j assigned,

v_{ij} = weighting factor corresponding to negative deviation for goal i with priority j assigned,

d_i^+ = positive deviation from the target of goal i, defined as

$$d_i^+ = \begin{cases} E[f_i(\boldsymbol{x},\boldsymbol{\xi})] - b_i, & E[f_i(\boldsymbol{x},\boldsymbol{\xi})] > b_i \\ 0, & E[f_i(\boldsymbol{x},\boldsymbol{\xi})] \le b_i, \end{cases}$$

d_i^- = negative deviation from the target of goal i, defined as

$$d_i^- = \begin{cases} 0, & E[f_i(\boldsymbol{x},\boldsymbol{\xi})] \ge b_i \\ b_i - E[f_i(\boldsymbol{x},\boldsymbol{\xi})], & E[f_i(\boldsymbol{x},\boldsymbol{\xi})] < b_i, \end{cases}$$

f_i = a function in goal constraints,
g_j = a function in real constraints,
h_k = a function in real constraints,
b_i = the target value according to goal i,

$\boldsymbol{\xi}$ = stochastic vector of parameters,
l = number of priorities,
m = number of goal constraints,
p = number of real constraints.

4.3 Convexity

Convexity is an interesting issue in optimization theory. A mathematical programming model is called convex if both objective function and feasible set are convex. For the expected value models, we have the following result on convexity.

Theorem 4.1 *Assume that, for each fixed* $\boldsymbol{\xi}$*, the functions* $f(\boldsymbol{x},\boldsymbol{\xi})$*,* $g_j(\boldsymbol{x},\boldsymbol{\xi})$*,* $j=1,2,\cdots,p$ *are convex in* $\boldsymbol{x}$*, and the functions* $h_k(\boldsymbol{x},\boldsymbol{\xi})$*,* $k=1,2,\cdots,p$ *are linear in* $\boldsymbol{x}$*. Then the expected value model*

$$\begin{cases} \min \ E[f(\boldsymbol{x},\boldsymbol{\xi})] \\ \textit{subject to:} \\ \qquad E[g_j(\boldsymbol{x},\boldsymbol{\xi})] \le 0, \quad j=1,2,\cdots,p \\ \qquad E[h_k(\boldsymbol{x},\boldsymbol{\xi})] = 0, \quad k=1,2,\cdots,q \end{cases} \tag{4.13}$$

is a convex programming.

Proof. For each fixed $\boldsymbol{\xi}$, since the function $f(\boldsymbol{x},\boldsymbol{\xi})$ is convex in $\boldsymbol{x}$, we have

$$f(\lambda\boldsymbol{x}_1+(1-\lambda)\boldsymbol{x}_2,\boldsymbol{\xi}) \le \lambda f(\boldsymbol{x}_1,\boldsymbol{\xi})+(1-\lambda)f(\boldsymbol{x}_2,\boldsymbol{\xi})$$

for any given solutions $\boldsymbol{x}_1,\boldsymbol{x}_2$ and scalar $\lambda\in[0,1]$. It follows from the definition of expectation operator that

$$E[f(\lambda\boldsymbol{x}_1+(1-\lambda)\boldsymbol{x}_2,\boldsymbol{\xi})] \le \lambda E[f(\boldsymbol{x}_1,\boldsymbol{\xi})]+(1-\lambda)E[f(\boldsymbol{x}_2,\boldsymbol{\xi})]$$

which proves the convexity of the objective function $E[f(\boldsymbol{x},\boldsymbol{\xi})]$ in $\boldsymbol{x}$.

For any feasible solutions $\boldsymbol{x}_1$ and $\boldsymbol{x}_2$ constrained by

$$\begin{cases} E[g_j(\boldsymbol{x},\boldsymbol{\xi})] \le 0, \quad j=1,2,\cdots,p \\ E[h_k(\boldsymbol{x},\boldsymbol{\xi})] = 0, \quad k=1,2,\cdots,q, \end{cases}$$

let us prove the convexity of feasible set by verifying that $\lambda\boldsymbol{x}_1+(1-\lambda)\boldsymbol{x}_2$ is feasible for any scalar $\lambda\in[0,1]$. By the convexity of the functions $g_j(\boldsymbol{x},\boldsymbol{\xi})$, $j=1,2,\cdots,p$, we know that

$$g_j(\lambda\boldsymbol{x}_1+(1-\lambda)\boldsymbol{x}_2,\boldsymbol{\xi}) \le \lambda g_j(\boldsymbol{x}_1,\boldsymbol{\xi})+(1-\lambda)g_j(\boldsymbol{x}_2,\boldsymbol{\xi}), \quad j=1,2,\cdots,p$$

which yields that

$$E[g_j(\lambda \boldsymbol{x}_1 + (1-\lambda)\boldsymbol{x}_2, \boldsymbol{\xi})] \le \lambda E[g_j(\boldsymbol{x}_1, \boldsymbol{\xi})] + (1-\lambda)E[g_j(\boldsymbol{x}_2, \boldsymbol{\xi})] \le 0 \quad (4.14)$$

for $j = 1, 2, \cdots, p$. By the linearity of the functions $h_k(\boldsymbol{x}, \boldsymbol{\xi})$, $k = 1, 2, \cdots, q$, we have

$$h_k(\lambda \boldsymbol{x}_1 + (1-\lambda)\boldsymbol{x}_2, \boldsymbol{\xi}) = \lambda h_k(\boldsymbol{x}_1, \boldsymbol{\xi}) + (1-\lambda)h_k(\boldsymbol{x}_2, \boldsymbol{\xi}), \quad k = 1, 2, \cdots, q$$

which implies that

$$E[h_k(\lambda \boldsymbol{x}_1 + (1-\lambda)\boldsymbol{x}_2, \boldsymbol{\xi})] = \lambda E[h_k(\boldsymbol{x}_1, \boldsymbol{\xi})] + (1-\lambda)E[h_k(\boldsymbol{x}_2, \boldsymbol{\xi})] = 0 \quad (4.15)$$

for $k = 1, 2, \cdots, q$. It follows from (4.14) and (4.15) that $\lambda \boldsymbol{x}_1 + (1-\lambda)\boldsymbol{x}_2$ is feasible. Hence the feasible set is convex.

The expected value model is proven a convex programming.

4.4 Stochastic Programming with Recourse

For a stochastic decision-making problem, we may make an original activity $\boldsymbol{x}$ to minimize the cost function $f(\boldsymbol{x}, \boldsymbol{\xi})$. In many real cases, we have a chance to select an emergency activity $\boldsymbol{y}$ after the stochastic vector $\boldsymbol{\xi}$ is realized. This will cause an extra cost $Q(\boldsymbol{x}, \boldsymbol{\xi})$ called *recourse function*. Thus we have a *stochastic programming with recourse*

$$\min_{\boldsymbol{x}} E_{\boldsymbol{\xi}} \left[f(\boldsymbol{x}, \boldsymbol{\xi}) + Q(\boldsymbol{x}, \boldsymbol{\xi}) \right] \quad (4.16)$$

which is clearly a special expected value model, where the recourse function $Q(\boldsymbol{x}, \boldsymbol{\xi})$ could be chosen as

$$Q(\boldsymbol{x}, \boldsymbol{\xi}) = \min_{\boldsymbol{y}} \left\{ q(\boldsymbol{y}) \mid G_j(\boldsymbol{y}|\boldsymbol{x}, \boldsymbol{\xi}) \le 0, \ j = 1, 2, \cdots, p \right\} \quad (4.17)$$

where $q(\boldsymbol{y})$ is a cost function, and $G_j(\boldsymbol{y}|\boldsymbol{x}, \boldsymbol{\xi})$ are constraint functions of $\boldsymbol{y}$ given decision $\boldsymbol{x}$ and realized parameter $\boldsymbol{\xi}$ for $j = 1, 2, \cdots, p$.

Stochastic programming with recourse can also be regarded as a two-stage dynamic decision problem.

4.5 Stochastic Simulation-based Genetic Algorithms

From the mathematical viewpoint, there is no difference between deterministic optimization and expected value model except for the fact that there exist multiple integrals in the latter. In this section, we introduce a stochastic simulation-based genetic algorithm for solving expected value models and give some numerical examples to illustrate this algorithm.

In order to compute a multiple integral, we can employ the technique of stochastic simulation, which is based on the assumption that the numbers with which we are dealing are obtained genuinely at random. Now we consider a multiple integral. For example, we want to calculate $\int_{\Re^t} f(\boldsymbol{x}, \boldsymbol{\xi})\phi(\boldsymbol{\xi})d\boldsymbol{\xi}$. If the points $\boldsymbol{\xi}_1, \boldsymbol{\xi}_2, \cdots, \boldsymbol{\xi}_N$ are independent random vectors with the probability density function $\phi(\boldsymbol{\xi})$, then

$$\frac{1}{N}\sum_{i=1}^{N} f(\boldsymbol{x}, \boldsymbol{\xi}_i)$$

is a random variable whose expectation is the value of the integral and whose standard deviation is $O(N^{-\frac{1}{2}})$. In contrast to the classical method of multiple integral by iteration, the number of sampling points required to obtain a given degree of accuracy is independent of the number of dimensions, which makes the stochastic simulation very attractive for large numbers of dimensions.

In the stochastic simulation-based genetic algorithm, the initialization process, selection, crossover, and mutation operations are the same as those in the genetic algorithm described in Chapter 2, except for the fact that we have to employ stochastic simulation to compute the multiple integrals in the expected value models.

Genetic Algorithm Procedure

Step 0. *Input parameters pop_size, P_c and P_m.*

Step 1. *Initialize pop_size chromosomes in which stochastic simulations may be employed to compute the multiple integrals of constraint functions.*

Step 2. *Update the chromosomes by crossover and mutation operations in which the feasibility of offspring may be checked by stochastic simulations.*

Step 3. *Calculate the objective values for all chromosomes by stochastic simulations.*

Step 4. *Compute the fitness of each chromosome by rank-based evaluation function based on the objective values.*

Step 5. *Select the chromosomes by spinning the roulette wheel.*

Step 6. *Repeat the second to fifth steps a given number of cycles.*

Step 7. *Report the best chromosome as the optimal solution.*

The computer code for the stochastic simulation-based genetic algorithm to expected value models has been written in C language. To illustrate the effectiveness of the genetic algorithm, a set of numerical examples has been done, and the results are successful. Here we give some numerical examples which are all performed on a personal computer with the following parameters: the population size is 30, the probability of crossover P_c is 0.3, the probability of mutation P_m is 0.2, and the parameter a in the rank-based evaluation function is 0.05.

Example 1: Let us reconsider the newsboy problem described at the beginning of this chapter. We assume that the selling price is $a = 6$, the price at the recycling center is $b = 0.2$, the ordering cost is $c = 4$, and the demand ξ is a normally distributed variable $\mathcal{N}(100, 100)$. This is a very simple numerical example for genetic algorithms. A run of the stochastic simulation-based genetic algorithm with 100 generations shows that the optimal number of newspapers to order is

$$x^* = 96$$

whose expected profit is 178.76.

Example 2: This example is a stochastic optimization with three decision variables and three stochastic parameters [49],

$$\begin{cases} \max f(\boldsymbol{x}) = \displaystyle\int_{\Re^3} \big[(x_1 - \xi_1) \cdot \sin(\pi x_1) + (x_2 - \xi_2) \cdot \sin(4\pi x_2) \\ \qquad\qquad +(x_3 - \xi_3) \cdot \sin(10\pi x_3)\big] \phi(\xi_1, \xi_2, \xi_3) d\xi_1 d\xi_2 d\xi_3 \\ \text{subject to:} \\ \qquad 0 \le x_1 \le 5, \quad 0 \le x_2 \le 5, \quad 0 \le x_3 \le 5 \end{cases}$$

where $\phi(\xi_1, \xi_2, \xi_3)$ is the jointly normal density function which has the following form,

$$\phi(\xi_1, \xi_2, \xi_3) = (2\pi)^{-\frac{3}{2}} (\det C)^{\frac{1}{2}} \exp\left\{ -\frac{1}{2} \sum_{i=1}^{3} \sum_{j=1}^{3} c_{ij} (\xi_i - u_i)(\xi_j - u_j) \right\}$$

where $u_1 = 1$, $u_2 = 2$, $u_3 = 3$, the positive definite matrix $C = (c_{ij})$ is given by

$$c_{ij} = \begin{cases} 2, & i = j \\ 1, & i \ne j, \end{cases} \qquad i = 1, 2, 3, \; j = 1, 2, 3$$

and $\det C$ is the determinant of C.

A run of the stochastic simulation-based genetic algorithm shows that in 1000 iterations the best solution of this example is 8.0146; in 2000 iterations the best solution is 8.9584; in 2500 iterations the best solution is 8.9747; in 3000 iterations the best solution is 8.9906 with

$$x_1^* = 4.5065, \quad x_2^* = 4.6279, \quad x_3^* = 0.1459.$$

The time complexity of this example is the sum of the time spent for the stochastic simulation and the time spent for the genetic algorithm, where the computation time for stochastic simulation is exactly proportional to the number of sampling points. In performing the algorithm with 1000 generations, the CPU time spent for the genetic algorithm is 58.3 seconds on a personal computer.

4.6 Notes

Expected value models are indeed a popular method for dealing with stochastic optimization problems. However, we are not always concerned with maximizing expected profit or minimizing expected cost. In fact, sometimes we have to consider the so-called *risk*, referred to as the probability that some unfavorable event will occur.

Given two alternatives of investments with different risks but identical expected profit, some people (for this case, risk-seekers) may select the riskier investment; some people (for this case, risk-averters) will select the less-risky investment; and some people who are indifferent to risk will think both investments equally good. The expected value models are just constructed under the attitude of risk indifference.

There also are many situations in which expected value models are not applicable. For example, it is well-known that some people enjoy buying lottery tickets, even though the expected return of lottery tickets is always negative. According to the result of the expected value model, we should never take part in a lottery. However, the real case is just the opposite of expected value models. The main reason is that the cost is very small compared with the potential income.

As opposed to expected value models, we will introduce two other types of stochastic programming—chance-constrained programming (CCP) and dependent-chance programming (DCP)—in the remaining part of this book.

Chapter 5

Chance-Constrained Programming

As one active type of stochastic programming developed by Charnes and Cooper [21], chance-constrained programming (CCP) models the stochastic decision systems with assumptions that the constraints will hold at least α of time, where α is referred to as the *confidence level* provided as an appropriate safety margin by the decision-maker.

The basic solution technique of CCP is to convert the stochastic constraints to their respective deterministic equivalents according to the predetermined confidence levels, then to solve the deterministic models by traditional solution procedure. Unfortunately, the converting process is usually hard and only successful for some special cases. However, with the development of modern computers, complex CCP models without deterministic equivalents have been able to solve by intelligent computations, for example, stochastic simulation-based genetic algorithms.

It is also well-known that the concept of CCP has been extended to chance-constrained goal programming (CCGP) and chance-constrained multiobjective programming (CCMOP).

This chapter introduces the general theory of CCP. We will provide a spectrum of CCP models and list some known deterministic equivalents. A stochastic simulation-based genetic algorithm is also designed to solve CCP models and is illustrated by some numerical examples.

5.1 Chance-Constrained Programming Models

Let us consider a mathematical programming with stochastic parameters,

$$\begin{cases} \max\ f(\boldsymbol{x}, \boldsymbol{\xi}) \\ \text{subject to:} \\ \qquad g_j(\boldsymbol{x}, \boldsymbol{\xi}) \leq 0, \quad j = 1, 2, \cdots, p \end{cases} \tag{5.1}$$

where $\boldsymbol{x}$ is an n-dimensional decision vector, $\boldsymbol{\xi}$ is a stochastic vector, $f(\boldsymbol{x}, \boldsymbol{\xi})$ is the return function, and $g_j(\boldsymbol{x}, \boldsymbol{\xi})$ are stochastic constraint functions, $j = 1, 2, \cdots, p$. In fact, this stochastic programming is not well-defined since the meanings of max as well as of the constraints are not clear at all.

In order to model this type of problem correctly, we may employ the following CCP model:

$$\begin{cases} \max\ \overline{f} \\ \text{subject to:} \\ \qquad \Pr\left\{f(\boldsymbol{x}, \boldsymbol{\xi}) \geq \overline{f}\right\} \geq \beta \\ \qquad \Pr\left\{g_j(\boldsymbol{x}, \boldsymbol{\xi}) \leq 0, j = 1, 2, \cdots, p\right\} \geq \alpha \end{cases} \tag{5.2}$$

where $\Pr\{\cdot\}$ denotes the probability of the event in $\{\cdot\}$, and α and β are predetermined confidence levels to constraints and objective, respectively.

A point $\boldsymbol{x}$ is feasible if and only if the probability measure of the event $\{g_j(\boldsymbol{x}, \boldsymbol{\xi}) \leq 0, j = 1, 2, \cdots, p\}$ is at least α. In other words, the constraints will be violated at most $(1 - \alpha)$ of time.

No matter what the types of stochastic parameter $\boldsymbol{\xi}$ and functional form f are, for each given decision $\boldsymbol{x}$, $f(\boldsymbol{x}, \boldsymbol{\xi})$ is a stochastic variable for which we denote its probability density function by $\phi_{f(\boldsymbol{x},\boldsymbol{\xi})}(f)$. Thus there are multiple possible values $\overline{f}$ such that $\Pr\left\{f(\boldsymbol{x}, \boldsymbol{\xi}) \geq \overline{f}\right\} \geq \beta$. In view of maximizing the objective value $\overline{f}$, the objective value $\overline{f}$ should be the maximum value that the return function $f(\boldsymbol{x}, \boldsymbol{\xi})$ achieves with at least probability level β, i.e.,

$$\overline{f} = \max\left\{f \mid \Pr\left\{f(\boldsymbol{x}, \boldsymbol{\xi}) \geq f\right\} \geq \beta\right\}. \tag{5.3}$$

This is illustrated in Figure 5.1.

The probabilistic constraints in CCP (5.2) are called joint chance constraints. Sometimes, the chance constraints are separately considered as

$$\Pr\{g_j(\boldsymbol{x}, \boldsymbol{\xi}) \leq 0\} \geq \alpha_j, \quad j = 1, 2, \cdots, p \tag{5.4}$$

which are referred to as separate chance constraints. Or more generally,

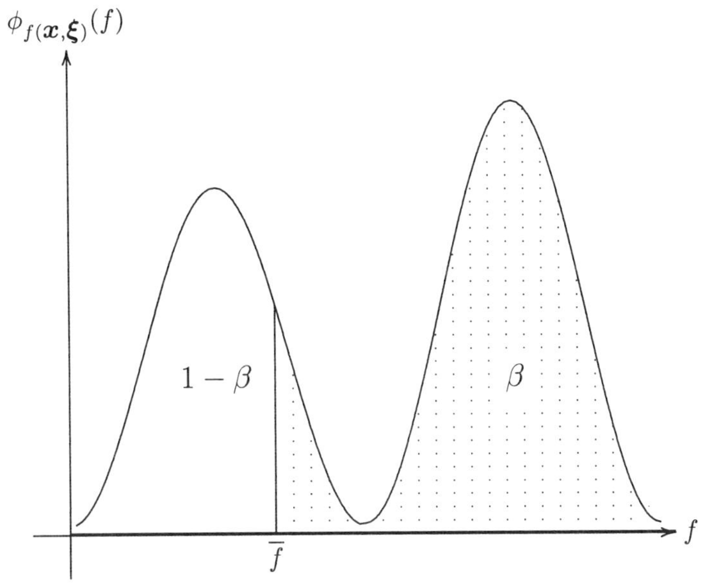

Figure 5.1: Probability Density Function $\phi_{f(\boldsymbol{x},\boldsymbol{\xi})}(f)$ and Objective Value $\overline{f}$

mixed chance constraints are used,

$$\begin{cases} \Pr\{g_j(\boldsymbol{x},\boldsymbol{\xi}) \le 0,\ j = 1, 2, \cdots, k_1\} \ge \alpha_1 \\ \Pr\{g_j(\boldsymbol{x},\boldsymbol{\xi}) \le 0,\ j = k_1+1, k_1+2, \cdots, k_2\} \ge \alpha_2 \\ \quad \cdots \\ \Pr\{g_j(\boldsymbol{x},\boldsymbol{\xi}) \le 0,\ j = k_{t-1}+1, k_{t-1}+2, \cdots, p\} \ge \alpha_t \end{cases} \tag{5.5}$$

where $1 \le k_1 < k_2 < \cdots < k_{t-1} < p$.

Analogously, for a minimization problem, we have

$$\begin{cases} \min\ \overline{f} \\ \text{subject to:} \\ \qquad \Pr\left\{f(\boldsymbol{x},\boldsymbol{\xi}) \le \overline{f}\right\} \ge \beta \\ \qquad \Pr\left\{g_j(\boldsymbol{x},\boldsymbol{\xi}) \le 0, j = 1, 2, \cdots, p\right\} \ge \alpha \end{cases} \tag{5.6}$$

where the objective value $\overline{f}$ should be the minimum value that the cost function $f(\boldsymbol{x},\boldsymbol{\xi})$ achieves with at least confidence level β.

As an extension of single-objective CCP, CCMOP may be written as follows:

$$
\begin{cases}
\max \ \left[\overline{f}_1, \overline{f}_2, \cdots, \overline{f}_m\right] \\
\text{subject to:} \\
\qquad \Pr\left\{f_i(\boldsymbol{x}, \boldsymbol{\xi}) \geq \overline{f}_i\right\} \geq \beta_i, \quad i = 1, 2, \cdots, m \\
\qquad \Pr\left\{g_j(\boldsymbol{x}, \boldsymbol{\xi}) \leq 0\right\} \geq \alpha_j, \quad j = 1, 2, \cdots, p
\end{cases}
\tag{5.7}
$$

where α_j and β_i are confidence levels to the jth constraints and ith objectives, and $\overline{f}_i$ are the maximum values that the return functions $f_i(\boldsymbol{x}, \boldsymbol{\xi})$ achieve with at least confidence levels β_i, $j = 1, 2, \cdots, p$, $i = 1, 2, \cdots, m$, respectively.

We can also formulate a stochastic decision system as a CCGP according to the priority structure and target levels set by the decision-maker:

$$
\begin{cases}
\min \sum\limits_{j=1}^{l} P_j \sum\limits_{i=1}^{m} (u_{ij} d_i^+ + v_{ij} d_i^-) \\
\text{subject to:} \\
\qquad \Pr\left\{f_i(\boldsymbol{x}, \boldsymbol{\xi}) + d_i^- - d_i^+ = b_i\right\} \geq \beta_i, \quad i = 1, 2, \cdots, m \\
\qquad \Pr\left\{g_j(\boldsymbol{x}, \boldsymbol{\xi}) \leq 0\right\} \geq \alpha_j, \qquad\qquad\quad j = 1, 2, \cdots, p \\
\qquad d_i^-, d_i^+ \geq 0, \qquad\qquad\qquad\qquad\qquad i = 1, 2, \cdots, m
\end{cases}
\tag{5.8}
$$

where

P_j = the preemptive priority factor which expresses the relative importance of various goals, $P_j \gg P_{j+1}$, for all j,

u_{ij} = weighting factor corresponding to positive deviation for goal i with priority j assigned,

v_{ij} = weighting factor corresponding to negative deviation for goal i with priority j assigned,

d_i^+ = positive deviation from the target of goal i,

d_i^- = negative deviation from the target of goal i,

f_i = a function in goal constraints,

g_j = a function in system constraints,

b_i = the target value according to goal i,

l = number of priorities,

m = number of goal constraints,

p = number of real constraints.

Remark 1: For each fixed feasible solution $\boldsymbol{x}$, i.e., the one satisfying $\Pr\{g_j(\boldsymbol{x}, \boldsymbol{\xi}) \leq 0\} \geq \alpha_j$, $j = 1, 2, \cdots, p$, since $\boldsymbol{\xi}$ is a stochastic vector, $f_i(\boldsymbol{x}, \boldsymbol{\xi})$ will be also a stochastic variable. Thus we have to explain the meaning of the goal constraint $\Pr\{f_i(\boldsymbol{x}, \boldsymbol{\xi}) + d_i^- - d_i^+ = b_i\} \geq \beta_i$. In fact, the positive and negative deviations should be understood as the minimal nonnegative values of d_i^+ and d_i^- such that

$$\Pr\left\{d_i^+ \geq f_i(\boldsymbol{x},\boldsymbol{\xi}) - b_i\right\} \geq \beta_i, \quad \Pr\left\{d_i^- \geq b_i - f_i(\boldsymbol{x},\boldsymbol{\xi})\right\} \geq \beta_i \tag{5.9}$$

for $i = 1, 2, \cdots, m$, respectively.

Remark 2: In a deterministic goal programming, there is at most one positive quantity of d_i^- and d_i^+. However, for a chance-constrained goal programming, it is possible that both d_i^- and d_i^+ are positive.

Remark 3: We also notice that CCP is not convex for many cases of practical interest, including uniform, exponential, and normal distributions, unless additional conditions are imposed.

Remark 4: Sometimes, the decision variables (or some of them) are assumed only integer values. This type of CCP is called *chance-constrained integer programming* or *chance-constrained mixed integer programming*, respectively.

5.2 Deterministic Equivalents

The traditional solution methods require conversion of the chance constraints to their respective deterministic equivalents. As we know, this process is usually hard to perform and only successful for some special cases. We will consider the following form of chance constraint,

$$\Pr\{g(\boldsymbol{x},\boldsymbol{\xi}) \leq 0\} \geq \alpha. \tag{5.10}$$

It is clear that the chance constraints (5.4) are a set of these forms, and the stochastic objective constraint $\Pr\{f(\boldsymbol{x},\boldsymbol{\xi}) \geq \overline{f}\} \geq \beta$ coincides with this form by defining $g(\boldsymbol{x},\boldsymbol{\xi}) = \overline{f} - f(\boldsymbol{x},\boldsymbol{\xi})$. Since the stochastic goal constraint $\Pr\{f(\boldsymbol{x},\boldsymbol{\xi}) + d^- - d^+ = b\} \geq \beta$ is understood as choosing the minimal nonnegative values of d^- and d^+ such that $\Pr\{d^- \geq b - f(\boldsymbol{x},\boldsymbol{\xi})\} \geq \beta$ and $\Pr\{d^+ \geq f(\boldsymbol{x},\boldsymbol{\xi}) - b\} \geq \beta$, the former and the latter coincide with the form (5.10) by defining $g(\boldsymbol{x},\boldsymbol{\xi}) = b - f(\boldsymbol{x},\boldsymbol{\xi}) - d^-$ and $g(\boldsymbol{x},\boldsymbol{\xi}) = f(\boldsymbol{x},\boldsymbol{\xi}) - b - d^+$, respectively. This section summarizes some known results.

Case I: Assume that the function $g(\boldsymbol{x},\boldsymbol{\xi})$ has the form $g(\boldsymbol{x},\boldsymbol{\xi}) = h(\boldsymbol{x}) - \xi$. Then the chance constraint (5.10) can be written in the following form,

$$\Pr\{h(\boldsymbol{x}) \leq \xi\} \geq \alpha \tag{5.11}$$

where $h(\boldsymbol{x})$ is a (linear or nonlinear) function of decision vector $\boldsymbol{x}$ and ξ is a random number with cumulative probability distribution $\Phi(\cdot)$.

It is clear that, for each given confidence level $\alpha(0 \le \alpha \le 1)$, there exists a number K_α (maybe multiple or ∞) such that

$$\Pr\{K_\alpha \le \xi\} = \alpha \tag{5.12}$$

and the probability $\Pr\{K_\alpha \le \xi\}$ will increase if K_α is replaced by a smaller number. Hence $\Pr\{h(\boldsymbol{x}) \le \xi\} \ge \alpha$ if and only if $h(\boldsymbol{x}) \le K_\alpha$.

Notice that the equation $\Pr\{K_\alpha \le \xi\} = 1 - \Phi(K_\alpha)$ always holds, and we have, by (5.12),

$$K_\alpha = \Phi^{-1}(1-\alpha)$$

where Φ^{-1} is the inverse function of Φ. Sometimes, the solution of equation (5.12) is not unique. Equivalently, the function Φ^{-1} is multivalued. For this case, we should choose it as the largest one, i.e.,

$$K_\alpha = \sup\left\{K \mid K = \Phi^{-1}(1-\alpha)\right\}.$$

Thus the deterministic equivalent to (5.11) is obtained and shown by the following form,

$$h(\boldsymbol{x}) \le K_\alpha. \tag{5.13}$$

For example, we have the following chance constraint,

$$\begin{cases} \Pr\{3x_1 + 4x_2 \le \xi_1\} \ge 0.80 \\ \Pr\left\{x_1^2 - x_2^3 \le \xi_2\right\} \ge 0.90 \end{cases} \tag{5.14}$$

where ξ_1 is an exponentially distributed variable $\mathcal{EXP}(2)$ whose probability distribution is denoted by Φ_1 and ξ_2 is a normally distributed variable $\mathcal{N}(2,1)$ whose probability distribution is denoted by Φ_2. Then by the formula (5.13), we know that the chance constraint (5.14) is equivalent to

$$\begin{cases} 3x_1 + 4x_2 \le \Phi_1^{-1}(1-0.80) = 0.446 \\ x_1^2 - x_2^3 \le \Phi_2^{-1}(1-0.90) = 0.719. \end{cases} \tag{5.15}$$

Case II: Analogous to Case I, assume that the function $g(\boldsymbol{x}, \boldsymbol{\xi}) = \xi - h(\boldsymbol{x})$. Then the chance constraint (5.10) can be written in the following form,

$$\Pr\{h(\boldsymbol{x}) \ge \xi\} \ge \alpha \tag{5.16}$$

where $h(\boldsymbol{x})$ is a (linear or nonlinear) function of decision vector $\boldsymbol{x}$ and ξ is a stochastic number having cumulative probability distribution $\Phi(\cdot)$.

It is clear that, for each given confidence level $\alpha(0 \le \alpha \le 1)$, there exists a number K_α such that

$$\Pr\{K_\alpha \ge \xi\} = \alpha \tag{5.17}$$

and the probability $\Pr\{K_\alpha \geq \xi\}$ will increase if K_α is replaced by a larger number. Hence $\Pr\{h(\boldsymbol{x}) \geq \xi\} \geq \alpha$ if and only if $h(\boldsymbol{x}) \geq K_\alpha$.

Notice that the equation $\Pr\{K_\alpha \geq \xi\} = \Phi(K_\alpha)$ always holds. Then we have

$$K_\alpha = \Phi^{-1}(\alpha)$$

where Φ^{-1} is the inverse function of Φ. Sometimes, the solution of equation (5.17) is not unique. Equivalently, the function Φ^{-1} is multivalued. For this case, we should choose it as the smallest one, i.e.,

$$K_\alpha = \inf\left\{K \mid K = \Phi^{-1}(\alpha)\right\}.$$

Thus the deterministic equivalent to (5.16) is obtained and shown by the following form,

$$h(\boldsymbol{x}) \geq K_\alpha. \tag{5.18}$$

Case III: Assume that the function $g(\boldsymbol{x}, \boldsymbol{\xi})$ has the form

$$g(\boldsymbol{x}, \boldsymbol{\xi}) = a_1x_1 + a_2x_2 + \cdots + a_nx_n - b.$$

Thus the chance constraint (5.10) can be written in the following form,

$$\Pr\left\{\sum_{i=1}^{n} a_ix_i \leq b\right\} \geq \alpha \tag{5.19}$$

where a_i and b are independently stochastic variables with normal distributions. Then the function

$$y(\boldsymbol{x}) = \sum_{i=1}^{n} a_ix_i - b$$

is also normally distributed with the following characteristics,

$$E(y(\boldsymbol{x})) = \sum_{i=1}^{n} E(a_i)x_i - E(b),$$
$$V(y(\boldsymbol{x})) = \sum_{i=1}^{n} V(a_i)x_i^2 + V(b)$$

where $E(\cdot)$ and $V(\cdot)$ are expected value and variance operators, respectively. We notice that

$$\frac{\sum_{i=1}^{n} a_ix_i - b - \left(\sum_{i=1}^{n} E(a_i)x_i - E(b)\right)}{\sqrt{\sum_{i=1}^{n} V(a_i)x_i^2 + V(b)}}$$

must be standardized normally distributed, i.e., $\mathcal{N}(0,1)$, and the inequality $\sum_{i=1}^{n} a_i x_i \le b$ is equivalent to

$$\frac{\sum\limits_{i=1}^{n} a_i x_i - b - \left(\sum\limits_{i=1}^{n} E(a_i)x_i - E(b)\right)}{\sqrt{\sum\limits_{i=1}^{n} V(a_i)x_i^2 + V(b)}} \le -\frac{\sum\limits_{i=1}^{n} E(a_i)x_i - E(b)}{\sqrt{\sum\limits_{i=1}^{n} V(a_i)x_i^2 + V(b)}}.$$

Hence the chance constraint (5.19) is equivalent to

$$\Pr\left\{\eta \le -\frac{\sum\limits_{i=1}^{n} E(a_i)x_i - E(b)}{\sqrt{\sum\limits_{i=1}^{n} V(a_i)x_i^2 + V(b)}}\right\} \ge \alpha \tag{5.20}$$

where η is the standardized normally distributed variable with the distribution

$$\Phi(\eta) = \frac{1}{\sqrt{2\pi}} \int_{-\infty}^{\eta} \exp\left(-\frac{t^2}{2}\right) dt.$$

Then the constraint set (5.20) holds if and only if

$$\Phi^{-1}(\alpha) \le -\frac{\sum\limits_{i=1}^{n} E(a_i)x_i - E(b)}{\sqrt{\sum\limits_{i=1}^{n} V(a_i)x_i^2 + V(b)}}, \tag{5.21}$$

that is,

$$\sum_{i=1}^{n} E(a_i)x_i + \Phi^{-1}(\alpha)\sqrt{\sum_{i=1}^{n} V(a_i)x_i^2 + V(b)} \le E(b). \tag{5.22}$$

This constraint is the deterministic equivalent of the chance constraint (5.19).

For example, suppose that the chance constraint set has the following form,

$$\Pr\{a_1x_1 + a_2x_2 + a_2x_3 \le b\} \ge 95\% \tag{5.23}$$

where a_1, a_2, a_3, and b are normally distributed variables $\mathcal{N}(1,1)$, $\mathcal{N}(2,1)$, $\mathcal{N}(3,1)$, and $\mathcal{N}(4,1)$, respectively. Then the formula (5.22) yields the deterministic equivalent of (5.23) as follows,

$$x_1 + 2x_2 + 3x_3 + 1.645\sqrt{x_1^2 + x_2^2 + x_3^2 + 1} \le 4 \tag{5.24}$$

by the fact that $\Phi^{-1}(95\%) = 1.645$.

5.3 Some Properties

We have discussed the deterministic equivalents of chance constraints. In this section, we present some properties of the following CCP model,

$$\min Ef(\boldsymbol{x}, \boldsymbol{\xi}) \tag{5.25}$$

subject to

$$\Pr\{g_j(\boldsymbol{x}, \boldsymbol{\xi}) \leq 0, j = 1, 2, \cdots, p\} \geq \alpha \tag{5.26}$$

where $\boldsymbol{x}$ is a decision vector, $\boldsymbol{\xi}$ is a stochastic vector with a joint density function $\phi(\boldsymbol{\xi})$, and E is an expected value operator on $\boldsymbol{\xi}$.

Now we define a new function

$$h(\boldsymbol{x}, \boldsymbol{\xi}) = \begin{cases} \alpha - 1, & \text{if } g_j(\boldsymbol{x}, \boldsymbol{\xi}) \leq 0, \ j = 1, 2, \cdots, p \\ \alpha, & \text{otherwise.} \end{cases} \tag{5.27}$$

That is, for each fixed decision $\boldsymbol{x}$, $h(\boldsymbol{x}, \boldsymbol{\xi})$ is $\alpha - 1$ on the region

$$\Xi = \{\boldsymbol{\xi} | g_j(\boldsymbol{x}, \boldsymbol{\xi}) \leq 0, j = 1, 2, \cdots, p\}$$

and α on the complement Ξ^c. Then we have, by the definition of expected value operator,

$$\begin{aligned}
& Eh(\boldsymbol{x}, \boldsymbol{\xi}) \\
= \ & \int h(\boldsymbol{x}, \boldsymbol{\xi}) \phi(\boldsymbol{\xi}) d\boldsymbol{\xi} \\
= \ & (\alpha - 1) \int_{\Xi} \phi(\boldsymbol{\xi}) d\boldsymbol{\xi} + \alpha \int_{\Xi^c} \phi(\boldsymbol{\xi}) d\boldsymbol{\xi} \\
= \ & (\alpha - 1) \Pr\left\{ \begin{array}{c} g_j(\boldsymbol{x}, \boldsymbol{\xi}) \leq 0 \\ j = 1, 2, \cdots, p \end{array} \right\} + \alpha \left[1 - \Pr\left\{ \begin{array}{c} g_j(\boldsymbol{x}, \boldsymbol{\xi}) \leq 0 \\ j = 1, 2, \cdots, p \end{array} \right\} \right] \\
= \ & \alpha - \Pr\{g_j(\boldsymbol{x}, \boldsymbol{\xi}) \leq 0, \ j = 1, 2, \cdots, p\}.
\end{aligned}$$

Therefore $Eh(\boldsymbol{x}, \boldsymbol{\xi}) \leq 0$ if and only if the chance constraint (5.26) holds. This fact provides a relationship between expected value model and CCP. We conclude it with the following theorem.

Theorem 5.1 *A CCP*

$$\begin{cases} \min \ Ef(\boldsymbol{x}, \boldsymbol{\xi}) \\ \textit{subject to:} \\ \qquad \Pr\{g_j(\boldsymbol{x}, \boldsymbol{\xi}) \leq 0, j = 1, 2, \cdots, p\} \geq \alpha \end{cases}$$

is equivalent to an expected value model

$$\begin{cases} \min\ Ef(\boldsymbol{x}, \boldsymbol{\xi}) \\ \textit{subject to:} \\ \qquad Eh(\boldsymbol{x}, \boldsymbol{\xi}) \le 0 \end{cases}$$

where the function $h(\boldsymbol{x}, \boldsymbol{\xi})$ *is defined by (5.27).*

The sets of chance constraints are, in general, not convex even if we assume convexity of all the functions $g_j(\boldsymbol{x}, \boldsymbol{\xi})$, $j = 1, 2, \cdots, p$. In order to assert the convexity of chance constraint set, we have to add some assumptions.

First we introduce some concepts. A real-valued function is called *quasi-concave* if

$$f\left(\lambda \boldsymbol{x} + (1-\lambda)\boldsymbol{y}\right) \ge \min\left\{f(\boldsymbol{x}), f(\boldsymbol{y})\right\} \tag{5.28}$$

for all $\boldsymbol{x}, \boldsymbol{y} \in \Re^n$ and $\lambda \in [0, 1]$. For any given constant c, let $\boldsymbol{x}_1$ and $\boldsymbol{x}_2$ be any two points such that $f(\boldsymbol{x}_1) \ge c$ and $f(\boldsymbol{x}_2) \ge c$. Then by the quasi-concavity of function $f(\boldsymbol{x})$, we have

$$f(\lambda \boldsymbol{x}_1 + (1-\lambda)\boldsymbol{x}_2) \ge \min\{f(\boldsymbol{x}_1), f(\boldsymbol{x}_2)\} \ge c$$

for any $\lambda \in [0, 1]$, which implies that the set $\{\boldsymbol{x} | f(\boldsymbol{x}) \ge c\}$ is convex for any c. Conversely, if the set $\{\boldsymbol{x} | f(\boldsymbol{x}) \ge c\}$ is convex for any c, then for any given points $\boldsymbol{x}_1$ and $\boldsymbol{x}_2$, the set $\{\boldsymbol{x} | f(\boldsymbol{x}) \ge c\}$ is convex for $c = \min\{f(\boldsymbol{x}_1), f(\boldsymbol{x}_2)\}$ and contains the two points $\boldsymbol{x}_1$ and $\boldsymbol{x}_2$. Thus for any number $\lambda \in [0, 1]$, we have $\lambda \boldsymbol{x}_1 + (1-\lambda)\boldsymbol{x}_2 \in \{\boldsymbol{x} | f(\boldsymbol{x}) \ge c\}$, which implies that $f\left(\lambda \boldsymbol{x}_1 + (1-\lambda)\boldsymbol{x}_2\right) \ge \min\left\{f(\boldsymbol{x}_1), f(\boldsymbol{x}_2)\right\}$. Hence the function f is quasi-concave. Therefore, the quasi-concavity of a function f is equivalent to the property that the set $\{\boldsymbol{x} | f(\boldsymbol{x}) \ge c\}$ is convex for every c.

A real-valued function $f(x)$ defined on the real line $\Re$ is called *unimodal* about a mode v if the function $f(x)$ is nonincreasing as x goes away from the mode v. If the dimension $n = 1$, then the quasi-concavity is equivalent to the unimodality.

A nonnegative function f is called *logconcave* if $\log f$ is concave, i.e.,

$$\log f(\lambda \boldsymbol{x} + (1-\lambda)\boldsymbol{y}) \ge \lambda \log f(\boldsymbol{x}) + (1-\lambda) \log f(\boldsymbol{y}), \tag{5.29}$$

or equivalently,

$$f\left(\lambda \boldsymbol{x} + (1-\lambda)\boldsymbol{y}\right) \ge \left[f(\boldsymbol{x})\right]^{\lambda} \left[f(\boldsymbol{y})\right]^{1-\lambda} \tag{5.30}$$

for all $\boldsymbol{x}, \boldsymbol{y} \in \Re^n$, and $\lambda \in [0, 1]$. Logconcave functions have been proved quasi-concave.

Now let F be a function defined on a collection $\mathcal{A}$ of convex sets. Then the function F is called quasi-concave if

$$F(\lambda A_1 + (1-\lambda)A_2) \geq \min\{F(A_1), F(A_2)\} \tag{5.31}$$

for all $A_1, A_2 \in \mathcal{A}$ and scalar $\lambda \in [0,1]$.

Lemma 5.1 *If* $g_j(\boldsymbol{x}, \boldsymbol{\xi}), j = 1, 2, \cdots, p$ *are jointly convex in* $(\boldsymbol{x}, \boldsymbol{\xi})$ *and the probability measure* Pr *is quasi-concave, then the chance constraint set*

$$\mathcal{X} = \left\{\boldsymbol{x} \mid \Pr\{g_j(\boldsymbol{x}, \boldsymbol{\xi}) \leq 0,\ j = 1, 2, \cdots, p\} \geq \alpha\right\}$$

is convex for any confidence level α *with* $0 \leq \alpha \leq 1$.

Proof. At first we define a set-valued function of decision $\boldsymbol{x}$,

$$\Xi(\boldsymbol{x}) = \{\boldsymbol{\xi} | g_j(\boldsymbol{x}, \boldsymbol{\xi}) \leq 0,\ j = 1, 2, \cdots, p\}.$$

In order to prove the convexity of $\mathcal{X}$, let $\boldsymbol{x}_1, \boldsymbol{x}_2 \in \mathcal{X}$ and $\lambda \in [0,1]$ be given. Then for any $\boldsymbol{\xi}_1 \in \Xi(\boldsymbol{x}_1)$ and $\boldsymbol{\xi}_2 \in \Xi(\boldsymbol{x}_2)$, we have

$$g_j(\boldsymbol{x}_i, \boldsymbol{\xi}_i) \leq 0, \quad j = 1, 2, \cdots, p, \quad i = 1, 2.$$

By the joint convexity of the functions $g_j(\boldsymbol{x}, \boldsymbol{\xi})$ in $(\boldsymbol{x}, \boldsymbol{\xi})$, $j = 1, 2, \cdots, p$, we have

$$g_j\left[\lambda\boldsymbol{x}_1 + (1-\lambda)\boldsymbol{x}_2, \lambda\boldsymbol{\xi}_1 + (1-\lambda)\boldsymbol{\xi}_2\right] \leq \lambda g_j(\boldsymbol{x}_1, \boldsymbol{\xi}_1) + (1-\lambda)g_j(\boldsymbol{x}_2, \boldsymbol{\xi}_2) \leq 0$$

for all $j = 1, 2, \cdots, p$. That is,

$$\lambda\boldsymbol{\xi}_1 + (1-\lambda)\boldsymbol{\xi}_2 \in \Xi(\lambda\boldsymbol{x}_1 + (1-\lambda)\boldsymbol{x}_2)$$

which implies that

$$\lambda\Xi(\boldsymbol{x}_1) + (1-\lambda)\Xi(\boldsymbol{x}_2) \subset \Xi(\lambda\boldsymbol{x}_1 + (1-\lambda)\boldsymbol{x}_2).$$

It follows from the quasi-concavity of the probability measure Pr that

$$\begin{aligned}\Pr\left[\Xi(\lambda\boldsymbol{x}_1 + (1-\lambda)\boldsymbol{x}_2)\right] &\geq \Pr\left[\lambda\Xi(\boldsymbol{x}_1) + (1-\lambda)\Xi(\boldsymbol{x}_2)\right] \\ &\geq \min\left\{\Pr\left[\Xi(\boldsymbol{x}_1)\right], \Pr\left[\Xi(\boldsymbol{x}_2)\right]\right\} \\ &\geq \alpha\end{aligned}$$

which yields that

$$\lambda\boldsymbol{x}_1 + (1-\lambda)\boldsymbol{x}_2 \in \mathcal{X}.$$

The convexity of the chance constraint set $\mathcal{X}$ is proved.

Theorem 5.2 *Assume that the function $f(\boldsymbol{x}, \boldsymbol{\xi})$ is convex in $\boldsymbol{x}$ for each $\boldsymbol{\xi}$, and the functions $g_j(\boldsymbol{x}, \boldsymbol{\xi}), j = 1, 2, \cdots, p$ are jointly convex in $(\boldsymbol{x}, \boldsymbol{\xi})$. If the probability measure* Pr *is quasi-concave, then the CCP model*

$$\begin{cases} \min \; Ef(\boldsymbol{x}, \boldsymbol{\xi}) \\ \textit{subject to:} \\ \qquad \Pr\{g_j(\boldsymbol{x}, \boldsymbol{\xi}) \le 0, j = 1, 2, \cdots, p\} \ge \alpha \end{cases}$$

is convex.

Proof. The convexity of feasible set has been proved by Lemma 5.1 under the assumptions that the functions $g_j(\boldsymbol{x}, \boldsymbol{\xi})$, $j = 1, 2, \cdots, p$ are jointly convex in $(\boldsymbol{x}, \boldsymbol{\xi})$ and the probability measure Pr is quasi-concave. Thus the theorem is proved if we can show the convexity of objective function $Ef(\boldsymbol{x}, \boldsymbol{\xi})$ in $\boldsymbol{x}$. For any given $\boldsymbol{x}_1, \boldsymbol{x}_2 \in \Re^n$ and $\lambda \in [0, 1]$, we have, by the convexity of $f(\boldsymbol{x}, \boldsymbol{\xi})$ in $\boldsymbol{x}$ for each $\boldsymbol{\xi}$,

$$\begin{aligned} Ef\left[\lambda \boldsymbol{x}_1 + (1-\lambda)\boldsymbol{x}_2, \boldsymbol{\xi}\right] &\le E\left[\lambda f(\boldsymbol{x}_1, \boldsymbol{\xi}) + (1-\lambda) f(\boldsymbol{x}_2, \boldsymbol{\xi})\right] \\ &= \lambda Ef(\boldsymbol{x}_1, \boldsymbol{\xi}) + (1-\lambda) Ef(\boldsymbol{x}_2, \boldsymbol{\xi}) \end{aligned}$$

which implies that $Ef(\boldsymbol{x}, \boldsymbol{\xi})$ is a convex function in $\boldsymbol{x}$.

Note: We listed some properties of convexity of CCP models. In fact, they are results only of theoretical significance because it is almost impossible to verify the quasi-concavity of the probability measure Pr in practice.

5.4 Stochastic Simulations

The difference between CCP and deterministic mathematical programming is that there exist chance constraints in the former. Thus we need to pay more attention to the chance constraints.

When the constraints are easy to handle, we can convert the chance constraints to their deterministic equivalents. But if the constraints fail to be regular or are hard to handle, it is more convenient to deal with chance constraints by the technique of stochastic simulations.

Checking Stochastic Systems Constraints

Now we consider the following chance constraint

$$\Pr\{g_j(\boldsymbol{x}, \boldsymbol{\xi}) \le 0, \; j = 1, 2, \cdots, k\} \ge \alpha \tag{5.32}$$

where $\boldsymbol{\xi}$ is a stochastic vector with a cumulative probability distribution $\Phi(\boldsymbol{\xi})$. For any given decision $\boldsymbol{x}$, we use the following stochastic simulation technique to check whether the chance constraint (5.32) holds. We generate N independent random vectors $\boldsymbol{\xi}_1, \boldsymbol{\xi}_2, \cdots, \boldsymbol{\xi}_N$, from the probability distribution $\Phi(\boldsymbol{\xi})$, where the generating methods have been well-documented in Chapter 3. Let N' be the number of occasions on which

$$g_j(\boldsymbol{x}, \boldsymbol{\xi}_i) \leq 0, \quad j = 1, 2, \cdots, k,$$

for $i = 1, 2, \cdots, N$ (i.e., the number of random vectors satisfying the constraints). Then, by the law of large numbers, the probability

$$\Pr\{g_j(\boldsymbol{x}, \boldsymbol{\xi}) \leq 0, j = 1, 2, \cdots, k\}$$

can be estimated by N'/N. This means that a chance constraint (5.32) holds if and only if $N'/N \geq \alpha$. Certainly, this estimation is approximate and may change from one simulation to another. But it is available to real practice problems since the determination of the confidence level α itself is also not very precise. Now we summarize the above simulation process as the following steps.

Step 1. Set $N' = 0$.

Step 2. Generate $\boldsymbol{\xi}$ from its probability distribution $\Phi(\boldsymbol{\xi})$.

Step 3. If $g_j(\boldsymbol{x}, \boldsymbol{\xi}) \leq 0$ for $j = 1, 2, \cdots, k$, then $N' + +$.

Step 4. Repeat the second and third steps N times.

Step 5. If $N'/N \geq \alpha$, return FEASIBLE, else return INFEASIBLE.

Handling Stochastic Objective Constraints

For the following stochastic objective constraint with a vector of stochastic parameters $\boldsymbol{\xi}$,

$$\Pr\left\{f(\boldsymbol{x}, \boldsymbol{\xi}) \geq \overline{f}\right\} \geq \beta, \tag{5.33}$$

we sometimes need to find the maximal value of $\overline{f}$ such that (5.33) holds. The stochastic simulation is also available to this type of problem. We generate N independent random vectors $\boldsymbol{\xi}_i$, $i = 1, 2, \cdots, N$, from the probability distribution $\Phi(\boldsymbol{\xi})$. Then we get a sequence of $\{f_1, f_2, \cdots, f_N\}$ where $f_i = f(\boldsymbol{x}, \boldsymbol{\xi}_i)$, $i = 1, 2, \cdots, N$, respectively. We take N' as the integer part of βN. By the law of large numbers, the N'th greatest element in $\{f_1, f_2, \cdots, f_N\}$ may be regarded as the estimation of $\overline{f}$.

Step 1. Generate N vectors $\{\boldsymbol{\xi}_1, \boldsymbol{\xi}_2, \cdots, \boldsymbol{\xi}_N\}$ from the distribution $\Phi(\boldsymbol{\xi})$.

Step 2. Set $f_i = f(\boldsymbol{x}, \boldsymbol{\xi}_i)$ for $i = 1, 2, \cdots, N$.

Step 3. Set N' as the integer part of βN.

Step 4. Return the N'th greatest element in $\{f_1, f_2, \cdots, f_N\}$.

Handling Stochastic Goal Constraints

Consider the following stochastic goal constraint with a vector of stochastic parameters $\boldsymbol{\xi}$

$$\Pr\left\{f(\boldsymbol{x},\boldsymbol{\xi})+d^- - d^+ = b\right\} \ge \beta. \tag{5.34}$$

By the meaning of this goal constraint, we should find the minimal nonnegative values of d^- and d^+ such that

$$\Pr\{d^- \ge b - f(\boldsymbol{x},\boldsymbol{\xi})\} \ge \beta, \quad \Pr\{d^+ \ge f(\boldsymbol{x},\boldsymbol{\xi}) - b\} \ge \beta.$$

Similar to the simulation process for handling a stochastic objective constraint, we get a sequence of $\{f_1^-, f_2^-, \cdots, f_N^-\}$ where $f_i^- = b - f(\boldsymbol{x},\boldsymbol{\xi}_i)$ by generating $\boldsymbol{\xi}_i$ from the probability distribution $\Phi(\boldsymbol{\xi})$, $i = 1,2,\cdots,N$, respectively. We take N' as the integer part of βN. Then the N'th least element in $\{f_1^-, f_2^-, \cdots, f_N^-\}$ is regarded as the negative deviation d^- provided that it is nonnegative. If the N'th least element is negative, then we set $d^- = 0$. Analogously, we make a sequence of $\{f_1^+, f_2^+, \cdots, f_N^+\}$ where $f_i^+ = f(\boldsymbol{x},\boldsymbol{\xi}_i) - b$ and $\boldsymbol{\xi}_i$ are generated from the probability distribution $\Phi(\boldsymbol{\xi})$, $i = 1,2,\cdots,N$, respectively. We also take N' as the integer part of βN. Then the N'th least element in $\{f_1^+, f_2^+, \cdots, f_N^+\}$ is regarded as the positive deviation d^+. Certainly, if $d^+ < 0$, then we set $d^+ = 0$.

Step 1. Generate N vectors $\{\boldsymbol{\xi}_1, \boldsymbol{\xi}_2, \cdots, \boldsymbol{\xi}_N\}$ from the distribution $\Phi(\boldsymbol{\xi})$.
Step 2. Set $f_i^- = b - f(\boldsymbol{x},\boldsymbol{\xi}_i)$ and $f_i^+ = f(\boldsymbol{x},\boldsymbol{\xi}_i) - b$ for $i = 1,2,\cdots,N$.
Step 3. Set N' as the integer part of βN.
Step 4. Set f^- as the N'th least element in $\{f_1^-, f_2^-, \cdots, f_N^-\}$.
Step 5. Set f^+ as the N'th least element in $\{f_1^+, f_2^+, \cdots, f_N^+\}$.
Step 6. $d^- = f^- \vee 0$, $d^+ = f^+ \vee 0$.

5.5 Stochastic Simulation-based Genetic Algorithms

We have known that the classical solution technique of CCP is to convert the stochastic constraints to their respective deterministic equivalents according to the predetermined confidence levels. Since this process is usually hard and successful only for some special cases, Iwamura and Liu [63] provided a stochastic simulation-based genetic algorithm for solving CCP, CCMOP, and CCGP.

In this section we introduce the stochastic simulation-based genetic algorithm and give some numerical examples to illustrate this algorithm. In fact, the initialization process, selection, crossover, and mutation operations are the same as those in the genetic algorithm described in Chapter 2, except for the fact that we have to employ stochastic simulation to check the feasibility of new offspring and to handle stochastic objective and goal constraints as discussed in Section 5.4.

Genetic Algorithm Procedure

Step 0. *Input parameters pop_size, P_c and P_m.*

Step 1. *Initialize pop_size chromosomes in which stochastic simulations may be employed to check the feasibility.*

Step 2. *Update the chromosomes by crossover and mutation operations in which the feasibility of offspring may be checked by stochastic simulations.*

Step 3. *Calculate the objective values for all chromosomes by stochastic simulations.*

Step 4. *Compute the fitness of each chromosome by rank-based evaluation function based on the objective values.*

Step 5. *Select the chromosomes by spinning the roulette wheel.*

Step 6. *Repeat the second to fifth steps a given number of cycles.*

Step 7. *Report the best chromosome as the optimal solution.*

The computer code for the genetic algorithm to CCP has been written in C language. To illustrate the effectiveness of the genetic algorithm, a set of numerical examples has been done, and the results are successful. Here we give some numerical examples which are all performed on a personal computer with the following parameters: the population size is 30, the probability of crossover P_c is 0.3, the probability of mutation P_m is 0.2, and the parameter a in the rank-based evaluation function is 0.05.

Example 1: First we consider a simple CCP model,

$$\begin{cases} \max\ x_1x_2(x_3+x_4) \\ \text{subject to:} \\ \qquad \Pr\left\{\xi_1x_1^2+\xi_2x_2^2+\xi_3x_3^2+\xi_4x_4^2 \le 100\right\} \ge 0.90 \\ \qquad x_1,x_2,x_3,x_4 \ge 0 \end{cases} \tag{5.35}$$

where ξ_1 is a uniformly distributed variable $\mathcal{U}(2,3)$, ξ_2 is a normally distributed variable $\mathcal{N}(2,1)$, ξ_3 is an exponentially distributed variable $\mathcal{EXP}(3)$, and ξ_4 is a Cauchy distributed variable $\mathcal{C}(3,2)$.

A run of the stochastic simulation-based genetic algorithm with 100 generations shows that the optimal solution is

$$(x_1^*,x_2^*,x_3^*,x_4^*) = (3.1751,\ 3.1208,\ 2.2650,\ 1.7028)$$

with optimal objective value 39.316. And we also have

$$\Pr\left\{\xi_1 x_1^{*2} + \xi_2 x_2^{*2} + \xi_3 x_3^{*2} + \xi_4 x_4^{*2} \le 100\right\} \approx 0.90.$$

The time complexity of this problem is the sum of the time spent for the stochastic simulation and the time spent for the genetic algorithm, where the computation time for stochastic simulation is exactly proportional to the number of sampling points.

Example 2: Let us consider the following single-objective CCP in which there are three decision variables and nine stochastic parameters,

$$\begin{cases} \max \overline{f} \\ \text{subject to:} \\ \qquad \Pr\left\{\xi_1 x_1 + \xi_2 x_2 + \xi_3 x_3 \ge \overline{f}\right\} \ge 0.90 \\ \qquad \Pr\left\{\eta_1 x_1^2 + \eta_2 x_2^2 + \eta_3 x_3^2 \le 8\right\} \ge 0.80 \\ \qquad \Pr\left\{\tau_1 x_1^3 + \tau_2 x_2^3 + \tau_3 x_3^3 \le 15\right\} \ge 0.85 \\ \qquad x_1, x_2, x_3 \ge 0 \end{cases} \tag{5.36}$$

where ξ_1, η_1, and τ_1 are uniformly distributed variables $\mathcal{U}(1,2)$, $\mathcal{U}(2,3)$, and $\mathcal{U}(3,4)$, respectively, ξ_2, η_2, and τ_2 are normally distributed variables $\mathcal{N}(1,1)$, $\mathcal{N}(2,1)$, and $\mathcal{N}(3,1)$, respectively, and ξ_3, η_3, and τ_3 are exponentially distributed variables $\mathcal{EXP}(1)$, $\mathcal{EXP}(2)$, and $\mathcal{EXP}(3)$, respectively,

Each stochastic simulation will be performed with 2000 cycles. A run of the stochastic simulation-based genetic algorithm with 200 generations shows that the optimal solution is

$$(x_1^*, x_2^*, x_3^*) = (1.5296,\ 0.4226,\ 0.6608)$$

with objective value $\overline{f}^* = 2.386$. In fact, we also have

$$\begin{cases} \Pr\left\{\xi_1 x_1^* + \xi_2 x_2^* + \xi_3 x_3^* \ge \overline{f}^*\right\} \approx 0.90, \\ \Pr\left\{\eta_1 x_1^{*2} + \eta_2 x_2^{*2} + \eta_3 x_3^{*2} \le 8\right\} \approx 0.80, \\ \Pr\left\{\tau_1 x_1^{*3} + \tau_2 x_2^{*3} + \tau_3 x_3^{*3} \le 15\right\} \approx 0.85. \end{cases}$$

Example 3: Now we solve the following CCGP model by the stochastic simulation-based genetic algorithm,

$$
\left\{
\begin{array}{l}
\text{lexmin } \{d_1^-, d_2^-, d_3^-\} \\
\text{subject to:} \\
\qquad \Pr\left\{\tau_1 x_1 + \tau_2 x_2 + \tau_3 x_3 + d_1^- - d_1^+ = 10\right\} \ge 0.90 \\
\qquad x_1 + d_2^- - d_2^+ = 4 \\
\qquad x_2 + x_3 + d_3^- - d_3^+ = 2 \\
\qquad \Pr\left\{
\begin{array}{l}
\eta_1 x_1 + x_2 + x_3 \le \xi_1 \\
x_1 + \eta_2 x_2 + x_3 \le \xi_2 \\
x_1 + x_2 + \eta_3 x_3 \le \xi_3
\end{array}
\right\} \ge 0.8 \\
\qquad x_1, x_2, x_3 \ge 0
\end{array}
\right.
\tag{5.37}
$$

where the parameters $\xi_1, \xi_2, \xi_3, \eta_1$, and τ_1 are uniformly distributed variables $\mathcal{U}(8,10)$, $\mathcal{U}(10,12)$, $\mathcal{U}(5,7)$, $\mathcal{U}(1,2)$, and $\mathcal{U}(2,3)$, respectively, η_2 and τ_2 are exponentially distributed variables $\mathcal{EXP}(2)$ and $\mathcal{EXP}(3)$, respectively, and η_3 and τ_3 are normally distributed variables $\mathcal{N}(2,1)$ and $\mathcal{N}(3,1)$, respectively.

A run of the stochastic simulation-based genetic algorithm with 400 generations shows that the optimal solution for the CCGP is

$$(x_1^*, x_2^*, x_3^*) = (4.0001,\ 1.0291,\ 0.1045)$$

which can satisfy the first and second goals, but the negative deviation of the third goal is 0.8664. Furthermore, we have

$$\Pr\left\{\tau_1 x_1^* + \tau_2 x_2^* + \tau_3 x_3^* \ge 10\right\} \approx 0.90$$

and

$$
\Pr\left\{
\begin{array}{l}
\eta_1 x_1^* + x_2^* + x_3^* \le \xi_1 \\
x_1^* + \eta_2 x_2^* + x_3^* \le \xi_2 \\
x_1^* + x_2^* + \eta_3 x_3^* \le \xi_3
\end{array}
\right\} \approx 0.8.
$$

5.6 Notes

In this chapter we introduced the general formulations of CCP, CCMOP, and CCGP, and showed some of their deterministic equivalents and mathematical properties.

Stochastic simulations have also been designed to check stochastic system constraints as well as to handle stochastic objective constraints and goal constraints.

The stochastic simulation-based genetic algorithm provides an effective means to solve complex CCP, CCMOP, and CCGP models. An advantage of this approach is to obtain the global optima fairly well. The other advantage is that we do not need to convert the stochastic constraints to their deterministic equivalents, where the translation is usually impossible to do. This ensures that we can deal with general CCP models. The effectiveness of the stochastic simulation-based genetic algorithm has been proven by many numerical experiments and is illustrated by some test problems at the end of this chapter.

Chapter 6

Applications of Chance-Constrained Programming

In this chapter, we provide some examples to illustrate the modeling idea of chance-constrained programming (CCP), chance-constrained multiobjective programming (CCMOP), and chance-constrained goal programming (CCGP). We will present the following applications:

- Production Process
- Feed Mixture Problem
- Stochastic Resource Allocation
- Open Inventory Network
- Capital Budgeting

6.1 Production Process

This is a modification of an example of Kall and Wallace [68]. Let us consider a weekly production plan of an oil refinery for crude oil (raw_1 and raw_2), for supplying gasoline ($prod_1$) to a distribution system of gas stations and fuel oil ($prod_2$) to power plants.

It is known that the productivities $\pi(raw_1, prod_1)$ and $\pi(raw_2, prod_2)$ (i.e., the output of gas from raw_1 and output of fuel from raw_2) may change randomly, whereas the other productivities are deterministic. They are assumed to be

$$\pi(raw_1, prod_1) = 2 + \eta_1, \quad \pi(raw_1, prod_2) = 3,$$
$$\pi(raw_2, prod_1) = 6, \qquad \pi(raw_2, prod_2) = 3.4 - \eta_2$$

where η_1 is a uniformly distributed variable $\mathcal{U}(-0.8, 0.8)$, and η_2 is an exponentially distributed variable $\mathcal{EXP}(0.4)$.

The weekly demands of the clients (gas stations and power plants), h_1 for gas and h_2 for fuel, are also varying randomly and are represented by

$$h_1 = 180 + \xi_1, \qquad h_2 = 162 + \xi_2$$

where ξ_1 and ξ_2 are normally distributed variables $\mathcal{N}(0, 12)$ and $\mathcal{N}(0, 9)$, respectively.

Let x_1 and x_2 be the quantities of raw_1 and raw_2 to be processed in one week, respectively. The production costs per unit of the raw materials are $c_1 = 2$ for raw_1 and $c_2 = 3$ for raw_2. The total cost is thus $2x_1 + 3x_2$.

The production capacity (i.e., the maximal total amount of raw materials) is assumed to be 100. Thus we have to restrict the production plan by $x_1 + x_2 \le 100$.

If the weekly production plan (x_1, x_2) has to be fixed in advance and cannot be changed during the week, and clients expect their actual demand to be satisfied during the corresponding week, then we have the following constraints,

$$(2 + \eta_1)x_1 + 6x_2 \ge 180 + \xi_1, \qquad 3x_1 + (3.4 - \eta_2)x_2 \ge 162 + \xi_2.$$

Note that these constraints are not clear at all since some stochastic variables are included. One feasible way is to employ chance constraints. For example, we may impose confidence levels α_1 and α_2 on the two clients and obtain

$$\Pr\{(2 + \eta_1)x_1 + 6x_2 \ge 180 + \xi_1\} \ge \alpha_1,$$
$$\Pr\{3x_1 + (3.4 - \eta_2)x_2 \ge 162 + \xi_2\} \ge \alpha_2.$$

We hope that the total production cost is as low as possible. Different from the stochastic programming with recourse employed in [68], we formulate a CCP model for this production process as follows:

$$\begin{cases} \min f(\boldsymbol{x}) = 2x_1 + 3x_2 \\ \text{subject to:} \\ \qquad \Pr\{(2+\eta_1)x_1 + 6x_2 \geq 180 + \xi_1\} \geq \alpha_1 \\ \qquad \Pr\{3x_1 + (3.4 - \eta_2)x_2 \geq 162 + \xi_2\} \geq \alpha_2 \\ \qquad x_1 + x_2 \leq 100 \\ \qquad x_1, x_2 \geq 0. \end{cases} \tag{6.1}$$

When the confidence levels α_1 and α_2 are assumed to be 0.8 and 0.7, respectively, then the optimal production plan is

$$(x_1^*, x_2^*) = (31.95, 22.65)$$

with production cost $f(x_1^*, x_2^*) = 131.85$. The result is obtained by running the stochastic simulation-based genetic algorithm with 500 generations. Furthermore, we have

$$\Pr\{(2+\eta_1)x_1^* + 6x_2^* \geq 180 + \xi_1\} \approx 0.88,$$

$$\Pr\{3x_1^* + (3.4 - \eta_2)x_2^* \geq 162 + \xi_2\} \approx 0.70.$$

6.2 Feed Mixture Problem

Van de Panne and Popp [141] presented a CCP model for a feed mixture problem, which is to select four materials to mix in order to design a cattle feed mix subject to protein and fat constraints with the objective of minimizing cost.

Let x_1, x_2, x_3, and x_4 be the percentage levels of the four materials. Then we have, at first, $x_1 + x_2 + x_3 + x_4 = 1$.

Suppose that the protein contents per unit of the four materials are 2.3, 5.6, 11.1, and 1.3. If the protein content of feed is not allowed to be lower than 5, then we have

$$2.3x_1 + 5.6x_2 + 11.1x_3 + 1.3x_4 \geq 5.$$

The fat contents of the four materials are η_1, η_2, η_3, and η_4, which are assumed normally distributed variables $\mathcal{N}(12.0, 0.2809^2)$, $\mathcal{N}(11.9, 0.1936^2)$, $\mathcal{N}(41.8, 20.25^2)$, and $\mathcal{N}(52.1, 0.6241^2)$, respectively. If the fat content of feed is required to be larger than or equal to 21 with probability level $\alpha (0 < \alpha < 1)$, then we have a chance constraint

$$\Pr\{\eta_1 x_1 + \eta_2 x_2 + \eta_3 x_3 + \eta_4 x_4 \geq 21\} \geq \alpha.$$

The prices of the four materials are assumed to be 24.55, 26.75, 39.00, and 40.50. Then the total cost of per unit of feed is

$$f(\boldsymbol{x}) = 24.55x_1 + 26.75x_2 + 39.00x_3 + 40.50x_4.$$

Thus the CCP model for the feed mixture problem can be written as follows:

$$\begin{cases} \min f(\boldsymbol{x}) = 24.55x_1 + 26.75x_2 + 39.00x_3 + 40.50x_4 \\ \text{subject to:} \\ \qquad x_1 + x_2 + x_3 + x_4 = 1 \\ \qquad 2.3x_1 + 5.6x_2 + 11.1x_3 + 1.3x_4 \geq 5 \\ \qquad \Pr\{\eta_1 x_1 + \eta_2 x_2 + \eta_3 x_3 + \eta_4 x_4 \geq 21\} \geq \alpha \\ \qquad x_1, x_2, x_3, x_4 \geq 0. \end{cases} \tag{6.2}$$

When α is assigned to be 0.8, a run of the stochastic simulation-based genetic algorithm with 1000 generations shows that the optimal solution is

$$(x_1^*,\ x_2^*,\ x_3^*,\ x_4^*) = (0.001,\ 0.739,\ 0.053,\ 0.199)$$

which means that the cost per unit of feed $f(x_1^*, x_2^*, x_3^*, x_4^*) = 30.25$ and the actual reliability of fat content is just 80%.

6.3 Stochastic Resource Allocation

Let us consider a stochastic resource allocation problem in which there are multiple locations of resources and multiple users. The task of stochastic resource allocation is to determine the outputs that result from various combinations of resources such that certain goals of supply are achieved. As an example, our object of study is a water supply-allocation system in which there are 3 locations of water and 4 users. The scheme of the water supply-allocation system is shown in Figure 6.1.

In order to determine an optimal water allocation plan, we use 8 decision variables $x_1, x_2, \cdots, x_8$ to represent an action, where x_1, x_2, x_3 are quantities ordered from $input_1$ to outputs 1,2,3 respectively; x_4, x_5, x_6 from $input_2$ to outputs 2,3,4 respectively; and x_7, x_8 from $input_3$ to outputs 3,4 respectively.

We note that the inputs are available outside resources. They have their own properties. For example, the maximum quantities supplied by the three resources are marked by ξ_1, ξ_2, and ξ_3, which are two-parameter lognormally distributed variables $\mathcal{LOGN}(1.56, 0.56^2)$, $\mathcal{LOGN}(1.36, 0.45^2)$,

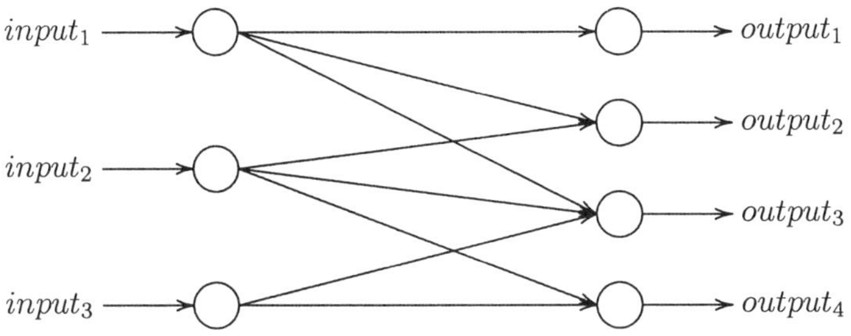

Figure 6.1: A Supply-Allocation System

and $\mathcal{LOGN}(0.95, 0.38^2)$, respectively. Thus at first we have the following constraints,

$$x_1 + x_2 + x_3 \le \xi_1, \qquad x_4 + x_5 + x_6 \le \xi_2, \qquad x_7 + x_8 \le \xi_3. \tag{6.3}$$

To handle the stochastic constraint (6.3), let $\alpha_1 = 0.9$, $\alpha_2 = 0.7$, and $\alpha_3 = 0.8$ be assigned as confidence levels of the three chance constraints, respectively. Then we have the following chance constraints,

$$\begin{cases} \Pr\{x_1 + x_2 + x_3 \le \xi_1\} \ge 0.9, \\ \Pr\{x_4 + x_5 + x_6 \le \xi_2\} \ge 0.7, \\ \Pr\{x_7 + x_8 \le \xi_3\} \ge 0.8. \end{cases}$$

The other clear constraints are $x_i \ge 0$, $i = 1, 2, \cdots, 8$, which means that the quantities ordered from the resources are nonnegative.

The management goals are assumed to satisfy the demands of four users. Suppose that $3, 1, 2$, and 3 are the demands of four users. We also suppose that the following target levels and priority structure have been set by the manager. At the first priority level, we should satisfy the demand of $output_1$, i.e.,

$$x_1 + d_1^- - d_1^+ = 3$$

where d_1^- will be minimized. At the second priority level, the demand of $output_2$ should be fulfilled, i.e.,

$$x_2 + x_4 + d_2^- - d_2^+ = 1$$

where d_2^- will be minimized. At the third priority level, we should fulfill the demand of $output_3$, i.e.,

$$x_3 + x_5 + x_7 + d_3^- - d_3^+ = 2$$

where d_3^- will be minimized. At the last priority level, the demand of $output_4$ should be met, i.e.,

$$x_6 + x_8 + d_4^- - d_4^+ = 3$$

where d_4^- will be minimized.

Then a CCGP associated with this problem is formulated as follows:

$$\begin{cases} \text{lexmin}\left\{d_1^-, d_2^-, d_3^-, d_4^-\right\} \\ \text{subject to:} \\ \qquad x_1 + d_1^- - d_1^+ = 3 \\ \qquad x_2 + x_4 + d_2^- - d_2^+ = 1 \\ \qquad x_3 + x_5 + x_7 + d_3^- - d_3^+ = 2 \\ \qquad x_6 + x_8 + d_4^- - d_4^+ = 3 \\ \qquad \Pr\{x_1 + x_2 + x_3 \le \xi_1\} \ge 0.9 \\ \qquad \Pr\{x_4 + x_5 + x_6 \le \xi_2\} \ge 0.7 \\ \qquad \Pr\{x_7 + x_8 \le \xi_3\} \ge 0.8 \\ \qquad x_i \ge 0, \quad i = 1, 2, \cdots, 8. \end{cases} \tag{6.4}$$

A run of stochastic simulation-based genetic algorithm with 3000 generations shows that the optimal solution is

$$(x_1, x_2, x_3, x_4, x_5, x_6, x_7, x_8) = (3.01, 0.00, 0.07, 1.31, 0.99, 0.15, 0.47, 1.07)$$

which can satisfy the first two goals, but the negative deviations of the third and fourth goals are 0.47 and 1.78, respectively.

6.4 Open Inventory Network

Usually, a network is described by nodes $\{1, 2, \cdots, p\}$ and arcs $\{1, 2, \cdots, n\}$. An arc k will be denoted by $k \sim (i, j)$, indicating that it starts at node i and ends at node j. As an extension, Liu and Esogbue [97] developed an open inventory network which regards the outer world as an external node denoted by ∞.

Now we take the stochastic inventory problems and reservoir operations as the background of an open inventory network. Then the nodes may represent locations or reservoirs, the external node may represent the market or user, and the arcs may represent orders, transportation, or water release.

For each node i (not including ∞!), let a_i and ξ_i be the state and stochastic term, respectively. Then $\xi_i > 0$ denotes inputs, $\xi_i < 0$ outputs. For an inventory problem, a_i represents the inventory level, ξ_i the stochastic demand; for a reservoir operation, a_i represents the volume in storage, ξ_i the stochastic inflow.

For each arc $k \sim (i, j)$, we denote the flow by x_k, which is a decision variable. Then the decision $x_k > 0$ implies moving from i to j, $x_k < 0$ moving from j to i. For an inventory problem, a decision represents the quantity ordered from outside or transported from other locations; for a reservoir operation, a decision represents the water released or drawn from other reservoirs.

We will call the above network an *open inventory network*, which is one where arcs correspond to decisions, nodes to locations or reservoirs, and the external node to the outer world. We mention that the term *open* means that the total amount in this system can vary because of the external node and stochastic term.

Generally, a network problem is called capacitated if $-\infty < x_k < +\infty$ for all arcs k, $k = 1, 2, \cdots, n$. Otherwise, the network is uncapacitated. Most networks are a mixture of these two cases. Thus we will suppose that the flows x_k's are constrained by $q_k \le x_k \le Q_k$, $k = 1, 2, \cdots, n$, respectively. Since each node i (not including ∞!) is a warehouse or reservoir, their states a_i's have physical constraints,

$$v_i \le a_i \le V_i, \quad i = 1, 2, \cdots, p. \tag{6.5}$$

For example, $v_i = 0$, $V_i =$ the maximum volume in storage.

Let $\boldsymbol{a} = (a_1, a_2, \cdots, a_p)$ be the vector of states, $\boldsymbol{\xi} = (\xi_1, \xi_2, \cdots, \xi_p)$ the vector of stochastic terms having joint probability density function $\phi(\boldsymbol{\xi})$ which may be separable or degenerate, and $\boldsymbol{x} = (x_1, x_2, \ldots, x_n)$ the decision constrained by the set

$$D = \left\{ \boldsymbol{x} \in \Re^n \mid q_i \le x_i \le Q_i, \quad i = 1, 2, \cdots, n \right\} \tag{6.6}$$

where q_i and Q_i are not necessarily positive and finite. For example, q_i and Q_i are water demand and maximum release quantity allowed by the downstream, respectively, in a reservoir operation problem.

The state $\boldsymbol{a}'$ after a decision and a stochastic term is described by the following state transition equation,

$$\boldsymbol{a}' = \boldsymbol{a} + t(\boldsymbol{x}) + \boldsymbol{\xi} \tag{6.7}$$

where $t()$ is a vector-valued function: $\Re^n \to \Re^p$.

In Figure 6.2, there are four nodes labeled as 1, 2, 3, 4, an external node represented by a dashed ellipse, and nine arcs listed as $(1, \infty)$, $(1, 2)$, $(1, 3)$, $(1, 4)$, $(2, \infty)$, $(2, 4)$, $(3, \infty)$, $(3, 4)$, and $(4, \infty)$. In this open inventory

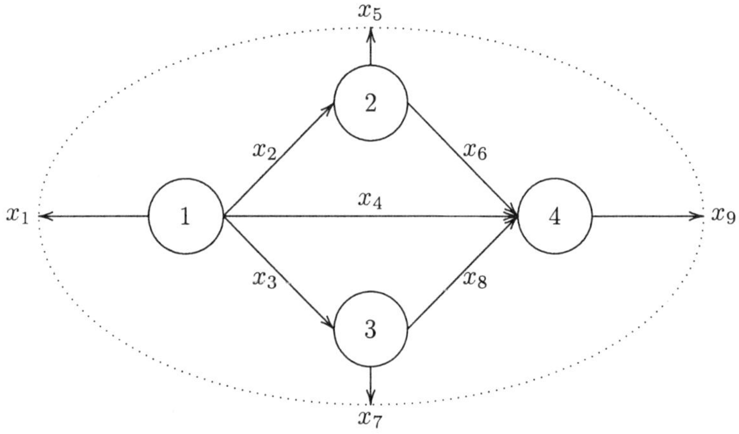

Figure 6.2: An Open Inventory Network

network, the function $t()$ is as follows,

$$t(\boldsymbol{x}) = \begin{pmatrix} -x_1 - x_2 - x_3 - x_4 \\ x_2 - x_5 - x_6 \\ x_3 - x_7 - x_8 \\ x_4 + x_6 + x_8 - x_9 \end{pmatrix}^T.$$

If we write $t_1(\boldsymbol{x}) = -x_1 - x_2 - x_3 - x_4$, $t_2(\boldsymbol{x}) = x_2 - x_5 - x_6$, $t_3(\boldsymbol{x}) = x_3 - x_7 - x_8$, and $t_4(\boldsymbol{x}) = x_4 + x_6 + x_8 - x_9$, then we have

$$t(\boldsymbol{x}) = \big(t_1(\boldsymbol{x}), t_2(\boldsymbol{x}), t_3(\boldsymbol{x}), t_4(\boldsymbol{x})\big).$$

One of the basic network optimization problems is the *shortest-path problem*, which is concerned with finding the shortest path between two given nodes in a network, where the measure of path may be distance, time, money, and so on. The *minimum cost flow problem* is connected with minimizing the cost of moving a given quantity of a commodity from a given origin to a given destination in a network which has not only a capacity but also a unit cost associated with each arc. The *maximal flow problem* is related to maximizing the flow of some commodity through the arcs of a network from a given origin to a given destination, where each arc has a capacity of flow.

The shortest-path problem and minimum cost flow problem assume essentially that the initial state and destination state of a network are known, and then find an action under some optimality criterion such that the destination state is reached. The maximal flow problem attempts to discover the maximum flow, or equivalently, the maximum destination state of a given node. However, the *optimal operation problem* of the open inventory network does not assume that the destination state is known in advance. In fact, the optimal operation problem arises in connection with finding the best destination state under some evaluation criterion, subject to the capacity constraints of nodes and arcs, from a given initial state. For this case, the optimal operating policy should be presented for the sake of reaching the best destination state.

An optimal operation model for open inventory networks is the so-called fuzzy criterion model based on dynamic programming proposed by Liu and Esogbue [87][97]. If the decision must be taken in the constraint set defined by (6.6) regardless of the physical constraints of the nodes, then the network can be described by the vector of *imaginary* states (not including the external node!) which are the states after decisions and stochastic inflows. When the imaginary states are less than the dead inventory levels, the demand is not fulfilled, and the difference represents the shortage quantity; when the imaginary states are larger than the largest physical volumes of storage, the amount exceeds the capacity of the warehouses or reservoirs, and the difference represents the degree of exceeding level or flood. Usually, there exists the best state at which we define the value of a fuzzy criterion as 1. When the inventory level goes away from the best state, the value of the fuzzy criterion decreases. Thus the set of all satisfactory states is a fuzzy criterion set whose fuzzy criterion function is the satisfactory degree of elements. Here the fuzzy criterion function is denoted by $\mu(\cdot)$.

For a given K-stage decision process, let $\mu_1, \mu_2, \cdots, \mu_K$ be the fuzzy criterion functions at the stages $1, 2, \cdots, K$, respectively. Assume that $\rho_1, \rho_2, \cdots, \rho_K$ are coefficients of convex combination representing the relative importance among $\mu_1, \mu_2, \cdots, \mu_K$. If the objective is related to maximizing the weighted sum of all fuzzy criterion functions over their respective stages, then the fuzzy criterion model is written as

$$\sup_{\boldsymbol{x}_k, k=1,2,\cdots,K} \sum_{k=1}^{K} \rho_i \int_{\Re^p} \mu_k(\boldsymbol{a}_k + t(\boldsymbol{x}_k) + \boldsymbol{\xi})\phi_k(\boldsymbol{\xi})d\boldsymbol{\xi} \tag{6.8}$$

with a state transition function

$$\boldsymbol{a}_{k+1} = \boldsymbol{a}_k + t(\boldsymbol{x}_k) + \boldsymbol{\xi} \tag{6.9}$$

for $k = 1, 2, \cdots, K-1$. The associated dynamic fuzzy criterion model is given by

$$\begin{cases} f_K(\boldsymbol{a}) & = \sup_{\boldsymbol{x} \in D_K} L_K(\boldsymbol{a} + t(\boldsymbol{x})) \\ f_k(\boldsymbol{a}) & = \sup_{\boldsymbol{x} \in D_k} \Big\{ \theta_k L_k(\boldsymbol{a} + t(\boldsymbol{x})) \\ & \qquad + (1 - \theta_k) \int_{\Re^p} f_{k+1}(\boldsymbol{a} + t(\boldsymbol{x}) + \boldsymbol{\xi}) \phi_k(\boldsymbol{\xi}) d\boldsymbol{\xi} \Big\} \\ k & \leq K - 1 \end{cases} \tag{6.10}$$

where

$$L_k(\boldsymbol{y}) = \int_{\Re^p} \mu_k(\boldsymbol{y} + \boldsymbol{\xi}) \phi_k(\boldsymbol{\xi}) d\boldsymbol{\xi} \tag{6.11}$$

and $\theta_k = \rho_k / (\rho_k + \rho_{k+1} + \cdots + \rho_K)$, $k = 1, 2, \cdots, K$, respectively.

Fuzzy criterion models are able to incorporate expert knowledge via the fuzzy criterion functions μ_k's, so they conform to the spirit of modern decision-making theory. However, fuzzy criterion models only serve long-term and dynamic decision making. Sometimes, we should operate the open inventory network in detail. Chance-constrained programming will be employed to model such an open inventory network in this section.

Since each node i is a location or reservoir, the state a_i must be non-negative. For an inventory system, the state $a_i \geq 0$; for a reservoir system, $a_i \geq v_i$ where v_i is the dead volume in storage of the node i. On the other hand, the state a_i must be less than the largest physical volume in storage V_i. That is, no matter what type of node it is, we always have $a_i \leq V_i$. Hence we should find a decision $\boldsymbol{x}$ in D such that the state a_i' after a decision and a stochastic term satisfies $v_i \leq a_i' \leq V_i$, i.e.,

$$v_i \leq a_i + t_i(\boldsymbol{x}) + \xi_i \leq V_i, \quad i = 1, 2, \cdots, p \tag{6.12}$$

where $t(\boldsymbol{x}) = (t_1(\boldsymbol{x}), t_2(\boldsymbol{x}), \cdots, t_p(\boldsymbol{x}))$ and each $t_i(\boldsymbol{x})$ is a real-valued function. Since there is a vector of stochastic terms $\boldsymbol{\xi} = (\xi_1, \xi_2, \cdots, \xi_p)$ in equation (6.12), we do not know whether the given decision $\boldsymbol{x}$ meets the constraints before the stochastic vector is realized. However, by the formalism of CCP, we may predetermine a confidence level α for the stochastic constraints (6.12) and formulate the following inequality,

$$\Pr\{v_i \leq a_i + t_i(\boldsymbol{x}) + \xi_i \leq V_i, i = 1, 2, \cdots, p\} \geq \alpha \tag{6.13}$$

which is a joint chance constraint, where $\Pr\{\cdot\}$ denotes the probability of the event $\{\cdot\}$. This chance constraint may be regarded as an added term of the constraint set D. Thus a decision $\boldsymbol{x}$ in D is feasible if and only if the probability measure of the set $\{\boldsymbol{\xi}|v_i \leq a_i + t_i(\boldsymbol{x}) + \xi_i \leq V_i, i = 1, 2, \cdots, p\}$ is at least α. Note that equation (6.12) is equivalent to

$$v_i - a_i - t_i(\boldsymbol{x}) \leq \xi_i \leq V_i - a_i - t_i(\boldsymbol{x}), \quad i = 1, 2, \cdots, p,$$

that is, the vector of stochastic terms $\boldsymbol{\xi} = (\xi_1, \xi_2, \cdots, \xi_p)$ should lie on the hypercube

$$[v_1 - a_1 - t_1(\boldsymbol{x}), V_1 - a_1 - t_1(\boldsymbol{x})] \times \cdots \times [v_p - a_p - t_p(\boldsymbol{x}), V_p - a_p - t_p(\boldsymbol{x})].$$

Thus we have

$$\begin{aligned} & \Pr\{v_i \leq a_i + t_i(\boldsymbol{x}) + \xi_i \leq V_i, i = 1, 2, \cdots, p\} \\ = & \int_{v_1 - a_1 - t_1(\boldsymbol{x})}^{V_1 - a_1 - t_1(\boldsymbol{x})} \cdots \int_{v_p - a_p - t_p(\boldsymbol{x})}^{V_p - a_p - t_p(\boldsymbol{x})} \phi(\xi_1, \cdots, \xi_p) d\xi_1 \cdots d\xi_p \end{aligned}$$

which yields the deterministic equivalent of chance constraint (6.13) as follows,

$$\int_{v_1 - a_1 - t_1(\boldsymbol{x})}^{V_1 - a_1 - t_1(\boldsymbol{x})} \cdots \int_{v_p - a_p - t_p(\boldsymbol{x})}^{V_p - a_p - t_p(\boldsymbol{x})} \phi(\xi_1, \cdots, \xi_p) d\xi_1 \cdots d\xi_p \geq \alpha.$$

We can also formulate the joint chance constraint as separate chance constraints,

$$\Pr\{v_i \leq a_i + t_i(\boldsymbol{x}) + \xi_i \leq V_i\} \geq \alpha_i, \quad i = 1, 2, \cdots, p \tag{6.14}$$

where α_i are predetermined confidence levels to the respective constraints, $i = 1, 2, \cdots, p$. Now we suppose that $\phi(\xi_1, \xi_2, \cdots, \xi_p)$ is separable, i.e., $\phi(\xi_1, \xi_2, \cdots, \xi_p) = \phi_1(\xi_1)\phi_2(\xi_2) \cdots \phi_p(\xi_p)$. Then we have

$$\begin{aligned} & \Pr\{v_i \leq a_i + t_i(\boldsymbol{x}) + \xi_i \leq V_i\} \\ = & \int_{v_i - a_i - t_i(\boldsymbol{x})}^{V_i - a_i - t_i(\boldsymbol{x})} \phi_i(\xi_i) d\xi_i \\ = & \Phi_i(V_i - a_i - t_i(\boldsymbol{x})) - \Phi_i(v_i - a_i - t_i(\boldsymbol{x})) \end{aligned}$$

where Φ_i are the cumulative probability distributions of ξ_i, $i = 1, 2, \cdots, p$, respectively. Hence the chance constraints (6.14) are equivalent to

$$\Phi_i(V_i - a_i - t_i(\boldsymbol{x})) - \Phi_i(v_i - a_i - t_i(\boldsymbol{x})) \geq \alpha_i, \quad i = 1, 2, \cdots, p. \tag{6.15}$$

We should mention that the chance constraint set is, in general, not convex.

Recall the definition of the set D. A decision $\boldsymbol{x}$ in D implies that the decision $\boldsymbol{x}$ will satisfy the demands of users and does not exceed the capacities of arcs. If such a decision $\boldsymbol{x}$ can actually be performed, that is, the decision meets the constraints (6.12) or the chance constraints (6.14), then the decision is usually considered acceptable. Thus the simplest problem is formulated by the following CCP,

$$\begin{cases} \text{Find } \boldsymbol{x} \text{ in } D \\ \text{subject to:} \\ \qquad \Pr\{v_i \le a_i + t_i(\boldsymbol{x}) + \xi_i \le V_i\} \ge \alpha_i, \quad i = 1, 2, \cdots, p. \end{cases} \tag{6.16}$$

where v_i, V_i, a_i, and α_i are given parameters, $i = 1, 2, \cdots, p$, and the decision vector is $\boldsymbol{x} = (x_1, x_2, \cdots, x_n)$. Or equivalently,

$$\begin{cases} \text{Find } \boldsymbol{x} \text{ in } D \\ \text{subject to:} \\ \qquad \Phi_i(V_i - a_i - t_i(\boldsymbol{x})) - \Phi_i(v_i - a_i - t_i(\boldsymbol{x})) \ge \alpha_i, \quad i = 1, 2, \cdots, p. \end{cases}$$

Although any decision $\boldsymbol{x}$ given by the CCP (6.16) is considered acceptable, the decision-maker is interested in some special class of decisions. For example, we may hope that (i) the sum of all flows is as little as possible, i.e., minimizing the function $f_1(\boldsymbol{x}) = |x_1| + |x_2| + \cdots + |x_n|$; (ii) the sum of transportation costs is as little as possible, i.e., minimizing the cost function $f_2(\boldsymbol{x}) = c_1|x_1| + c_2|x_2| + \cdots + c_n|x_n|$, and so on. When some objective function $f(\boldsymbol{x})$ is selected (without loss of generality, suppose that $f(\boldsymbol{x})$ will be minimized), we can model the open inventory network as the following CCP,

$$\begin{cases} \min f(\boldsymbol{x}) \\ \text{subject to:} \\ \qquad \Pr\{v_i \le a_i + t_i(\boldsymbol{x}) + \xi_i \le V_i\} \ge \alpha_i, \quad i = 1, 2, \cdots, p \\ \qquad \boldsymbol{x} \in D. \end{cases} \tag{6.17}$$

This CCP is equivalent to

$$\begin{cases} \min f(\boldsymbol{x}) \\ \text{subject to:} \\ \qquad \Phi_i(V_i - a_i - t_i(\boldsymbol{x})) - \Phi_i(v_i - a_i - t_i(\boldsymbol{x})) \ge \alpha_i, \quad i = 1, 2, \cdots, p \\ \qquad \boldsymbol{x} \in D. \end{cases}$$

Since there are multiple potential objective functions in an open inventory network, we may extend single-objective CCP to the multiobjective case,

$$\begin{cases} \min\,[f_1(\boldsymbol{x}), f_2(\boldsymbol{x}), \cdots, f_m(\boldsymbol{x})] \\ \text{subject to:} \\ \qquad \Pr\{v_i \le a_i + t_i(\boldsymbol{x}) + \xi_i \le V_i\} \ge \alpha_i, \quad i = 1, 2, \cdots, p \\ \qquad \boldsymbol{x} \in D \end{cases} \tag{6.18}$$

which has the following deterministic equivalent form,

$$\begin{cases} \min\,[f_1(\boldsymbol{x}), f_2(\boldsymbol{x}), \cdots, f_m(\boldsymbol{x})] \\ \text{subject to:} \\ \qquad \Phi_i(V_i - a_i - t_i(\boldsymbol{x})) - \Phi_i(v_i - a_i - t_i(\boldsymbol{x})) \ge \alpha_i, \quad i = 1, 2, \cdots, p \\ \qquad \boldsymbol{x} \in D. \end{cases}$$

When some management targets are given, the objective function may minimize the deviations, positive, negative, or both, with a certain priority structure set by the decision-maker. Then we can also formulate the stochastic open inventory network as a CCGP model,

$$\begin{cases} \min \sum\limits_{j=1}^{l} P_j \sum\limits_{i=1}^{m} (u_{ij} d_i^+ + v_{ij} d_i^-) \\ \text{subject to:} \\ \qquad f_i(\boldsymbol{x}) + d_i^- - d_i^+ = b_i, & i = 1, 2, \cdots, m \\ \qquad \Pr\{v_i \le a_i + t_i(\boldsymbol{x}) + \xi_i \le V_i\} \ge \alpha_j, & j = 1, 2, \cdots, p \\ \qquad \boldsymbol{x} \in D \\ \qquad d_i^-, d_i^+ \ge 0, & i = 1, 2, \cdots, m \end{cases} \tag{6.19}$$

where P_j = the preemptive priority factor which expresses the relative importance of various goals, $P_j \gg P_{j+1}$, for all j, u_{ij} = weighting factor corresponding to positive deviation for goal i with priority j assigned, v_{ij} = weighting factor corresponding to negative deviation for goal i with priority j assigned, d_i^+ = positive deviation from the target of goal i, d_i^- = negative deviation from the target of goal i, f_i = a function in goal constraints, b_i = the target value according to goal i, l = number of priorities, and m = number of goal constraints.

Let us turn our attention to the open inventory network (a reservoir system) illustrated in Figure 6.2. We suppose that all the capacity vectors of nine arcs form a deterministic set D in which each element $\boldsymbol{x} = (x_1, x_2, \cdots, x_9)$ is constrained by

$$\begin{array}{lll} 10 \le x_1 \le 50, & 0 \le x_2 \le 10, & 0 \le x_3 \le 10, \\ 0 \le x_4 \le 15, & 15 \le x_5 \le 60, & -5 \le x_6 \le 5, \\ 15 \le x_7 \le 60, & -5 \le x_8 \le 5, & 20 \le x_9 \le 70. \end{array}$$

The stochastic terms (inflows) are two-parameter lognormally distributed variables $\mathcal{LOGN}(\mu_i, \sigma_i^2)$, $i = 1, 2, 3, 4$, respectively. We suppose that the values of parameters (μ_i, σ_i) of the four reservoirs are

$$(2.24, 1.12), \quad (1.60, 1.28), \quad (1.87, 1.45), \quad (1.30, 1.34),$$

respectively. We also suppose that the values of parameters (v_i, V_i) of the four reservoirs are $(10, 120)$, $(20, 100)$, $(10, 80)$, and $(0, 90)$, respectively.

If we assume that the probability that the given decision $\boldsymbol{x}$ in D satisfies the constraints (6.12) should be larger than or equal to a confidence level $\alpha = 0.90$, and the objective is to minimize the total sum of flows, then the optimal operation problem of open inventory network is formulated by the following chance-constrained programming,

$$\begin{cases} \min |x_1| + |x_2| + |x_3| + |x_4| + |x_5| + |x_6| + |x_7| + |x_8| + |x_9| \\ \text{subject to:} \\ \qquad 10 \le x_1 \le 50, \quad 0 \le x_2 \le 10, \quad 0 \le x_3 \le 10 \\ \qquad 0 \le x_4 \le 15, \quad 15 \le x_5 \le 60, \quad -5 \le x_6 \le 5 \\ \qquad 15 \le x_7 \le 60, \quad -5 \le x_8 \le 5, \quad 20 \le x_9 \le 70 \\ \qquad \Pr\left\{ \begin{array}{l} 10 \le 70 - x_1 - x_2 - x_3 - x_4 + \xi_1 \le 120 \\ 20 \le 80 + x_2 - x_5 - x_6 + \xi_2 \le 100 \\ 10 \le 60 + x_3 - x_7 - x_8 + \xi_3 \le 80 \\ 0 \le 50 + x_4 + x_6 + x_8 - x_9 + \xi_4 \le 90 \end{array} \right\} \ge 0.90 \end{cases}$$

where 70, 80, 60, and 50 are the initial volumes in storage of the four reservoirs, respectively. A run of the stochastic simulation-based genetic algorithm with 3000 generations shows that the optimal solution is

$$\boldsymbol{x}^* = (31.8,\ 0.0,\ 0.1,\ 0.1,\ 43.6,\ 1.3,\ 47.0,\ 0.0,\ 20.2)$$

whose actual reliability level is about 0.90 and the sum of all flows is 144.1.

6.5 Capital Budgeting

The original capital budgeting is concerned with maximizing the total net profit subject to a budget constraint by selecting an appropriate combination of projects. With the requirement of considering uncertainty of future demand and multiple conflicting goals, chance-constrained integer goal programming was employed to model capital budgeting by Keown and Martin [73] in the working capital management and by Keown and Taylor [75] in the production area. In addition, De et al. [30] extended CCGP to the zero-one case and applied it to capital budgeting problems.

Consider a company which has the opportunity to purchase machines in a plant. Suppose that there are n types of machines available. We use x_i to denote the numbers of type i machines selected, $i = 1, 2, \cdots, n$, respectively. Then all the variables x_i's are nonnegative integers. Let a_i be the level of funds that needs to be allocated to type i machine and a be the total capital available for distribution. Then we have

$$a_1x_1 + a_2x_2 + \cdots + a_nx_n \le a. \tag{6.20}$$

That is, the total cost spent for machines cannot exceed the amount available.

The other constraint is the maximum space availability limitation for the machines. Suppose that b_i are the spaces used by type i machine, $i = 1, 2, \cdots, n$, respectively. If the total available space is b, then we have the following constraint,

$$b_1x_1 + b_2x_2 + \cdots + b_nx_n \le b. \tag{6.21}$$

We suppose that different machines produce different products. Let η_i be the production capacity of the type i machine for product i. Then the total products i are $\eta_i x_i$, $i = 1, 2, \cdots, n$, respectively. We also assume that the future demands for products i are ξ_i, $i = 1, 2, \cdots, n$. Since the production should satisfy the future demand, we have

$$\eta_i x_i \ge \xi_i, \quad i = 1, 2, \cdots, n. \tag{6.22}$$

If c_i are the net profits per type i machine, $i = 1, 2, \cdots, n$, then the total net profit is $c_1x_1 + c_2x_2 + \cdots + c_nx_n$. Assume that our objective is to maximize the total net profit, i.e.,

$$\max c_1x_1 + c_2x_2 + \cdots + c_nx_n, \tag{6.23}$$

then we have a deterministic model for capital budgeting based on integer programming,

$$\begin{cases} \max c_1x_1 + c_2x_2 + \cdots + c_nx_n \\ \text{subject to:} \\ \qquad a_1x_1 + a_2x_2 + \cdots + a_nx_n \le a \\ \qquad b_1x_1 + b_2x_2 + \cdots + b_nx_n \le b \\ \qquad \eta_i x_i \ge \xi_i, \quad i = 1, 2, \cdots, n \\ \qquad x_i, i = 1, 2, \cdots, n, \quad \text{nonnegative integers.} \end{cases} \tag{6.24}$$

The capital budgeting problem (6.24) is clearly a general case of the knapsack problem, which is concerned with trying to fill a knapsack to a maximum total value, i.e.,

$$\begin{cases} \max c_1x_1 + c_2x_2 + \cdots + c_nx_n \\ \text{subject to:} \\ \qquad a_1x_1 + a_2x_2 + \cdots + a_nx_n \le a \\ \qquad x_i, i = 1, 2, \cdots, n, \quad \text{nonnegative integers} \end{cases} \tag{6.25}$$

where $(c_1, c_2, \cdots, c_n)$ and $(a_1, a_2, \cdots, a_n)$ are the respective values and weights of the n objects and a is the overall weight limitation.

Certainly, real capital budgeting problems are much more complex than the above-mentioned model. However, it is enough for illustrating the chance-constrained integer programming.

Now let us model the capital budgeting problems by chance-constrained integer programming based on [73][75][30].

In practice, the production capacities η_i and future demands ξ_i are not necessarily deterministic. Here we suppose that they are stochastic variables. Let ψ_i and ϕ_i denote the probability density functions of η_i and ξ_i, $i = 1, 2, \cdots, n$, respectively. Then the constraints $\eta_i x_i \ge \xi_i$ are stochastic. If the manager gives α_i as the probabilities of meeting the demands of products i, $i = 1, 2, \cdots, n$, respectively, then we have the following chance constraints,

$$\Pr\{\eta_i x_i \ge \xi_i\} \ge \alpha_i, \quad i = 1, 2, \cdots, n. \tag{6.26}$$

Thus, a chance-constrained integer programming is immediately formulated as follows,

$$\begin{cases} \max c_1x_1 + c_2x_2 + \cdots + c_nx_n \\ \text{subject to:} \\ \qquad a_1x_1 + a_2x_2 + \cdots + a_nx_n \le a \\ \qquad b_1x_1 + b_2x_2 + \cdots + b_nx_n \le b \\ \qquad \Pr\{\eta_i x_i \ge \xi_i\} \ge \alpha_i, \quad i = 1, 2, \cdots, n \\ \qquad x_i, i = 1, 2, \cdots, n, \quad \text{nonnegative integers} \end{cases} \tag{6.27}$$

where the separate chance constraints $\Pr\{c_i x_i \ge d_i\} \ge \alpha_i$, $i = 1, 2, \cdots, n$ may be replaced by a joint form

$$\Pr\{\eta_i x_i \ge \xi_i, i = 1, 2, \cdots, n\} \ge \alpha$$

or some mixed forms of chance constraints.

If the net profits c_i are also stochastic, $i = 1, 2, \cdots, n$, then the total profit $c_1x_1 + c_2x_2 + \cdots + c_nx_n$ is clearly a stochastic variable. Thus we have to maximize the level that the total profit can achieve with at least probability β. That is, we should maximize the objective value $\overline{f}$ such that

$$\Pr\left\{c_1x_1 + c_2x_2 + \cdots + c_nx_n \ge \overline{f}\right\} \ge \beta.$$

Hence the chance-constrained integer programming model may be formulated as follows,

$$\begin{cases} \max\ \overline{f} \\ \text{subject to:} \\ \qquad \Pr\left\{c_1x_1 + c_2x_2 + \cdots + c_nx_n \ge \overline{f}\right\} \ge \beta \\ \qquad a_1x_1 + a_2x_2 + \cdots + a_nx_n \le a \\ \qquad b_1x_1 + b_2x_2 + \cdots + b_nx_n \le b \\ \qquad \Pr\{\eta_ix_i \ge \xi_i\} \ge \alpha_i, \quad i = 1, 2, \cdots, n \\ \qquad x_i, i = 1, 2, \cdots, n, \quad \text{nonnegative integers.} \end{cases} \tag{6.28}$$

We may also set the following target levels and priority structure:

Priority 1: Budget goal: The total cost spent for machines should not exceed the amount available,

$$a_1x_1 + a_2x_2 + \cdots + a_nx_n + d_1^- - d_1^+ = a$$

where d_1^+ will be minimized.

Priority 2: Space goal: The total space used by the machines should not exceed the space available,

$$b_1x_1 + b_2x_2 + \cdots + b_nx_n + d_2^- - d_2^+ = b$$

where d_2^+ will be minimized.

Priority 3: Profit goal: The total profit should achieve a given level c (if c is a very large number, then this goal means that the total profit should be as large as possible),

$$c_1x_1 + c_2x_2 + \cdots + c_nx_n + d_3^- - d_3^+ = c$$

where d_3^- will be minimized.

We also suppose that the probability of satisfying the demand is at least α, i.e., $\Pr\{\eta_ix_i \ge \xi_i, i = 1, 2, \cdots, n\} \ge \alpha$, and all the variables x_i,

$i = 1, 2, \cdots, n$ are nonnegative integers. Then we have a CCGP as follows,

$$\begin{cases} \text{lexmin } \left\{ d_1^+, d_2^+, d_3^- \right\} \\ \text{subject to:} \\ \qquad a_1 x_1 + a_2 x_2 + \cdots + a_n x_n + d_1^- - d_1^+ = a \\ \qquad b_1 x_1 + b_2 x_2 + \cdots + b_n x_n + d_2^- - d_2^+ = b \\ \qquad c_1 x_1 + c_2 x_2 + \cdots + c_n x_n + d_3^- - d_3^+ = c \\ \qquad \Pr\left\{ \eta_i x_i \ge \xi_i, i = 1, 2, \cdots, n \right\} \ge \alpha \\ \qquad x_i, i = 1, 2, \cdots, n, \quad \text{nonnegative integers.} \end{cases} \tag{6.29}$$

Theoretically, if all of the parameters a_i, b_i, and c_i are stochastic, $i = 1, 2, \cdots, n$, then we have to assign confidence levels β_1, β_2, and β_3 to the budget, space, and profit goals, respectively. Thus we have the following CCGP model,

$$\begin{cases} \text{lexmin } \left\{ d_1^+, d_2^+, d_3^- \right\} \\ \text{subject to:} \\ \qquad \Pr\{a_1 x_1 + a_2 x_2 + \cdots + a_n x_n + d_1^- - d_1^+ = a\} \ge \beta_1 \\ \qquad \Pr\{b_1 x_1 + b_2 x_2 + \cdots + b_n x_n + d_2^- - d_2^+ = b\} \ge \beta_2 \\ \qquad \Pr\{c_1 x_1 + c_2 x_2 + \cdots + c_n x_n + d_3^- - d_3^+ = c\} \ge \beta_3 \\ \qquad \Pr\left\{ \eta_i x_i \ge \xi_i, i = 1, 2, \cdots, n \right\} \ge \alpha \\ \qquad x_i, i = 1, 2, \cdots, n, \quad \text{nonnegative integers.} \end{cases} \tag{6.30}$$

Chapter 7

Dependent-Chance Programming

A complex stochastic decision system usually undertakes multiple tasks called events, and the decision-maker wishes to maximize the chance functions which are represented by the probabilities of satisfying these events. In order to model this type of decision system, Liu [88] provided a theoretical framework of the third type of stochastic programming, called *dependent-chance programming* (DCP) (including dependent-chance multiobjective programming (DCMOP) and dependent-chance goal programming (DCGP)).

Roughly speaking, DCP involves maximizing some chance functions of events in a so-called uncertain environment. In deterministic models, expected value models, and chance-constrained programming (CCP), the feasible set is essentially assumed to be deterministic after the real problem is modeled. That is, an optimal solution is always given regardless of whether it can be performed in practice. However, the given solution may be impossible to perform if the realization of uncertain parameter is unfavorable. Thus the DCP model never assumes that the feasible set is deterministic. In fact, the feasible set of dependent-chance programming is described by an uncertain environment. Although a deterministic solution is given by the DCP model, this solution needs to be performed as far as possible. This special feature of DCP is very different from the other existing stochastic programming techniques. However, such problems do exist in the real world. Some real and potential applications of DCP have been presented by Liu and Ku [85], Liu [86], and Liu and Iwamura [89].

In order to understand the idea of DCP correctly, we strongly remind the reader that the feasible set of DCP is stochastic rather than deterministic!

In this chapter, we introduce the concepts of uncertain environments, events, chance functions, and induced constraints appearing in the area of DCP. We also provide a spectrum of DCP, DCMOP, and DCGP models. Finally, a stochastic simulation-based genetic algorithm is presented to solve DCP models and is illustrated by some numerical examples.

7.1 Background: Supply-Allocation System

Many decision systems, including supply-allocation systems, can be represented by Figure 7.1.

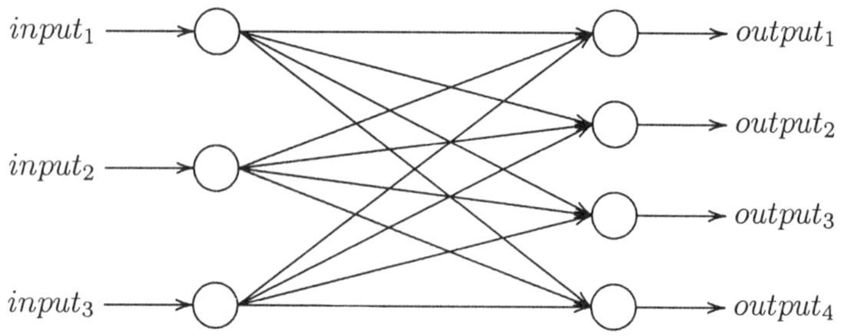

Figure 7.1: A Supply-Allocation System

As an illustrative example, in Figure 7.1 there are 3 inputs representing 3 locations of resources and 4 outputs representing the demands of 4 users. We must answer the following two types of questions.

(a) Supply problems. In order to achieve certain goals in the future, a decision must be made concerning present and future actions to be taken. That is, we must determine the optimal combination of *inputs* in advance, for example, to determine the quantities ordered from the 3 inputs.

(b) Allocation problems. One of the basic allocation problems is the optimal allocation of the resources. The task of this part is to determine the *outputs* that result from various combinations of resources such that certain goals are achieved.

Certainly, in this system supply and allocation problems should not be separate.

In order to answer the above two types of problems, we use 12 decision variables $x_1, x_2, \cdots, x_{12}$ to represent an action, where x_1, x_2, x_3, x_4 are quantities ordered from $input_1$ to outputs 1,2,3,4 respectively; x_5, x_6, x_7, x_8 from $input_2$; $x_9, x_{10}, x_{11}, x_{12}$ from $input_3$. In practice, some variables may vanish because of some physical constraints.

We note that the inputs are available outside resources. Thus they have their own properties. For example, the maximum quantities supplied by the three resources are marked by ξ_1, ξ_2, ξ_3, which may be stochastic variables characterized by probability density functions ϕ_1, ϕ_2, ϕ_3, respectively. Thus at first we have the following constraint,

$$\begin{cases} x_1 + x_2 + x_3 + x_4 & \leq & \xi_1 \\ x_5 + x_6 + x_7 + x_8 & \leq & \xi_2 \\ x_9 + x_{10} + x_{11} + x_{12} & \leq & \xi_3. \end{cases} \tag{7.1}$$

If at least one of ξ_1, ξ_2, and ξ_3 is really stochastic, then this constraint is not clear at all because we cannot make a decision before knowing the realization of ξ_1, ξ_2, and ξ_3. We will call this type of constraint *uncertain environment*, and in this case the *stochastic environment* (the other subtopic is fuzzy environment). The other clear constraint is

$$x_i \geq 0, \quad i = 1, 2, \cdots, 12 \tag{7.2}$$

which represents that the quantities ordered from the resources are nonnegative.

Since our object of study is a decision system, some decision criteria for such a system unquestionably exist. We will regard each criterion as an evaluation of a certain event in this system. For example, the four outputs have their own quantities of demand marked by c_1, c_2, c_3, and c_4, respectively. Then we have the following four events:

$$\begin{aligned} x_1 + x_5 + x_9 &= c_1, \\ x_2 + x_6 + x_{10} &= c_2, \\ x_3 + x_7 + x_{11} &= c_3, \\ x_4 + x_8 + x_{12} &= c_4. \end{aligned} \tag{7.3}$$

These equalities mean that the decision should satisfy the demands of users. In view of the uncertainty of this system, we are not sure whether a decision can be performed before knowing the realization of stochastic variables. Thus we have to employ the so-called *chance functions* to evaluate these four events. They are

$$\begin{aligned} f_1(\boldsymbol{x}) &= \Pr\{x_1 + x_5 + x_9 = c_1\}, \\ f_2(\boldsymbol{x}) &= \Pr\{x_2 + x_6 + x_{10} = c_2\}, \\ f_3(\boldsymbol{x}) &= \Pr\{x_3 + x_7 + x_{11} = c_3\}, \\ f_4(\boldsymbol{x}) &= \Pr\{x_4 + x_8 + x_{12} = c_4\}, \end{aligned} \tag{7.4}$$

where $\Pr\{\cdot\}$ denotes the probability of the event in $\{\cdot\}$.

Usually, we hope to maximize the four chance functions $f_1(\boldsymbol{x})$, $f_2(\boldsymbol{x})$, $f_3(\boldsymbol{x})$ and $f_4(\boldsymbol{x})$ (i.e., to increase the reliability levels of the four events as high as possible). Here we remind the reader once more that the decision vector $\boldsymbol{x}$ does possess some uncertainty even though it is not a random vector. In fact, the randomness of decision vector $\boldsymbol{x}$ is caused by the stochastic parameters ξ_1, ξ_2, ξ_3, and ξ_4 in the uncertain environment.

In addition, we may wish to use $input_3$ as little as possible because of some economic or political reasons. Thus the fifth event is to minimize the quantity ordered from $input_3$ and described by

$$\min f_5(\boldsymbol{x}) = x_9 + x_{10} + x_{11} + x_{12} \tag{7.5}$$

which is a deterministic objective.

Until now we have formulated a stochastic programming model for the supply-allocation problem in an uncertain environment as follows,

$$\begin{cases} \max f_1(\boldsymbol{x}) = \Pr\{x_1 + x_5 + x_9 = c_1\} \\ \max f_2(\boldsymbol{x}) = \Pr\{x_2 + x_6 + x_{10} = c_2\} \\ \max f_3(\boldsymbol{x}) = \Pr\{x_3 + x_7 + x_{11} = c_3\} \\ \max f_4(\boldsymbol{x}) = \Pr\{x_4 + x_8 + x_{12} = c_4\} \\ \min f_5(\boldsymbol{x}) = x_9 + x_{10} + x_{11} + x_{12} \\ \text{subject to:} \\ \qquad x_1 + x_2 + x_3 + x_4 \le \xi_1 \\ \qquad x_5 + x_6 + x_7 + x_8 \le \xi_2 \\ \qquad x_9 + x_{10} + x_{11} + x_{12} \le \xi_3 \\ \qquad x_i \ge 0, \quad i = 1, 2, \cdots, 12 \end{cases} \tag{7.6}$$

where ξ_1, ξ_2, and ξ_3 are stochastic variables characterized by density functions ϕ_1, ϕ_2, and ϕ_3, respectively. In this stochastic programming model, we cannot discuss the realization of each decision component in isolation. For example, we have to consider all of x_1, x_2, x_3, and x_4 simultaneously but separately. This means that some variables as well as the chance functions are stochastically dependent. We will call the stochastic programming in (7.6) *dependent-chance programming* (DCP).

We use the term DCP for the following reasons: (i) some constraints are stochastic; (ii) some objectives are chances of certain events; (iii) some decision variables are stochastically dependent; and (iv) the chances of some events are dependent. Chance dependence means that we cannot consider the reliability level of each individual event in isolation.

7.2 Stochastic Sets

In deterministic mathematical programming, expected value models, and CCP, the feasible sets are essentially represented by deterministic sets, which are normally defined as collections of elements $x \in X$. Each single element can either belong or not belong to a set A with $A \subset X$. Such a deterministic set can be described in different ways: one can either list the elements that belong to the set; describe the set analytically by a sequence of equalities and inequalities (constraints); or define the member elements by using the characteristic function, in which 1 indicates membership and 0 nonmembership. As an extension, we use a probability function to describe a feasible set. Probability is 1 means the statement *x belongs to A* is true, 0 the statement is false. When the boundaries of a feasible set are defined by some stochastic factors, the probability function does allow various values between 0 and 1. This case arises in stochastic constraints of stochastic mathematical programming. In order to describe such sets, we employ the term *stochastic set.* Analogous to the definition of fuzzy set, we define the stochastic set as follows.

Definition 7.1 *If Ω is a collection of objects denoted generally by x, then the stochastic set A in Ω is defined as a set of ordered pairs:*

$$A = \{(x, \mu_A(x)) \mid x \in \Omega\} \tag{7.7}$$

where $\mu_A(x)$ is called the probability function of x in A.

In the above definition, the statement that $\mu_A(x)$ is the probability function of x in A means that the probability of realization of x in A is $\mu_A(\boldsymbol{x})$ in some given stochastic environment.

For example, we suppose that the water marks ξ_1 and ξ_2 of a reservoir and a river have probability density functions ϕ_1 and ϕ_2, respectively. How much water can we draw from the reservoir and river? We cannot answer this question deterministically. Assume that $\boldsymbol{x} = (x_1, x_2)$ denotes a vector whose first element x_1 is the water quantity drawn from the reservoir, and whose second element x_2 is drawn from the river. Theoretically, all possible realizing vectors $\boldsymbol{x}$ form the first quadrant of Euclidean plane. Let $\Omega = \Re_2^+$ be the first quadrant of $\Re^2$ and A the set of all possible realizing vectors satisfying $1 \le x_1 + x_2 \le 5$. Recall the stochastic constraints $x_1 \le \xi_1$, $x_2 \le \xi_2$ (i.e., we cannot draw more water than the available volumes in storage). Thus A is a stochastic set whose probability function can be written as follows,

$$\mu_A(\boldsymbol{x}) = \Pr\{0 \le x_1 \le \xi_1; \quad 0 \le x_2 \le \xi_2; \quad 1 \le x_1 + x_2 \le 5\}$$

which is equivalent to

$$\mu_A(\boldsymbol{x}) = \begin{cases} \displaystyle\int_{x_1}^{+\infty} \phi_1(\xi)d\xi \cdot \int_{x_2}^{+\infty} \phi_2(\xi)d\xi, & x_1 \geq 0, x_2 \geq 0, 1 \leq x_1 + x_2 \leq 5 \\ 0, & \text{otherwise.} \end{cases}$$

We note that the probability function $\mu_A(x)$ is determined by two factors. One is from the realizations of stochastic variables, for example, $x_1 \leq \xi_1$ and $x_2 \leq \xi_2$, and the other is from the real constraints given by the decision-maker or physical system, for example, $x_1 \geq 0, x_2 \geq 0$ and $1 \leq x_1 + x_2 \leq 5$.

From the definition of stochastic sets, we know that $\mu_A(\boldsymbol{x}) = 0$ means that $\boldsymbol{x}$ is impossible to be realized; $\mu_A(\boldsymbol{x}) = 1$ implies that we can reach $\boldsymbol{x}$ for any realizations of stochastic variables; and $\mu_A(\boldsymbol{x}) = \alpha(0 < \alpha < 1)$ represents that the probability that $\boldsymbol{x}$ can be performed is α.

If $\mu_A(\boldsymbol{x})$ only maps Ω to the two points 0 and 1, A is a deterministic set and the probability function $\mu_A(\boldsymbol{x})$ is identical to the characteristic function.

Similar to the concept of the α-level set in fuzzy set theory, we define the α-level set of a stochastic set as follows.

Definition 7.2 *The set of elements that belong to the stochastic set A, at least to the probability α, is called the α-level set, represented by*

$$A_\alpha = \left\{x \in \Omega \;\middle|\; \mu_A(x) \geq \alpha\right\}. \tag{7.8}$$

Now let us consider the following type of CCP:

$$\begin{cases} \max\ Ef(\boldsymbol{x}, \boldsymbol{\xi}) \\ \text{subject to:} \\ \qquad \Pr\{g_j(\boldsymbol{x}, \boldsymbol{\xi}) \leq 0, j = 1, 2, \cdots, p\} \geq \alpha \end{cases} \tag{7.9}$$

where $\boldsymbol{x}$ is a decision vector, $\boldsymbol{\xi}$ is a stochastic vector, $f(\boldsymbol{x}, \boldsymbol{\xi})$ is the return function, E denotes the expected value operator on $\boldsymbol{\xi}$, $g_j(\boldsymbol{x}, \boldsymbol{\xi})$ are stochastic constraint functions, $j = 1, 2, \cdots, p$, $\Pr\{\cdot\}$ denotes the probability of the event in $\{\cdot\}$, and α is a predetermined confidence level. A point $\boldsymbol{x}$ is feasible if and only if the probability measure of the set $\{\boldsymbol{\xi} | g_j(\boldsymbol{x}, \boldsymbol{\xi}) \leq 0, j = 1, 2, \cdots, p\}$ is at least α. In other words, the constraints will be violated at most $(1 - \alpha)$ of time. It is clear that we can represent the stochastic constraint $g_j(\boldsymbol{x}, \boldsymbol{\xi}) \leq 0, j = 1, 2, \cdots, p$ by a stochastic set

$$S = \left\{(\boldsymbol{x}, \mu_S(\boldsymbol{x})) \;\middle|\; \boldsymbol{x} \in R^n\right\} \tag{7.10}$$

where the probability function $\mu_S(\boldsymbol{x})$ is defined by

$$\mu_S(\boldsymbol{x}) = \Pr\left\{g_j(\boldsymbol{x}, \boldsymbol{\xi}) \leq 0, j = 1, 2, \cdots, p\right\}. \tag{7.11}$$

The chance constraint set in (7.9) is just the α-level set S_α of the stochastic set S defined by equation (7.10). Thus CCP (7.9) reads as

$$\max_{\boldsymbol{x} \in S_\alpha} Ef(\boldsymbol{x}, \boldsymbol{\xi}). \tag{7.12}$$

We also note that when $\alpha = 1$ the optimal solution is just a fat solution since $\boldsymbol{x} \in S_1$ is always feasible for any realization of stochastic term $\boldsymbol{\xi}$. Certainly, this form of CCP does not do anything more than (7.9).

7.3 Uncertain Environment

Different from deterministic mathematical programming, expected value model, and CCP, we cannot say that a point is feasible or not when the problem is defined in an uncertain environment generally represented by

$$g_j(\boldsymbol{x}, \boldsymbol{\xi}) \le 0, \quad j = 1, 2, \cdots, p. \tag{7.13}$$

We have to say that a point $\boldsymbol{x}$ is feasible with probability α, where α is the value of probability function $\mu_S(\boldsymbol{x})$, which is represented by

$$\mu_S(\boldsymbol{x}) = \Pr\left\{g_j(\boldsymbol{x}, \boldsymbol{\xi}) \le 0,\ j = 1, 2, \cdots, p\right\}. \tag{7.14}$$

Let $\boldsymbol{x} = (x_1, x_2, \cdots, x_n)$. For the sake of clarity, we call $\boldsymbol{x}$ a decision vector, and x_i, $i = 1, 2, \cdots, n$ decision components throughout this book. Sometimes the term decision is omitted for brevity.

We noted in Section 7.1 that some decision components are stochastically dependent. Two components x' and x'' are called stochastically dependent if the realization of x' is dependent on x'' and vice versa, where dependence means that the chance of each of x' and x'' is a function of at least x' and x''. However, unfortunately, the probability function itself does not provide exact information regarding which components are stochastically dependent. Thus we have to analyze them from the uncertain environment.

Let us consider the uncertain environment represented by (7.1). We will find that $\{x_1, x_2, x_3, x_4\}$ is a stochastically dependent group because the realization of any one of them is dependent on the others. Moreover, the chance of each one is a function of all of x_1, x_2, x_3, and x_4 when we want to realize all of them simultaneously. In fact,

$$f(x_i) = \int_{x_1+x_2+x_3+x_4}^{+\infty} \phi_1(\xi) d\xi, \quad i = 1, 2, 3, 4$$

where $f(x_i)$ is the chance function of realization of x_i for $i = 1, 2, 3, 4$. Similar reason shows that $\{x_5, x_6, x_7, x_8\}$ and $\{x_9, x_{10}, x_{11}, x_{12}\}$ are two other stochastic dependent groups. On the other hand, there is no stochastic relationship among the above three groups. This property is extremely important for discussing the multiple objective case.

In this book, we suppose that we know the following relationship among the decision components proposed by Liu [88].

Stochastic Relationship: *There is a known partition of n components of a decision vector into k groups such that these k groups are mutually stochastically independent and in each group any elements are stochastically dependent and have the same chance to appear if they need to be realized simultaneously.*

For the supply-allocation system, if we only want to satisfy *output*$_1$ and *output*$_2$, then the components $x_1, x_2, x_5, x_6, x_9, x_{10}$ need to be realized simultaneously. Thus, by the partition of 12 decision components into $\{x_1, x_2, x_3, x_4\}$, $\{x_5, x_6, x_7, x_8\}$, and $\{x_9, x_{10}, x_{11}, x_{12}\}$, we know that x_1 and x_2 are stochastically dependent and their chances of occurrence are

$$f(x_i) = \int_{x_1+x_2}^{+\infty} \phi_1(\xi)d\xi, \qquad i = 1, 2$$

respectively, because the decision components x_3 and x_4 do not need to be realized. The same case occurs also in $\{x_5, x_6\}$ and $\{x_9, x_{10}\}$.

In practice, this stochastic relationship is always clear and can be obtained easily. We mention that the algorithm for DCMOP and DCGP cannot work if we do not input such a stochastic relationship among decision variables into the computer program. Although the stochastic relationship can be easily recognized from the uncertain environment itself by human brains, until now we have not found a way to teach the computer to recognize the stochastic relationship automatically from the uncertain environment.

7.4 Events and Chance Functions

In a stochastic decision system, we have three types of objective functions for different evaluation criteria.

(i) Expected value, for example, expected cost minimization, expected profit maximization, etc. This is also available to the deterministic case if the parameters are regarded as degenerate stochastic variables.

(ii) Target with a limit on chance, i.e., given a chance which is usually represented by a confidence level, the target with a lower/upper limit on chance is to be optimized.

(iii) Chance of a certain event, i.e., given an event, the chance of this event is to be optimized.

Types (i) and (ii) are well-discussed in the research areas of expected value model and CCP, respectively. Here we consider type (iii). We suppose that the chance of each given event will be maximized. Otherwise, we can define the chance as the probability of its complement. We have announced that the chance function is a probability of a certain event. For example, the following equality

$$x_1 + x_5 + x_9 = c_1$$

means satisfying the demand of $output_1$ in the supply-allocation system. In fact, the decision vectors $\boldsymbol{x} = (x_1, x_2, \cdots, x_{12})$ meeting the event also form a stochastic set (Deterministic set is a special stochastic set!). We denote this event by E. Let $\mu_E(\boldsymbol{x})$ be the characteristic function of the event E. Then we have

$$\mu_E(\boldsymbol{x}) = \begin{cases} 1, & x_1 + x_5 + x_9 = c_1 \\ 0, & \text{otherwise.} \end{cases}$$

We are now concerned with the questions: What is the probability of this event that can be realized in an uncertain environment? How do we represent the chance function of this event?

Recall that the event E is composed of all possible decisions

$$\boldsymbol{x} = (x_1, x_2, \cdots, x_{12})$$

meeting the demand (i.e., $x_1+x_5+x_9 = c_1$). However, we are only interested in three components of them, x_1, x_5, and x_9 but not the others. That is, we are only concerned with the realizations of x_1, x_5, and x_9, which meet the given event $x_1 + x_5 + x_9 = c_1$. The realizations of other components will be ignored. Let $V(E)$ denote the set of all components of $\boldsymbol{x}$ which are necessary to the event E. We note that only x_1, x_5, and x_9 are necessary components to the event $x_1 + x_5 + x_9 = c_1$, thus $V(E) = \{x_1, x_5, x_9\}$.

Generally, let the single chance function of a given event E be $f(\boldsymbol{x})$ and suppose that the uncertain environment of our problem is generally represented by

$$g_j(\boldsymbol{x}, \boldsymbol{\xi}) \le 0, \quad j = 1, 2, \cdots, p \tag{7.15}$$

where $\boldsymbol{\xi}$ is a stochastic vector. Since we are interested in only one event, this event will claim precedence over all other potential events, thus the chance function $f(\boldsymbol{x})$ will be the maximum probability of realizations of components in $V(E)$ when $\boldsymbol{x} \in E$ (means that the components in $V(E)$ meet the event). Otherwise we define the chance function as zero, i.e.,

$$f(\boldsymbol{x}) = \begin{cases} \max\limits_{\boldsymbol{y} \in E^*} \Pr\{g_j(\boldsymbol{y}, \boldsymbol{\xi}) \le 0, j = 1, 2, \cdots, p\}, & \boldsymbol{x} \in E \\ 0, & \boldsymbol{x} \notin E \end{cases} \tag{7.16}$$

where

$$E^* = \left\{ \boldsymbol{y} = (y_1, y_2, \cdots, y_n) \;\middle|\; \begin{array}{r} y_j = x_j \text{ if } y_j \in V(E) \\ j = 1, \cdots, n \end{array} \right\}. \tag{7.17}$$

Note that for any element $\boldsymbol{y} = (y_1, y_2, \cdots, y_n)$ in E^*, the decision components $y_j \in V(E)$ are fixed and equal to x_j, and the remaining components are arbitrary such that $\boldsymbol{y} \in E$.

In practice, for each given decision $\boldsymbol{x} = (x_1, x_2, \cdots, x_n) \in E$, it is not difficult to determine the values x_j^* of decision components out of $V(E)$ for the optimal solution $\boldsymbol{y}^*(\boldsymbol{x})$ in (7.16),

$$\boldsymbol{y}^*(\boldsymbol{x}) = (y_1, y_2, \cdots, y_n): \quad y_j = \begin{cases} x_j, & y_j \in V(E) \\ x_j^*, & y_j \notin V(E), \end{cases} \qquad 1 \le j \le n \tag{7.18}$$

such that

$$f(\boldsymbol{x}) = \Pr\{g_j(\boldsymbol{y}^*(\boldsymbol{x}), \boldsymbol{\xi}) \le 0, \ j = 1, 2, \cdots, p\} \tag{7.19}$$

when $\boldsymbol{x} \in E$. Therefore, the chance function of the event E is

$$f(\boldsymbol{x}) = \begin{cases} \Pr\{g_j(\boldsymbol{y}^*(\boldsymbol{x}), \boldsymbol{\xi}) \le 0, \ j = 1, 2, \cdots, p\}, & \boldsymbol{x} \in E \\ 0, & \boldsymbol{x} \notin E. \end{cases} \tag{7.20}$$

Usually, the point $\boldsymbol{y}^*(\boldsymbol{x})$ associated with $\boldsymbol{x}$ occurs at some extreme place. For example, in the supply-allocation system the values x_j^* of decision components out of $V(E)$ should be assigned 0 for any $\boldsymbol{x} \in E$. We will call the constraints

$$g_j(\boldsymbol{y}^*(\boldsymbol{x}), \boldsymbol{\xi}) \le 0, \quad j = 1, 2, \cdots, p \tag{7.21}$$

the *induced constraints* on the event E at the point $\boldsymbol{x}$. The induced constraints will play an important role in calculating the chance functions by using stochastic simulation technique.

7.5 Dependent-Chance Programming

In this section, we consider single-objective DCP. A typical formulation of DCP is represented as maximizing a chance function subject to an uncertain environment,

$$\begin{cases} \max \ f(\boldsymbol{x}) \\ \text{subject to:} \\ \qquad g_j(\boldsymbol{x}, \boldsymbol{\xi}) \le 0, \quad j = 1, 2, \cdots, p \end{cases} \tag{7.22}$$

where $\boldsymbol{x}$ is an n-dimensional decision vector, $f(\boldsymbol{x})$ is a chance function of certain event, and the constraints $g_j(\boldsymbol{x}, \boldsymbol{\xi}) \le 0$, $j = 1, 2, \cdots, p$ are an uncertain environment.

We now go back to the supply-allocation system. Suppose that the stochastic constraint is (7.1) together with $x_i \ge 0$, $i = 1, 2, \cdots, 12$. Then this constraint can be represented by a stochastic set S with probability function

$$\mu_S(\boldsymbol{x}) = \begin{cases} \displaystyle\int_{x'}^{+\infty} \phi_1(\xi)d\xi \cdot \int_{x''}^{+\infty} \phi_2(\xi)d\xi \cdot \int_{x'''}^{+\infty} \phi_3(\xi)d\xi, & x_i \geq 0, \ \forall i \\ 0, & \text{otherwise} \end{cases}$$

where $x' = x_1 + x_2 + x_3 + x_4$, $x'' = x_5 + x_6 + x_7 + x_8$, and $x''' = x_9 + x_{10} + x_{11} + x_{12}$. Here we suppose that ϕ_1, ϕ_2, and ϕ_3 are two-parameter lognormal densities with parameters $u = 1.56, 1.36, 0.95$, and $\sigma = 0.56, 0.45, 0.38$, respectively. The single interesting event is to satisfy the demand $c_1 = 6$ of *output*$_1$ (i.e., $x_1 + x_5 + x_9 = c_1$). Thus the event E is represented by

$$E = \left\{\boldsymbol{x} = (x_1, x_2, \cdots, x_{12}) \;\middle|\; x_1 + x_5 + x_9 = c_1 = 6\right\}.$$

Then the chance function associated with the event E is

$$f(\boldsymbol{x}) = \begin{cases} \displaystyle\max_{\boldsymbol{y} \in E^*} \Pr \left\{ \begin{array}{l} y_1 + y_2 + y_3 + y_4 \leq \xi_1 \\ y_5 + y_6 + y_7 + y_8 \leq \xi_2 \\ y_9 + y_{10} + y_{11} + y_{12} \leq \xi_3 \end{array} \right\}, & \boldsymbol{x} \in E \\ 0, & \boldsymbol{x} \notin E. \end{cases}$$

For any given decision $\boldsymbol{x}$, since there is only one event E, the induced constraints on the event E at the point $\boldsymbol{x}$ should be

$$x_1 \leq \xi_1, \quad x_5 \leq \xi_2, \quad x_9 \leq \xi_3 \tag{7.23}$$

by taking $x_i = 0$ for all $i \neq 1, 5, 9$. The chance function $f(\boldsymbol{x})$ is then written as

$$f(\boldsymbol{x}) = \begin{cases} \Pr\{x_1 \leq \xi_1, \, x_5 \leq \xi_2, \, x_9 \leq \xi_3\}, & \boldsymbol{x} \in E \\ 0, & \boldsymbol{x} \notin E. \end{cases}$$

Note that

$$\Pr \left\{ \begin{array}{l} x_1 \leq \xi_1 \\ x_5 \leq \xi_2 \\ x_9 \leq \xi_3 \end{array} \right\} = \int_{x_1}^{+\infty} \phi_1(\xi)d\xi \cdot \int_{x_5}^{+\infty} \phi_2(\xi)d\xi \cdot \int_{x_9}^{+\infty} \phi_3(\xi)d\xi.$$

Thus the model is equivalent to

$$\begin{cases} \max \ f(\boldsymbol{x}) \\ \text{subject to:} \\ \qquad x_i \geq 0, \ i = 1, 2, \cdots, 9 \end{cases}$$

which is conventional mathematical programming.

A run of the computer program for this problem shows that the optimal solution is $\boldsymbol{x}^* = (x_1^*, x_2^*, \cdots, x_{12}^*)$ in which all x_i^* are zero except for

$$x_1^* = 2.6, \qquad x_5^* = 2.1, \qquad x_9^* = 1.3$$

with $f(\boldsymbol{x}^*) = 0.71$. That is, the reliability level of this event is 71% if we give priority to the performance of $\boldsymbol{x}^*$.

7.6 Dependent-Chance Multiobjective Programming

Since a complex decision system usually undertakes multiple tasks, there undoubtedly exist multiple potential objectives (some of them are chance functions) in a decision process, for example, maximizing the chance of accomplishing each task. A typical formulation of DCMOP is represented as maximizing a vector of chance functions subject to an uncertain environment,

$$\begin{cases} \max \left[f_1(\boldsymbol{x}), f_2(\boldsymbol{x}), \cdots, f_m(\boldsymbol{x})\right] \\ \text{subject to:} \\ \qquad g_j(\boldsymbol{x}, \boldsymbol{\xi}) \le 0, \quad j = 1, 2, \cdots, p \end{cases} \tag{7.24}$$

where $f(\boldsymbol{x})$ is a vector of m real-valued functions $f_i(\boldsymbol{x})$, $i = 1, 2, \cdots, m$ in which some are chance functions.

We have given a solution procedure for computing a single chance function in an uncertain environment. Next we consider the multiple objective case. If some of $f_1(\boldsymbol{x}), f_2(\boldsymbol{x}), \cdots, f_m(\boldsymbol{x})$ are not chance functions, then we can obtain their values immediately. Without loss of generality, suppose that all of $f_1(\boldsymbol{x}), f_2(\boldsymbol{x}), \cdots, f_m(\boldsymbol{x})$ are chance functions. Each chance function $f_i(\boldsymbol{x})$ represents a probability of a certain event

$$E_i = \left\{\boldsymbol{x} = (x_1, x_2, \cdots, x_n) \mid \boldsymbol{x} \text{ meets the event } i\right\} \tag{7.25}$$

for each i with $1 \le i \le m$. We write

$$E = E_1 \cap E_2 \cap \cdots \cap E_m \tag{7.26}$$

and

$$V(E) = V(E_1) \cup V(E_2) \cup \cdots \cup V(E_m) \tag{7.27}$$

where $\boldsymbol{x} \in E$ means that the decision vector $\boldsymbol{x}$ can satisfy all of the events $E_1, E_2, \cdots, E_m$, and $V(E_i)$ are the sets of all necessary components to the events i, $i = 1, 2, \cdots, m$, respectively. Thus $V(E)$ is the set of all necessary components to the m events. We also define $E^*, E_i^*, i = 1, 2, \cdots, m$ as follows,

$$E^* = \{\boldsymbol{y} = (y_1, y_2, \cdots, y_n) \mid y_j = x_j \text{ if } y_j \in V(E),\, j = 1, 2, \cdots, n\},$$

$$E_i^* = \{\boldsymbol{y} = (y_1, y_2, \cdots, y_n) \mid y_j = x_j \text{ if } y_j \in V(E_i),\, j = 1, 2, \cdots, n\}$$

for $i = 1, 2, \cdots, m$. That is, the decision components $y_j \in V(E)$ are fixed and equal to x_j, and the remaining components are arbitrary such that $\boldsymbol{y} \in E_i$.

Based on the stochastic relationship, let $D(E)$ and $D(E_i)$ denote the sets of all components which are stochastically dependent of at least one element in $V(E)$ and $V(E_i)$, $i = 1, 2, \cdots, m$, respectively. Thus we have $V(E) \subset D(E)$ and $V(E_i) \subset D(E_i)$, $i = 1, 2, \cdots, m$.

Now let $\mu_S(\boldsymbol{x})$ be the probability function associated with the uncertain environment. Generally speaking, we have

$$\max_{\boldsymbol{y} \in E_i^*} \mu_S(\boldsymbol{y}) \geq f_i(\boldsymbol{x}) \geq \max_{\boldsymbol{y} \in E^*} \mu_S(\boldsymbol{y}), \quad i = 1, 2, \cdots, m \tag{7.28}$$

in which the first inequality means that the probability of realization of E_i in a multievent case is usually less than or equal to that in a single-event case because we cannot perform the event at the expense of others; the second means that the probability of realization of E_i in a multievent case is usually larger than or equal to the probability of realization of all events because some events are stochastically independent. That is, the realization of one event is not necessarily dependent on the realization of all others.

Now we discuss the relationship between decision vectors and their respective chance functions. In fact, our way is to realize each event, say E_i, as much as possible but not sacrifice the chances of other events. Thus we have to treat all elements in the stochastically dependent set $D(E_i)$ of $V(E_i)$ at an equitable level. On the other hand, we are not concerned with the elements out of $V(E)$ because they do not make any contribution to the events we are going to realize. Thus we must consider all the elements in and only in $D(E_i) \cap V(E)$ simultaneously for the event E_i. By the stochastic relationship, we know that all of the elements in $D(E_i) \cap V(E)$ (a subset of $V(E)$) are stochastic independent of any other elements in $V(E)$. Hence we can perform the elements in $D(E_i) \cap V(E)$ as much as possible. Therefore we have

$$f_i(\boldsymbol{x}) = \begin{cases} \max\limits_{\boldsymbol{y} \in E_i^*} \Pr\{g_j(\boldsymbol{y}, \boldsymbol{\xi}) \leq 0,\, j = 1, 2, \cdots, p\}, & \boldsymbol{x} \in E_i \\ 0, & \boldsymbol{x} \notin E_i \end{cases}$$

where the sets E_i^* are defined as

$$E_i^* = \{\boldsymbol{y} = (y_1, \cdots, y_n) \in E_i \mid y_j = x_j \text{ if } y_j \in D(E_i) \cap V(E), j = 1, \cdots, n\}$$

for $i = 1, 2, \cdots, m$, respectively. Usually, we can determine $\boldsymbol{y}_i^*(\boldsymbol{x})$ such that the induced constraints on the events E_i at the point $\boldsymbol{x}$ are

$$g_j(\boldsymbol{y}_i^*(\boldsymbol{x}), \boldsymbol{\xi}) \le 0, \quad j = 1, 2, \cdots, p$$

which yield the chance functions $f_i(\boldsymbol{x})$ as follows,

$$f_i(\boldsymbol{x}) = \begin{cases} \Pr\left\{g_j(\boldsymbol{y}_i^*(\boldsymbol{x}), \boldsymbol{\xi}) \le 0, \, j = 1, 2, \cdots, p\right\}, & \boldsymbol{x} \in E_i \\ 0, & \boldsymbol{x} \notin E_i \end{cases}$$

for $i = 1, 2, \cdots, m$, respectively.

After constructing a relationship between decision vectors and chance functions, we can calculate the chance functions directly or by the technique of stochastic simulations for complex stochastic constraints. Then we can solve DCMOP by utility theory if complete information of the preference function is given by the decision-maker or search for all of the efficient solutions if no information is available. In practice, the decision-maker can provide only partial information. In this case, we have to employ the so-called interactive methods such as feasible region reduction, weighting vector space reduction, criterion cone contraction, or line search (Steuer [136]).

7.7 Dependent-Chance Goal Programming

DCGP may be considered as an extension of goal programming in a complex stochastic decision system. When some management targets are given, the objective function may minimize the deviations, positive, negative, or both, with a certain priority structure set by the decision-maker. Then we may formulate the stochastic decision system as the following DCGP,

$$\begin{cases} \min \sum\limits_{j=1}^{l} P_j \sum\limits_{i=1}^{m} (u_{ij} d_i^+ + v_{ij} d_i^-) \\ \text{subject to:} \\ \qquad f_i(\boldsymbol{x}) + d_i^- - d_i^+ = b_i, \quad i = 1, 2, \cdots, m \\ \qquad g_j(\boldsymbol{x}, \boldsymbol{\xi}) \le 0, \qquad\qquad j = 1, 2, \cdots, p \\ \qquad d_i^-, d_i^+ \ge 0, \qquad\qquad i = 1, 2, \cdots, m \end{cases} \tag{7.29}$$

where

P_j = the preemptive priority factor, which expresses the relative importance of various goals, $P_j \gg P_{j+1}$, for all j,

u_{ij} = weighting factor corresponding to positive deviation for goal i with priority j assigned,

v_{ij} = weighting factor corresponding to negative deviation for goal i with priority j assigned,
d_i^+ = positive deviation from the target of goal i,
d_i^- = negative deviation from the target of goal i,
$\boldsymbol{x}$ = n-dimensional decision vector,
f_i = a chance function or a conventional real-valued function $\Re^n \to \Re^1$ in goal constraints,
g_j = a real-valued function in the uncertain environment,
b_i = the target value according to goal i,
l = number of priorities,
m = number of goal constraints.

The key problem of solving DCGP is to calculate the values of all $f_i(\boldsymbol{x})$ for a given solution $\boldsymbol{x}$. In the first priority level, we suppose that there are t goals, which are listed as

$$f_i(\boldsymbol{x}) + d_i^- - d_i^+ = b_i, \qquad i = 1, 2, \cdots, t.$$

If some of $f_1(\boldsymbol{x}), f_2(\boldsymbol{x}), \cdots, f_t(\boldsymbol{x})$ are conventional real-valued functions, then we can obtain their respective deviations immediately. Without loss of generality, we assume that all of them are chance functions. Similar to the case of DCMOP, each chance function $f_i(\boldsymbol{x})$ represents a probability of a certain event denoted by E_i. We write

$$E = E_1 \cap E_2 \cap \cdots \cap E_t$$

and

$$V(E) = V(E_1) \cup V(E_2) \cup \cdots \cup V(E_t).$$

Then, mentioning that the goals in the higher-priority level will be satisfied as much as possible regardless of the lower-priority goals, by a similar discussion of the multiobjective case, we have

$$f_i(\boldsymbol{x}) = \begin{cases} \max\limits_{\boldsymbol{y} \in E_i^*} \Pr\{g_j(\boldsymbol{y}, \boldsymbol{\xi}) \le 0,\ j = 1, 2, \cdots, p\}, & \boldsymbol{x} \in E_i \\ 0, & \boldsymbol{x} \notin E_i \end{cases}$$

where the sets E_i^* are defined as

$$E_i^* = \left\{\boldsymbol{y} = (y_1, \cdots, y_n) \in E_i \;\middle|\; y_j = x_j \text{ if } y_j \in D(E_i) \cap V(E), j = 1, \cdots, n\right\}$$

for $i = 1, 2, \cdots, t$, respectively. Usually, we can determine $\boldsymbol{y}_i^*(\boldsymbol{x})$ such that the induced constraints on the events E_i at the point $\boldsymbol{x}$ are

$$g_j(\boldsymbol{y}_i^*(\boldsymbol{x}), \boldsymbol{\xi}) \le 0, \quad j = 1, 2, \cdots, p$$

which yield the chance functions $f_i(\boldsymbol{x})$ as follows,

$$f_i(\boldsymbol{x}) = \begin{cases} \Pr\{g_j(\boldsymbol{y}_i^*(\boldsymbol{x}), \boldsymbol{\xi}) \le 0, j = 1, 2, \cdots, p\}, & \boldsymbol{x} \in E_i \\ 0, & \boldsymbol{x} \notin E_i \end{cases}$$

for $i = 1, 2, \cdots, t$, respectively.

In the second priority level, a similar process will yield the respective deviations except for the fact that E is replaced by

$$E = E_1 \cap \cdots \cap E_t \cap E_{t+1} \cap \cdots \cap E_{t'}$$

and

$$V(E) = V(E_1) \cup \cdots \cup V(E_t) \cup V(E_{t+1}) \cup \cdots \cup V(E_{t'})$$

where $E_{t+1}, E_{t+2}, \cdots, E_{t'}$ are the events associated with the chance functions $f_{t+1}(\boldsymbol{x}), f_{t+2}(\boldsymbol{x}), \cdots, f_{t'}(\boldsymbol{x})$, which are assumed the goals in this priority level, because the decisions on events $E_1, E_2, \cdots, E_t$ have been made in the higher-priority level and the remaining decisions for lower-priority goals must follow the state resulting from the higher-priority decisions.

Certainly, the successive levels will be similarly discussed until all conventional real-valued and chance functions are calculated. Thus all deviations can be obtained for any given decision $\boldsymbol{x}$.

We can solve DCGP model by combining the above process and the techniques for solving nonlinear goal programming.

7.8 Preemptive Solution

In the deterministic case as well as the expected value model and chance-constrained programming, a solution is always assumed to be able to perform in practice, even though such an assumption is questionable. Thus we can perform either the components of a solution $\boldsymbol{x}$ one by one, or all of them at the same time. Theoretically, there is no difference between the two ways.

However, we cannot guarantee this point in a stochastic environment because the feasible set is stochastic rather than deterministic. In the stochastic case, an important problem is how to perform the solution $\boldsymbol{x}^*$. In order to coincide with the modeling idea of DCGP, analogous to the structure of preemptive goal programming, there is a hierarchy of importance among the components of a solution vector, where the structure of hierarchy is identical to that of objectives. Then the satisfaction of higher-order components is always preferred over lower-order components. This means that we will perform the components in $V(E_1) \cup V(E_2) \cup \cdots \cup V(E_t)$ at the first level, and then perform the components in the successive priority levels. In water resource management systems, the managers do perform their plan in this way.

7.9 Stochastic Simulation for Chance Functions

According to the earlier analysis, $f_i(\boldsymbol{x})$ is the probability of realizing the decision components in $D(E_i) \cap V(E)$. In practice, it is not difficult to obtain the induced constraints from the uncertain environment. Let $g_j(\boldsymbol{y}^*(\boldsymbol{x}), \boldsymbol{\xi}) \le 0$, $j = 1, 2, \cdots, p$ be the induced constraints on the event E_i at the point $\boldsymbol{x}$. Then the chance function $f_i(\boldsymbol{x})$ is given by

$$f_i(\boldsymbol{x}) = \Pr\left\{g_j(\boldsymbol{y}^*(\boldsymbol{x}), \boldsymbol{\xi}) \le 0,\ j = 1, 2, \cdots, p\right\}.$$

When the induced constraints are easy to handle, we can employ some numerical integration method. But if the induced constraints fail to be regular or are hard to calculate, it is more convenient to compute chance functions by a stochastic simulation process. Without loss of generality, we suppose that $\boldsymbol{\xi}$ is a stochastic vector with a separate or joint probability distribution Φ. For any given decision $\boldsymbol{x}$, we use the following stochastic simulation technique to estimate $f_i(\boldsymbol{x})$. We generate N independent random vectors $\boldsymbol{\xi}_k$, $k = 1, 2, \cdots, N$ from the probability distribution Φ, where the generating methods have been well-documented in Chapter 3. Let N' be the number of occasions on which

$$g_j(\boldsymbol{y}^*(\boldsymbol{x}), \boldsymbol{\xi}_k) \le 0, \quad j = 1, 2, \cdots, p,$$

for $k = 1, 2, \cdots, N$ (i.e., the number of random vectors satisfying the induced constraints). Then, by the law of large numbers, $f_i(\boldsymbol{x})$ can be estimated by

$$f_i(\boldsymbol{x}) = \frac{N'}{N}. \tag{7.30}$$

Step 1. Set $N' = 0$.
Step 2. Generate $\boldsymbol{\xi}$ from its probability distribution $\Phi(\boldsymbol{\xi})$.
Step 3. If $g_j(\boldsymbol{y}^*(\boldsymbol{x}), \boldsymbol{\xi}) \le 0$ for $j = 1, 2, \cdots, p$, then $N'{+}{+}$.
Step 4. Repeat the second and third steps N times.
Step 5. Return N'/N.

7.10 Stochastic Simulation-based Genetic Algorithms

We can combine the technique of stochastic simulation with other available methods to form a solution process for solving DCP models. In view of the complexity of objective functions, genetic algorithms will play an active role in searching for optimal solutions. Generally, the stochastic simulation-based genetic algorithm has the following steps:

Genetic Algorithm Procedure

Step 0. *Input parameters pop_size, P_c and P_m.*

Step 1. *Initialize pop_size chromosomes.*

Step 2. *Update the chromosomes by crossover and mutation operations.*

Step 3. *Calculate the objective values for all chromosomes by stochastic simulation.*

Step 4. *Compute the fitness of each chromosome by rank-based evaluation function based on the objective values.*

Step 5. *Select the chromosomes by spinning the roulette wheel.*

Step 6. *Repeat the second to fifth steps a given number of cycles.*

Step 7. *Report the best chromosome as the optimal solution.*

The computer code for the stochastic simulation-based genetic algorithms to DCP has been written in C language. Here we give two numerical examples performed on a personal computer with the following parameters: the population size is 30, the probability of crossover P_c is 0.3, the probability of mutation P_m is 0.2, and the parameter a in the rank-based evaluation function is 0.05. Each stochastic simulation in the evolution process will be performed 3000 cycles.

Example 1: Now let us consider a single-objective DCP model,

$$\begin{cases} \max f(\boldsymbol{x}) = \Pr\left\{x_1 + x_2^2 + x_3^3 = 10\right\} \\ \text{subject to:} \\ \qquad x_1^2 + x_2^2 + x_3^2 + x_4^2 \le \xi_1 \\ \qquad \xi_2\left(x_1 x_2 x_3\right) \ge \xi_3 \\ \qquad x_1, x_2, x_3, x_4 \ge 0 \end{cases}$$

where ξ_1, ξ_2, and ξ_3 are uniformly distributed variable $\mathcal{U}[8,20]$, normally distributed variable $\mathcal{N}(5,1)$, and exponentially distributed variable $\mathcal{EXP}(2)$, respectively.

Clearly, the single event is to fulfill $x_1+x_2^2+x_3^3 = 10$ with $x_1, x_2, x_3 \ge 0$. Since the decision component x_4 does not make any contribution to the event, the induced constraints on this event are

$$\begin{cases} x_1^2 + x_2^2 + x_3^2 \le \xi_1 \\ \xi_2\left(x_1 x_2 x_3\right) \ge \xi_3 \end{cases}$$

by taking $x_4 = 0$. Thus the chance function $f(\boldsymbol{x})$ of this event can be represented by

$$f(\boldsymbol{x}) = \begin{cases} \Pr\left\{ \begin{array}{l} x_1^2 + x_2^2 + x_3^2 \le \xi_1 \\ \xi_2 (x_1 x_2 x_3) \ge \xi_3 \end{array} \right\}, & x_1 + x_2^2 + x_3^3 = 10,\ x_1, x_2, x_3 \ge 0 \\ 0, & \text{otherwise} \end{cases}$$

which can be estimated by the technique of stochastic simulation. We will sample a chromosome $V = (x_1, x_2, x_3)$ from the hypercube $\Omega = [0,1] \times [0,1] \times [0,1]$, and translate it to a feasible solution meeting the event by taking

$$x_1' = \frac{x_1}{Q}, \quad x_2' = \frac{x_2}{\sqrt{Q}}, \quad x_3' = \frac{x_3}{\sqrt[3]{Q}}$$

where $Q = (x_1 + x_2^2 + x_3^3)/10$. It is clear that $x_1' + {x_2'}^2 + {x_3'}^3 = 10$.

A run of the stochastic simulation-based genetic algorithm with 300 generations shows that the optimal solution is

$$(x_1^*,\ x_2^*,\ x_3^*,\ x_4^*) = (1.6304,\ 1.9400,\ 1.6638,\ 0)$$

whose reliability level is $f(\boldsymbol{x}^*) = 89.7\%$.

Example 2: Let us now turn our attention to the following DCGP,

$$\begin{cases} \text{lexmin}\left\{d_1^-, d_2^- + d_3^-, d_4^+\right\} \\ \text{subject to:} \\ \qquad f_1(\boldsymbol{x}) + d_1^- - d_1^+ = 0.96 \\ \qquad f_2(\boldsymbol{x}) + d_2^- - d_2^+ = 0.90 \\ \qquad f_3(\boldsymbol{x}) + d_3^- - d_3^+ = 0.90 \\ \qquad f_4(\boldsymbol{x}) + d_4^- - d_4^+ = 0 \\ \qquad x_1 + x_2 + x_5 \le \xi_1 \\ \qquad x_3 + x_4 \le \xi_2 \\ \qquad x_6 + x_7 \le \xi_3 \\ \qquad x_i \ge 0, \quad i = 1, 2, \cdots, 7 \\ \qquad d_i^-, d_i^+ \ge 0, \quad i = 1, 2, 3, 4 \end{cases}$$

where ξ_1, ξ_2, and ξ_3 are uniformly distributed variable $\mathcal{U}[5,7]$, normally distributed variable $\mathcal{N}(4,1)$, and exponentially distributed variable $\mathcal{EXP}(3)$, respectively, and

$$\begin{cases} f_1(\boldsymbol{x}) = \Pr\{x_1 + x_3^2 = 4\} \\ f_2(\boldsymbol{x}) = \Pr\{x_2^2 + x_4 = 2\} \\ f_3(\boldsymbol{x}) = \Pr\{x_5^2 + x_6^2 = 2\} \\ f_4(\boldsymbol{x}) = x_4 + x_6. \end{cases}$$

Note that the decision component x_7 never appears in the goal constraints.

From the stochastic environment, we know the following stochastic relationship: the seven decision components can be divided into three groups $\{x_1, x_2, x_5\}$, $\{x_3, x_4\}$, and $\{x_6, x_7\}$ such that these three groups are mutually stochastically independent and in each group any elements are stochastic dependent and have the same chance to appear if they need to be realized simultaneously.

In the first priority level, there is only one event denoted by E_1 in the stochastic environment, which should be fulfilled by $x_1 + x_3^2 = 4$. It is clear that $V(E_1) = \{x_1, x_3\}$ and the induced constraints on the event E_1 should be

$$\begin{cases} x_1 \le \xi_1 \\ x_3 \le \xi_2 \end{cases}$$

since the remaining components can be regarded as 0 temporarily for the event E_1 at the current priority level. Thus the chance function $f_1(\boldsymbol{x})$ of E_1 should be

$$f_1(\boldsymbol{x}) = \Pr\left\{x_1 + x_3^2 = 4\right\} = \begin{cases} \Pr\left\{x_1 \le \xi_1, x_3 \le \xi_2\right\}, & x_1 + x_3^2 = 4,\ \boldsymbol{x} \ge 0 \\ 0, & \text{otherwise.} \end{cases}$$

At the second priority level, there are two events E_2 and E_3 which should be fulfilled by $x_2^2 + x_4 = 2$ and $x_5^2 + x_6^2 = 2$, respectively. We also have $V(E_2) = \{x_2, x_4\}$ and $V(E_3) = \{x_5, x_6\}$. Write $E = E_1 \cap E_2 \cap E_3$, then $V(E) = V(E_1) \cup V(E_2) \cup V(E_3) = \{x_1, x_2, x_3, x_4, x_5, x_6\}$. Since

$$\begin{aligned} D(E_2) \cap V(E) &= \{x_1, x_2, x_5, x_3, x_4\} \cap \{x_1, x_2, x_3, x_4, x_5, x_6\} \\ &= \{x_1, x_2, x_3, x_4, x_5\}, \end{aligned}$$

the induced constraints on the event E_2 should be

$$\begin{cases} x_1 + x_2 + x_5 \le \xi_1 \\ x_3 + x_4 \le \xi_2 \end{cases}$$

which yield the chance function $f_2(\boldsymbol{x})$ of the event E_2 as follows,

$$\begin{aligned} f_2(\boldsymbol{x}) &= \Pr\left\{x_2^2 + x_4 = 2\right\} \\ &= \begin{cases} \Pr\{x_1 + x_2 + x_5 \le \xi_1, x_3 + x_4 \le \xi_2\}, & x_2^2 + x_4 = 2, \boldsymbol{x} \ge 0 \\ 0, & \text{otherwise.} \end{cases} \end{aligned}$$

It follows from

$$D(E_3) \cap V(E) = \{x_1, x_2, x_5, x_6, x_7\} \cap \{x_1, x_2, x_3, x_4, x_5, x_6\} = \{x_1, x_2, x_5, x_6\}$$

that the induced constraints on the event E_3 should be

$$\begin{cases} x_1 + x_2 + x_5 \le \xi_1 \\ x_6 \le \xi_3 \end{cases}$$

which yield the chance function $f_3(\boldsymbol{x})$ of the event E_3 as follows,

$$\begin{aligned} f_3(\boldsymbol{x}) &= \Pr\left\{x_5^2 + x_6^2 = 2\right\} \\ &= \begin{cases} \Pr\{x_1 + x_2 + x_5 \le \xi_1, x_6 \le \xi_3\}, & x_5^2 + x_6^2 = 2, \ \boldsymbol{x} \ge 0 \\ 0, & \text{otherwise.} \end{cases} \end{aligned}$$

At the third priority level there is no chance function. Thus we can get the deviations immediately.

We can sample the chromosome $V = (x_1, x_2, \cdots, x_7)$ from the hypercube $[0, 10]^7$ and translate it to a feasible solution meeting the demands in the following way,

$$x_1' = \frac{x_1}{Q_1}, \quad x_2' = \frac{x_2}{\sqrt{Q_2}}, \quad x_3' = \frac{x_3}{\sqrt{Q_1}},$$

$$x_4' = \frac{x_4}{Q_2}, \quad x_5' = \frac{x_5}{\sqrt{Q_3}}, \quad x_6' = \frac{x_6}{\sqrt{Q_3}}, \quad x_7' = x_7$$

where $Q_1 = (x_1 + x_3^2)/4$, $Q_2 = (x_2^2 + x_4)/2$, $Q_3 = (x_5^2 + x_6^2)/2$.

A run of the stochastic simulation-based genetic algorithm with 500 generations shows that the optimal solution is

$$\boldsymbol{x}^* = (2.4071,\ 1.3862,\ 1.2621,\ 0.0786,\ 1.4142,\ 0.0004,\ 0.0000)$$

which can satisfy the first two goals, but the third objective is 0.0790. In fact, we also have

$$f_1(\boldsymbol{x}^*) \approx 96\%, \quad f_2(\boldsymbol{x}^*) \approx 90\%, \quad f_3(\boldsymbol{x}^*) \approx 90\%, \quad f_4(\boldsymbol{x}^*) = 0.0790.$$

7.11 Notes

Following expected value models and CCP, this chapter introduced the third type of stochastic programming—DCP, DCMOP, and DCGP. The DCP models are available to the systems in which there are stochastic parameters and multiple events whose reliability levels need to be optimized. We also presented a stochastic simulation for computing the chance functions for any given decisions. Thus we can combine stochastic simulations with other available methods to form a solution process for solving DCP models. In view of the complexity of objective functions, stochastic simulation-based genetic algorithm is well worth mentioning in searching for optimal solutions and is illustrated by some numerical examples.

Certainly, we need more experiments and theory to determine the stochastic relationship among the decision components. Further applications of DCP are expected to be extended to a wide variety of real management problems in stochastic environments. Efficient algorithms for different cases remain to be designed to handle more complex stochastic decision systems.

Chapter 8

Modeling Stochastic Decision Systems

This chapter provides some illustrative examples to show how to model complex stochastic decision systems by using dependent-chance programming (DCP), dependent-chance multiobjective programming (DCMOP), and dependent-chance goal programming (DCGP). We will present the following applications:

- Water Supply-Allocation Problem
- Production Process
- Open Inventory Network
- Capital Budgeting

8.1 Water Supply-Allocation Problem

As a class of stochastic resource allocation problems, we consider a water supply-allocation problem shown in Figure 8.1.

In Figure 8.1 there are 3 inputs representing 3 reservoirs and 4 outputs representing the demands of 4 users. We must answer the following two types of questions.

(a) Supply problems. In order to achieve certain goals in the future, a decision must be made concerning present and future actions to be taken. That is, we must determine the optimal combination of *inputs* in advance, for example, to determine the quantities drawn from the 3 reservoirs.

(b) Allocation problems. One of the basic allocation problems is the optimal allocation of the water. The task of this part is to determine the

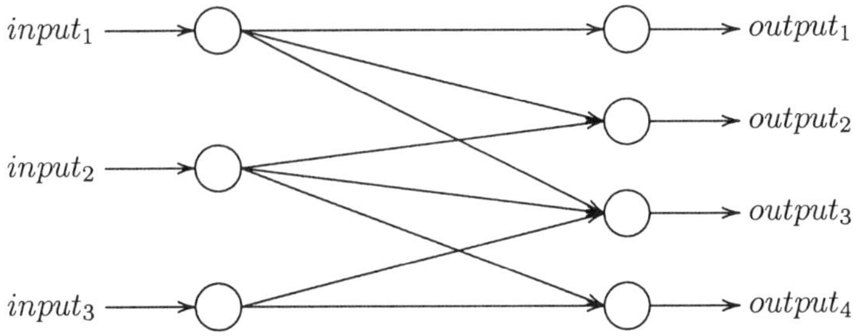

Figure 8.1: A Supply-Allocation System

outputs that result from various combinations of resources such that certain goals are achieved.

Certainly, in this system supply and allocation problems should not be separate.

In order to answer the above two types of problems, we use 8 decision variables $x_1, x_2, \cdots, x_8$ to represent an action, where x_1, x_2, x_3 are quantities ordered from $input_1$ to outputs 1,2,3 respectively; x_4, x_5, x_6 from $input_2$ to outputs 2,3,4 respectively; and x_7, x_8 from $input_3$ to outputs 3,4 respectively.

We note that the inputs are available outside resources, they have their own properties. For example, the maximum quantities supplied by the three resources are marked by ξ_1, ξ_2, ξ_3, which may be assumed to be stochastic variables characterized by probability density functions ϕ_1, ϕ_2, ϕ_3, respectively. Thus at first we have the following stochastic environment,

$$x_1 + x_2 + x_3 \le \xi_1, \quad x_4 + x_5 + x_6 \le \xi_2, \quad x_7 + x_8 \le \xi_3. \tag{8.1}$$

The other clear constraint is $\{x_i \ge 0, i = 1, 2, \cdots, 8\}$, which represents that the quantities ordered from the resources are nonnegative.

Since the object of study is a decision system, some decision criteria for such a system unquestionably exist. We will regard each criterion as an evaluation on a certain event in this system. For example, the four outputs have their own demands marked by c_1, c_2, c_3, and c_4, respectively. Then we have the following four events:

$$x_1 = c_1, \quad x_2 + x_4 = c_2, \quad x_3 + x_5 + x_7 = c_3, \quad x_6 + x_8 = c_4. \tag{8.2}$$

These equalities mean that the decisions should satisfy the demands. In view of the uncertainty of this system, we are not sure whether a decision can be performed before knowing the realization of stochastic variables.

Thus we have to employ chance functions to evaluate these four events. Let

$$\begin{aligned} f_1(\boldsymbol{x}) &= \Pr\{x_1 = c_1\}, & f_2(\boldsymbol{x}) &= \Pr\{x_2 + x_4 = c_2\}, \\ f_3(\boldsymbol{x}) &= \Pr\{x_3 + x_5 + x_7 = c_3\}, & f_4(\boldsymbol{x}) &= \Pr\{x_6 + x_8 = c_4\}. \end{aligned} \tag{8.3}$$

Usually, we hope to maximize the four chance functions (i.e., to increase the reliability levels of the four events as high as possible).

Up to now we have formulated a DCMOP model for the supply-allocation problem in an uncertain environment as follows,

$$\begin{cases} \max f_1(\boldsymbol{x}) = \Pr\{x_1 = c_1\} \\ \max f_2(\boldsymbol{x}) = \Pr\{x_2 + x_4 = c_2\} \\ \max f_3(\boldsymbol{x}) = \Pr\{x_3 + x_5 + x_7 = c_3\} \\ \max f_4(\boldsymbol{x}) = \Pr\{x_6 + x_8 = c_4\} \\ \text{subject to:} \\ \qquad x_1 + x_2 + x_3 \le \xi_1 \\ \qquad x_4 + x_5 + x_6 \le \xi_2 \\ \qquad x_7 + x_8 \le \xi_3 \\ \qquad x_i \ge 0, \quad i = 1, 2, \cdots, 8. \end{cases} \tag{8.4}$$

The stochastic feasible set S will be defined by the following probability function

$$\mu_S(\boldsymbol{x}) = \Pr\left\{\begin{array}{l} x_1 + x_2 + x_3 \le \xi_1 \\ x_4 + x_5 + x_6 \le \xi_2 \\ x_7 + x_8 \le \xi_3 \\ x_i \ge 0, i = 1, \cdots, 8 \end{array}\right\}. \tag{8.5}$$

It is easy to obtain the following stochastic relationship. These decision components can be divided into three groups $\{x_1, x_2, x_3\}$, $\{x_4, x_5, x_6\}$, and $\{x_7, x_8\}$, which are mutually stochastically independent and in each group any elements are stochastically dependent and have the same chance to appear if they need to be realized simultaneously. We also have,

$$\begin{aligned} V(E_1) &= \{x_1\}, & V(E_2) &= \{x_2, x_4\}, \\ V(E_3) &= \{x_3, x_5, x_7\}, & V(E_4) &= \{x_6, x_8\}, \end{aligned}$$

and it is clear that $V(E) = \{x_1, x_2, \cdots, x_8\}$ if we define $E = E_1 \cap E_2 \cap E_3 \cap E_4$. It follows from the stochastic relationship that

$$\begin{aligned} D(E_1) &= \{x_1, x_2, x_3\}, & D(E_2) &= \{x_1, x_2, x_3, x_4, x_5, x_6\}, \\ D(E_3) &= \{x_1, x_2, x_3, x_4, x_5, x_6, x_7, x_8\}, & D(E_4) &= \{x_4, x_5, x_6, x_7, x_8\}. \end{aligned}$$

The induced constraint on the event E_1 is $\{x_1 + x_2 + x_3 \le \xi_1\}$; on the event E_2 is $\{x_1 + x_2 + x_3 \le \xi_1, x_4 + x_5 + x_6 \le \xi_2\}$; on the event E_3 is $\{x_1 + x_2 + x_3 \le \xi_1, x_4 + x_5 + x_6 \le \xi_2, x_7 + x_8 \le \xi_3\}$; and on the event E_4 is $\{x_4 + x_5 + x_6 \le \xi_2, x_7 + x_8 \le \xi_3\}$. Hence we have, for $\boldsymbol{x} \in E_1 \cap E_2 \cap E_3 \cap E_4$,

$$\begin{cases} f_1(\boldsymbol{x}) = \Pr\{x_1 + x_2 + x_3 \le \xi_1\} \\ f_2(\boldsymbol{x}) = \Pr\{x_1 + x_2 + x_3 \le \xi_1, x_4 + x_5 + x_6 \le \xi_2\} \\ f_3(\boldsymbol{x}) = \Pr\left\{\begin{array}{l} x_1 + x_2 + x_3 \le \xi_1 \\ x_4 + x_5 + x_6 \le \xi_2 \\ x_7 + x_8 \le \xi_3 \end{array}\right\} \\ f_4(\boldsymbol{x}) = \Pr\{x_4 + x_5 + x_6 \le \xi_2, x_7 + x_8 \le \xi_3\}. \end{cases} \tag{8.6}$$

Equivalently, since ξ_1, ξ_2 and ξ_3 are independently distributed variables, we have for each $\boldsymbol{x} \in E_1 \cap E_2 \cap E_3 \cap E_4$,

$$\begin{cases} f_1(\boldsymbol{x}) = \displaystyle\int_{x_1+x_2+x_3}^{+\infty} \phi_1(\xi)d\xi \\ f_2(\boldsymbol{x}) = \displaystyle\int_{x_1+x_2+x_3}^{+\infty} \phi_1(\xi)d\xi \cdot \int_{x_4+x_5+x_6}^{+\infty} \phi_2(\xi)d\xi \\ f_3(\boldsymbol{x}) = \displaystyle\int_{x_1+x_2+x_3}^{+\infty} \phi_1(\xi)d\xi \cdot \int_{x_4+x_5+x_6}^{+\infty} \phi_2(\xi)d\xi \cdot \int_{x_7+x_8}^{+\infty} \phi_3(\xi)d\xi \\ f_4(\boldsymbol{x}) = \displaystyle\int_{x_4+x_5+x_6}^{+\infty} \phi_2(\xi)d\xi \cdot \int_{x_7+x_8}^{+\infty} \phi_3(\xi)d\xi. \end{cases} \tag{8.7}$$

Then we can calculate the chance functions $f_1(\boldsymbol{x}), f_2(\boldsymbol{x}), f_3(\boldsymbol{x})$, and $f_4(\boldsymbol{x})$ by stochastic simulation according to (8.6) or by numerical integration method according to (8.7).

Now let the demands of four outputs be $(c_1, c_2, c_3, c_4) = (1, 2, 2, 3)$. We also suppose that the stochastic parameters ξ_1, ξ_2, and ξ_3 are two-parameter lognormally distributed variables $\mathcal{LOGN}(1.56, 0.56^2)$, $\mathcal{LOGN}(1.36, 0.45^2)$, and $\mathcal{LOGN}(0.95, 0.38^2)$, respectively. If the weights of the four objectives, interpreted as the relative preferences of some decision-maker, are labeled w_1, w_2, w_3, w_4, then the DCMOP is transformed into a single-objective DCP. When (w_1, w_2, w_3, w_4) is assumed to be $(3, 1, 2, 3)$, a run of the stochastic simulation-based genetic algorithm shows that the optimal action is

$$(x_1^*, x_2^*, x_3^*, x_4^*, x_5^*, x_6^*, x_7^*, x_8^*) = (1.00, 1.90, 1.44, 0.10, 0.54, 1.63, 0.02, 1.37),$$

and the chances of four outputs are 62%, 55%, 52%, and 84%.

Now let us examine this problem from a different angle. In the same uncertain environment, the management goals with some priority structure and target levels given by the decision-maker are listed as follows:

Priority 1: The chance of meeting the demand of the first user should achieve the desired level 90%, i.e.,

$$\Pr\{x_1 = c_1\} + d_1^- - d_1^+ = 0.90$$

where d_1^- is to be minimized.

Priority 2: The chance of meeting the demand of the second user should achieve the desired level 85%, i.e.,

$$\Pr\{x_2 + x_4 = c_2\} + d_2^- - d_2^+ = 0.85$$

where d_2^- is to be minimized.

Priority 3: The chances of meeting demands of the third and fourth users should achieve the desired levels 70% and 50%, and the weighting factors are 2 and 1, respectively, i.e.,

$$\Pr\{x_3 + x_5 + x_7 = c_3\} + d_3^- - d_3^+ = 0.70,$$
$$\Pr\{x_6 + x_8 = c_4\} + d_4^- - d_4^+ = 0.50$$

where $2d_3^- + d_4^-$ is to be minimized.

Priority 4: Draw water from the third location of resource as little as possible, i.e.,

$$x_7 + x_8 + d_5^- - d_5^+ = 0$$

where d_5^+ is to be minimized.

Then the DCGP for this management problem is formulated as follows:

$$\begin{cases} \text{lexmin}\left\{d_1^-, d_2^-, 2d_3^- + d_4^-, d_5^+\right\} \\ \text{subject to:} \\ \qquad \Pr\{x_1 = c_1\} + d_1^- - d_1^+ = 0.90 \\ \qquad \Pr\{x_2 + x_4 = c_2\} + d_2^- - d_2^+ = 0.85 \\ \qquad \Pr\{x_3 + x_5 + x_7 = c_3\} + d_3^- - d_3^+ = 0.70 \\ \qquad \Pr\{x_6 + x_8 = c_4\} + d_4^- - d_4^+ = 0.5 \\ \qquad x_7 + x_8 + d_5^- - d_5^+ = 0 \\ \qquad x_1 + x_2 + x_3 \le \xi_1 \\ \qquad x_4 + x_5 + x_6 \le \xi_2 \\ \qquad x_7 + x_8 \le \xi_3 \\ \qquad x_i \ge 0, \quad i = 1, 2, \cdots, 8 \\ \qquad d_j^-, d_j^+ \ge 0, \quad j = 1, 2, \cdots, 5. \end{cases} \tag{8.8}$$

In the first priority level, there is only one goal: $\Pr\{x_1 = c_1\} + d_1^- - d_1^+ = 0.90$. For this case, we have

$$E_1 = \left\{(x_1, x_2, \cdots, x_8) \mid x_1 = c_1\right\}.$$

Thus we have $V(E) = V(E_1) = \{x_1\}$ and $D(E_1) = \{x_1, x_2, x_3\}$ and $D(E_1) \cap V(E) = \{x_1\}$. The induced constraint on the event E_1 is then $x_1 \le \xi_1$. Hence the chance function of the first event is

$$\Pr\{x_1 = c_1\} = \Pr\left\{x_1 = c_1 \le \xi_1\right\}. \tag{8.9}$$

In the second priority level, there is also one goal: $\Pr\{x_2 + x_4 = c_2\} + d_2^- - d_2^+ = 0.85$. Thus, we have

$$E_2 = \left\{(x_1, x_2, \cdots, x_8) \mid x_2 + x_4 = c_2\right\}$$

and $V(E) = V(E_1) \cup V(E_2) = \{x_1, x_2, x_4\}$, $D(E_2) = \{x_1, x_2, x_3, x_4, x_5, x_6\}$, and $D(E_2) \cap V(E) = \{x_1, x_2, x_4\}$. The induced constraint on the event E_2 is $\{x_1 + x_2 \le \xi_1, x_4 \le \xi_2\}$. Thus the chance function of the second event is

$$\Pr\{x_2 + x_4 = c_2\} = \Pr\left\{x_1 + x_2 \le \xi_1,\ x_4 \le \xi_2\right\}. \tag{8.10}$$

In the third priority level, there are two goals, $\Pr\{x_3 + x_5 + x_7 = c_3\} + d_3^- - d_3^+ = 0.70$ and $\Pr\{x_6 + x_8 = c_4\} + d_4^- - d_4^+ = 0.5$. We have

$$E_3 = \left\{(x_1, x_2, \cdots, x_8) \mid x_3 + x_5 + x_7 = c_3\right\},$$

$$E_4 = \left\{(x_1, x_2, \cdots, x_8) \mid x_6 + x_8 = c_4\right\}$$

and

$$
\begin{aligned}
&V(E_3) = \{x_3, x_5, x_7\},\\
&V(E_4) = \{x_6, x_8\},\\
&V(E) = V(E_1) \cup V(E_2) \cup V(E_3) \cup V(E_4) = \{x_1, x_2, \cdots, x_8\},\\
&D(E_3) = \{x_1, x_2, \cdots, x_8\},\\
&D(E_4) = \{x_4, x_5, \cdots, x_8\}.
\end{aligned}
$$

By $D(E_3) \cap V(E) = \{x_1, x_2, \cdots, x_8\}$, the induced constraint on the event E_3 is

$$x_1 + x_2 + x_3 \le \xi_1, \quad x_4 + x_5 + x_6 \le \xi_2, \quad x_7 + x_8 \le \xi_3,$$

and by $D(E_4) \cap V(E) = \{x_4, x_5, \cdots, x_8\}$, the induced constraint on the event E_4 should be

$$x_4 + x_5 + x_6 \le \xi_2, \quad x_7 + x_8 \le \xi_3.$$

Hence the chance functions of the third and fourth events are

$$\Pr\{x_3 + x_5 + x_7 = c_3\} = \Pr\left\{\begin{array}{l} x_1 + x_2 + x_3 \le \xi_1 \\ x_4 + x_5 + x_6 \le \xi_2 \\ x_7 + x_8 \le \xi_3 \end{array}\right\} \tag{8.11}$$

and

$$\Pr\{x_6 + x_8 = c_4\} = \Pr\left\{x_4 + x_5 + x_6 \le \xi_2, x_7 + x_8 \le \xi_3\right\} \tag{8.12}$$

respectively.

In the last priority level, there is no chance function. Thus we can get the values of deviations immediately. Under the same assumption on parameters, based on the stochastic simulation on (8.9), (8.10), (8.11), and (8.12), a run of the genetic algorithm shows that the optimal solution is

$$(x_1^*, x_2^*, x_3^*, x_4^*, x_5^*, x_6^*, x_7^*, x_8^*) = (1.00, 1.67, 1.96, 0.33, 0.03, 1.28, 0.01, 1.72)$$

which satisfies the first, second, and fourth goals with reliability levels 99%, 85%, and 85%, respectively, but the reliability level of the third goal is 47%, which is less than the desired level 70%, and the total quantity drawn from the third location is 1.73.

8.2 Production Process

Let us reconsider the production process in Section 6.1. It is a weekly production plan of an oil refinery for crude oil (raw_1 and raw_2, respectively), for supplying gasoline ($prod_1$) to a distribution system of gas stations and fuel oil ($prod_2$) to power plants.

It is known that the productivities $\pi(raw_1, prod_1)$ and $\pi(raw_2, prod_2)$ (i.e., the output of gas from raw_1 and output of fuel from raw_2) may change randomly, whereas the other productivities are deterministic. They are assumed to be

$$\pi(raw_1, prod_1) = 2 + \eta_1, \quad \pi(raw_1, prod_2) = 3,$$

$$\pi(raw_2, prod_1) = 6, \qquad \pi(raw_2, prod_2) = 3.4 - \eta_2$$

where η_1 is a uniformly distributed variable $\mathcal{U}[-0.8, 0.8]$ and η_2 is an exponentially distributed variable $\mathcal{EXP}(0.4)$.

The weekly demands of the clients (gas stations and power plants), h_1 for gas and h_2 for fuel, are also varying randomly and represented by

$$h_1 = 180 + \xi_1, \qquad h_2 = 162 + \xi_2$$

where ξ_1 and ξ_2 are normally distributed variables $\mathcal{N}(0, 12)$ and $\mathcal{N}(0, 9)$, respectively.

The production costs per unit of the raw materials are $c_1 = 2$ for raw_1 and $c_2 = 3$ for raw_2. The total cost is thus $2x_1 + 3x_2$.

The production capacity (i.e., the maximal total amount of raw materials) is assumed to be 100. Thus we have $x_1 + x_2 \le 100$.

If the weekly production plan (x_1, x_2) has to be fixed in advance and cannot be changed during the week, and clients expect their actual demands to be satisfied during the corresponding week, then we have the following constraints,

$$(2 + \eta_1)x_1 + 6x_2 \ge 180 + \xi_1, \quad 3x_1 + (3.4 - \eta_2)x_2 \ge 162 + \xi_2.$$

This is clearly an uncertain environment.

We hope the chance that the total production cost is less than 140 is as high as possible. That is, what production plan ensures that total production cost does not exceed 140 and has the highest reliability level to satisfy the actual demands of clients? The associated DCP is written as follows,

$$\begin{cases} \max f(\boldsymbol{x}) = \Pr\{2x_1 + 3x_2 \le 140\} \\ \text{subject to:} \\ \qquad x_1 + x_2 \le 100 \\ \qquad (2 + \eta_1)x_1 + 6x_2 \ge 180 + \xi_1 \\ \qquad 3x_1 + (3.4 - \eta_2)x_2 \ge 162 + \xi_2 \\ \qquad x_1, x_2 \ge 0. \end{cases} \tag{8.13}$$

For this single-objective DCP, we do not need to discuss the stochastic relationship among the decision components. We will search for a solution (x_1, x_2) such that $\{x_1 + x_2 \le 100, x_1, x_2 \ge 0\}$ is satisfied at first, and then maximizes the chance function

$$f(\boldsymbol{x}) = \begin{cases} p(\boldsymbol{x}), & 2x_1 + 3x_2 \le 140 \\ 0, & 2x_1 + 3x_2 > 140 \end{cases}$$

where

$$p(\boldsymbol{x}) = \Pr\left\{ \begin{array}{l} (2+\eta_1)x_1 + 6x_2 \ge 180 + \xi_1 \\ 3x_1 + (3.4 - \eta_2)x_2 \ge 162 + \xi_2 \end{array} \right\}.$$

A run of the stochastic simulation-based genetic algorithm shows that the optimal solution is

$$(x_1^*, x_2^*) = (34.74, 23.51)$$

with the highest chance 84% and the associated total production cost is just 140.

If the manager wants to consider the reliability levels of clients separately, then we may set the priority structure and target levels as follows:

Priority 1: Total production cost should not exceed 140.

Priority 2: The chance of satisfying the gas stations should achieve 95%.

Priority 3: The chance of satisfying the power plants should achieve 90%.

Then the DCGP associated with this problem is formulated as

$$\begin{cases} \text{lexmin}\left\{d_1^+, d_2^-, d_3^-\right\} \\ \text{subject to:} \\ \qquad 2x_1 + 3x_2 + d_1^- - d_1^+ = 140 \\ \qquad \Pr\{(2+\eta_1)x_1 + 6x_2 \ge 180 + \xi_1\} + d_2^- - d_2^+ = 0.95 \\ \qquad \Pr\{3x_1 + (3.4 - \eta_2)x_2 \ge 162 + \xi_2\} + d_3^- - d_3^+ = 0.90 \\ \qquad x_1 + x_2 \le 100 \\ \qquad x_1, x_2 \ge 0. \end{cases} \tag{8.14}$$

This model is easy to handle since the chance functions can be calculated by stochastic simulations clearly. A run of the genetic algorithm shows that the optimal solution is

$$(x_1^*, x_2^*) = (35.774, 22.817)$$

which can satisfy the first two goals, but the reliability level of the third goal is 85%, which is less than the desired level 90%.

8.3 Open Inventory Network

Recall the open inventory network discussed in Section 6.4. The simplest model based on DCP for the optimal operation problem of an open inventory network is

$$\begin{cases} \max f(\boldsymbol{x}) = \Pr\{\boldsymbol{x}\} \\ \text{subject to:} \\ \qquad v_i \le a_i + t_i(\boldsymbol{x}) + \xi_i \le V_i, \quad i = 1, 2, \cdots, p \\ \qquad \boldsymbol{x} \in D \end{cases} \tag{8.15}$$

which is related to finding a decision $\boldsymbol{x}$ in D maximizing the probability that the decision can actually be performed. Notice that a decision $\boldsymbol{x} \in D$ can actually be performed if and only if the realization of $\boldsymbol{\xi}$ meets $v_i \le a_i + t_i(\boldsymbol{x}) + \xi_i \le V_i$, $i = 1, 2, \cdots, p$. In fact, this model attempts to find the safest solution (i.e., the one with the maximum probability that the open inventory system does not go wrong). Here we remind the reader once more that the feasible set is stochastic rather than deterministic. Thus the decision $\boldsymbol{x}$ does possess some uncertainty even though it is not a random vector. Sometimes, we may wish to maximize the reliability levels of the four reservoirs separately. Generally speaking, we have m potential objective functions (some of them are chance functions). Then the problem may be formulated as the following DCMOP model,

$$\begin{cases} \max\,[f_1(\boldsymbol{x}), f_2(\boldsymbol{x}), \cdots, f_m(\boldsymbol{x})] \\ \text{subject to:} \\ \qquad v_i \le a_i + t_i(\boldsymbol{x}) + \xi_i \le V_i, \quad i = 1, 2, \cdots, p \\ \qquad \boldsymbol{x} \in D. \end{cases} \tag{8.16}$$

In order to balance the multiple conflicting objectives, open inventory networks may also be modeled by the following DCGP according to the target levels and priority structure set by the decision maker,

$$\begin{cases} \min \sum_{j=1}^{l} P_j \sum_{i=1}^{m} (u_{ij} d_i^+ + v_{ij} d_i^-) \\ \text{subject to:} \\ \qquad f_i(\boldsymbol{x}) + d_i^- - d_i^+ = b_i, \quad i = 1, 2, \cdots, m \\ \qquad v_i \le a_i + t_i(\boldsymbol{x}) + \xi_i \le V_i, \quad i = 1, 2, \cdots, p \\ \qquad \boldsymbol{x} \in D \\ \qquad d_i^-, d_i^+ \ge 0, \quad i = 1, 2, \cdots, m \end{cases} \tag{8.17}$$

where P_j = the preemptive priority factor which expresses the relative importance of various goals, $P_j \gg P_{j+1}$, for all j, u_{ij} = weighting factor corresponding to positive deviation for goal i with priority j assigned, v_{ij} = weighting factor corresponding to negative deviation for goal i with priority j assigned, d_i^+ = positive deviation from the target of goal i, d_i^- = negative deviation from the target of goal i, $\boldsymbol{x}$ = n-dimensional decision vector, f_i = a chance function or conventional real-valued function $\Re^n \to \Re^1$, in goal constraints, b_i = the target value according to goal i, l = number of priorities, and m = number of goal constraints.

Now we are going to employ the stochastic simulation-based genetic algorithm to solve DCP models for the optimal operation problems of open inventory networks. The parameters in the genetic algorithm are defined as follows: the population size is 30, the probability of crossover P_c is 0.3, the probability of mutation P_m is 0.2, the parameter a in the rank-based evaluation function is 0.05, and the number of cycles in the stochastic simulation is 5000.

Let us consider the open inventory network illustrated by Figure 6.2. We suppose that all the capacity vectors of nine arcs form a deterministic set D in which each element $\boldsymbol{x} = (x_1, x_2, \cdots, x_9)$ is constrained by

$$\begin{array}{lll} 10 \le x_1 \le 50, & 0 \le x_2 \le 10, & 0 \le x_3 \le 10, \\ 0 \le x_4 \le 15, & 15 \le x_5 \le 60, & -5 \le x_6 \le 5, \\ 15 \le x_7 \le 60, & -5 \le x_8 \le 5, & 20 \le x_9 \le 70. \end{array}$$

The stochastic terms (in this case the inflows) are assumed to be two-parameter lognormally distributed variables $\mathcal{LOGN}(\mu_i, \sigma_i^2)$ for $i = 1, 2, 3, 4$. We suppose that the values of parameters (μ_i, σ_i) of the four reservoirs are

$$(2.24, 1.12), \quad (1.60, 1.28), \quad (1.87, 1.45), \quad (1.30, 1.34),$$

respectively. We also suppose that the values of parameters (v_i, V_i) of the four reservoirs are $(10, 120)$, $(20, 100)$, $(10, 80)$, and $(0, 90)$, respectively.

If the manager is not concerned with the reliability level of each reservoir, but the reliability level of the whole system, then the goal of management is to find the safest solution $\boldsymbol{x}$ in D. In order to solve the problem, we may formulate it by the following single-objective DCP model,

$$\begin{cases} \max\ f(\boldsymbol{x}) = \Pr\{\boldsymbol{x}\} \\ \text{subject to:} \\ \qquad 10 \le 70 - x_1 - x_2 - x_3 - x_4 + \xi_1 \le 120 \\ \qquad 20 \le 80 + x_2 - x_5 - x_6 + \xi_2 \le 100 \\ \qquad 10 \le 60 + x_3 - x_7 - x_8 + \xi_3 \le 80 \\ \qquad 0 \le 50 + x_4 + x_6 + x_8 - x_9 + \xi_4 \le 90 \\ \qquad (x_1, x_2, \cdots, x_9) \in D. \end{cases} \tag{8.18}$$

It is clear that, if $\boldsymbol{x} \in D$, then the chance function should be

$$f(\boldsymbol{x}) = \Pr\left\{\begin{array}{l} 10 \le 70 - x_1 - x_2 - x_3 - x_4 + \xi_1 \le 120 \\ 20 \le 80 + x_2 - x_5 - x_6 + \xi_2 \le 100 \\ 10 \le 60 + x_3 - x_7 - x_8 + \xi_3 \le 80 \\ 0 \le 50 + x_4 + x_6 + x_8 - x_9 + \xi_4 \le 90 \end{array}\right\},$$

otherwise, $f(\boldsymbol{x}) = 0$. A run of the stochastic simulation-based genetic algorithm with 1000 generations shows that the optimal solution (i.e., the safest action) is

$$\boldsymbol{x}^* = (37.1,\ 2.8,\ 4.6,\ 9.2,\ 54.7,\ 3.4,\ 50.7,\ 3.3,\ 65.3)$$

whose reliability level is 92.7% and the total sum of flows is 231.1.

Now let us examine this problem from a different angle. In the same uncertain environment, the management goals with some priority structure set by the decision-maker are listed as follows:

Priority 1: The chance of the reservoir 1 should achieve the desired level 96%.

Priority 2: The chance of the whole network should achieve the desired level 90%.

Priority 3: The sum of all flows is as little as possible.

In order to meet these management goals as many as possible, we can employ the following DCGP model,

$$\begin{cases} \text{lexmin}\left\{d_1^-, d_2^-, d_3^+\right\} \\ \text{subject to:} \\ \qquad f_1(\boldsymbol{x}) + d_1^- - d_1^+ = 0.96 \\ \qquad f_2(\boldsymbol{x}) + d_2^- - d_2^+ = 0.90 \\ \qquad \sum_{i=1}^{9} x_i + d_3^- - d_3^+ = 0 \\ \qquad 10 \le 70 - x_1 - x_2 - x_3 - x_4 + \xi_1 \le 120 \\ \qquad 20 \le 80 + x_2 - x_5 - x_6 + \xi_2 \le 100 \\ \qquad 10 \le 60 + x_3 - x_7 - x_8 + \xi_3 \le 80 \\ \qquad 0 \le 50 + x_4 + x_6 + x_8 - x_9 + \xi_4 \le 90 \\ \qquad (x_1, x_2, \cdots, x_9) \in D \\ \qquad d_i^+, d_i^- \ge 0, \quad i = 1, 2, 3 \end{cases} \tag{8.19}$$

where the chance functions $f_1(\boldsymbol{x})$ and $f_2(\boldsymbol{x})$ represent the probability levels that the reservoir and the whole network do not go wrong, respectively. By the stochastic relationship, it is easy to derive that

$$f_1(\boldsymbol{x}) = \Pr\{10 \le 70 - x_1 - x_2 - x_3 - x_4 + \xi_1 \le 120\} \tag{8.20}$$

and

$$f_2(\boldsymbol{x}) = \Pr\left\{\begin{array}{l} 10 \le 70 - x_1 - x_2 - x_3 - x_4 + \xi_1 \le 120 \\ 20 \le 80 + x_2 - x_5 - x_6 + \xi_2 \le 100 \\ 10 \le 60 + x_3 - x_7 - x_8 + \xi_3 \le 80 \\ 0 \le 50 + x_4 + x_6 + x_8 - x_9 + \xi_4 \le 90 \end{array}\right\}. \tag{8.21}$$

A run of stochastic simulation-based genetic algorithm with 2000 generations shows that the optimal solution is

$$\boldsymbol{x}^* = (31.3,\ 2.3,\ 0.0,\ 3.3,\ 37.3,\ -1.0,\ 48.5,\ 0.1,\ 30.1)$$

which can satisfy the first two goals, but the total sum of flows is 153.9.

8.4 Capital Budgeting

We model capital budgeting problems by chance-constrained integer programming in Chapter 6. In this section we construct some DCP models for them.

The simplest model based on integer DCP for capital budgeting is

$$\begin{cases} \max \ \Pr\{\eta_i x_i \ge \xi_i, \ i = 1, 2, \cdots, n\} \\ \text{subject to:} \\ \qquad a_1 x_1 + a_2 x_2 + \cdots + a_n x_n \le a \\ \qquad b_1 x_1 + b_2 x_2 + \cdots + b_n x_n \le b \\ \qquad x_i, i = 1, 2, \cdots, n, \quad \text{nonnegative integers} \end{cases} \tag{8.22}$$

which is concerned with finding the safest solution (i.e., the one with the maximum probability that the productions meet the demands), where a is the total capital available for distribution, b is the total available space, a_i are the levels of funds that need to be allocated to type i machine, b_i are the spaces used by type i machine, η_i are the production capacities of the type i machine for product i, ξ_i are the future demands for product i, and x_i are the number of type i machines selected, $i = 1, 2, \cdots, n$, respectively. In addition, the decision variables x_i's are all nonnegative integers.

Sometimes, we may wish to maximize the reliability levels of all types of demands separately. Then the problem may be formulated as the following DCMOP model,

$$\begin{cases} \max \ \left[\Pr\{\eta_1 x_1 \ge \xi_1\}, \Pr\{\eta_2 x_2 \ge \xi_2\}, \cdots, \Pr\{\eta_n x_n \ge \xi_n\}\right] \\ \text{subject to:} \\ \qquad a_1 x_1 + a_2 x_2 + \cdots + a_n x_n \le a \\ \qquad b_1 x_1 + b_2 x_2 + \cdots + b_n x_n \le b \\ \qquad x_i, i = 1, 2, \cdots, n, \quad \text{nonnegative integers.} \end{cases} \tag{8.23}$$

In order to balance the multiple conflicting objectives, capital budgeting may be modeled by the following DCGP according to the target levels and priority structure set by the decision-maker,

$$\begin{cases} \min \sum_{j=1}^{l} P_j \sum_{i=1}^{n} (u_{ij} d_i^+ + v_{ij} d_i^-) \\ \text{subject to:} \\ \qquad \Pr\{\eta_i x_i \ge \xi_i\} + d_i^- - d_i^+ = \alpha_i, \quad i = 1, 2, \cdots, n \\ \qquad a_1 x_1 + a_2 x_2 + \cdots + a_n x_n \le a \\ \qquad b_1 x_1 + b_2 x_2 + \cdots + b_n x_n \le b \\ \qquad d_i^-, d_i^+ \ge 0, \quad i = 1, 2, \cdots, n \\ \qquad x_i, i = 1, 2, \cdots, n, \quad \text{nonnegative integers.} \end{cases} \tag{8.24}$$

where P_j = the preemptive priority factor which expresses the relative importance of various goals, $P_j \gg P_{j+1}$, for all j, u_{ij} = weighting factor corresponding to positive deviation for goal i with priority j assigned, v_{ij} = weighting factor corresponding to negative deviation for goal i with priority j assigned, d_i^+ = positive deviation from the target of goal i, d_i^- = negative deviation from the target of goal i, α_i = the target value according to goal i, l = number of priorities.

If some of the parameters a, b, a_i and b_i, $i = 1, 2, \cdots, n$ in (8.24) are assumed stochastic, then the feasible set described by

$$\begin{cases} a_1x_1 + a_2x_2 + \cdots + a_nx_n \le a \\ b_1x_1 + b_2x_2 + \cdots + b_nx_n \le b \\ x_i, i = 1, 2, \cdots, n, \quad \text{nonnegative integers} \end{cases}$$

is a stochastic environment.

Now we suppose that there are 5 types of machines which produce 5 different products. We assume that the production capacities of type i machines are lognormally distributed variables. Here the probability density functions $\phi_i(\eta_i)$ of production capacities of type i machines are

$$\phi_i(\eta_i) = \begin{cases} \dfrac{1}{\sqrt{2\pi}\sigma_i\eta_i} \exp\left[-\dfrac{(\ln\eta_i - \mu_i)^2}{2\sigma_i^2}\right], & 0 \le c_i < \infty \\ 0, & \text{otherwise} \end{cases} \tag{8.25}$$

where (μ_i, σ_i) are (3.0,1.0), (4.0,1.6), (5.0,1.6), (4.0,1.2), and (3.0,0.8), $i = 1, 2, 3, 4, 5$, respectively. We also assume that the demands ξ_i of products i have exponential distributions. That is, their probability density functions are

$$\psi_i(\xi_i) = \begin{cases} \dfrac{1}{\beta_i} \exp\left(-\dfrac{\xi_i}{\beta_i}\right), & 0 \le d_i < \infty \\ 0, & \text{otherwise} \end{cases} \tag{8.26}$$

where β_i are 10, 15, 20, 18, and 16, $i = 1, 2, 3, 4, 5$, respectively.

The levels of funds a_i that need to be allocated to type i machines are 300, 800, 700, 900, and 1000, $i = 1, 2, \cdots, 5$, respectively, and the total capital available for distribution a is 12500. In addition, the spaces b_i used by type i machines are 20, 30, 50, 30, and 10, $i = 1, 2, \cdots, 5$, respectively, and the maximum available space b is 500.

If we want to find a capital budgeting plan with the maximum probability that the productions meet the demands, then we can model it by the following integer DCP model,

$$\begin{cases} \max \Pr\{\eta_i x_i \geq \xi_i, i = 1, 2, \cdots, 5\} \\ \text{subject to:} \\ \qquad 300x_1 + 800x_2 + 700x_3 + 900x_4 + 1000x_5 \leq 12500 \\ \qquad 20x_1 + 30x_2 + 50x_3 + 30x_4 + 10x_5 \leq 500 \\ \qquad x_i, i = 1, 2, \cdots, 5, \quad \text{nonnegative integers} \end{cases}$$

where x_i, $i = 1, 2, \cdots, 5$ are decision variables representing the numbers of type i machines selected. A run of the stochastic simulation-based genetic algorithm with 300 generations shows that the optimal capital budgeting is

$$(x_1^*, x_2^*, x_3^*, x_4^*, x_5^*) = (6, 3, 2, 3, 4)$$

whose reliability level is 85.06%.

We set the following target levels and priority structure for a capital budgeting problem:

Strict constraint: Space availability limitation,

$$20x_1 + 30x_2 + 50x_3 + 30x_4 + 10x_5 \leq 500.$$

Priority 1: The probability level of meeting the demand ξ_1 should achieve 97%, i.e.,

$$\Pr\{\eta_1 x_1 \geq \xi_1\} + d_1^- - d_1^+ = 0.97$$

where d_1^- is to be minimized.

Priority 2: The probability level of meeting the demand ξ_2 should achieve 95%, i.e.,

$$\Pr\{\eta_2 x_2 \geq \xi_2\} + d_2^- - d_2^+ = 0.95$$

where d_2^- is to be minimized.

Priority 3: The probability level of meeting the demands ξ_3, ξ_4 and ξ_5 should achieve 90%, i.e.,

$$\Pr\{\eta_i x_i \geq \xi_i, i = 3, 4, 5\} + d_3^- - d_3^+ = 0.90$$

where d_3^- is to be minimized.

Priority 4: The total capital used for buying machines should not exceed 12500, i.e.,

$$300x_1 + 800x_2 + 700x_3 + 900x_4 + 1000x_5 + d_4^- - d_4^+ = 12500$$

where d_4^+ is to be minimized.

According to the above-mentioned priority structure and target levels, the following DCGP model is formulated,

$$\begin{cases} \text{lexmin}\left\{d_1^-, d_2^-, d_3^-, d_4^+\right\} \\ \text{subject to:} \\ \qquad \Pr\left\{\eta_1 x_1 \ge \xi_1\right\} + d_1^- - d_1^+ = 0.97 \\ \qquad \Pr\left\{\eta_2 x_2 \ge \xi_2\right\} + d_2^- - d_2^+ = 0.95 \\ \qquad \Pr\left\{\eta_i x_i \ge \xi_i, i = 3,4,5\right\} + d_3^- - d_3^+ = 0.90 \\ \qquad 300x_1 + 800x_2 + 700x_3 + 900x_4 + 1000x_5 + d_4^- - d_4^+ = 12500 \\ \qquad 20x_1 + 30x_2 + 50x_3 + 30x_4 + 10x_5 \le 500 \\ \qquad d_i^-, d_i^+ \ge 0, \quad i = 1,2,3,4 \\ \qquad x_i, i = 1,2,\cdots,5, \quad \text{nonnegative integers.} \end{cases}$$

A run of the stochastic simulation-based genetic algorithm with 400 generations shows that the optimal capital budgeting is

$$(x_1^*,\ x_2^*,\ x_3^*,\ x_4^*,\ x_5^*) = (5,\ 4,\ 2,\ 4,\ 4)$$

which satisfies the first three goals, but the fourth objective is 1200. In fact, we also have

$$\Pr\left\{\eta_1 x_1^* \ge \xi_1\right\} = 97.65\%,$$
$$\Pr\left\{\eta_2 x_2^* \ge \xi_2\right\} = 95.34\%,$$
$$\Pr\left\{\eta_i x_i^* \ge \xi_i, i = 3,4,5\right\} = 91.89\%$$

and the total capital to be distributed is 13700.

Chapter 9

Chance-Constrained Programming with Fuzzy Coefficients

As a type of stochastic programming developed by Charnes and Cooper [21], chance-constrained programming (CCP) provides a means of allowing the decision-maker to consider objectives and constraints in terms of the probability of their attainment. That is, CCP models stochastic decision systems with assumptions that the constraints will hold at least α of time, where α is referred to as the confidence level. For this case, the term *chance* is represented by the probability that the constraints are satisfied. CCP with stochastic parameters has been documented in Chapter 5.

However, the term *fuzzy programming* has been used in different ways in the past. Here we define fuzzy programming as mathematical programming with fuzzy parameters. Analogous to chance-constrained programming with stochastic parameters, in a fuzzy decision system we assume that the constraints will hold with at least possibility α, and the *chance* is represented by the possibility that the constraints are satisfied.

In this chapter, we will introduce a spectrum of CCP, chance-constrained multiobjective programming (CCMOP), and chance-constrained goal programming (CCGP) models with fuzzy rather than stochastic coefficients constructed by Liu and Iwamura [90][91], and present the crisp equivalents of chance constraints for some special cases. We also propose a technique of fuzzy simulation for the chance constraints which are usually hard to convert to their crisp equivalents in practice. Finally, a fuzzy simulation-based genetic algorithm is designed for solving this type of problem and is illustrated by some numerical examples.

9.1 Chance-Constrained Programming Models

A mathematical programming with fuzzy coefficients should have the following form:

$$\begin{cases} \max f(\boldsymbol{x}, \boldsymbol{\xi}) \\ \text{subject to:} \\ \qquad g_j(\boldsymbol{x}, \boldsymbol{\xi}) \leq 0, \quad j = 1, 2, \cdots, p \end{cases} \tag{9.1}$$

where $\boldsymbol{x}$ is a decision vector, $\boldsymbol{\xi}$ is a vector of fuzzy parameters, $f(\boldsymbol{x}, \boldsymbol{\xi})$ is the return function, and $g_j(\boldsymbol{x}, \boldsymbol{\xi})$ are constraint functions, $j = 1, 2, \cdots, p$. However, this fuzzy programming is not well-defined since the meanings of max as well as of the constraints are not clear at all.

Therefore we have to present some meaningful forms of fuzzy programming. Following the idea of CCP proposed by Charnes and Cooper [21], Liu and Iwamura [90][91] suggested a spectrum of CCP models with fuzzy coefficients. A single-objective CCP with fuzzy coefficients may be written as follows,

$$\begin{cases} \max \overline{f} \\ \text{subject to:} \\ \qquad \text{Pos}\left\{f(\boldsymbol{x}, \boldsymbol{\xi}) \geq \overline{f}\right\} \geq \beta \\ \qquad \text{Pos}\left\{g_j(\boldsymbol{x}, \boldsymbol{\xi}) \leq 0, \, j = 1, 2, \cdots, p\right\} \geq \alpha \end{cases} \tag{9.2}$$

where α and β are predetermined confidence levels to the constraints and objective, and $\text{Pos}\{\cdot\}$ denotes the possibility of the event in $\{\cdot\}$.

Thus a point $\boldsymbol{x}$ is feasible if and only if the possibility measure of the set $\{\boldsymbol{\xi} | g_j(\boldsymbol{x}, \boldsymbol{\xi}) \leq 0, j = 1, 2, \cdots, p\}$ is at least α.

For any given decision $\boldsymbol{x}$, $f(\boldsymbol{x}, \boldsymbol{\xi})$ is clearly a fuzzy number. Thus there are multiple possible values $\overline{f}$ such that $\text{Pos}\left\{f(\boldsymbol{x}, \boldsymbol{\xi}) \geq \overline{f}\right\} \geq \beta$. In view of maximizing the objective value $\overline{f}$, the objective value $\overline{f}$ should be the maximal value that the return function $f(\boldsymbol{x}, \boldsymbol{\xi})$ can achieve with at least possibility β, i.e.,

$$\overline{f} = \max_{f} \left\{ f \mid \text{Pos}\left\{f(\boldsymbol{x}, \boldsymbol{\xi}) \geq f\right\} \geq \beta \right\}. \tag{9.3}$$

Sometimes we formulate the fuzzy decision problem as a CCP with separate chance constraints as follows,

$$\begin{cases} \max \overline{f} \\ \text{subject to:} \\ \qquad \text{Pos}\left\{f(\boldsymbol{x}, \boldsymbol{\xi}) \geq \overline{f}\right\} \geq \beta \\ \qquad \text{Pos}\left\{g_j(\boldsymbol{x}, \boldsymbol{\xi}) \leq 0\right\} \geq \alpha_j, \quad j = 1, 2, \cdots, p \end{cases} \tag{9.4}$$

where the parameters α_j are predetermined confidence levels to the constraints, $j = 1, 2, \cdots, p$, respectively.

For a minimization problem, the objective value $\overline{f}$ should be the minimal value that the cost function $f(\boldsymbol{x}, \boldsymbol{\xi})$ can achieve with at least possibility β. Thus we have the following model,

$$\begin{cases} \min \overline{f} \\ \text{subject to:} \\ \qquad \text{Pos}\left\{f(\boldsymbol{x}, \boldsymbol{\xi}) \le \overline{f}\right\} \ge \beta \\ \qquad \text{Pos}\left\{g_j(\boldsymbol{x}, \boldsymbol{\xi}) \le 0\right\} \ge \alpha_j, \quad j = 1, 2, \cdots, p. \end{cases} \tag{9.5}$$

As an extension of single-objective CCP with fuzzy coefficients, CCMOP may be written as follows,

$$\begin{cases} \max \ \left[\overline{f}_1, \overline{f}_2, \cdots, \overline{f}_m\right] \\ \text{subject to:} \\ \qquad \text{Pos}\left\{f_i(\boldsymbol{x}, \boldsymbol{\xi}) \ge \overline{f}_i\right\} \ge \beta_i, \quad i = 1, 2, \cdots, m \\ \qquad \text{Pos}\{g_j(\boldsymbol{x}, \boldsymbol{\xi}) \le 0\} \ge \alpha_j, \quad j = 1, 2, \cdots, p \end{cases} \tag{9.6}$$

where β_i are confidence levels to the ith objectives, and the objective values $\overline{f}_i$ should be the maximal values that the return functions $f(\boldsymbol{x}, \boldsymbol{\xi})$ can achieve with at least possibilities β_i, $i = 1, 2, \cdots, m$, respectively.

We can also formulate the fuzzy decision system as a chance-constrained goal programming according to the priority structure and target levels set by the decision-maker:

$$\begin{cases} \min \sum\limits_{j=1}^{l} P_j \sum\limits_{i=1}^{m} (u_{ij} d_i^+ + v_{ij} d_i^-) \\ \text{subject to:} \\ \qquad \text{Pos}\left\{f_i(\boldsymbol{x}, \boldsymbol{\xi}) + d_i^- - d_i^+ = b_i\right\} \ge \beta_i, \quad i = 1, 2, \cdots, m \\ \qquad \text{Pos}\left\{g_j(\boldsymbol{x}, \boldsymbol{\xi}) \le 0\right\} \ge \alpha_j, \qquad\qquad j = 1, 2, \cdots, p \\ \qquad d_i^-, d_i^+ \ge 0, \qquad\qquad\qquad\qquad\quad i = 1, 2, \cdots, m \end{cases} \tag{9.7}$$

where

P_j = the preemptive priority factor which expresses the relative importance of various goals, $P_j \gg P_{j+1}$, for all j,

u_{ij} = weighting factor corresponding to positive deviation for goal i with priority j assigned,

v_{ij} = weighting factor corresponding to negative deviation for goal i with priority j assigned,

d_i^+ = positive deviation from the target of goal i,
d_i^- = negative deviation from the target of goal i,
$\boldsymbol{x}$ = n-dimensional decision vector,
f_i = a function in goal constraints,
g_j = a function in real constraints,
b_i = the target value according to goal i,
$\boldsymbol{\xi}$ = fuzzy vector of parameters,
l = number of priorities,
m = number of goal constraints,
p = number of real constraints.

For each fixed feasible solution $\boldsymbol{x}$ (i.e., the one satisfying $\text{Pos}\{g_j(\boldsymbol{x},\boldsymbol{\xi}) \le 0\} \ge \alpha_j$, $j = 1, 2, \cdots, p$), since $\boldsymbol{\xi}$ is a fuzzy vector, $f_i(\boldsymbol{x},\boldsymbol{\xi})$ is clearly a fuzzy number. This leads to the fact that there are multiple potential values of d_i^- and d_i^+ such that $\text{Pos}\{f_i(\boldsymbol{x},\boldsymbol{\xi}) + d_i^- - d_i^+ = b_i\} \ge \beta_i$. For this case, the positive and negative deviations are understood as the minimal nonnegative values of d_i^+ and d_i^- such that

$$\text{Pos}\left\{d_i^+ \ge f_i(\boldsymbol{x},\boldsymbol{\xi}) - b_i\right\} \ge \beta_i, \quad \text{Pos}\left\{d_i^- \ge b_i - f_i(\boldsymbol{x},\boldsymbol{\xi})\right\} \ge \beta_i \tag{9.8}$$

for $i = 1, 2, \cdots, m$, respectively.

If the fuzzy vector $\boldsymbol{\xi}$ degenerates to the crisp case, then the two possibilities $\text{Pos}\left\{d_i^+ \ge f_i(\boldsymbol{x},\boldsymbol{\xi}) - b_i\right\}$ and $\text{Pos}\left\{d_i^- \ge b_i - f_i(\boldsymbol{x},\boldsymbol{\xi})\right\}$ should be always 1 provided that $\beta_i > 0$, and (9.8) should become

$$d_i^+ = [f_i(\boldsymbol{x},\boldsymbol{\xi}) - b_i] \vee 0, \quad d_i^- = [b_i - f_i(\boldsymbol{x},\boldsymbol{\xi})] \vee 0.$$

This coincides with the crisp goal programming.

9.2 Crisp Equivalents

One way of solving CCP with fuzzy coefficients is to convert the chance constraint

$$\text{Pos}\left\{g(\boldsymbol{x},\boldsymbol{\xi}) \le 0\right\} \ge \alpha \tag{9.9}$$

to its crisp equivalent and then solve the equivalent crisp models by the traditional solution process. Please note that the fuzzy system constraints $\text{Pos}\{g_j(\boldsymbol{x},\boldsymbol{\xi}) \le 0\} \ge \alpha_j$, $j = 1, 2, \cdots, p$ are a set of this form, and the fuzzy objective constraint $\text{Pos}\{f(\boldsymbol{x},\boldsymbol{\xi}) \ge \overline{f}\} \ge \beta$ coincides with this form by defining $g(\boldsymbol{x},\boldsymbol{\xi}) = \overline{f} - f(\boldsymbol{x},\boldsymbol{\xi})$. Since the fuzzy goal constraint $\text{Pos}\{f(\boldsymbol{x},\boldsymbol{\xi}) + d^- - d^+ = b\} \ge \beta$ is understood as $\text{Pos}\{d^- \ge b - f(\boldsymbol{x},\boldsymbol{\xi})\} \ge \beta$ and $\text{Pos}\{d^+ \ge f(\boldsymbol{x},\boldsymbol{\xi}) - b\} \ge \beta$, the former and the latter coincide with the form (9.9) by defining $g(\boldsymbol{x},\boldsymbol{\xi}) = b - f(\boldsymbol{x},\boldsymbol{\xi}) - d^-$ and $g(\boldsymbol{x},\boldsymbol{\xi}) = f(\boldsymbol{x},\boldsymbol{\xi}) - b - d^+$, respectively. This section presents some known results.

Case I: Assume that the function $g(\boldsymbol{x}, \boldsymbol{\xi})$ has the form $g(\boldsymbol{x}, \boldsymbol{\xi}) = h(\boldsymbol{x}) - \xi$, then the chance constraint (9.9) can be written in the following form,

$$\text{Pos}\{h(\boldsymbol{x}) \le \xi\} \ge \alpha \tag{9.10}$$

where $h(\boldsymbol{x})$ is a (linear or nonlinear) function of decision vector $\boldsymbol{x}$ and ξ is a fuzzy number with membership function $\mu(\xi)$.

It is clear that, for any given confidence level α $(0 \le \alpha \le 1)$, there exist some values K_α (maybe $+\infty$ or $-\infty$) such that

$$\text{Pos}\{K_\alpha \le \xi\} = \alpha. \tag{9.11}$$

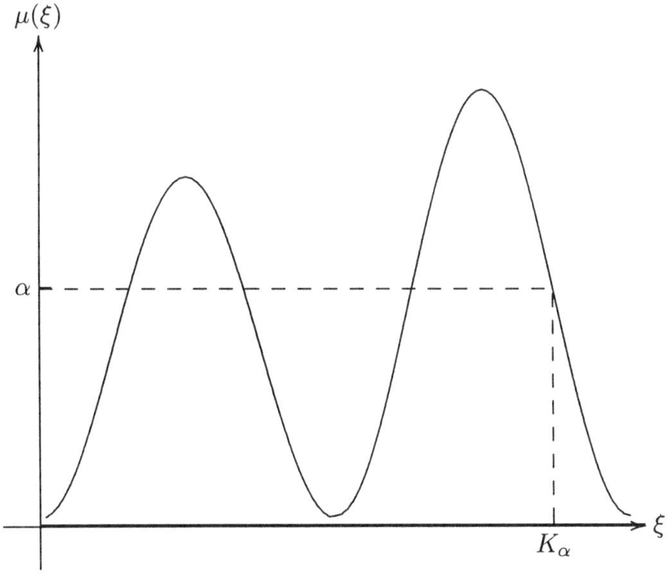

Figure 9.1: Membership Function $\mu(\xi)$, K_α, and α

We note that the possibility $\text{Pos}\{K_\alpha \le \xi\}$ will increase if the number K_α is replaced by a smaller number K'_α since

$$\begin{aligned} \text{Pos}\{K_\alpha \le \xi\} &= \sup\{\mu(\xi) \mid \xi \ge K_\alpha\} \\ &\le \sup\{\mu(\xi) \mid \xi \ge K'_\alpha\} \\ &= \text{Pos}\{K'_\alpha \le \xi\}. \end{aligned}$$

Thus the crisp equivalent of chance constraint (9.10) will be

$$h(\boldsymbol{x}) \le K_\alpha \tag{9.12}$$

provided that K_α is the largest value satisfying (9.11).

In fact, the largest value K_α is determined by

$$K_\alpha = \sup\left\{K \mid K = \mu^{-1}(\alpha)\right\} \tag{9.13}$$

where μ^{-1} is the inverse function of μ.

Case II: Assume that the function $g(\boldsymbol{x}, \boldsymbol{\xi}) = \xi - h(\boldsymbol{x})$. Then chance constraint (9.9) can be written in the following form,

$$\text{Pos}\left\{h(\boldsymbol{x}) \geq \xi\right\} \geq \alpha \tag{9.14}$$

where $h(\boldsymbol{x})$ is a (linear or nonlinear) function of decision vector $\boldsymbol{x}$ and ξ is a fuzzy number with membership function $\mu(\xi)$.

It is clear that, for any given confidence level α $(0 \leq \alpha \leq 1)$, there exist some values K_α (maybe $+\infty$ or $-\infty$) such that

$$\text{Pos}\left\{K_\alpha \geq \xi\right\} = \alpha. \tag{9.15}$$

We note that the possibility $\text{Pos}\left\{K_\alpha \geq \xi\right\}$ will increase if the number K_α is replaced by a larger number K'_α since

$$\begin{aligned}\text{Pos}\left\{K_\alpha \geq \xi\right\} &= \sup\left\{\mu(\xi) \mid \xi \leq K_\alpha\right\}\\ &\leq \sup\left\{\mu(\xi) \mid \xi \leq K'_\alpha\right\}\\ &= \text{Pos}\left\{K'_\alpha \geq \xi\right\}.\end{aligned}$$

The crisp equivalent of chance constraint (9.14) will be

$$h(\boldsymbol{x}) \geq K_\alpha \tag{9.16}$$

where K_α is the smallest value satisfying (9.15), i.e.,

$$K_\alpha = \inf\left\{K \mid K = \mu^{-1}(\alpha)\right\}$$

where μ^{-1} is the inverse function of μ.

Case III: Assume that, in chance constraint (9.9), the function $g(\boldsymbol{x}, \boldsymbol{\xi})$ is linear for the components of $\boldsymbol{\xi}$. For example, let $\boldsymbol{\xi} = (\xi_1, \xi_2, \cdots, \xi_t)$ be a t-dimensional vector. The linearity of $g(\boldsymbol{x}, \boldsymbol{\xi})$ on $\boldsymbol{\xi}$ implies that we can rewrite $g(\boldsymbol{x}, \boldsymbol{\xi})$ as follows,

$$g(\boldsymbol{x}, \boldsymbol{\xi}) = h_1(\boldsymbol{x})\xi_1 + h_2(\boldsymbol{x})\xi_2 + \cdots + h_t(\boldsymbol{x})\xi_t + h_0(\boldsymbol{x}) \tag{9.17}$$

where the functions $h_k(\boldsymbol{x})$ are not necessarily linear or positive for $k = 0, 1, 2, \cdots, t$. If $\xi_1, \xi_2, \cdots, \xi_t$ are general fuzzy numbers, then the membership function of $g(\boldsymbol{x}, \boldsymbol{\xi})$ will be very complex. Here we suppose that all of ξ_k's are trapezoidal fuzzy numbers, denoted by quadruples

$$\xi_k = (r_{k1}, r_{k2}, r_{k3}, r_{k4}), \quad k = 1, 2, \cdots, t.$$

Now we define two functions

$$h_k^+(\boldsymbol{x}) = \begin{cases} h_k(\boldsymbol{x}), & h_k(\boldsymbol{x}) \ge 0 \\ 0, & h_k(\boldsymbol{x}) < 0 \end{cases}$$

and

$$h_k^-(\boldsymbol{x}) = \begin{cases} 0, & h_k(\boldsymbol{x}) \ge 0 \\ -h_k(\boldsymbol{x}), & h_k(\boldsymbol{x}) < 0 \end{cases}$$

for $k = 1, 2, \cdots, t$. Then the functions $h_k^+(\boldsymbol{x})$ and $h_k^-(\boldsymbol{x})$ are all nonnegative and $h_k(\boldsymbol{x}) = h_k^+(\boldsymbol{x}) - h_k^-(\boldsymbol{x})$. Thus we have

$$\begin{aligned} g(\boldsymbol{x}, \boldsymbol{\xi}) &= \sum_{k=1}^{t} h_k(\boldsymbol{x})\xi_k + h_0(\boldsymbol{x}) \\ &= \sum_{k=1}^{t} \left[h_k^+(\boldsymbol{x}) - h_k^-(\boldsymbol{x})\right] \xi_k + h_0(\boldsymbol{x}) \\ &= \sum_{k=1}^{t} \left[h_k^+(\boldsymbol{x})\xi_k + h_k^-(\boldsymbol{x})\xi_k'\right] + h_0(\boldsymbol{x}) \end{aligned}$$

where ξ_k' are also trapezoidal fuzzy numbers,

$$\xi_k' = (-r_{k4}, -r_{k3}, -r_{k2}, -r_{k1}), \quad k = 1, 2, \cdots, t.$$

By the addition and multiplication operations of trapezoidal fuzzy numbers, the function $g(\boldsymbol{x}, \boldsymbol{\xi})$ is also a trapezoidal fuzzy number determined by the quadruple

$$g(\boldsymbol{x}, \boldsymbol{\xi}) = \begin{pmatrix} \sum_{k=1}^{t} \left[r_{k1}h_k^+(\boldsymbol{x}) - r_{k4}h_k^-(\boldsymbol{x})\right] + h_0(\boldsymbol{x}) \\ \sum_{k=1}^{t} \left[r_{k2}h_k^+(\boldsymbol{x}) - r_{k3}h_k^-(\boldsymbol{x})\right] + h_0(\boldsymbol{x}) \\ \sum_{k=1}^{t} \left[r_{k3}h_k^+(\boldsymbol{x}) - r_{k2}h_k^-(\boldsymbol{x})\right] + h_0(\boldsymbol{x}) \\ \sum_{k=1}^{t} \left[r_{k4}h_k^+(\boldsymbol{x}) - r_{k1}h_k^-(\boldsymbol{x})\right] + h_0(\boldsymbol{x}) \end{pmatrix}^T.$$

From Lemma 3.1, we know that the crisp equivalent of chance constraint (9.9) has the following form,

$$\begin{aligned}(1-\alpha)\sum_{k=1}^{t}\left[r_{k1}h_k^+(\boldsymbol{x})-r_{k4}h_k^-(\boldsymbol{x})\right]\\+\alpha\sum_{k=1}^{t}\left[r_{k2}h_k^+(\boldsymbol{x})-r_{k3}h_k^-(\boldsymbol{x})\right]+h_0(\boldsymbol{x})\le 0.\end{aligned}\tag{9.18}$$

9.3 Fuzzy Simulations

Although chance constraints can be represented as an explicit form for some special cases, we need numerical methods for general cases. Liu and Iwamura [90][91] had suggested a series of *fuzzy simulations* to check the fuzzy system constraints

$$\text{Pos}\left\{g_j(\boldsymbol{x},\boldsymbol{\xi})\le 0, j=1,2,\cdots,k\right\}\ge\alpha$$

and to handle fuzzy objective constraints

$$\text{Pos}\left\{f(\boldsymbol{x},\boldsymbol{\xi})\ge\overline{f}\right\}\ge\beta$$

as well as to handle fuzzy goal constraints

$$\text{Pos}\left\{f(\boldsymbol{x},\boldsymbol{\xi})+d^- - d^+ = b\right\}\ge\beta.$$

In this section, we introduce the technique of fuzzy simulations.

Checking Fuzzy System Constraints

From the definition of operations over fuzzy numbers, we say

$$\text{Pos}\left\{g_j(\boldsymbol{x},\boldsymbol{\xi})\le 0, j=1,2,\cdots,k\right\}\ge\alpha \tag{9.19}$$

for a given decision vector $\boldsymbol{x}$ if and only if there is a crisp vector $\boldsymbol{\xi}^0$ such that $g_j(\boldsymbol{x},\boldsymbol{\xi}^0)\le 0, j=1,2,\cdots,k$ and $\mu(\boldsymbol{\xi}^0)\ge\alpha$. Thus, we can generate a crisp vector $\boldsymbol{\xi}^0$ uniformly from the fuzzy vector $\boldsymbol{\xi}$ such that $\mu(\boldsymbol{\xi}^0)\ge\alpha$ (i.e., the α-level set of fuzzy vector $\boldsymbol{\xi}$). If the α-level set of the fuzzy vector $\boldsymbol{\xi}$ is too complex to determine, we can sample a vector $\boldsymbol{\xi}^0$ from a hypercube Ω containing the α-level set and then accept or reject it, depending on whether $\mu(\boldsymbol{\xi}^0)\ge\alpha$ or not. Certainly, in order to speed up the simulation process, the hypercube Ω should be designed as small as possible. If $\boldsymbol{\xi}^0$ satisfies that $g_j(\boldsymbol{x},\boldsymbol{\xi}^0)\le 0, j=1,2,\cdots,k$, then we can believe that $\text{Pos}\left\{g_j(\boldsymbol{x},\boldsymbol{\xi})\le 0, j=1,2,\cdots,k\right\}\ge\alpha$. If not, we will regenerate a crisp vector $\boldsymbol{\xi}^0$ from the α-level set of fuzzy vector $\boldsymbol{\xi}$ and check the constraints again. After a given number N of cycles, if there is no crisp vector $\boldsymbol{\xi}^0$ generated such that $g_j(\boldsymbol{x}, \boldsymbol{\xi}^0) \leq 0, j = 1, 2, \cdots, k$, then we believe that the given decision vector $\boldsymbol{x}$ is infeasible.

Step 1. Generate $\boldsymbol{\xi}^0$ uniformly from the α-level set of fuzzy vector $\boldsymbol{\xi}$.
Step 2. If $g_j(\boldsymbol{x}, \boldsymbol{\xi}^0) \leq 0, j = 1, 2, \cdots, k$, return FEASIBLE.
Step 3. Repeat the first and second steps N times.
Step 4. Return INFEASIBLE.

Handling Fuzzy Objective Constraints

For a fuzzy objective constraint with a vector of fuzzy parameters $\boldsymbol{\xi}$,

$$\text{Pos}\left\{f(\boldsymbol{x}, \boldsymbol{\xi}) \geq \overline{f}\right\} \geq \beta, \tag{9.20}$$

in view of the purpose of maximizing $\overline{f}$, we should find the maximal value $\overline{f}$ such that (9.20) holds for a given decision vector $\boldsymbol{x}$. First we set $\overline{f} = -\infty$. Then we generate a crisp vector $\boldsymbol{\xi}^0$ uniformly from the fuzzy vector $\boldsymbol{\xi}$ such that $\mu(\boldsymbol{\xi}^0) \geq \beta$ (i.e., the β-level set of fuzzy vector $\boldsymbol{\xi}$). We set $\overline{f} = f(\boldsymbol{x}, \boldsymbol{\xi}^0)$ provided that $\overline{f} < f(\boldsymbol{x}, \boldsymbol{\xi}^0)$. Repeat this process N times. The value $\overline{f}$ is regarded as the objective value at the point $\boldsymbol{x}$.

Step 1. Set $\overline{f} = -\infty$.
Step 2. Generate $\boldsymbol{\xi}^0$ uniformly from the β-level set of fuzzy vector $\boldsymbol{\xi}$.
Step 3. If $\overline{f} < f(\boldsymbol{x}, \boldsymbol{\xi}^0)$, then we set $\overline{f} = f(\boldsymbol{x}, \boldsymbol{\xi}^0)$.
Step 4. Repeat the second and third steps N times.
Step 5. Return $\overline{f}$.

Handling Fuzzy Goal Constraints

In chance-constrained goal programming with fuzzy coefficients there may be the following type of fuzzy goal constraint,

$$\text{Pos}\left\{f(\boldsymbol{x}, \boldsymbol{\xi}) + d^- - d^+ = b\right\} \geq \beta, \tag{9.21}$$

that is, as we defined, we should find the minimal nonnegative values of d^- and d^+ for each fixed decision $\boldsymbol{x}$ such that

$$\text{Pos}\{d^- \geq b - f(\boldsymbol{x}, \boldsymbol{\xi})\} \geq \beta, \quad \text{Pos}\{d^+ \geq f(\boldsymbol{x}, \boldsymbol{\xi}) - b\} \geq \beta.$$

First we set $d^- = d^+ = +\infty$. Then we generate a crisp vector $\boldsymbol{\xi}^0$ from the β-level set of fuzzy vector $\boldsymbol{\xi}$. If $d^- > b - f(\boldsymbol{x}, \boldsymbol{\xi}^0)$, then we set $d^- = [b - f(\boldsymbol{x}, \boldsymbol{\xi}^0)] \vee 0$. Similarly, if $d^+ > f(\boldsymbol{x}, \boldsymbol{\xi}^0) - b$, then we set $d^+ = [f(\boldsymbol{x}, \boldsymbol{\xi}^0) - b] \vee 0$. Repeat the above process N times by generating new crisp vector $\boldsymbol{\xi}^0$. The values of d^+ and d^- are regarded as the positive and negative deviations at the point $\boldsymbol{x}$, respectively. Notice that d^+ and d^- generated by this process are undoubtedly nonnegative.

Step 1. Set $d^+ = d^- = +\infty$.
Step 2. Generate $\boldsymbol{\xi}^0$ uniformly from the β-level set of fuzzy vector $\boldsymbol{\xi}$.
Step 3. If $d^+ > f(\boldsymbol{x}, \boldsymbol{\xi}^0) - b$, then we set $d^+ = [f(\boldsymbol{x}, \boldsymbol{\xi}^0) - b] \vee 0$.
Step 4. If $d^- > b - f(\boldsymbol{x}, \boldsymbol{\xi}^0)$, then we set $d^- = [b - f(\boldsymbol{x}, \boldsymbol{\xi}^0)] \vee 0$.
Step 5. Repeat the second and third and/or fourth steps N times.
Step 6. Return d^+ and d^-.

9.4 Fuzzy Simulation-based Genetic Algorithms

For CCP models with fuzzy coefficients, if the chance constraints can be converted to their respective crisp equivalents, then CCP can be solved by numerous methods to crisp mathematical programming.

In this section, we focus our attention on complex CCP models which are not assumed to be able to convert to crisp equivalents. We will introduce a fuzzy simulation-based genetic algorithm for solving CCP with fuzzy coefficients. In fact, the initialization process, selection, crossover, and mutation operations are the same as those in the genetic algorithm described in Chapter 2, except for the fact that we have to employ fuzzy simulation to check fuzzy system constraints and to handle fuzzy objective and goal constraints as discussed in Section 9.3.

Genetic Algorithm Procedure

Step 0. *Input parameters pop_size, P_c and P_m.*

Step 1. *Initialize pop_size chromosomes in which fuzzy simulations may be employed to check the feasibility.*

Step 2. *Update the chromosomes by crossover and mutation operations in which the feasibility of offspring may be checked by fuzzy simulations.*

Step 3. *Calculate the objective values for all chromosomes by fuzzy simulations.*

Step 4. *Compute the fitness of each chromosome by rank-based evaluation function based on the objective values.*

Step 5. *Select the chromosomes by spinning the roulette wheel.*

Step 6. *Repeat the second to fifth steps a given number of cycles.*

Step 7. *Report the best chromosome as the optimal solution.*

The computer code for the fuzzy simulation-based genetic algorithm for CCP models with fuzzy coefficients has been written in C language. To illustrate the effectiveness of genetic algorithm, a set of numerical examples has been done, and the results are successful. Here we give some numerical examples performed on a personal computer with the following parameters: the population size is 30, the probability of crossover P_c is 0.2, the probability of mutation P_m is 0.3, and the parameter a in the rank-based evaluation function is 0.05.

Example 1: Let us consider the following single-objective CCP with fuzzy coefficients,

$$\begin{cases} \max 2x_1 + 3x_2 \\ \text{subject to:} \\ \qquad \text{Pos}\left\{\tilde{a}x_1 + x_2 \le \tilde{b}\right\} \ge 0.90 \\ \qquad \text{Pos}\left\{x_1 + \tilde{c}x_2 \le \tilde{d}\right\} \ge 0.85 \\ \qquad x_1 + x_2 \le 100 \\ \qquad x_1, x_2 \ge 0 \end{cases} \tag{9.22}$$

where $\tilde{a}$ is a trapezoidal fuzzy number $(1, 1.5, 2.5, 3)$, $\tilde{b}$ is a fuzzy number with membership function

$$\mu_{\tilde{b}}(\xi) = \exp\left[-\frac{1}{10}|\xi - 150|\right],$$

$\tilde{c}$ is a triangular fuzzy number $(1, 2, 3)$, and $\tilde{d}$ is a fuzzy number with membership function

$$\mu_{\tilde{d}}(\xi) = \exp\left[-\frac{1}{10}|\xi - 130|\right].$$

In order to perform fuzzy simulation to check whether the given solution $\boldsymbol{x}$ is feasible, we can take α-level sets of $\tilde{a}, \tilde{b}, \tilde{c}$, and $\tilde{d}$ as $[1, 3]$, $[140, 160]$, $[1, 3]$, and $[120, 140]$, respectively. A run of the fuzzy simulation-based genetic algorithm with 200 generations shows that the best solution is

$$(x_1^*, x_2^*) = (62.56, 37.33)$$

whose value of objective function is 237.11. Furthermore, we have

$$\text{Pos}\left\{\tilde{a}x_1^* + x_2^* \le \tilde{b}\right\} = 1.00, \qquad \text{Pos}\left\{x_1^* + \tilde{c}x_2^* \le \tilde{d}\right\} = 0.85.$$

Example 2: This example is a CCGP with fuzzy coefficients,

$$\left\{\begin{array}{l} \text{lexmin}\left\{d_1^-, d_2^-\right\} \\ \text{subject to:} \\ \qquad x_1 + x_2 + d_1^- - d_1^+ = 2 \\ \qquad x_3 + d_2^- - d_2^+ = 3 \\ \qquad \text{Pos}\left\{\tilde{a}_1 x_1 + \tilde{a}_2 x_2 + \tilde{a}_3 x_3 \le \tilde{b}\right\} \ge 0.80 \\ \qquad x_1, x_2, x_3, d_1^-, d_1^+, d_2^-, d_2^+ \ge 0 \end{array}\right. \tag{9.23}$$

where $\tilde{a}_1$ is a trapezoidal fuzzy number $(1, 2, 3, 4)$, $\tilde{a}_2$ has a membership function

$$\mu_{\tilde{a}_2}(\xi) = \exp\left[-(\xi - 2)^2\right],$$

$\tilde{a}_3$ has a membership function

$$\mu_{\tilde{a}_3}(\xi) = \begin{cases} \dfrac{1}{\xi}, & \xi \ge 1 \\ 0, & \text{otherwise} \end{cases}$$

and $\tilde{b}$ is a triangular fuzzy number $(3, 4, 5)$. A run of the fuzzy simulation-based genetic algorithm with 600 generations shows that the optimal solution is

$$(x_1^*,\ x_2^*,\ x_3^*) = (0.045,\ 1.957,\ 1.073)$$

which can satisfy the first goal, but the negative deviation of the second goal is 1.927. Moreover, we have

$$\text{Pos}\left\{\tilde{a}_1 x_1^* + \tilde{a}_2 x_2^* + \tilde{a}_3 x_3^* \le \tilde{b}\right\} = 0.80.$$

Example 3: Now we consider the following CCGP with fuzzy coefficients occurring in both system constraints and goal constraints,

$$\left\{\begin{array}{l} \text{lexmin}\left\{d_1^-, d_2^-, d_3^- + d_3^+\right\} \\ \text{subject to:} \\ \qquad \text{Pos}\left\{\tilde{c}_1 x_1 x_3 + d_1^- - d_1^+ = 2\right\} \ge 0.9 \\ \qquad \text{Pos}\left\{x_2 + d_2^- - d_2^+ = \tilde{c}_2\right\} \ge 0.8 \\ \qquad x_4 + d_3^- - d_3^+ = 4 \\ \qquad \text{Pos}\left\{(\tilde{a}_1 x_1 + \tilde{a}_2 x_2)(\tilde{a}_3 x_3 + \tilde{a}_4 x_4) \le 25\right\} \ge 0.8 \\ \qquad x_1, x_2, x_3, x_4, d_i^-, d_i^+ \ge 0, \quad i = 1, 2, 3 \end{array}\right.$$

where $\tilde{a}_1 = (1, 2, 3)$ is a triangular fuzzy number, $\tilde{a}_2$ is a fuzzy number with membership function

$$\mu_{\tilde{a}_2}(z) = \exp\left[-(z-1)^2\right],$$

$\tilde{a}_3 = (2, 2.5, 3.5, 4)$ is a trapezoidal fuzzy number, $\tilde{a}_4$ is a fuzzy number with membership function

$$\mu_{\tilde{a}_4}(z) = \frac{1}{1+(z-2)^2},$$

the fuzzy coefficient in goal constraints $\tilde{c}_1 = (0.5, 1, 1.5)$ is triangular, and $\tilde{c}_2$ has a membership function,

$$\mu_{\tilde{c}_2}(z) = \exp\left[-(z-2)^2\right].$$

In order to apply fuzzy simulation technique to handling fuzzy system constraints and fuzzy goal constraints, we conservatively take the hypercubes containing the α-level sets of fuzzy numbers $\tilde{a}_1, \tilde{a}_2, \tilde{a}_3, \tilde{a}_4, \tilde{c}_1$, and $\tilde{c}_2$ as $[1.5, 2.5]$, $[0.5, 1.5]$, $[2, 4]$, $[1, 3]$, $[0.8, 1.2]$, and $[1.5, 2.5]$, respectively. For this example, each fuzzy simulation will be performed 2000 cycles. A run of the fuzzy simulation-based genetic algorithm with 800 generations shows that the optimal solution is

$$(x_1^*,\, x_2^*,\, x_3^*,\, x_4^*) = (1.1511,\, 1.5394,\, 1.6603,\, 3.0555)$$

which satisfies the first two goals, but the third objective is 0.9445. Furthermore, we have,

$$\begin{aligned}
&\text{Pos}\left\{\tilde{c}_1 x_1^* x_3^* \ge 2\right\} = 0.904 \approx 0.9,\\
&\text{Pos}\left\{x_2^* \ge \tilde{c}_2\right\} = 0.807 \approx 0.8,\\
&\text{Pos}\left\{(\tilde{a}_1 x_1^* + \tilde{a}_2 x_2^*)(\tilde{a}_3 x_3^* + \tilde{a}_4 x_4^*) \le 25\right\} = 0.801 \approx 0.8.
\end{aligned}$$

9.5 Capital Budgeting

Recall the capital budgeting problems discussed in Chapter 6. We have discussed the chance constraints

$$\Pr\left\{\eta_i x_i \ge \xi_i\right\} \ge \alpha_i, \quad i = 1, 2, \cdots, n$$

where η_i and ξ_i are assumed stochastic variables with known probability density functions and α_i are predetermined confidence levels for $i = 1, 2, \cdots, n$. It is well-known that the density functions are generated by repetitions of experiments. However, in many cases, we have no such experiment when we initiate the machines in a plant. For this case, we have to regard η_i and ξ_i as fuzzy numbers and construct their membership functions by some expert knowledge.

In this section, we assume that the membership functions of η_i and ξ_i are all given. If we hope that the possibility of satisfying the demands ξ_i are at least possibilities α_i, $i = 1, 2, \cdots, n$, respectively, then we have chance constraints in a fuzzy environment as follows,

$$\text{Pos}\{\eta_i x_i \geq \xi_i\} \geq \alpha_i, \quad i = 1, 2, \cdots, n.$$

More generally, assume that we can substitute some products for others. For example, we have p classes of demands denoted by ξ_j, and the production capacities of the type i machines for the product classes j are η_{ij}, $i = 1, 2, \cdots, n$, $j = 1, 2, \cdots, p$, respectively. Then the chance constraints are written as

$$\text{Pos}\{\eta_{1j} x_1 + \eta_{2j} x_2 + \cdots + \eta_{nj} x_n \geq \xi_j\} \geq \alpha_j, \quad j = 1, 2, \cdots, p \tag{9.24}$$

or written as a joint form

$$\text{Pos}\{\eta_{1j} x_1 + \eta_{2j} x_2 + \cdots + \eta_{nj} x_n \geq \xi_j, j = 1, 2, \cdots, p\} \geq \alpha \tag{9.25}$$

where α is a predetermined confidence level. In some special cases (for example, all fuzzy numbers are assumed trapezoidal), the chance constraints (9.24) can be converted to crisp equivalents.

The simplest integer CCP with fuzzy coefficients for capital budgeting is

$$\begin{cases} \max c_1 x_1 + c_2 x_2 + \cdots + c_n x_n \\ \text{subject to:} \\ \qquad a_1 x_1 + a_2 x_2 + \cdots + a_n x_n \leq a \\ \qquad b_1 x_1 + b_2 x_2 + \cdots + b_n x_n \leq b \\ \qquad \text{Pos}\{\eta_{1j} x_1 + \eta_{2j} x_2 + \cdots + \eta_{nj} x_n \geq \xi_j, j = 1, 2, \cdots, p\} \geq \alpha \\ \qquad x_i, i = 1, 2, \cdots, n, \quad \text{nonnegative integers.} \end{cases}$$

In order to balance the multiple conflicting objectives, capital budgeting may also be modeled by the following CCGP with fuzzy coefficients according to the target levels and priority structure set by the decision-maker,

$$\begin{cases} \text{lexmin} \left\{ d_1^+, d_2^+, d_3^- \right\} \\ \text{subject to:} \\ \qquad a_1x_1 + a_2x_2 + \cdots + a_nx_n + d_1^- - d_1^+ = a \\ \qquad b_1x_1 + b_2x_2 + \cdots + b_nx_n + d_2^- - d_2^+ = b \\ \qquad c_1x_1 + c_2x_2 + \cdots + c_nx_n + d_3^- - d_3^+ = c \\ \qquad \text{Pos}\left\{ \eta_{1j}x_1 + \eta_{2j}x_2 + \cdots + \eta_{nj}x_n \ge \xi_j, j = 1, 2, \cdots, p \right\} \ge \alpha \\ \qquad x_i, i = 1, 2, \cdots, n, \quad \text{nonnegative integers.} \end{cases}$$

Let us now consider some numerical examples. Suppose that we have five types of machines. When the objective is concerned with maximizing the total profit, the capital budgeting model is formulated as follows,

$$\begin{cases} \max\ 3x_1 + x_2 + 2x_3 + 3x_4 + x_5 \\ \text{subject to:} \\ \qquad 2x_1 + x_2 + 3x_3 + 6x_4 + 4x_5 \le 50 \\ \qquad 7x_1 + 6x_2 + 4x_3 + 8x_4 + x_5 \le 100 \\ \qquad \text{Pos}\left\{ \begin{array}{l} \eta_{11}x_1 + \eta_{21}x_2 + \eta_{31}x_3 \ge \xi_1 \\ \eta_{32}x_3 + \eta_{42}x_4 + \eta_{52}x_5 \ge \xi_2 \end{array} \right\} \ge 0.9 \\ \qquad x_1, x_2, x_3, x_4, x_5, \quad \text{nonnegative integers} \end{cases}$$

where η_{11} is a triangular fuzzy number (13,14,15), η_{21} is a fuzzy number with membership function

$$\mu_{\eta_{21}}(u) = \exp\left[-(u-8)^2\right],$$

η_{31} is a fuzzy number with membership function

$$\mu_{\eta_{31}}(u) = \begin{cases} \dfrac{1}{u-9}, & u \ge 10 \\ 0, & u < 10, \end{cases}$$

the demand of the first product ξ_1 is a fuzzy number with membership function

$$\mu_{\xi_1}(u) = \exp\left[-|u-50|\right],$$

η_{32} is a trapezoidal fuzzy number (8,9,10,11), η_{42} is a triangular fuzzy number (10,11,12), η_{52} is a fuzzy number with membership function

$$\mu_{\eta_{52}}(u) = \exp\left[-|u-10|\right],$$

and the demand of the second product ξ_2 is a triangular fuzzy number (30,40,50). A run of the fuzzy simulation-based genetic algorithm with 300 generations shows that the optimal solution is

$$(x_1^*, x_2^*, x_3^*, x_4^*, x_5^*) = (10, 0, 7, 0, 1)$$

whose total profit is 45.

Now let us set the following target levels and priority structure:

Priority 1: Budget goal, i.e., the total cost spent for machines should not exceed the amount available,

$$2x_1 + x_2 + 3x_3 + 6x_4 + 4x_5 + d_1^- - d_1^+ = 50$$

where d_1^+ will be minimized.

Priority 2: Space goal, i.e., the total space used by the machines should not exceed the space available,

$$7x_1 + 6x_2 + 4x_3 + 8x_4 + x_5 + d_2^- - d_2^+ = 100$$

where d_2^+ will be minimized.

Priority 3: Profit goal, i.e., the total profit should achieve a given level,

$$3x_1 + x_2 + 2x_3 + 3x_4 + x_5 + d_3^- - d_3^+ = 50$$

where d_3^- will be minimized.

Then we can model the capital budgeting problem by the following integer CCGP with fuzzy coefficients,

$$\begin{cases} \text{lexmin } \left\{d_1^+, d_2^+, d_3^-\right\} \\ \text{subject to:} \\ \qquad 2x_1 + x_2 + 3x_3 + 6x_4 + 4x_5 + d_1^- - d_1^+ = 50 \\ \qquad 7x_1 + 6x_2 + 4x_3 + 8x_4 + x_5 + d_2^- - d_2^+ = 100 \\ \qquad 3x_1 + x_2 + 2x_3 + 3x_4 + x_5 + d_3^- - d_3^+ = 50 \\ \qquad \text{Pos}\left\{ \begin{array}{l} \eta_{11}x_1 + \eta_{21}x_2 + \eta_{31}x_3 \geq \xi_1 \\ \eta_{32}x_3 + \eta_{42}x_4 + \eta_{52}x_5 \geq \xi_2 \end{array} \right\} \geq 0.9 \\ \qquad x_1, x_2, x_3, x_4, x_5, \quad \text{nonnegative integers} \end{cases}$$

where the parameters are defined as above. A run of the fuzzy simulation-based genetic algorithm with 400 generations shows that the optimal solution is

$$(x_1^*, x_2^*, x_3^*, x_4^*, x_5^*) = (10, 0, 7, 0, 1)$$

which can satisfy the first two goals, but the negative deviation of the third goal is 5.

9.6 Notes

As opposed to CCP models with stochastic parameters, this chapter provided a spectrum of CCP, CCMOP, and CCGP models with fuzzy coefficients.

We also listed some techniques of fuzzy simulations for checking fuzzy system constraints, for handling fuzzy objective constraints, and for handling fuzzy goal constraints. A fuzzy simulation-based genetic algorithm was also designed for solving CCP models and was illustrated by some numerical examples.

The time complexity of the fuzzy simulation-based genetic algorithm for solving CCP models is the sum of the time spent for the fuzzy simulation and the time spent for the genetic algorithm, where the computation time for fuzzy simulation has to be spent since we have assumed that there is no direct method to substitute for it.

Chapter 10

Dependent-Chance Programming in Fuzzy Environments

Following the idea of dependent-chance programming (DCP) in stochastic environment, Liu [99] provided a series of DCP, dependent-chance multiobjective programming (DCMOP), and dependent-chance goal programming (DCGP) models in fuzzy environments.

In this chapter, we will introduce the concepts of uncertain environments, events, chance functions, and induced constraints for fuzzy cases. We also outline the framework of DCP in a fuzzy environment. Finally, a fuzzy simulation-based genetic algorithm is employed for solving some numerical examples of DCP models.

10.1 Dependent-Chance Programming

Uncertain environments, events, chance functions, and induced constraints are key elements in the framework of DCP in a stochastic environment. Let us redefine them in fuzzy environments.

By *uncertain environment* (in this case the *fuzzy environment*) we mean the solution set constrained by some uncertain conditions and generally represented by

$$g_j(\boldsymbol{x}, \boldsymbol{\xi}) \leq 0, \quad j = 1, 2, \cdots, p \tag{10.1}$$

where $\boldsymbol{x}$ is a decision vector and $\boldsymbol{\xi}$ is a vector of fuzzy parameters. Although $\boldsymbol{x}$ is a decision vector, it indeed possesses some uncertain properties caused by the uncertainty of $\boldsymbol{\xi}$ since the realization of decision vector $\boldsymbol{x}$ is dependent on the realization of parameter vector $\boldsymbol{\xi}$. And, the uncertain properties (for example, possibility) of $\boldsymbol{x}$ can be derived from (10.1) and the characteristics of $\boldsymbol{\xi}$.

A complex decision system usually undertakes multiple tasks and should satisfy some interior requirements. By *events* we mean these tasks and interior requirements. Let the events be generally represented by a solution set of $\boldsymbol{x} = (x_1, x_2, \cdots, x_n)$ meeting, for example, $x_1 + x_2 = c$, which means that the demand of some client should be fulfilled.

The term *chance function* is the possibility measure of events, and is represented by the possibility of satisfying an event, for example, $f(\boldsymbol{x}) = \text{Pos}\{x_1 + x_2 = c\}$, where $\text{Pos}\{\cdot\}$ denotes the possibility of the event in $\{\cdot\}$.

Now the problem is how to represent the chance functions by the uncertain environment. Let E be a single event in a fuzzy decision system. The event E can be satisfied by an appropriate decision vector $\boldsymbol{x} = (x_1, x_2, \cdots, x_n)$. Usually, the realization of E relates only to partial elements in $\{x_1, x_2, \cdots, x_n\}$ rather than the whole. Let $V(E)$ denote the set of all decision components of $\boldsymbol{x}$ which are necessary to the event E. Thus the possibility of realizing the event E is dependent only on the realization of the elements of $V(E)$. Since there is only one event E in the fuzzy decision system, the chance function of the event E should be the maximal possibility of realization of components in $V(E)$ when $\boldsymbol{x} \in E$, otherwise we regard the chance function as zero, i.e.,

$$f(\boldsymbol{x}) = \begin{cases} \max\limits_{\boldsymbol{y} \in E^*} \text{Pos}\left\{g_j(\boldsymbol{y}, \boldsymbol{\xi}) \le 0, j = 1, 2, \cdots, p\right\}, & \boldsymbol{x} \in E \\ 0, & \boldsymbol{x} \notin E \end{cases} \tag{10.2}$$

where $\boldsymbol{x} \in E$ means that the decision vector $\boldsymbol{x}$ meets the event E, and

$$E^* = \left\{\boldsymbol{y} = (y_1, y_2, \cdots, y_n) \mid y_j = x_j \text{ if } y_j \in V(E), j = 1, 2, \cdots, n\right\}. \tag{10.3}$$

Note that for any element $\boldsymbol{y} = (y_1, y_2, \cdots, y_n)$ in E^*, the decision components $y_j \in V(E)$ are fixed and equal to x_j and the remaining components are arbitrary such that $\boldsymbol{y} \in E$. Usually, it is not difficult to determine the values x_j^* of decision components out of $V(E)$ for the optimal solution $\boldsymbol{y}^*(\boldsymbol{x})$ in (10.2) for each given decision $\boldsymbol{x}$ such that

$$\boldsymbol{y}^*(\boldsymbol{x}) = (y_1, y_2, \cdots, y_n): \quad y_j = \begin{cases} x_j, & y_j \in V(E) \\ x_j^*, & y_j \notin V(E), \end{cases} \qquad j = 1, 2, \cdots, n.$$

In fact, the decision components x_j^* usually take the values at some extreme places. Therefore, the chance function of the event E should be

$$f(\boldsymbol{x}) = \begin{cases} \text{Pos}\left\{g_j(\boldsymbol{y}^*(\boldsymbol{x}), \boldsymbol{\xi}) \le 0, j = 1, 2, \cdots, p\right\}, & \boldsymbol{x} \in E \\ 0, & \boldsymbol{x} \notin E \end{cases} \tag{10.4}$$

where the constraints

$$g_j(\boldsymbol{y}^*(\boldsymbol{x}), \boldsymbol{\xi}) \le 0, \quad j = 1, 2, \cdots, p \tag{10.5}$$

are called *induced constraints* on the event E at the point $\boldsymbol{x}$. Until now we have represented a chance function for a single event clearly.

A typical formulation of single-objective DCP in a fuzzy environment is given as follows:

$$\begin{cases} \max\ f(\boldsymbol{x}) \\ \text{subject to:} \\ \qquad g_j(\boldsymbol{x}, \boldsymbol{\xi}) \le 0, \quad j = 1, 2, \cdots, p \end{cases} \tag{10.6}$$

where $\boldsymbol{x}$ is an n-dimensional decision vector, $\boldsymbol{\xi}$ is a fuzzy vector of parameters, $f(\boldsymbol{x})$ is a chance function of certain event, and the uncertain environment is described by the fuzzy environment constrained as $g_j(\boldsymbol{x}, \boldsymbol{\xi}) \le 0, j = 1, 2, \cdots, p$. Note that in a DCP model the feasible set, represented by the uncertain environment, is never assumed crisp.

10.2 Dependent-Chance Multiobjective Programming

Since a complex decision system usually undertakes multiple tasks, there undoubtedly exist multiple potential objectives (some of them are chance functions) in the decision process. A typical formulation of DCMOP with fuzzy parameters is given as follows,

$$\begin{cases} \max\ f(\boldsymbol{x}) = [f_1(\boldsymbol{x}), f_2(\boldsymbol{x}), \cdots, f_m(\boldsymbol{x})] \\ \text{subject to:} \\ \qquad g_j(\boldsymbol{x}, \boldsymbol{\xi}) \le 0, \quad j = 1, 2, \cdots, p \end{cases} \tag{10.7}$$

where $f(\boldsymbol{x})$ is a vector of m functions $f_i(\boldsymbol{x})$, $i = 1, 2, \cdots, m$ in which some of them are chance functions.

In order to represent the chance functions for multiple events, let us introduce the fuzzy relationship among the decision components $x_1, x_2, \cdots, x_n$. Recall the following stochastic relationship among the decision components discussed in Chapter 7. There is a known partition of n components of a decision vector into k groups such that these k groups are mutually stochastically independent and in each group any elements are stochastically dependent and have the same chance to appear if they need to be realized simultaneously. Now for the fuzzy case, we say that decision components are fuzzy dependent if the realization of each component is dependent on the others, where dependence means that the chance (here the possibility) of each component is a function of all of them. We call the set of fuzzy dependent components a fuzzy dependent group. Two groups are called fuzzy independent if each element in one group is not fuzzy dependent on any element in the other group. k groups are called mutually fuzzy independent if any two groups are fuzzy independent. Analogous to stochastic relationship, we assume the following fuzzy relationship for the fuzzy case.

Fuzzy Relationship: *There is a known partition of n components of a decision vector into k groups such that these k groups are mutually fuzzy independent and in each group any elements are fuzzy dependent and have the same chance to appear if they need to be realized simultaneously.*

Based on the fuzzy relationship, let $D(E)$ denote the set of all components which are fuzzy dependent on at least one element in $V(E)$ for an event E. Notice that the set $D(E)$ can be determined easily.

For the multiobjective case, without loss of generality, we assume that there exist m events E_i with chance functions $f_i(\boldsymbol{x})$, $i = 1, 2, \cdots, m$, respectively. We write,

$$E = E_1 \cap E_2 \cap \cdots \cap E_m$$

and

$$V(E) = V(E_1) \cup V(E_2) \cup \cdots \cup V(E_m),$$

where $\boldsymbol{x} \in E$ means that the decision vector $\boldsymbol{x}$ can satisfy all of the events $E_1, E_2, \cdots, E_m$, and $V(E)$ is the set of all necessary components to the m events. Based on the fuzzy relationship, let $D(E)$, $D(E_i), i = 1, 2, \cdots, m$ be the sets of all components which are fuzzy dependent on at least one element of $V(E)$, $V(E_i), i = 1, 2, \cdots, m$, respectively. Since all events are at the same priority level, we should realize each event E_i as much as possible but not sacrifice the chances of other events. On the one hand, we should treat all elements in $D(E_i)$ at an equitable level; on the other hand, we are not interested in any elements out of $V(E)$ because they do not make any contributions to the m events. By the fuzzy relationship, we know that all elements in $D(E_i) \cap V(E)$ (a subset of $V(E)$) are fuzzy independent on any other elements of $V(E)$. Hence we can perform the elements in $D(E_i) \cap V(E)$ as much as possible for the event E_i, $i = 1, 2, \cdots, m$, respectively. Therefore we have

$$f_i(\boldsymbol{x}) = \begin{cases} \max\limits_{\boldsymbol{y} \in E_i^*} \text{Pos}\left\{g_j(\boldsymbol{y}, \boldsymbol{\xi}) \le 0,\ j = 1, 2, \cdots, p\right\}, & \boldsymbol{x} \in E_i \\ 0, & \boldsymbol{x} \notin E_i \end{cases} \tag{10.8}$$

where the sets E_i^* are defined by

$$E_i^* = \left\{ \boldsymbol{y} = (y_1, y_2, \cdots, y_n) \;\middle|\; \begin{array}{r} y_j = x_j \text{ if } y_j \in D(E_i) \cap V(E) \\ j = 1, 2, \cdots, n \end{array} \right\} \tag{10.9}$$

for $i = 1, 2, \cdots, m$, respectively. That is, for any element $\boldsymbol{y} = (y_1, y_2, \cdots, y_n)$ in E_i^*, the decision components $y_j \in D(E_i) \cap V(E)$ are fixed and equal to x_j and the remaining components are arbitrary such that $\boldsymbol{y} \in E_i$. It is also easy to determine $\boldsymbol{y}_i^*(\boldsymbol{x})$ for each given decision $\boldsymbol{x}$ such that the induced constraints on the events E_i have the following forms,

$$g_j(\boldsymbol{y}_i^*(\boldsymbol{x}), \boldsymbol{\xi}) \le 0, \quad j = 1, 2, \cdots, p \tag{10.10}$$

and the chance functions of the events E_i should be

$$f_i(\boldsymbol{x}) = \begin{cases} \text{Pos}\left\{g_j(\boldsymbol{y}_i^*(\boldsymbol{x}), \boldsymbol{\xi}) \le 0, j = 1, 2, \cdots, p\right\}, & \boldsymbol{x} \in E_i \\ 0, & \boldsymbol{x} \notin E_i \end{cases} \tag{10.11}$$

for $i = 1, 2, \cdots, m$, respectively.

10.3 Dependent-Chance Goal Programming

DCGP in fuzzy environment may be considered as an extension of goal programming in a complex uncertain decision system. When some management targets are given, the objective function may minimize the deviations, positive, negative, or both, with a certain priority structure. Thus we can formulate a fuzzy decision system as a DCGP according to the priority structure and target levels set by the decision-maker,

$$\begin{cases} \min \sum\limits_{j=1}^{l} P_j \sum\limits_{i=1}^{m} (u_{ij} d_i^+ + v_{ij} d_i^-) \\ \text{subject to:} \\ \qquad f_i(\boldsymbol{x}) + d_i^- - d_i^+ = b_i, \quad i = 1, 2, \cdots, m \\ \qquad g_j(\boldsymbol{x}, \boldsymbol{\xi}) \le 0, \qquad\qquad j = 1, 2, \cdots, p \\ \qquad d_i^-, d_i^+ \ge 0, \qquad\qquad i = 1, 2, \cdots, m \end{cases} \tag{10.12}$$

where

P_j = the preemptive priority factor which expresses the relative importance of various goals, $P_j \gg P_{j+1}$, for all j,

u_{ij} = weighting factor corresponding to positive deviation for goal i with priority j assigned,

v_{ij} = weighting factor corresponding to negative deviation for goal i with priority j assigned,

d_i^+ = positive deviation from the target of goal i,

d_i^- = negative deviation from the target of goal i,

f_i = a chance function or a conventional real-valued function $\Re^n \to \Re$ in goal constraints,

b_i = the target value according to goal i,
l = number of priorities,
m = number of goal constraints.

For DCGP models, since there are multiple priority levels, we should consider the goals in turn from higher-priority level to lower-priority level.

In the first priority level, we assume that there are t events represented by $E_1, E_2, \cdots, E_t$. Define

$$E = E_1 \cap E_2 \cap \cdots \cap E_t$$

and

$$V(E) = V(E_1) \cup V(E_2) \cup \cdots \cup V(E_t).$$

A similar discussion with a multiobjective case can yield the induced constraints and chance functions $f_1(\boldsymbol{x}), f_2(\boldsymbol{x}), \cdots, f_t(\boldsymbol{x})$ for the t events. Therefore we have

$$f_i(\boldsymbol{x}) = \begin{cases} \max\limits_{\boldsymbol{y} \in E_i^*} \text{Pos}\left\{g_j(\boldsymbol{y}, \boldsymbol{\xi}) \le 0,\ j = 1, 2, \cdots, p\right\}, & \boldsymbol{x} \in E_i \\ 0, & \boldsymbol{x} \notin E_i \end{cases} \tag{10.13}$$

where the sets E_i^* are defined by

$$E_i^* = \left\{ \boldsymbol{y} = (y_1, y_2, \cdots, y_n) \;\middle|\; \begin{array}{r} y_j = x_j \text{ if } y_j \in D(E_i) \cap V(E) \\ j = 1, 2, \cdots, n \end{array} \right\} \tag{10.14}$$

for $i = 1, 2, \cdots, t$, respectively. That is, for any element $\boldsymbol{y} = (y_1, y_2, \cdots, y_n)$ in E_i^*, the decision components $y_j \in D(E_i) \cap V(E)$ are fixed and equal to x_j and the remaining components are arbitrary such that $\boldsymbol{y} \in E_i$. It is also easy to determine $\boldsymbol{y}_i^*(\boldsymbol{x})$ for each given decision $\boldsymbol{x}$ such that the induced constraints on the events E_i have the following forms,

$$g_j(\boldsymbol{y}_i^*(\boldsymbol{x}), \boldsymbol{\xi}) \le 0, \quad j = 1, 2, \cdots, p \tag{10.15}$$

and the chance functions of the events E_i should be

$$f_i(\boldsymbol{x}) = \begin{cases} \text{Pos}\left\{g_j(\boldsymbol{y}_i^*(\boldsymbol{x}), \boldsymbol{\xi}) \le 0,\ j = 1, 2, \cdots, p\right\}, & \boldsymbol{x} \in E_i \\ 0, & \boldsymbol{x} \notin E_i \end{cases} \tag{10.16}$$

for $i = 1, 2, \cdots, t$, respectively. Thus we can calculate all the chance functions $f_i(\boldsymbol{x})$ and obtain the deviations d_i^+ and d_i^- for $i = 1, 2, \cdots, t$.

In the second priority level, we assume that there are events E_{t+1}, E_{t+2}, $\cdots$, $E_{t'}$. A similar process can produce the induced constraints and chance functions $f_{t+1}(\boldsymbol{x}), f_{t+2}(\boldsymbol{x}), \cdots, f_{t'}(\boldsymbol{x})$ for the events $E_{t+1}, E_{t+2}, \cdots, E_{t'}$, respectively, provided that we follow the state resulting from the first priority decisions by defining

$$E = E_1 \cap E_2 \cap \cdots \cap E_t \cap E_{t+1} \cap E_{t+2} \cap \cdots \cap E_{t'}$$

and

$V(E) = V(E_1) \cup V(E_2) \cup \cdots \cup V(E_t) \cup V(E_{t+1}) \cup V(E_{t+2}) \cup \cdots \cup V(E_{t'})$.

Generally, the goals in the successive priority levels will be discussed in a similar way provided that we follow the state resulting from the higher-priority decisions.

10.4 Fuzzy Simulation for Chance Functions

Fuzzy simulation [90][91] has been applied to handling fuzzy system constraints like $\text{Pos}\{g_j(\boldsymbol{x}, \boldsymbol{\xi}) \leq 0, j = 1, 2, \cdots, p\} \geq \alpha$ and fuzzy objective constraints like $\text{Pos}\{f(\boldsymbol{x}, \boldsymbol{\xi}) \geq \bar{f}\} \geq \alpha$ as well as fuzzy goal constraints like $\text{Pos}\{f(\boldsymbol{x}, \boldsymbol{\xi}) + d^- - d^+ = b\} \geq \alpha$.

In this section, we will show how to compute the chance functions for given events by the technique of fuzzy simulation. Now let E be an event in a fuzzy decision system. Suppose that the induced constraints on the event E at the point $\boldsymbol{x}$ are

$$g_j(\boldsymbol{y}, \boldsymbol{\xi}) \leq 0, \quad j = 1, 2, \cdots, p$$

where $\boldsymbol{y}$ is derived from the point $\boldsymbol{x}$. Then the chance function of the event E should be

$$f(\boldsymbol{x}) = \begin{cases} \text{Pos}\{g_j(\boldsymbol{y}, \boldsymbol{\xi}) \leq 0, \, j = 1, 2, \cdots, p\}, & \boldsymbol{x} \in E \\ 0, & \boldsymbol{x} \notin E. \end{cases}$$

If $\boldsymbol{x} \notin E$, then we get $f(\boldsymbol{x}) = 0$ immediately. For each fixed decision $\boldsymbol{x} \in E$, we set $f(\boldsymbol{x}) = 0$ at first. Then we generate a crisp vector $\boldsymbol{\xi}^0$ from the fuzzy vector $\boldsymbol{\xi}$. In practice, we are not interested in the decision vectors with too low possibility. Thus we can predetermine a level, say α_0, and then generate $\boldsymbol{\xi}^0$ uniformly from the α_0-level set of fuzzy vector $\boldsymbol{\xi}$. If the α_0-level set of the fuzzy vector $\boldsymbol{\xi}$ is too complex to determine, we can sample a vector $\boldsymbol{\xi}^0$ from a hypercube Ω containing the α_0-level set and then accept or reject it, depending on whether $\mu(\boldsymbol{\xi}^0) \geq \alpha_0$ or not. Certainly, the smaller the hypercube, the more effective the fuzzy simulation. If $g_j(\boldsymbol{y}, \boldsymbol{\xi}^0) \leq 0, j = 1, 2, \cdots, p$ and $f(\boldsymbol{x}) < \mu(\boldsymbol{\xi}^0)$, then we set $f(\boldsymbol{x}) = \mu(\boldsymbol{\xi}^0)$. Repeating this process a given number N of times, the value $f(\boldsymbol{x})$ is regarded as its estimation. We now summarize the fuzzy simulation as follows.

Step 1. Set $f(\boldsymbol{x}) = 0$.
Step 2. Generate $\boldsymbol{\xi}^0$ uniformly from the α_0-level set of fuzzy vector $\boldsymbol{\xi}$.
Step 3. If $g_j(\boldsymbol{y}, \boldsymbol{\xi}^0) \leq 0, j = 1, 2, \cdots, p$ and $f(\boldsymbol{x}) < \mu(\boldsymbol{\xi}^0)$, then we set

$$f(\boldsymbol{x}) = \mu(\boldsymbol{\xi}^0).$$

Step 4. Repeat the second and third steps for N times.
Step 5. Return $f(\boldsymbol{x})$.

10.5 Fuzzy Simulation-based Genetic Algorithms

For CCP, CCMOP, and CCGP models, Iwamura and Liu [63] provided a stochastic simulation-based genetic algorithm for stochastic cases; Liu and Iwamura [90][91] provided a fuzzy simulation-based genetic algorithm for fuzzy models. The DCP, DCMOP, and DCGP models in a stochastic environment have also been solved by the stochastic simulation-based genetic algorithm (see [86][88][89]).

In fact, the fuzzy simulation-based genetic algorithm is also suitable for solving DCP models in a fuzzy environment provided that we compute the chance functions by the technique of fuzzy simulation.

Genetic Algorithm Procedure

Step 0. *Input parameters pop_size, P_c and P_m.*

Step 1. *Initialize pop_size chromosomes.*

Step 2. *Update the chromosomes by crossover and mutation operations.*

Step 3. *Calculate the objective values for all chromosomes by fuzzy simulation.*

Step 4. *Compute the fitness of each chromosome by rank-based evaluation function based on the objective values.*

Step 5. *Select the chromosomes by spinning the roulette wheel.*

Step 6. *Repeat the second to fifth steps a given number of cycles.*

Step 7. *Report the best chromosome as the optimal solution.*

The computer code for the fuzzy simulation-based genetic algorithm for DCP in a fuzzy environment has been written in C language. Here we give some numerical examples performed on a personal computer with the following parameters: the population size is 30, the probability of crossover P_c is 0.3, the probability of mutation P_m is 0.2, and the parameter a in the rank-based evaluation function is 0.05. Each fuzzy simulation in the evolution process will be performed 2000 cycles.

Example 1: Let us first consider the following simple example of a single-objective DCP model,

$$\begin{cases} \max\ f(\boldsymbol{x}) = \text{Pos}\left\{x_1^2 + x_2^2 + x_3^2 = 1\right\} \\ \text{subject to:} \\ \qquad x_1 + x_2 + x_3 \le \tilde{a} \\ \qquad \tilde{b}(x_1 + x_2)x_3 \ge \tilde{c} \\ \qquad x_1, x_2, x_3 > 0 \end{cases}$$

where $\tilde{a}$ and $\tilde{b}$ are two fuzzy numbers with membership functions

$$\mu_{\tilde{a}}(\xi) = \exp\left(-|\xi - 1|\right), \quad \mu_{\tilde{b}}(\xi) = \frac{1}{1 + (\xi - 10)^2},$$

respectively, and $\tilde{c}$ is a trapezoidal fuzzy number $(0, 1, 2, 3)$.

Clearly, the single event is to meet $x_1^2 + x_2^2 + x_3^2 = 1$ with nonnegativity condition $x_1, x_2, x_3 > 0$. The induced constraints on the event are

$$\begin{cases} x_1 + x_2 + x_3 \le \tilde{a} \\ \tilde{b}(x_1 + x_2)x_3 \ge \tilde{c}. \end{cases}$$

Thus the chance function $f(\boldsymbol{x})$ of this event can be represented by

$$f(\boldsymbol{x}) = \begin{cases} \text{Pos}\left\{ \begin{array}{l} x_1 + x_2 + x_3 \le \tilde{a} \\ \tilde{b}(x_1 + x_2)x_3 \ge \tilde{c} \end{array} \right\}, & x_1^2 + x_2^2 + x_3^2 = 1,\ x_1, x_2, x_3 > 0 \\ 0, & \text{otherwise} \end{cases}$$

which can be computed by the fuzzy simulation technique. We can sample the chromosome $V = (x_1, x_2, x_3)$ from the hypercube $[0, 1] \times [0, 1] \times [0, 1]$ and translate it to a solution meeting the constraint $x_1^2 + x_2^2 + x_3^2 = 1$ in the following way,

$$x_i' = \frac{x_i}{\sqrt{x_1^2 + x_2^2 + x_3^2}}, \qquad i = 1, 2, 3$$

which ensures that ${x_1'}^2 + {x_2'}^2 + {x_3'}^2 = 1$.

A run of the fuzzy simulation-based genetic algorithm with 400 generations shows that the optimal solution is

$$(x_1^*,\ x_2^*,\ x_3^*) = (0.08656,\ 0.00331,\ 0.99624)$$

which ensures that the possibility of satisfying the event achieves $f(\boldsymbol{x}^*) = 0.9175$.

Example 2: Let us now turn our attention to the following DCGP,

$$\begin{cases} \text{lexmin}\left\{d_1^-, d_2^- + d_3^-, d_4^+\right\} \\ \text{subject to:} \\ \qquad f_1(\boldsymbol{x}) + d_1^- - d_1^+ = 0.98 \\ \qquad f_2(\boldsymbol{x}) + d_2^- - d_2^+ = 0.95 \\ \qquad f_3(\boldsymbol{x}) + d_3^- - d_3^+ = 0.90 \\ \qquad f_4(\boldsymbol{x}) + d_4^- - d_4^+ = 0 \\ \qquad x_1 + x_2 + x_5 \le \tilde{a} \\ \qquad x_3 + x_4 \le \tilde{b} \\ \qquad x_6 + x_7 \le \tilde{c} \\ \qquad x_i \ge 0, \quad i = 1, 2, \cdots, 7 \\ \qquad d_i^-, d_i^+ \ge 0, \quad i = 1, 2, 3, 4 \end{cases}$$

where $\tilde{a}$ is a trapezoidal fuzzy number $(3,4,5,6)$, $\tilde{b}$ is a triangular fuzzy number $(2,3,4)$, and $\tilde{c}$ is a fuzzy number with membership function $\mu_{\tilde{c}}(\xi) = 1/[1+(\xi-2)^2]$, and

$$\begin{cases} f_1(\boldsymbol{x}) = \text{Pos}\{x_1^2 + x_3^2 = 9\} \\ f_2(\boldsymbol{x}) = \text{Pos}\{x_2 + x_4 = 3\} \\ f_3(\boldsymbol{x}) = \text{Pos}\{x_5^2 + x_6 = 7\} \\ f_4(\boldsymbol{x}) = x_4 + x_6. \end{cases}$$

Note that the decision component x_7 never appears in the goal constraints.

From the fuzzy environment, we know the following fuzzy relationship: the seven decision components can be divided into three groups $\{x_1, x_2, x_5\}$, $\{x_3, x_4\}$, and $\{x_6, x_7\}$ such that these three groups are mutually fuzzy independent and in each group any elements are fuzzy dependent and have the same chance to appear if they need to be realized simultaneously.

In the first priority level, there is only one event denoted by E_1 in the fuzzy environment, which should be fulfilled by $x_1^2 + x_3^2 = 9$. It is clear that $V(E_1) = \{x_1, x_3\}$ and the induced constraints on the event E_1 should be

$$\begin{cases} x_1 \le \tilde{a} \\ x_3 \le \tilde{b} \end{cases}$$

since the remaining components can be regarded as 0 temporarily for the event E_1 at the current priority level. Thus the chance function $f_1(\boldsymbol{x})$ of the event E_1 should be

$$f_1(\boldsymbol{x}) = \text{Pos}\left\{x_1^2 + x_3^2 = 9\right\} = \begin{cases} \text{Pos}\left\{x_1 \le \tilde{a}, x_3 \le \tilde{b}\right\}, & x_1^2 + x_3^2 = 9, \boldsymbol{x} \ge 0 \\ 0, & \text{otherwise.} \end{cases}$$

At the second priority level, there are two events E_2 and E_3 which should be fulfilled by $x_2 + x_4 = 3$ and $x_5^2 + x_6 = 7$, respectively. We also have $V(E_2) = \{x_2, x_4\}$ and $V(E_3) = \{x_5, x_6\}$. Write $E = E_1 \cap E_2 \cap E_3$, then $V(E) = V(E_1) \cup V(E_2) \cup V(E_3) = \{x_1, x_2, x_3, x_4, x_5, x_6\}$. Since

$$\begin{aligned} D(E_2) \cap V(E) &= \{x_1, x_2, x_5, x_3, x_4\} \cap \{x_1, x_2, x_3, x_4, x_5, x_6\} \\ &= \{x_1, x_2, x_3, x_4, x_5\}, \end{aligned}$$

the induced constraints on the event E_2 should be

$$\begin{cases} x_1 + x_2 + x_5 \le \tilde{a} \\ x_3 + x_4 \le \tilde{b} \end{cases}$$

which yield the chance function $f_2(\boldsymbol{x})$ of the event E_2 as follows,

$$\begin{aligned} f_2(\boldsymbol{x}) &= \text{Pos}\,\{x_2 + x_4 = 3\} \\ &= \begin{cases} \text{Pos}\left\{x_1 + x_2 + x_5 \le \tilde{a}, x_3 + x_4 \le \tilde{b}\right\}, & x_2 + x_4 = 3, \boldsymbol{x} \ge 0 \\ 0, & \text{otherwise.} \end{cases} \end{aligned}$$

It follows from

$$D(E_3) \cap V(E) = \{x_1, x_2, x_5, x_6, x_7\} \cap \{x_1, x_2, x_3, x_4, x_5, x_6\} = \{x_1, x_2, x_5, x_6\}$$

that the induced constraints on the event E_3 should be

$$\begin{cases} x_1 + x_2 + x_5 \le \tilde{a} \\ x_6 \le \tilde{c} \end{cases}$$

which yield the chance function $f_3(\boldsymbol{x})$ of the event E_3 as follows,

$$\begin{aligned} f_3(\boldsymbol{x}) &= \text{Pos}\left\{x_5^2 + x_6 = 7\right\} \\ &= \begin{cases} \text{Pos}\,\{x_1 + x_2 + x_5 \le \tilde{a}, x_6 \le \tilde{c}\}, & x_5^2 + x_6 = 7, \boldsymbol{x} \ge 0 \\ 0, & \text{otherwise.} \end{cases} \end{aligned}$$

At the third priority level there is no chance function. Thus we can get the deviations immediately.

We may sample the chromosome $V = (x_1, x_2, \cdots, x_6)$ from the hypercube $[0,1]^6$ and translate it to a feasible solution in the following way,

$$\begin{aligned} x_1' &= \frac{x_1}{\sqrt{Q_1}}, & x_2' &= \frac{x_2}{Q_2}, & x_3' &= \frac{x_3}{\sqrt{Q_1}} \\ x_4' &= \frac{x_4}{Q_2}, & x_5' &= \frac{x_5}{\sqrt{Q_3}}, & x_6' &= \frac{x_6}{Q_3} \end{aligned}$$

where $Q_1 = (x_1^2 + x_3^2)/9$, $Q_2 = (x_2 + x_4)/3$ and $Q_3 = (x_5^2 + x_6)/7$, which ensures that ${x_1'}^2 + {x_3'}^2 = 9$, $x_2' + x_4' = 3$ and ${x_5'}^2 + x_6' = 7$.

A run of the fuzzy simulation-based genetic algorithm with 1000 generations shows that the optimal solution is

$$\boldsymbol{x}^* = (0.0000, 2.9186, 3.0000, 0.0814, 2.1611, 2.3296, 0.0000)$$

which can satisfy the first goal, but the second and third objectives are 0.0315 and 2.4110, respectively. Furthermore, we have

$$f_1(\boldsymbol{x}^*) = 1.0000, \quad f_2(\boldsymbol{x}^*) = 0.9185, \quad f_3(\boldsymbol{x}^*) = 0.9020, \quad f_4(\boldsymbol{x}^*) = 2.4110.$$

10.6 Notes

In this chapter we provided a spectrum of DCP, DCMOP, and DCGP models in a fuzzy environment as opposed to DCP models in a stochastic environment. We also introduced the concepts of uncertain environment, event, chance function, induced constraints, and uncertain relationship for fuzzy cases. Finally we illustrated the effectiveness of the fuzzy simulation-based genetic algorithm for some DCP models.

Chapter 11

Fuzzy Programming with Fuzzy Decisions

Traditionally, mathematical programming models produce crisp decision vectors such that some objectives achieve the optimal values. However, for practical purposes, sometimes we should provide a fuzzy decision rather than a crisp one. Bouchon-Meunier et al. [15] surveyed various approaches to maximizing a numerical function over a fuzzy set. Buckley and Hayashi [17] presented a fuzzy genetic algorithm for maximizing a real-valued function by selecting an optimal fuzzy set and applying the fuzzy genetic algorithm to fuzzy optimization, fuzzy maximum flow problem, fuzzy regression, and tuning a fuzzy controller.

More generally, Liu and Iwamura [101] provided a spectrum of chance-constrained programming (CCP), chance-constrained multiobjective programming (CCMOP), and chance constrained goal programming (CCGP) with fuzzy decisions. In addition, Liu [100] constructed a framework of dependent-chance programming (DCP) models with fuzzy decisions and extended it to dependent-chance multiobjective programming (DCMOP) and dependent-chance goal programming (DCGP).

In this chapter, we introduce both CCP and DCP models with fuzzy decisions. Fuzzy simulation-based genetic algorithms have also been designed for solving these models and are illustrated by some numerical examples.

11.1 Fuzzy Decisions

On the one hand, actual controllers are not completely precise. On the other hand, management decisions sometimes cannot be precisely performed in practice even if we had provided crisp values. It is thus reasonable to suppose that we should provide fuzzy rather than crisp decisions not only for control problems but also for decision making. Furthermore, each decision may be restricted in a reference collection of fuzzy sets (not necessarily finite or countable) which are determined by the property of decision systems. For example,

(a) A decision may be represented by a linguistic variable such as *large*, *medium*, *small*, *nil*.

(b) A decision may be assigned a fuzzy set in the collection described by membership functions

$$\mu(x) = \frac{1}{1 + \|x - t\|} \tag{11.1}$$

where $t \in [0, 10]$.

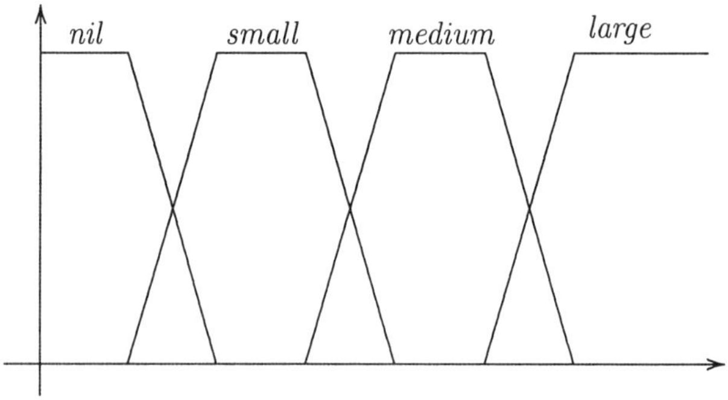

Figure 11.1: Membership Functions for *large*, *medium*, *small*, and *nil*

Assume that a fuzzy decision is described by an n-dimensional vector $\tilde{\boldsymbol{x}} = (\tilde{x}_1, \tilde{x}_2, \cdots, \tilde{x}_n)$ in which each component $\tilde{x}_i$ will be assigned an element in the reference collection of fuzzy sets X_i, $i = 1, 2, \cdots, n$, respectively. Notice that the reference collections are all predetermined. Thus each fuzzy decision vector must be taken from the Cartesian product

$$\mathcal{X} = X_1 \otimes X_2 \otimes \cdots \otimes X_n. \tag{11.2}$$

11.2 Chance-Constrained Programming Models

A single-objective CCP with fuzzy decisions may be written as follows,

$$\begin{cases} \max \overline{f} \\ \text{subject to:} \\ \qquad \text{Pos}\left\{f(\tilde{\boldsymbol{x}}, \boldsymbol{\xi}) \geq \overline{f}\right\} \geq \beta \\ \qquad \text{Pos}\left\{g_j(\tilde{\boldsymbol{x}}, \boldsymbol{\xi}) \leq 0, j = 1, 2, \cdots, p\right\} \geq \alpha \end{cases} \tag{11.3}$$

where $\tilde{\boldsymbol{x}}$ is a fuzzy decision vector in the reference collection $\mathcal{X}$ defined by (11.2), $\boldsymbol{\xi}$ is a vector of fuzzy parameters, $f(\tilde{\boldsymbol{x}}, \boldsymbol{\xi})$ is the return function, $g_j(\tilde{\boldsymbol{x}}, \boldsymbol{\xi})$ are constraint functions, $j = 1, 2, \cdots, p$, α and β are predetermined confidence levels for fuzzy constraints and fuzzy objective, respectively, and $\text{Pos}\{\cdot\}$ denotes the possibility of the event in $\{\cdot\}$.

A fuzzy solution $\tilde{\boldsymbol{x}}$ is feasible if and only if the possibility measure of the event $\{g_j(\tilde{\boldsymbol{x}}, \boldsymbol{\xi}) \leq 0, j = 1, 2, \cdots, p\}$ is at least α. For each fixed fuzzy solution $\tilde{\boldsymbol{x}}$, the objective value $\overline{f}$ should be the maximum value that the objective function $f(\tilde{\boldsymbol{x}}, \boldsymbol{\xi})$ achieves with at least possibility β.

Sometimes we formulate the fuzzy decision problem as a CCP with separate chance constraints as follows,

$$\begin{cases} \max \overline{f} \\ \text{subject to:} \\ \qquad \text{Pos}\left\{f(\tilde{\boldsymbol{x}}, \boldsymbol{\xi}) \geq \overline{f}\right\} \geq \beta \\ \qquad \text{Pos}\left\{g_j(\tilde{\boldsymbol{x}}, \boldsymbol{\xi}) \leq 0\right\} \geq \alpha_j, \quad j = 1, 2, \cdots, p \end{cases} \tag{11.4}$$

where α_j are predetermined confidence levels to the j-th constraints for $j = 1, 2, \cdots, p$, respectively.

Clearly, if the cost function $f(\tilde{\boldsymbol{x}}, \boldsymbol{\xi})$ is to be minimized, then the associated CCP model should be

$$\begin{cases} \min \overline{f} \\ \text{subject to:} \\ \qquad \text{Pos}\left\{f(\tilde{\boldsymbol{x}}, \boldsymbol{\xi}) \leq \overline{f}\right\} \geq \beta \\ \qquad \text{Pos}\left\{g_j(\tilde{\boldsymbol{x}}, \boldsymbol{\xi}) \leq 0\right\} \geq \alpha_j, \quad j = 1, 2, \cdots, p \end{cases} \tag{11.5}$$

where the objective value $\overline{f}$ should be the minimal value that the cost function $f(\tilde{\boldsymbol{x}}, \boldsymbol{\xi})$ achieves with at least possibility β.

As an extension of single-objective CCP, CCMOP may be written as follows:

$$\begin{cases} \max\ \left[\overline{f}_1, \overline{f}_2, \cdots, \overline{f}_m\right] \\ \text{subject to:} \\ \qquad \text{Pos}\left\{f_i(\tilde{\boldsymbol{x}}, \boldsymbol{\xi}) \geq \overline{f}_i\right\} \geq \beta_i, \quad i = 1, 2, \cdots, m \\ \qquad \text{Pos}\left\{g_j(\tilde{\boldsymbol{x}}, \boldsymbol{\xi}) \leq 0\right\} \geq \alpha_j, \quad j = 1, 2, \cdots, p \end{cases} \tag{11.6}$$

where $f_i(\tilde{\boldsymbol{x}}, \boldsymbol{\xi})$ are return functions, β_i are confidence levels for the ith objectives, and the objective values $\overline{f}_i$ should be the maximum values that the return functions $f_i(\tilde{\boldsymbol{x}}, \boldsymbol{\xi})$ achieve with at least possibilities β_i, $i = 1, 2, \cdots, m$, respectively.

We can also formulate a fuzzy decision system as a CCGP according to the priority structure and target levels set by the decision-maker,

$$\begin{cases} \min \sum_{j=1}^{l} P_j \sum_{i=1}^{m} (u_{ij} d_i^+ + v_{ij} d_i^-) \\ \text{subject to:} \\ \qquad \text{Pos}\left\{f_i(\tilde{\boldsymbol{x}}, \boldsymbol{\xi}) + d_i^- - d_i^+ = b_i\right\} \geq \beta_i, \quad i = 1, 2, \cdots, m \\ \qquad \text{Pos}\left\{g_j(\tilde{\boldsymbol{x}}, \boldsymbol{\xi}) \leq 0\right\} \geq \alpha_j, \quad j = 1, 2, \cdots, p \\ \qquad d_i^-, d_i^+ \geq 0, \quad i = 1, 2, \cdots, m \end{cases} \tag{11.7}$$

where

P_j = the preemptive priority factor which expresses the relative importance of various goals, $P_j \gg P_{j+1}$, for all j,

u_{ij} = weighting factor corresponding to positive deviation for goal i with priority j assigned,

v_{ij} = weighting factor corresponding to negative deviation for goal i with priority j assigned,

d_i^+ = positive deviation from the target of goal i,

d_i^- = negative deviation from the target of goal i,

b_i = the target value according to goal i,

l = number of priorities,

m = number of goal constraints.

Note that in CCGP models with fuzzy decisions, the positive and negative deviations are understood as the minimal nonnegative values of d_i^+ and d_i^- such that

$$\text{Pos}\left\{d_i^+ \geq f_i(\tilde{\boldsymbol{x}}, \boldsymbol{\xi}) - b_i\right\} \geq \beta_i, \quad \text{Pos}\left\{d_i^- \geq b_i - f_i(\tilde{\boldsymbol{x}}, \boldsymbol{\xi})\right\} \geq \beta_i \tag{11.8}$$

for $i = 1, 2, \cdots, m$, respectively.

11.3 Dependent-Chance Programming Models

Uncertain environments, events, chance functions, and induced constraints are key elements in the framework of DCP, DCMOP, and DCGP. In this section, we will revisit these concepts and provide a spectrum of DCP models with fuzzy rather than crisp decisions.

By uncertain environment we mean the solution set constrained by some uncertain conditions and generally represented by

$$g_j(\tilde{\boldsymbol{x}}, \boldsymbol{\xi}) \leq 0, \quad j = 1, 2, \cdots, p \tag{11.9}$$

where $\tilde{\boldsymbol{x}}$ is a fuzzy decision vector and $\boldsymbol{\xi}$ is a vector of fuzzy parameters. The fuzziness of feasibility of a decision vector $\tilde{\boldsymbol{x}}$ is caused by not only its fuzziness but also the uncertain parameter vector $\boldsymbol{\xi}$.

A complex decision system usually undertakes multiple tasks and should satisfy some interior requirements. By events we mean these tasks and interior requirements, and they are generally represented by a set of fuzzy solutions $\tilde{\boldsymbol{x}} = (\tilde{x}_1, \tilde{x}_2, \cdots, \tilde{x}_n)$ meeting, for example, $\tilde{x}_1 + \tilde{x}_2 = c$, which means that the demand c of some client should be fulfilled.

The term chance function is represented by the possibility of satisfying the event, for example, $f(\tilde{\boldsymbol{x}}) = \text{Pos}\{\tilde{x}_1 + \tilde{x}_2 = c\}$, where $\text{Pos}\{\cdot\}$ denotes the possibility of the event in $\{\cdot\}$.

Now the problem is how to represent the chance functions by the uncertain environment. We have answered this problem for the crisp decision case in Chapters 7 and 10. Here we analyze the case of fuzzy decisions. Let E be a single event in an uncertain decision system. The event E can be satisfied by an appropriate fuzzy decision vector $\tilde{\boldsymbol{x}} = (\tilde{x}_1, \tilde{x}_2, \cdots, \tilde{x}_n)$ with some degree of membership. Usually, the realization of E relates only to partial elements in $\{\tilde{x}_1, \tilde{x}_2, \cdots, \tilde{x}_n\}$ rather than the whole. Let $V(E)$ denote the set of all decision components of $\tilde{\boldsymbol{x}}$ which are necessary to the event E. Thus the possibility of realizing the event E is dependent only on the realization of the elements in $V(E)$. If there is only one event E in the uncertain decision system, then the chance function of the event E should be the maximal possibility of realizing the components in $V(E)$ with $\tilde{\boldsymbol{x}} \in E$, that is,

$$f(\tilde{\boldsymbol{x}}) = \max_{\tilde{\boldsymbol{y}} \in E^*} \text{Pos}\left\{g_j(\tilde{\boldsymbol{y}}, \boldsymbol{\xi}) \leq 0,\ j = 1, 2, \cdots, p\ \&\ \tilde{\boldsymbol{x}} \in E\right\}, \tag{11.10}$$

or equivalently,

$$f(\tilde{\boldsymbol{x}}) = \max_{\tilde{\boldsymbol{y}} \in E^*} \text{Pos}\left\{g_j(\tilde{\boldsymbol{y}}, \boldsymbol{\xi}) \leq 0, j = 1, 2, \cdots, p\right\} \wedge \text{Pos}\left\{\tilde{\boldsymbol{x}} \in E\right\} \tag{11.11}$$

where $\tilde{\boldsymbol{x}} \in E$ means that the fuzzy decision vector $\tilde{\boldsymbol{x}}$ meets the event E,

and

$$E^* = \left\{ \tilde{\boldsymbol{y}} = (\tilde{y}_1, \tilde{y}_2, \cdots, \tilde{y}_n) \;\middle|\; \begin{array}{c} \tilde{y}_j = \tilde{x}_j \text{ if } \tilde{y}_j \in V(E) \\ j = 1, 2, \cdots, n \end{array} \right\}. \tag{11.12}$$

Note that for any element $\tilde{\boldsymbol{y}} = (\tilde{y}_1, \tilde{y}_2, \cdots, \tilde{y}_n)$ in E^*, the fuzzy decision components $\tilde{y}_j \in V(E)$ are fixed and equal to $\tilde{x}_j$ and the remaining components are arbitrary. Usually, it is not difficult to determine the values $\tilde{x}_j^*$ of decision components out of $V(E)$ for the optimal solution $\tilde{\boldsymbol{y}}^*(\tilde{\boldsymbol{x}})$ in (11.10) for each given decision $\tilde{\boldsymbol{x}}$ such that

$$\tilde{\boldsymbol{y}}^*(\tilde{\boldsymbol{x}}) = (\tilde{y}_1, \tilde{y}_2, \cdots, \tilde{y}_n): \quad \tilde{y}_j = \begin{cases} \tilde{x}_j, & \tilde{y}_j \in V(E) \\ \tilde{x}_j^*, & \tilde{y}_j \notin V(E), \end{cases} \qquad j = 1, 2, \cdots, n.$$

In fact, the fuzzy decision components x_j^* usually take the fuzzy values at some extreme places. Therefore, the chance function of the event E should be

$$f(\tilde{\boldsymbol{x}}) = \text{Pos}\left\{g_j(\tilde{\boldsymbol{y}}^*(\tilde{\boldsymbol{x}}), \boldsymbol{\xi}) \le 0, j = 1, 2, \cdots, p\right\} \wedge \text{Pos}\left\{\tilde{\boldsymbol{x}} \in E\right\} \tag{11.13}$$

where the constraints

$$g_j(\tilde{\boldsymbol{y}}^*(\tilde{\boldsymbol{x}}), \boldsymbol{\xi}) \le 0, \quad j = 1, 2, \cdots, p \tag{11.14}$$

are called induced constraints on the event E at the fuzzy point $\tilde{\boldsymbol{x}}$. Up to now we have represented a chance function for a single event clearly.

A typical formulation of single-objective DCP with fuzzy decisions is thus defined as follows:

$$\begin{cases} \max \ f(\tilde{\boldsymbol{x}}) \\ \text{subject to:} \\ \qquad g_j(\tilde{\boldsymbol{x}}, \boldsymbol{\xi}) \le 0, \quad j = 1, 2, \cdots, p \end{cases} \tag{11.15}$$

where $\tilde{\boldsymbol{x}}$ is an n-dimensional fuzzy decision vector, $\boldsymbol{\xi}$ is a fuzzy vector of parameters, $f(\tilde{\boldsymbol{x}})$ is a chance function of an event, and the uncertain environment is constrained as $g_j(\tilde{\boldsymbol{x}}, \boldsymbol{\xi}) \le 0, j = 1, 2, \cdots, p$.

Since a complex decision system usually undertakes multiple tasks, there undoubtedly exist multiple potential objectives (some of them are chance functions) in the decision process. A typical formulation of DCMOP with fuzzy decisions is given as follows,

$$\begin{cases} \max \ f(\tilde{\boldsymbol{x}}) = \left[f_1(\tilde{\boldsymbol{x}}), f_2(\tilde{\boldsymbol{x}}), \cdots, f_m(\tilde{\boldsymbol{x}})\right] \\ \text{subject to:} \\ \qquad g_j(\tilde{\boldsymbol{x}}, \boldsymbol{\xi}) \le 0, \quad j = 1, 2, \cdots, p \end{cases} \tag{11.16}$$

where $f(\tilde{\boldsymbol{x}})$ is a vector of m functions $f_i(\tilde{\boldsymbol{x}})$ in which some of them are chance functions.

In order to represent the chance functions for multiple events, we assume that we know the fuzzy relationship among the fuzzy decision components $\tilde{x}_1, \tilde{x}_2, \cdots, \tilde{x}_n$ as defined in Section 10.2. That is, there is a known partition of n components of a decision vector into k groups such that these k groups are mutually fuzzy independent and in each group any elements are fuzzy dependent and have the same chance to appear if they need to be realized simultaneously.

Based on the fuzzy relationship, let $D(E)$ denote the set of all components which are fuzzy dependent on at least one element in $V(E)$ for an event E. Notice that the set $D(E)$ can easily be determined for real problems.

For the multiobjective case, without loss of generality, we assume that there exist m events E_i with chance functions $f_i(\tilde{\boldsymbol{x}})$, $i = 1, 2, \cdots, m$, respectively. We write,

$$E = E_1 \cap E_2 \cap \cdots \cap E_m$$

and

$$V(E) = V(E_1) \cup V(E_2) \cup \cdots \cup V(E_m),$$

where $\tilde{\boldsymbol{x}} \in E$ means that the fuzzy decision vector $\tilde{\boldsymbol{x}}$ should satisfy all of the events $E_1, E_2, \cdots, E_m$, and $V(E)$ is the set of all necessary components to the m events. Based on the fuzzy relationship, let $D(E)$, $D(E_i), i = 1, 2, \cdots, m$ be the sets of all components which are fuzzy dependent on at least one element of $V(E)$, $V(E_i), i = 1, 2, \cdots, m$, respectively. Since all events are at the same priority level, we should realize each event E_i as much as possible but not sacrifice the chances of other events. On the one hand, we should treat all elements in $D(E_i)$ at an equitable level; on the other hand, we are not interested in any elements out of $V(E)$ because they do not make any contributions to the m events. By the fuzzy relationship, we know that all elements in $D(E_i) \cap V(E)$ (a subset of $V(E)$) are fuzzy independent on any other elements in $V(E)$. Hence we can perform the elements in $D(E_i) \cap V(E)$ as much as possible for the event E_i. Therefore we have

$$f_i(\tilde{\boldsymbol{x}}) = \max_{\tilde{\boldsymbol{y}} \in E_i^*} \text{Pos}\left\{g_j(\tilde{\boldsymbol{y}}, \boldsymbol{\xi}) \le 0,\ j = 1, 2, \cdots, p\right\} \wedge \text{Pos}\left\{\tilde{\boldsymbol{x}} \in E_i\right\} \quad (11.17)$$

where the sets E_i^* are defined as

$$E_i^* = \left\{ \tilde{\boldsymbol{y}} = (\tilde{y}_1, \tilde{y}_2, \cdots, \tilde{y}_n) \;\middle|\; \begin{array}{r} \tilde{y}_j = \tilde{x}_j \text{ if } \tilde{y}_j \in D(E_i) \cap V(E) \\ j = 1, 2, \cdots, n \end{array} \right\} \quad (11.18)$$

for $i = 1, 2, \cdots, m$, respectively. It is assumed that we can determine $\tilde{\boldsymbol{y}}_i^*(\tilde{\boldsymbol{x}})$ for each given fuzzy solution $\tilde{\boldsymbol{x}}$ such that the induced constraints on the events E_i have the following forms,

$$g_j(\tilde{\boldsymbol{y}}_i^*(\tilde{\boldsymbol{x}}), \boldsymbol{\xi}) \le 0, \quad j = 1, 2, \cdots, p, \tag{11.19}$$

then the chance functions of E_i should be

$$f_i(\tilde{\boldsymbol{x}}) = \text{Pos}\left\{g_j(\tilde{\boldsymbol{y}}_i^*(\tilde{\boldsymbol{x}}), \boldsymbol{\xi}) \le 0,\ j = 1, 2, \cdots, p\right\} \wedge \text{Pos}\left\{\tilde{\boldsymbol{x}} \in E_i\right\} \tag{11.20}$$

for $i = 1, 2, \cdots, m$, respectively.

DCGP with fuzzy decisions may be considered as an extension of goal programming in a complex uncertain decision system. When some management targets are given, the objective function may minimize the deviations, positive, negative, or both, with a certain priority structure. Thus we can formulate a fuzzy decision system as a DCGP model according to the priority structure and target levels set by the decision-maker,

$$\begin{cases} \min \sum_{j=1}^{l} P_j \sum_{i=1}^{m} (u_{ij} d_i^+ + v_{ij} d_i^-) \\ \text{subject to:} \\ \qquad f_i(\tilde{\boldsymbol{x}}) + d_i^- - d_i^+ = b_i, \quad i = 1, 2, \cdots, m \\ \qquad g_j(\tilde{\boldsymbol{x}}, \boldsymbol{\xi}) \le 0, \qquad\qquad j = 1, 2, \cdots, p \\ \qquad d_i^-, d_i^+ \ge 0, \qquad\qquad i = 1, 2, \cdots, m \end{cases} \tag{11.21}$$

where

P_j = the preemptive priority factor which expresses the relative importance of various goals, $P_j \gg P_{j+1}$, for all j,

u_{ij} = weighting factor corresponding to positive deviation for goal i with priority j assigned,

v_{ij} = weighting factor corresponding to negative deviation for goal i with priority j assigned,

d_i^+ = positive deviation from the target of goal i,

d_i^- = negative deviation from the target of goal i,

f_i = a chance function or a conventional real-valued function in goal constraints,

b_i = the target value according to goal i,

l = number of priorities,

m = number of goal constraints.

For DCGP models, since there are multiple priority levels, we should consider the goals in turn from higher-priority level to lower-priority level.

In the first priority level, we assume that there are t events represented by $E_1, E_2, \cdots, E_t$. Define

$$E = E_1 \cap E_2 \cap \cdots \cap E_t$$

and

$$V(E) = V(E_1) \cup V(E_2) \cup \cdots \cup V(E_t).$$

A similar discussion with the multiobjective case can yield the induced constraints and chance functions $f_1(\tilde{\boldsymbol{x}}), f_2(\tilde{\boldsymbol{x}}), \cdots, f_t(\tilde{\boldsymbol{x}})$ for the t events. Therefore we have

$$f_i(\tilde{\boldsymbol{x}}) = \max_{\tilde{\boldsymbol{y}} \in E_i^*} \text{Pos}\{g_j(\tilde{\boldsymbol{y}}, \boldsymbol{\xi}) \le 0, j = 1, 2, \cdots, p\} \wedge \text{Pos}\{\tilde{\boldsymbol{x}} \in E_i\} \tag{11.22}$$

where the sets E_i^* are defined as

$$E_i^* = \left\{ \tilde{\boldsymbol{y}} = (\tilde{y}_1, \tilde{y}_2, \cdots, \tilde{y}_n) \;\middle|\; \begin{array}{r} \tilde{y}_j = \tilde{x}_j \text{ if } \tilde{y}_j \in D(E_i) \cap V(E) \\ j = 1, 2, \cdots, n \end{array} \right\} \tag{11.23}$$

for $i = 1, 2, \cdots, t$, respectively. It is assumed that we can determine $\tilde{\boldsymbol{y}}_i^*(\tilde{\boldsymbol{x}})$ for each given fuzzy solution $\tilde{\boldsymbol{x}}$ such that the induced constraints on the events E_i have the following forms,

$$g_j(\tilde{\boldsymbol{y}}_i^*(\tilde{\boldsymbol{x}}), \boldsymbol{\xi}) \le 0, \quad j = 1, 2, \cdots, p, \tag{11.24}$$

then the chance functions of E_i should be

$$f_i(\tilde{\boldsymbol{x}}) = \text{Pos}\{g_j(\tilde{\boldsymbol{y}}_i^*(\tilde{\boldsymbol{x}}), \boldsymbol{\xi}) \le 0, j = 1, 2, \cdots, p\} \wedge \text{Pos}\{\tilde{\boldsymbol{x}} \in E_i\} \tag{11.25}$$

for $i = 1, 2, \cdots, t$, respectively.

In the second priority level, we assume that there are events E_{t+1}, E_{t+2}, $\cdots$, $E_{t'}$. A similar process can also produce the induced constraints and chance functions $f_{t+1}(\tilde{\boldsymbol{x}}), f_{t+2}(\tilde{\boldsymbol{x}}), \cdots, f_{t'}(\tilde{\boldsymbol{x}})$ for the events E_{t+1}, E_{t+2}, $\cdots$, $E_{t'}$, respectively, provided that we follow the state resulting from the first priority decisions by defining

$$E = E_1 \cap E_2 \cap \cdots \cap E_t \cap E_{t+1} \cap E_{t+2} \cap \cdots \cap E_{t'}$$

and

$$V(E) = V(E_1) \cup V(E_2) \cup \cdots \cup V(E_t) \cup V(E_{t+1}) \cup V(E_{t+2}) \cup \cdots \cup V(E_{t'}).$$

Generally, the goals in the successive priority levels will be discussed in a similar way provided that we follow the state resulting from the higher-priority decisions.

11.4 Fuzzy Simulations

Liu and Iwamura [101] presented a computer technique of fuzzy simulations for checking fuzzy system constraint

$$\text{Pos}\{g_j(\tilde{\boldsymbol{x}}, \boldsymbol{\xi}) \le 0, j = 1, 2, \cdots, k\} \ge \alpha$$

as well as for handling fuzzy objective constraint

$$\text{Pos}\left\{f(\tilde{\boldsymbol{x}}, \boldsymbol{\xi}) \geq \overline{f}\right\} \geq \beta$$

and for handling fuzzy goal constraint

$$\text{Pos}\left\{f(\tilde{\boldsymbol{x}}, \boldsymbol{\xi}) + d^- - d^+ = b\right\} \geq \beta.$$

In addition to these, Liu [100] provided a fuzzy simulation for computing chance functions

$$f(\tilde{\boldsymbol{x}}) = \text{Pos}\left\{g_j(\tilde{\boldsymbol{x}}, \boldsymbol{\xi}) \leq 0,\ j = 1, 2, \cdots, p\right\}$$

where $\tilde{\boldsymbol{x}}$ and $\boldsymbol{\xi}$ are assumed fuzzy with membership functions $\nu(\cdot)$ and $\mu(\cdot)$, respectively. In this section we introduce the technique of fuzzy simulations.

Checking Fuzzy System Constraints

From the definition of operations over fuzzy numbers, we say

$$\text{Pos}\left\{g_j(\tilde{\boldsymbol{x}}, \boldsymbol{\xi}) \leq 0,\ j = 1, 2, \cdots, k\right\} \geq \alpha \tag{11.26}$$

for a given fuzzy decision vector $\tilde{\boldsymbol{x}}$ if and only if there are two crisp vectors $\boldsymbol{\xi}^0$ and $\tilde{\boldsymbol{x}}^0$ such that $g_j(\tilde{\boldsymbol{x}}^0, \boldsymbol{\xi}^0) \leq 0, j = 1, 2, \cdots, k$ and $\mu(\boldsymbol{\xi}^0) \wedge \nu(\tilde{\boldsymbol{x}}^0) \geq \alpha$. Thus, we can generate two crisp vectors $\boldsymbol{\xi}^0$ and $\tilde{\boldsymbol{x}}^0$ uniformly from the fuzzy vectors $\boldsymbol{\xi}$ and $\tilde{\boldsymbol{x}}$ such that $\mu(\boldsymbol{\xi}^0) \geq \alpha$ and $\nu(\tilde{\boldsymbol{x}}^0) \geq \alpha$ (i.e., the α-level sets of fuzzy vectors $\boldsymbol{\xi}$ and $\tilde{\boldsymbol{x}}$, respectively). If the α-level set of the fuzzy vector $\boldsymbol{\xi}$ is too complex to determine, we can sample a vector $\boldsymbol{\xi}^0$ from a hypercube Ω containing the α-level set and then accept or reject it, depending on whether $\mu(\boldsymbol{\xi}^0) \geq \alpha$ or not. Certainly, in order to speed up the simulation process, the hypercube Ω should be designed as small as possible. For the fuzzy decision $\tilde{\boldsymbol{x}}$, the sampling process is analogous to the case of $\boldsymbol{\xi}$. If the two crisp vectors $\boldsymbol{\xi}^0$ and $\tilde{\boldsymbol{x}}^0$ simultaneously satisfy that $g_j(\tilde{\boldsymbol{x}}^0, \boldsymbol{\xi}^0) \leq 0$ for $j = 1, 2, \cdots, k$, then we can believe that $\text{Pos}\left\{g_j(\tilde{\boldsymbol{x}}, \boldsymbol{\xi}) \leq 0, j = 1, 2, \cdots, k\right\} \geq \alpha$. If not, we will regenerate two crisp vectors $\boldsymbol{\xi}^0$ and $\tilde{\boldsymbol{x}}^0$ from the α-level sets of fuzzy vectors $\boldsymbol{\xi}$ and $\tilde{\boldsymbol{x}}$, respectively, and check the constraints again. After a given number N of cycles, if there are no crisp vectors $\boldsymbol{\xi}^0$ and $\tilde{\boldsymbol{x}}^0$ generated such that $g_j(\tilde{\boldsymbol{x}}^0, \boldsymbol{\xi}^0) \leq 0$ for $j = 1, 2, \cdots, k$, then we say that the given fuzzy decision vector $\tilde{\boldsymbol{x}}$ is infeasible for the chance constraint (11.26). Now we summarize the above process as follows.

Step 1. Generate $\boldsymbol{\xi}^0$ and $\tilde{\boldsymbol{x}}^0$ uniformly from the α-level sets of fuzzy vectors $\boldsymbol{\xi}$ and $\tilde{\boldsymbol{x}}$, respectively.

Step 2. If $g_j(\tilde{\boldsymbol{x}}^0, \boldsymbol{\xi}^0) \leq 0, j = 1, 2, \cdots, k$, return FEASIBLE.

Step 3. Repeat the first and second steps N times.

Step 4. Return INFEASIBLE.

Handling Fuzzy Objective Constraints

For a fuzzy objective constraint,

$$\text{Pos}\left\{f(\tilde{\boldsymbol{x}}, \boldsymbol{\xi}) \geq \overline{f}\right\} \geq \beta, \tag{11.27}$$

in view of the purpose of maximizing $\overline{f}$, we should find the maximal value $\overline{f}$ such that (11.27) holds for a given fuzzy decision vector $\tilde{\boldsymbol{x}}$. At first, we set $\overline{f} = -\infty$. Then we generate two crisp vectors $\boldsymbol{\xi}^0$ and $\tilde{\boldsymbol{x}}^0$ uniformly from the fuzzy vector $\boldsymbol{\xi}$ and $\tilde{\boldsymbol{x}}$, respectively, such that $\mu(\boldsymbol{\xi}^0) \wedge \nu(\tilde{\boldsymbol{x}}^0) \geq \beta$ (i.e., the β-level sets of fuzzy vectors $\boldsymbol{\xi}$ and $\tilde{\boldsymbol{x}}$, respectively). We set $\overline{f} = f(\tilde{\boldsymbol{x}}^0, \boldsymbol{\xi}^0)$ provided that $\overline{f} < f(\tilde{\boldsymbol{x}}^0, \boldsymbol{\xi}^0)$. Repeating this process N times, the value $\overline{f}$ is regarded as the objective value at the fuzzy decision $\tilde{\boldsymbol{x}}$. We summarize this process as follows.

Step 1. Set $\overline{f} = -\infty$.

Step 2. Generate $\boldsymbol{\xi}^0$ and $\tilde{\boldsymbol{x}}^0$ uniformly from the β-level sets of fuzzy vectors $\boldsymbol{\xi}$ and $\tilde{\boldsymbol{x}}$, respectively.

Step 3. If $\overline{f} < f(\tilde{\boldsymbol{x}}^0, \boldsymbol{\xi}^0)$, then we set $\overline{f} = f(\tilde{\boldsymbol{x}}^0, \boldsymbol{\xi}^0)$.

Step 4. Repeat the second and third steps N times.

Step 5. Return $\overline{f}$.

Handling Fuzzy Goal Constraints

In CCGP with fuzzy decisions there may be the following type of fuzzy goal constraint,

$$\text{Pos}\left\{f(\tilde{\boldsymbol{x}}, \boldsymbol{\xi}) + d^- - d^+ = b\right\} \geq \beta, \tag{11.28}$$

for which we should find the minimal nonnegative values of d^- and d^+ for the given fuzzy decision $\tilde{\boldsymbol{x}}$ such that

$$\text{Pos}\{d^- \geq b - f(\tilde{\boldsymbol{x}}, \boldsymbol{\xi})\} \geq \beta, \quad \text{Pos}\{d^+ \geq f(\tilde{\boldsymbol{x}}, \boldsymbol{\xi}) - b\} \geq \beta.$$

At first, we set $d^- = d^+ = +\infty$. Then we generate two crisp vectors $\boldsymbol{\xi}^0$ and $\tilde{\boldsymbol{x}}^0$ from the β-level sets of fuzzy vectors $\boldsymbol{\xi}$ and $\tilde{\boldsymbol{x}}$, respectively. If $d^- > b - f(\tilde{\boldsymbol{x}}^0, \boldsymbol{\xi}^0)$, then we set $d^- = [b - f(\tilde{\boldsymbol{x}}^0, \boldsymbol{\xi}^0)] \vee 0$. Similarly, if $d^+ > f(\tilde{\boldsymbol{x}}^0, \boldsymbol{\xi}^0) - b$, then we set $d^+ = [f(\tilde{\boldsymbol{x}}^0, \boldsymbol{\xi}^0) - b] \vee 0$. Repeat the above process N times by generating new crisp vectors $\boldsymbol{\xi}^0$ and $\tilde{\boldsymbol{x}}^0$. The values of d^+ and d^- are regarded as the positive and negative deviations at the fuzzy decision $\tilde{\boldsymbol{x}}$, respectively. Now we summarize this process as follows.

Step 1. Set $d^+ = d^- = +\infty$.

Step 2. Generate $\boldsymbol{\xi}^0$ and $\tilde{\boldsymbol{x}}^0$ uniformly from the β-level sets of fuzzy vectors $\boldsymbol{\xi}$ and $\tilde{\boldsymbol{x}}$, respectively.

Step 3. If $d^+ > f(\tilde{\boldsymbol{x}}^0, \boldsymbol{\xi}^0) - b$, then we set $d^+ = [f(\tilde{\boldsymbol{x}}^0, \boldsymbol{\xi}^0) - b] \vee 0$.

Step 4. If $d^- > b - f(\tilde{\boldsymbol{x}}^0, \boldsymbol{\xi}^0)$, then we set $d^- = [b - f(\tilde{\boldsymbol{x}}^0, \boldsymbol{\xi}^0)] \vee 0$.

Step 5. Repeat the second and third and/or fourth steps N times.

Step 6. Return d^+ and d^-.

Computing Chance Functions

Now let E be an event in a fuzzy decision system. Suppose that the induced constraints on the event E at the fuzzy solution $\tilde{\boldsymbol{x}}$ are $g_j(\tilde{\boldsymbol{y}}, \boldsymbol{\xi}) \le 0, j = 1, 2, \cdots, p$, where the fuzzy point $\tilde{\boldsymbol{y}}$ is derived from the fuzzy point $\tilde{\boldsymbol{x}}$. Then the chance function of the event E should be

$$f(\tilde{\boldsymbol{x}}) = \text{Pos}\left\{g_j(\tilde{\boldsymbol{y}}, \boldsymbol{\xi}) \le 0, j = 1, 2, \cdots, p\right\} \wedge \text{Pos}\left\{\tilde{\boldsymbol{x}} \in E\right\}. \tag{11.29}$$

Usually we do not have an analytic method to estimate general chance function $f(\tilde{\boldsymbol{x}})$. Thus we have to employ the following fuzzy simulation technique. For each fixed fuzzy decision $\tilde{\boldsymbol{x}}$, we set $f(\tilde{\boldsymbol{x}}) = 0$ at first. Then we generate crisp vectors $\boldsymbol{\xi}^0$ and $\tilde{\boldsymbol{y}}^0$ from the fuzzy vectors $\boldsymbol{\xi}$ and $\tilde{\boldsymbol{y}}$, respectively. In practice, we are not interested in the decision vectors with too low possibility. Thus we can predetermine a level, say α_0, then generate $\boldsymbol{\xi}^0$ and $\tilde{\boldsymbol{y}}^0$ uniformly from the α_0-level sets of fuzzy vectors $\boldsymbol{\xi}$ and $\tilde{\boldsymbol{y}}$, respectively. If $g_j(\tilde{\boldsymbol{y}}^0, \boldsymbol{\xi}^0) \le 0, j = 1, 2, \cdots, p$ and $f(\tilde{\boldsymbol{x}}) < \mu(\boldsymbol{\xi}^0) \wedge \nu(\tilde{\boldsymbol{y}}^0) \wedge \text{Pos}\{\tilde{\boldsymbol{x}} \in E\}$, then we set $f(\tilde{\boldsymbol{x}}) = \mu(\boldsymbol{\xi}^0) \wedge \nu(\tilde{\boldsymbol{y}}^0) \wedge \text{Pos}\{\tilde{\boldsymbol{x}} \in E\}$. Repeating this process a given number N of times, the value $f(\tilde{\boldsymbol{x}})$ is regarded as its estimation. The above process is summarized as follows.

Step 1. Set $f(\tilde{\boldsymbol{x}}) = 0$.

Step 2. Generate $\boldsymbol{\xi}^0$ and $\tilde{\boldsymbol{y}}^0$ uniformly from the α_0-level sets of fuzzy vectors $\boldsymbol{\xi}$ and $\tilde{\boldsymbol{y}}$, respectively.

Step 3. If $g_j(\tilde{\boldsymbol{y}}^0, \boldsymbol{\xi}^0) \le 0, j = 1, 2, \cdots, p$ and $f(\tilde{\boldsymbol{x}}) < \mu(\boldsymbol{\xi}^0) \wedge \nu(\tilde{\boldsymbol{y}}^0) \wedge \text{Pos}\{\tilde{\boldsymbol{x}} \in E\}$, then we set $f(\tilde{\boldsymbol{x}}) = \mu(\boldsymbol{\xi}^0) \wedge \nu(\tilde{\boldsymbol{y}}^0) \wedge \text{Pos}\{\tilde{\boldsymbol{x}} \in E\}$.

Step 4. Repeat the second and third steps N times.

Step 5. Return $f(\tilde{\boldsymbol{x}})$.

11.5 Fuzzy Simulation-based Genetic Algorithms

In this section we design a fuzzy simulation-based genetic algorithm for both CCP and DCP models with fuzzy decisions.

Representation Structure

Traditionally, we can code a solution by either a binary vector or a floating number vector. However, for a fuzzy solution (decision), we have to employ fuzzy chromosomes in which each gene is a fuzzy set rather than a crisp digital.

Here we use a fuzzy vector $V = (\tilde{x}_1, \tilde{x}_2, \cdots, \tilde{x}_n)$ as a fuzzy chromosome to represent a fuzzy solution to the CCP or DCP models, where n is the dimension and the components $\tilde{x}_i$ are sampled from the reference collections of fuzzy sets X_i for $i = 1, 2, \cdots, n$, respectively.

Initialization Process

We randomly sample fuzzy sets from the reference collection X_i for each fuzzy gene $\tilde{x}_i$ and form a fuzzy chromosome $V = (\tilde{x}_1, \tilde{x}_2, \cdots, \tilde{x}_n)$.

For CCP models, if the generated fuzzy chromosome $V = (\tilde{x}_1, \tilde{x}_2, \cdots, \tilde{x}_n)$ is proven infeasible by the fuzzy simulation, then we resample fuzzy sets until a feasible fuzzy chromosome is obtained. Repeating the above process *pop_size* times, we can make *pop_size* initial feasible fuzzy chromosomes $V_1, V_2, \cdots, V_{pop\_size}$.

For DCP models, since we are usually not interested in the decision vector with too low possibility, we may predetermine a hypercube Ω (if we cannot make such a hypercube Ω, then we set $\Omega = X_1 \otimes X_2 \otimes \cdots \otimes X_n$) and we search for the optimal fuzzy solution only in Ω. Certainly, the smaller the hypercube Ω, the more effective the initialization process. Hence, if the generated fuzzy chromosome is proven not in Ω, then we resample fuzzy sets until a fuzzy chromosome in Ω is obtained. Repeating the above process *pop_size* times, we can make *pop_size* initial fuzzy chromosomes $V_1, V_2, \cdots, V_{pop\_size}$ in Ω.

Evaluation Function

Let $V_1, V_2, \cdots, V_{pop\_size}$ be the *pop_size* fuzzy chromosomes at the current generation. No matter what type of mathematical programming (single-objective, multiobjective, or goal programming) it is, it is reasonable to assume that the user can give an order relationship among the *pop_size* fuzzy chromosomes $V_1, V_2, \cdots, V_{pop\_size}$ such that the *pop_size* chromosomes can be rearranged from good to bad. This arrangement is usually based on the values of objective functions obtained by fuzzy simulations. Now let a parameter $a \in (0, 1)$ in the genetic system be given. Then we can define the rank-based evaluation function as follows,

$$eval(V_i) = a(1-a)^{i-1}, \qquad i = 1, 2, \cdots, pop\_size. \tag{11.30}$$

Selection Process

The selection process is based on spinning the roulette wheel *pop_size* times. Each time we select a single fuzzy chromosome for a new population in the following way:

Step 1. Calculate the cumulative probability q_i for each fuzzy chromosome V_i,

$$\begin{aligned} q_0 &= 0, \\ q_i &= \sum_{j=1}^{i} eval(V_j), \quad i = 1, 2, \cdots, pop\_size. \end{aligned} \tag{11.31}$$

Step 2. Generate a random real number r in $(0, q_{pop\_size}]$.

Step 3. Select the ith chromosome V_i ($1 \le i \le pop\_size$) such that $q_{i-1} < r \le q_i$.

Step 4. Repeat the second and third steps *pop_size* times and obtain *pop_size* copies of fuzzy chromosomes.

Crossover Operation

We define a parameter P_c of a genetic system as the probability of crossover. This probability gives us the expected number $P_c \cdot pop\_size$ of chromosomes undergoing the crossover operation.

In order to determine the parents for crossover operation, let us do the following process repeatedly from $i = 1$ to *pop_size*: generating a random real number r from the interval $[0, 1]$, the fuzzy chromosome V_i is selected as a parent provided that $r < P_c$.

We denote the selected parents as $V_1', V_2', V_3', \cdots$ and divide them into the following pairs:

$$(V_1', V_2'), \quad (V_3', V_4'), \quad (V_5', V_6'), \quad \cdots$$

Let us illustrate the crossover operator on each pair by (V_1', V_2'). At first we randomly generate an integer between 1 and n as the crossover point denoted by n', then we exchange the genes after the n'th gene of the fuzzy chromosomes V_1' and V_2' and produce two children. If the children are proven feasible for CCP or are in the hypercube Ω for DCP, then we will replace the parents with them. Otherwise we redo the crossover operation.

Mutation Operation

We define a parameter P_m of a genetic system as the probability of mutation. This probability gives us the expected number of $P_m \cdot pop\_size$ of chromosomes undergoing the mutation operations.

Similar to the process of selecting parents for crossover operation, we repeat the following steps from $i = 1$ to *pop_size*: generating a random real number r from the interval $[0, 1]$, the fuzzy chromosome V_i is selected as a parent for mutation provided that $r < P_m$.

For each selected parent, denoted by $V = (\tilde{x}_1, \tilde{x}_2, \cdots, \tilde{x}_n)$, we mutate it in the following way. We randomly choose a mutation position n' between 1 and n, then we sample a new fuzzy set from the collection of fuzzy sets $X_{n'}$ and replace the n'th gene of V to form a new one, V'. If the fuzzy chromosome V' is proven infeasible for CCP or is not in the hypercube Ω for DCP, then we redo the mutation operation until a feasible one is obtained.

The Procedure

Following selection, crossover, and mutation, the new population is ready for its next evaluation. The genetic algorithm will terminate after a given number of cyclic repetitions of the above steps. We can summarize the fuzzy simulation-based genetic algorithm for solving CCP and DCP models with fuzzy decisions as follows.

Genetic Algorithm Procedure

Step 0. *Input parameters pop_size, a, P_c and P_m.*

Step 1. *Initialize pop_size fuzzy chromosomes in which fuzzy simulations may be employed to check the feasibility.*

Step 2. *Update the fuzzy chromosomes by crossover and mutation operations in which the feasibility of offspring may be checked by fuzzy simulations.*

Step 3. *Calculate the objective values for all fuzzy chromosomes by fuzzy simulations.*

Step 4. *Compute the fitness of each fuzzy chromosome by rank-based evaluation function based on the objective values.*

Step 5. *Select the fuzzy chromosomes by spinning the roulette wheel.*

Step 6. *Repeat the second to fifth steps a given number of cycles.*

Step 7. *Report the best chromosome as the optimal fuzzy solution.*

11.6 Numerical Experiments

The computer code for the fuzzy simulation-based genetic algorithm for fuzzy programming models with fuzzy decisions has been written in C language. Here we give some numerical examples performed on a personal computer with the following parameters: the population size is 30, the probability of crossover P_c is 0.3, the probability of mutation P_m is 0.2, the parameter a in the rank-based evaluation function is 0.05, and each fuzzy simulation will be performed 2000 cycles.

Example 1: Now let us consider the following single-objective CCP model with fuzzy decisions,

$$\begin{cases} \max \overline{f} \\ \text{subject to:} \\ \qquad \text{Pos}\left\{\tilde{c}_1\tilde{x}_1 + \tilde{c}_2\tilde{x}_2 + \tilde{c}_3\tilde{x}_3 \geq \overline{f}\right\} \geq 0.9 \\ \qquad \text{Pos}\left\{\tilde{a}_1\tilde{x}_1^2 + \tilde{a}_2\tilde{x}_2^2 + \tilde{a}_3\tilde{x}_3^2 \leq 100\right\} \geq 0.7 \\ \qquad \text{Pos}\left\{\tilde{x}_1\tilde{x}_2\tilde{x}_3 \leq \tilde{b}\right\} \geq 0.8 \end{cases}$$

where the fuzzy decision $\tilde{\boldsymbol{x}} = (\tilde{x}_1, \tilde{x}_2, \tilde{x}_3)$ will be generated in the Cartesian product $X_1 \otimes X_2 \otimes X_3$, the reference collection X_1 is composed of all triangular fuzzy numbers $(t-1, t, t+1)$ with $t \in [1, 5]$, X_2 is composed of all fuzzy numbers with membership functions $\mu_2(x) = \exp(-|x-t|)$ with $t \in [2, 10]$, X_3 is composed of all fuzzy numbers with membership functions $\mu_3(x) = 1/[1 + (x-t)^2]$ with $t \in [5, 8]$, the triangular fuzzy parameters $\tilde{a}_1 = (0, 1, 2)$, $\tilde{a}_2 = (1, 2, 3)$, $\tilde{a}_3 = (2, 3, 4)$, the trapezoidal fuzzy number $\tilde{b} = (20, 25, 28, 30)$, and $\tilde{c}_1$, $\tilde{c}_2$, and $\tilde{c}_3$ are fuzzy numbers with membership functions $\mu_{\tilde{c}_1}(x) = 1/[1 + |x-1|]$, $\mu_{\tilde{c}_2}(x) = 1/[1 + |x-2|]$ and $\mu_{\tilde{c}_3}(x) = 1/[1 + |x-3|]$, respectively.

A run of the fuzzy simulation-based genetic algorithm with 600 generations shows that the optimal fuzzy solution $(\tilde{x}_1^*, \tilde{x}_2^*, \tilde{x}_3^*)$ is

$$\begin{cases} \tilde{x}_1^* = (0.369, 1.369, 2.369) \\ \mu_{\tilde{x}_2^*}(x) = \exp\left[-|x - 5.336|\right] \\ \mu_{\tilde{x}_3^*}(x) = \dfrac{1}{1 + (x - 5.251)^2} \end{cases}$$

whose objective value is $\overline{f}^* = 30.4$.

Example 2: Now we turn our attention to the following CCGP with fuzzy decisions.

$$\begin{cases} \text{lexmin}\left\{d_1^-, d_2^-, d_3^-\right\} \\ \text{subject to:} \\ \qquad \text{Pos}\left\{\tilde{x}_1^2 + \tilde{x}_2^2 + d_1^- - d_1^+ = \tilde{b}\right\} \geq 0.95 \\ \qquad \text{Pos}\left\{\tilde{x}_3 + d_2^- - d_2^+ = \tilde{c}\right\} \geq 0.90 \\ \qquad \text{Pos}\left\{\tilde{x}_4 + d_3^- - d_3^+ = 4\right\} \geq 0.85 \\ \qquad \text{Pos}\left\{\tilde{a}_1\tilde{x}_1 + \tilde{a}_2\tilde{x}_2 + \tilde{a}_3\tilde{x}_3 + \tilde{a}_4\tilde{x}_4 \leq 10\right\} \geq 0.80 \\ \qquad d_i^-, d_i^+ \geq 0, \quad i = 1, 2, 3 \end{cases}$$

where $\tilde{a}_1, \tilde{a}_2, \tilde{a}_3$, and $\tilde{a}_4$ are triangular fuzzy numbers $(0,1,2), (1,2,3), (2,3,4)$, and $(3,4,5)$, respectively, $\tilde{b}$ and $\tilde{c}$ are fuzzy numbers with membership functions

$$\mu_{\tilde{b}}(x) = \frac{1}{1 + (x - 10)^2}, \qquad \mu_{\tilde{c}}(x) = \frac{1}{1 + |x - 3|}$$

respectively, and the fuzzy decision $(\tilde{x}_1, \tilde{x}_2, \tilde{x}_3, \tilde{x}_4)$ will be generated in the Cartesian product $X_1 \otimes X_2 \otimes X_3 \otimes X_4$, where the reference collection X_1 is a crisp interval $[1, 10]$ (a degenerate case), X_2 is composed of all triangular fuzzy numbers $(t-1, t, t+1)$ with $t \in [1, 10]$, X_3 is composed of all fuzzy numbers with membership functions $\mu_3(x) = \exp(-|x - t|)$ with $t \in [1, 10]$, and X_4 is composed of all fuzzy numbers with membership functions $\mu_4(x) = 1/[1 + |x - t|]$ with $t \in [1, 10]$.

In order to apply the fuzzy simulation technique to handling fuzzy system constraints and fuzzy goal constraints, we conservatively take the hypercubes containing the α-level sets of fuzzy numbers $\tilde{a}_1, \tilde{a}_2, \tilde{a}_3, \tilde{a}_4, \tilde{b}$, and $\tilde{c}$ as $[0.5, 1.5]$, $[1.5, 2.5]$, $[2.5, 3.5]$, $[3.5, 4.5]$, $[9, 11]$, and $[2, 4]$, respectively. A run of the fuzzy simulation-based genetic algorithm with 1000 generations shows that the optimal fuzzy solution $(\tilde{x}_1^*, \tilde{x}_2^*, \tilde{x}_3^*, \tilde{x}_4^*)$ is

$$\begin{cases} \tilde{x}_1^* = 2.951 \\ \tilde{x}_2^* = (0, 1, 2) \\ \mu_{\tilde{x}_3^*}(x) = \exp\left(-|x - 1.420|\right) \\ \mu_{\tilde{x}_4^*}(x) = \dfrac{1}{1 + |x - 1.001|} \end{cases}$$

which can satisfy the first goal, but the second and third objectives are 1.37 and 2.82, respectively.

Example 3: Now we consider a simple DCP model with fuzzy decisions,

$$\begin{cases} \max \ f(\tilde{\boldsymbol{x}}) = \text{Pos}\{\tilde{x}_1 + \tilde{x}_2 + \tilde{x}_3 + \tilde{x}_4 = 8\} \\ \text{subject to:} \\ \qquad \tilde{x}_1^2 + \tilde{x}_2^2 \le \tilde{a} \\ \qquad \tilde{x}_3^3 + \tilde{x}_4^3 \le \tilde{b} \end{cases}$$

where $\tilde{a}$ and $\tilde{b}$ are triangular fuzzy number (6,7,8) and trapezoidal fuzzy number (7,8,9,10), and the fuzzy decision $(\tilde{x}_1, \tilde{x}_2, \tilde{x}_3, \tilde{x}_4)$ will be generated in the Cartesian product $X_1 \otimes X_2 \otimes X_3 \otimes X_4$, where the reference collection X_1 is composed of all triangular fuzzy numbers $(t-1, t, t+1)$ with $t \in [1, 10]$, X_2 is composed of all fuzzy numbers with membership functions $\mu_2(\xi) = 1/[1 + (\xi - t)^2]$ with $t \in [2, 4]$, X_3 is composed of all fuzzy numbers with membership functions $\mu_3(\xi) = \exp[-|\xi - t|]$ with $t \in [1, 5]$, and X_4 is a closed interval [1,10] (a degenerate case).

For this case, we do not need to analyze the fuzzy relationship among the decision components. Since there is only one event in the decision system and all decision components are necessary to the event, the induced constraints are the uncertain environment itself. Thus the chance function $f(\tilde{\boldsymbol{x}})$ should be

$$\begin{aligned} f(\tilde{\boldsymbol{x}}) &= \text{Pos}\left\{\tilde{x}_1^2 + \tilde{x}_2^2 \le \tilde{a},\ \tilde{x}_3^3 + \tilde{x}_4^3 \le \tilde{b}\right\} \wedge \text{Pos}\{\tilde{x}_1 + \tilde{x}_2 + \tilde{x}_3 + \tilde{x}_4 = 8\} \\ &= \text{Pos}\left\{\tilde{x}_1^2 + \tilde{x}_2^2 \le \tilde{a},\ \tilde{x}_3^3 + \tilde{x}_4^3 \le \tilde{b},\ \tilde{x}_1 + \tilde{x}_2 + \tilde{x}_3 + \tilde{x}_4 = 8\right\}. \end{aligned}$$

A run of the fuzzy simulation-based genetic algorithm with 200 generations shows that the optimal fuzzy solution $\tilde{\boldsymbol{x}}^* = (\tilde{x}_1^*, \tilde{x}_2^*, \tilde{x}_3^*, \tilde{x}_4^*)$ is

$$\tilde{x}_1^* = (1.0265, 2.0265, 3.0265), \quad \mu_{\tilde{x}_2^*}(\xi) = \frac{1}{1 + (\xi - 2.1438)^2},$$
$$\mu_{\tilde{x}_3^*}(\xi) = \exp[-|\xi - 1.6784|], \quad \tilde{x}_4^* = 1.6367$$

whose objective value $f(\tilde{\boldsymbol{x}}^*) = 90.3\%$.

Example 4: We consider the following DCGP with fuzzy decisions in fuzzy environment,

$$\begin{cases} \text{lexmin}\left\{d_1^-, d_2^-, d_3^-\right\} \\ \text{subject to:} \\ \qquad f_1(\tilde{\boldsymbol{x}}) + d_1^- - d_1^+ = 0.95 \\ \qquad f_2(\tilde{\boldsymbol{x}}) + d_2^- - d_2^+ = 0.92 \\ \qquad f_3(\tilde{\boldsymbol{x}}) + d_3^- - d_3^+ = 0.90 \\ \qquad \tilde{x}_1 + \tilde{x}_2 \le \tilde{a} \\ \qquad \tilde{x}_3 + \tilde{x}_4 + \tilde{x}_5 \le \tilde{b} \\ \qquad d_i^-, d_i^+ \ge 0, \quad i = 1, 2, 3 \end{cases}$$

where the chance functions are

$$\begin{cases} f_1(\tilde{\boldsymbol{x}}) = \text{Pos}\{\tilde{x}_1^2 + \tilde{x}_3^2 = 10\} \\ f_2(\tilde{\boldsymbol{x}}) = \text{Pos}\{\tilde{x}_2 = 7\} \\ f_3(\tilde{\boldsymbol{x}}) = \text{Pos}\{\tilde{x}_4^2 + \tilde{x}_5^2 = 25\}, \end{cases}$$

$\tilde{a}$ is a trapezoidal fuzzy number $(7, 8, 9, 10)$, $\tilde{b}$ is a triangular fuzzy number $(4, 5, 6)$, and each component $\tilde{x}_i$ of the fuzzy decision $\tilde{\boldsymbol{x}} = (\tilde{x}_1, \tilde{x}_2, \tilde{x}_3, \tilde{x}_4, \tilde{x}_5)$ will be generated in the reference collection composed of all fuzzy numbers with membership functions $\mu(\xi) = 1/[1 + (\xi - t)^2]$ with $t \in [1, 8]$.

From the fuzzy environment, we know the following fuzzy relationship: the five decision components can be divided into two groups $\{\tilde{x}_1, \tilde{x}_2\}$ and $\{\tilde{x}_3, \tilde{x}_4, \tilde{x}_5\}$ such that these two groups are mutually fuzzy independent and in each group any elements are fuzzy dependent and have the same chance to appear if they need to be realized simultaneously.

In the first priority level, there is only one event denoted by E_1 in the fuzzy environment, which should be fulfilled by $\tilde{x}_1^2 + \tilde{x}_3^2 = 10$. It is clear that $V(E_1) = \{\tilde{x}_1, \tilde{x}_3\}$ and the induced constraints on the event E_1 should be

$$\begin{cases} \tilde{x}_1 + \tilde{1} \le \tilde{a} \\ \tilde{x}_3 + \tilde{1} + \tilde{1} \le \tilde{b} \end{cases}$$

since the remaining components can be regarded as $\tilde{1}$ temporarily for the event E_1 at the current priority level, where $\tilde{1}$ is the smallest fuzzy number with membership function $\mu(\xi) = 1/[1 + (\xi - 1)^2]$. Thus the chance function $f_1(\tilde{\boldsymbol{x}})$ of E_1 should be

$$f_1(\tilde{\boldsymbol{x}}) = \text{Pos}\left\{\tilde{x}_1 + \tilde{1} \le \tilde{a},\ \tilde{x}_3 + \tilde{1} + \tilde{1} \le \tilde{b}\right\} \wedge \text{Pos}\left\{\tilde{x}_1^2 + \tilde{x}_3^2 = 10\right\}.$$

At the second priority level, there is also one event E_2, which should be fulfilled by $\tilde{x}_2 = 7$. We have $V(E_2) = \{\tilde{x}_2\}$. Write $E = E_1 \cap E_2$, then

$V(E) = V(E_1) \cup V(E_2) = \{\tilde{x}_1, \tilde{x}_2, \tilde{x}_3\}$. Since

$$D(E_2) \cap V(E) = \{\tilde{x}_1, \tilde{x}_2\} \cap \{\tilde{x}_1, \tilde{x}_2, \tilde{x}_3\} = \{\tilde{x}_1, \tilde{x}_2\},$$

the induced constraint on the event E_2 should be $\tilde{x}_1 + \tilde{x}_2 \le \tilde{a}$, which yields the chance function $f_2(\tilde{\boldsymbol{x}})$ of the event E_2 as follows,

$$f_2(\tilde{\boldsymbol{x}}) = \text{Pos}\{\tilde{x}_1 + \tilde{x}_2 \le \tilde{a}\} \wedge \text{Pos}\{\tilde{x}_2 = 7\}.$$

At the third priority level, there is only one event E_3 fulfilled by $\tilde{x}_4^2 + \tilde{x}_5^2 = 25$. Thus we have $V(E_3) = \{\tilde{x}_4, \tilde{x}_5\}$ and $V(E) = V(E_1) \cup V(E_2) \cup V(E_3) = \{\tilde{x}_1, \tilde{x}_2, \tilde{x}_3, \tilde{x}_4, \tilde{x}_5\}$. It follows from

$$D(E_3) \cap V(E) = \{\tilde{x}_3, \tilde{x}_4, \tilde{x}_5\} \cap \{\tilde{x}_1, \tilde{x}_2, \tilde{x}_3, \tilde{x}_4, \tilde{x}_5\} = \{\tilde{x}_3, \tilde{x}_4, \tilde{x}_5\}$$

that the induced constraint on the event E_3 should be $\tilde{x}_3 + \tilde{x}_4 + \tilde{x}_5 \le \tilde{b}$, which yields the chance function $f_3(\tilde{\boldsymbol{x}})$ of event E_3 as follows,

$$f_3(\tilde{\boldsymbol{x}}) = \text{Pos}\left\{\tilde{x}_3 + \tilde{x}_4 + \tilde{x}_5 \le \tilde{b}\right\} \wedge \text{Pos}\left\{\tilde{x}_4^2 + \tilde{x}_5^2 = 25\right\}.$$

A run of the fuzzy simulation-based genetic algorithm with 1000 generations shows that the optimal fuzzy solution is $\tilde{\boldsymbol{x}}^* = (\tilde{x}_1^*, \tilde{x}_2^*, \tilde{x}_3^*, \tilde{x}_4^*, \tilde{x}_5^*)$, in which $\tilde{x}_i^*$ are fuzzy numbers with membership functions $\mu(\xi) = 1/[1 + (\xi - t_i^*)^2]$ where t_i^* are

$$2.8107, \quad 6.7051, \quad 1.0038, \quad 1.0022, \quad 4.3799,$$

$i = 1, 2, 3, 4, 5$, respectively. This fuzzy solution can satisfy the first two goals, but the third objective is 0.063. Furthermore, we have

$$f_1(\tilde{\boldsymbol{x}}^*) = 0.981, \quad f_2(\tilde{\boldsymbol{x}}^*) = 0.920, \quad f_3(\tilde{\boldsymbol{x}}^*) = 0.837.$$

11.7 Notes

This chapter introduced a spectrum of CCP and DCP models with fuzzy rather than crisp decisions, and thus expanded the applicability of fuzzy programming. A fuzzy simulation-based genetic algorithm for solving these models was also designed. Finally, we illustrated the effectiveness of the fuzzy simulation-based genetic algorithm with some numerical examples. Although the algorithm is a slow and costly way to find the optimal solution, it is indeed a powerful and easy-to-use tool for this type of problem.

Chapter 12

Minimax Chance-Constrained Programming Models

We have discussed chance-constrained programming (CCP) models for fuzzy decision systems in Chapters 9 and 11. In fact, these CCP models are essentially types of maximax models (optimistic models) which maximize the maximum possible return.

This chapter introduces a spectrum of minimax models (as opposed to maximax models) constructed by Liu [95] based on CCP, chance-constrained multiobjective programming (CCMOP), and chance-constrained goal programming (CCGP), which will select the alternative that provides the best of the worst possible return. Finally, a fuzzy simulation-based genetic algorithm is designed for solving minimax models and is illustrated by some numerical examples.

Notice that for our purpose, the distinctions between minimin and maximax and between minimax and maximin are unnecessary.

12.1 Maximax Models

Liu and Iwamura [91][101] have provided a spectrum of nonlinear CCP, CCMOP, and CCGP models with fuzzy coefficients and fuzzy decisions. In fact, they are essentially maximax models (optimistic models) which maximize the maximum possible return. In order to introduce minimax CCP models, let us discuss the maximax models at first.

A single-objective maximax CCP model is defined by [101] in the following form,

$$\begin{cases} \max \overline{f} \\ \text{subject to:} \\ \qquad \text{Pos}\left\{f(\tilde{\boldsymbol{x}}, \boldsymbol{\xi}) \geq \overline{f}\right\} \geq \beta \\ \qquad \text{Pos}\{g_j(\tilde{\boldsymbol{x}}, \boldsymbol{\xi}) \leq 0, j = 1, 2, \cdots, p\} \geq \alpha \end{cases} \tag{12.1}$$

where the fuzzy decision $\tilde{\boldsymbol{x}}$ is described by an n-dimensional vector

$$\tilde{\boldsymbol{x}} = (\tilde{x}_1, \tilde{x}_2, \cdots, \tilde{x}_n)$$

in which components $\tilde{x}_i$ will be assigned an element in the reference collection of fuzzy sets X_i, $i = 1, 2, \cdots, n$, respectively, thus each fuzzy decision vector must be taken from the Cartesian product

$$\mathcal{X} = X_1 \otimes X_2 \otimes \cdots \otimes X_n, \tag{12.2}$$

and $\boldsymbol{\xi}$ is a vector of fuzzy parameters, $f(\tilde{\boldsymbol{x}}, \boldsymbol{\xi})$ is the return function, $g_j(\tilde{\boldsymbol{x}}, \boldsymbol{\xi})$ are constraint functions, $j = 1, 2, \cdots, p$, α and β are predetermined confidence levels for fuzzy constraints and fuzzy objective, respectively.

For each fixed fuzzy solution $\tilde{\boldsymbol{x}}$, since $\overline{f}$ should be maximized, the objective value $\overline{f}$ will be the maximum value that the return function $f(\tilde{\boldsymbol{x}}, \boldsymbol{\xi})$ achieves with at least possibility β, i.e.,

$$\overline{f} = \max\left\{f \mid \text{Pos}\left\{f(\tilde{\boldsymbol{x}}, \boldsymbol{\xi}) \geq f\right\} \geq \beta\right\}. \tag{12.3}$$

Hence the above-mentioned CCP model is essentially equivalent to the following form,

$$\begin{cases} \max\limits_{\tilde{\boldsymbol{x}}} \max\limits_{\overline{f}} \overline{f} \\ \text{subject to:} \\ \qquad \text{Pos}\left\{f(\tilde{\boldsymbol{x}}, \boldsymbol{\xi}) \geq \overline{f}\right\} \geq \beta \\ \qquad \text{Pos}\{g_j(\tilde{\boldsymbol{x}}, \boldsymbol{\xi}) \leq 0, j = 1, 2, \cdots, p\} \geq \alpha \end{cases} \tag{12.4}$$

which is more clearly a maximax model.

Analogously, the CCP model with a minimizing return function

$$\begin{cases} \min \overline{f} \\ \text{subject to:} \\ \qquad \text{Pos}\left\{f(\tilde{\boldsymbol{x}}, \boldsymbol{\xi}) \leq \overline{f}\right\} \geq \beta \\ \qquad \text{Pos}\{g_j(\tilde{\boldsymbol{x}}, \boldsymbol{\xi}) \leq 0, j = 1, 2, \cdots, p\} \geq \alpha \end{cases} \tag{12.5}$$

is essentially equivalent to the following minimin form,

$$\begin{cases} \min\limits_{\tilde{\boldsymbol{x}}} \min\limits_{\overline{f}} \overline{f} \\ \text{subject to:} \\ \qquad \text{Pos}\left\{f(\tilde{\boldsymbol{x}}, \boldsymbol{\xi}) \le \overline{f}\right\} \ge \beta \\ \qquad \text{Pos}\left\{g_j(\tilde{\boldsymbol{x}}, \boldsymbol{\xi}) \le 0, j = 1, 2, \cdots, p\right\} \ge \alpha \end{cases} \tag{12.6}$$

where $\min \overline{f}$ should be the minimal value that the return function $f(\tilde{\boldsymbol{x}}, \boldsymbol{\xi})$ achieves with at least possibility β.

The maximax CCMOP model is given by

$$\begin{cases} \max \left[\overline{f}_1, \overline{f}_2, \cdots, \overline{f}_m\right] \\ \text{subject to:} \\ \qquad \text{Pos}\left\{f_i(\tilde{\boldsymbol{x}}, \boldsymbol{\xi}) \ge \overline{f}_i\right\} \ge \beta_i, \quad i = 1, 2, \cdots, m \\ \qquad \text{Pos}\left\{g_j(\tilde{\boldsymbol{x}}, \boldsymbol{\xi}) \le 0\right\} \ge \alpha_j, \quad j = 1, 2, \cdots, p \end{cases} \tag{12.7}$$

where α_j and β_i are confidence levels for the constraints and objectives, and $\overline{f}_i$ should be the maximum values that the return functions $f_i(\tilde{\boldsymbol{x}}, \boldsymbol{\xi})$ achieve with at least possibility levels β_i, $i = 1, 2, \cdots, m$, $j = 1, 2, \cdots, p$, respectively. For the same reason, with the single-objective case, this model is essentially equivalent to

$$\begin{cases} \max\limits_{\tilde{\boldsymbol{x}}} \left[\max\limits_{\overline{f}_1} \overline{f}_1, \ \max\limits_{\overline{f}_2} \overline{f}_2, \ \cdots, \ \max\limits_{\overline{f}_m} \overline{f}_m\right] \\ \text{subject to:} \\ \qquad \text{Pos}\left\{f_i(\tilde{\boldsymbol{x}}, \boldsymbol{\xi}) \ge \overline{f}_i\right\} \ge \beta_i, \quad i = 1, 2, \cdots, m \\ \qquad \text{Pos}\left\{g_j(\tilde{\boldsymbol{x}}, \boldsymbol{\xi}) \le 0\right\} \ge \alpha_j, \quad j = 1, 2, \cdots, p. \end{cases} \tag{12.8}$$

According to the priority structure and target levels set by the decision-maker, the CCGP model is formulated as follows,

$$\begin{cases} \min \sum\limits_{j=1}^{l} P_j \sum\limits_{i=1}^{m} (u_{ij} d_i^+ + v_{ij} d_i^-) \\ \text{subject to:} \\ \qquad \text{Pos}\left\{f_i(\tilde{\boldsymbol{x}}, \boldsymbol{\xi}) + d_i^- - d_i^+ = \tilde{b}_i\right\} \ge \beta_i, \quad i = 1, 2, \cdots, m \\ \qquad \text{Pos}\left\{g_j(\tilde{\boldsymbol{x}}, \boldsymbol{\xi}) \le 0\right\} \ge \alpha_j, \qquad j = 1, 2, \cdots, p \\ \qquad d_i^-, d_i^+ \ge 0, \qquad i = 1, 2, \cdots, m \end{cases} \tag{12.9}$$

where

P_j = the preemptive priority factor which expresses the relative importance of various goals, $P_j \gg P_{j+1}$, for all j,

u_{ij} = weighting factor corresponding to positive deviation for goal i with priority j assigned,

v_{ij} = weighting factor corresponding to negative deviation for goal i with priority j assigned,

d_i^+ = positive deviation from the target of goal i,

d_i^- = negative deviation from the target of goal i,

$\tilde{b}_i$ = the fuzzy target value according to goal i,

l = number of priorities,

m = number of goal constraints.

Note that in this CCGP model, the positive and negative deviations are understood as the *minimal* nonnegative values of d_i^+ and d_i^- such that

$$\text{Pos}\left\{d_i^+ \ge f_i(\tilde{\boldsymbol{x}}, \boldsymbol{\xi}) - \tilde{b}_i\right\} \ge \beta_i, \quad \text{Pos}\left\{d_i^- \ge \tilde{b}_i - f_i(\tilde{\boldsymbol{x}}, \boldsymbol{\xi})\right\} \ge \beta_i \tag{12.10}$$

for $i = 1, 2, \cdots, m$, respectively. Thus the CCGP is essentially a minimin model.

12.2 Minimax Models

In this section, we will introduce a spectrum of minimax CCP models [95], in which the underlying philosophy is based on selecting the alternative that provides the best of the worst possible return.

Since there are multiple values of $\overline{f}$ such that $\text{Pos}\{f(\tilde{\boldsymbol{x}}, \boldsymbol{\xi}) \le \overline{f}\} \ge \beta$, we may take the minimizing value of $\overline{f}$ as the objective function to be maximized. Thus, a single-objective minimax CCP model may be written as follows,

$$\begin{cases} \max\limits_{\tilde{\boldsymbol{x}}} \min\limits_{\overline{f}} \overline{f} \\ \text{subject to:} \\ \qquad \text{Pos}\left\{f(\tilde{\boldsymbol{x}}, \boldsymbol{\xi}) \le \overline{f}\right\} \ge \beta \\ \qquad \text{Pos}\left\{g_j(\tilde{\boldsymbol{x}}, \boldsymbol{\xi}) \le 0, j = 1, 2, \cdots, p\right\} \ge \alpha \end{cases} \tag{12.11}$$

where $\overline{f}$ will be the minimum value that the return function $f(\tilde{\boldsymbol{x}}, \boldsymbol{\xi})$ achieves with at least possibility β.

If the objective function is assumed to be minimized, then we have the following minimax model,

$$\begin{cases} \min\limits_{\tilde{\boldsymbol{x}}} \max\limits_{\overline{f}} \overline{f} \\ \text{subject to:} \\ \qquad \text{Pos}\left\{f(\tilde{\boldsymbol{x}}, \boldsymbol{\xi}) \geq \overline{f}\right\} \geq \beta \\ \qquad \text{Pos}\left\{g_j(\tilde{\boldsymbol{x}}, \boldsymbol{\xi}) \leq 0, j = 1, 2, \cdots, p\right\} \geq \alpha \end{cases} \tag{12.12}$$

where $\max \overline{f}$ should be the maximum value that the return function $f(\tilde{\boldsymbol{x}}, \boldsymbol{\xi})$ achieves with at least possibility β.

As an extension of single-objective case, the minimax CCMOP model is given by

$$\begin{cases} \max\limits_{\tilde{\boldsymbol{x}}} \left[\min\limits_{\overline{f}_1} \overline{f}_1, \min\limits_{\overline{f}_2} \overline{f}_2, \cdots, \min\limits_{\overline{f}_m} \overline{f}_m\right] \\ \text{subject to:} \\ \qquad \text{Pos}\left\{f_i(\tilde{\boldsymbol{x}}, \boldsymbol{\xi}) \leq \overline{f}_i\right\} \geq \beta_i, \quad i = 1, 2, \cdots, m \\ \qquad \text{Pos}\left\{g_j(\tilde{\boldsymbol{x}}, \boldsymbol{\xi}) \leq 0\right\} \geq \alpha_j, \quad j = 1, 2, \cdots, p \end{cases} \tag{12.13}$$

where α_j and β_i are confidence levels for the constraints and objectives, and $\overline{f}_i$ should be the minimum values that the return functions $f_i(\tilde{\boldsymbol{x}}, \boldsymbol{\xi})$ achieve with at least possibility levels β_i, $i = 1, 2, \cdots, m$, $j = 1, 2, \cdots, p$, respectively.

According to the priority structure and target levels set by the decision-maker, the CCGP model is written as follows,

$$\begin{cases} \min \sum\limits_{j=1}^{l} P_j \sum\limits_{i=1}^{m} (u_{ij} d_i^+ + v_{ij} d_i^-) \\ \text{subject to:} \\ \qquad \text{Pos}\left\{f_i(\tilde{\boldsymbol{x}}, \boldsymbol{\xi}) + d_i^- - d_i^+ = \tilde{b}_i\right\} \geq \beta_i, \quad i = 1, 2, \cdots, m \\ \qquad \text{Pos}\left\{g_j(\tilde{\boldsymbol{x}}, \boldsymbol{\xi}) \leq 0\right\} \geq \alpha_j, \qquad j = 1, 2, \cdots, p \\ \qquad d_i^-, d_i^+ \geq 0, \qquad i = 1, 2, \cdots, m \end{cases} \tag{12.14}$$

where

P_j = the preemptive priority factor which expresses the relative importance of various goals, $P_j \gg P_{j+1}$, for all j,

u_{ij} = weighting factor corresponding to positive deviation for goal i with priority j assigned,

v_{ij} = weighting factor corresponding to negative deviation for goal i with priority j assigned,

d_i^+ = positive deviation from the target of goal i,
d_i^- = negative deviation from the target of goal i,
$\tilde{b}_i$ = the fuzzy target value according to goal i,
l = number of priorities,
m = number of goal constraints.

Notice that the CCGP model is essentially a minimax model if the positive and negative deviations are understood as the *maximal* nonnegative values (rather than minimum in the minimin models) of d_i^+ and d_i^- such that

$$\text{Pos}\left\{d_i^+ \le f_i(\tilde{\boldsymbol{x}}, \boldsymbol{\xi}) - \tilde{b}_i\right\} \ge \beta_i, \quad \text{Pos}\left\{d_i^- \le \tilde{b}_i - f_i(\tilde{\boldsymbol{x}}, \boldsymbol{\xi})\right\} \ge \beta_i \quad (12.15)$$

for $i = 1, 2, \cdots, m$, respectively, where the maximal nonnegative value means that if there are no positive values d_i^+ and d_i^- satisfying the above inequalities, then we set $d_i^+ = 0$ and $d_i^- = 0$.

We also note that there is no difference between the forms of minimin and minimax CCGP models. The CCGP is a minimin or minimax model, depending on whether the deviations are understood as the minimal or maximal values.

12.3 Minimax versus Maximax

In minimax and maximax CCP models there are the following two types of suboptimization to be considered,

$$\begin{aligned} \overline{f}_{\min} &= \min\{\overline{f} \mid \text{Pos}\{f(\tilde{\boldsymbol{x}}, \boldsymbol{\xi}) \le \overline{f}\} \ge \beta\}, \\ \overline{f}_{\max} &= \max\{\overline{f} \mid \text{Pos}\{f(\tilde{\boldsymbol{x}}, \boldsymbol{\xi}) \ge \overline{f}\} \ge \beta\}, \end{aligned} \quad (12.16)$$

respectively. No matter what the types of fuzzy decision $\tilde{\boldsymbol{x}}$, parameter $\boldsymbol{\xi}$, and functional form $f(\cdot,\cdot)$ are, $f(\tilde{\boldsymbol{x}}, \boldsymbol{\xi})$ can be regarded as a fuzzy number whose membership function is denoted by $\mu_{f(\tilde{\boldsymbol{x}},\boldsymbol{\xi})}(\cdot)$, which is able to derive from the membership functions of $\tilde{\boldsymbol{x}}$ and $\boldsymbol{\xi}$.

By the definition of possibility, we have

$$\text{Pos}\left\{f(\tilde{\boldsymbol{x}}, \boldsymbol{\xi}) \le \overline{f}\right\} = \sup_f \left\{\mu_{f(\tilde{\boldsymbol{x}},\boldsymbol{\xi})}(f) \mid f \le \overline{f}\right\}$$

and

$$\text{Pos}\left\{f(\tilde{\boldsymbol{x}}, \boldsymbol{\xi}) \ge \overline{f}\right\} = \sup_f \left\{\mu_{f(\tilde{\boldsymbol{x}},\boldsymbol{\xi})}(f) \mid f \ge \overline{f}\right\}.$$

Since $\overline{f}_{\min} = \min\left\{\overline{f} | \text{Pos}\{f(\tilde{\boldsymbol{x}}, \boldsymbol{\xi}) \le \overline{f}\} \ge \beta\right\}$, the minimum value $\overline{f}_{\min}$ should satisfy the following inequality

$$\text{Pos}\left\{f(\tilde{\boldsymbol{x}}, \boldsymbol{\xi}) \le \overline{f}_{\min}\right\} \ge \beta.$$

Furthermore we have $\mu_{f(\tilde{\boldsymbol{x}},\boldsymbol{\xi})}(\overline{f}_{\min}) \geq \beta$, otherwise, there will be at least one $f < \overline{f}_{\min}$ such that $\mu_{f(\tilde{\boldsymbol{x}},\boldsymbol{\xi})}(f) \geq \beta$, which implies that $\text{Pos}\{f(\tilde{\boldsymbol{x}},\boldsymbol{\xi}) \leq f\} \geq \beta$, a contradiction to the fact that $\overline{f}_{\min}$ is the minimum value of $\overline{f}$ satisfying

$$\text{Pos}\left\{f(\tilde{\boldsymbol{x}},\boldsymbol{\xi}) \leq \overline{f}\right\} \geq \beta.$$

Since it has been proven that $\mu_{f(\tilde{\boldsymbol{x}},\boldsymbol{\xi})}(\overline{f}_{\min}) \geq \beta$ holds, we have

$$\text{Pos}\left\{f(\tilde{\boldsymbol{x}},\boldsymbol{\xi}) \geq \overline{f}_{\min}\right\} = \sup_{f}\left\{\mu_{f(\tilde{\boldsymbol{x}},\boldsymbol{\xi})}(f) \mid f \geq \overline{f}_{\min}\right\} \geq \mu_{f(\tilde{\boldsymbol{x}},\boldsymbol{\xi})}(\overline{f}_{\min}) \geq \beta.$$

It follows from $\overline{f}_{\max} = \max\left\{\overline{f}|\text{Pos}\{f(\tilde{\boldsymbol{x}},\boldsymbol{\xi}) \geq \overline{f}\} \geq \beta\right\}$ that

$$\overline{f}_{\max} \geq \overline{f}_{\min} \tag{12.17}$$

always holds. This result is shown in Figure 12.1.

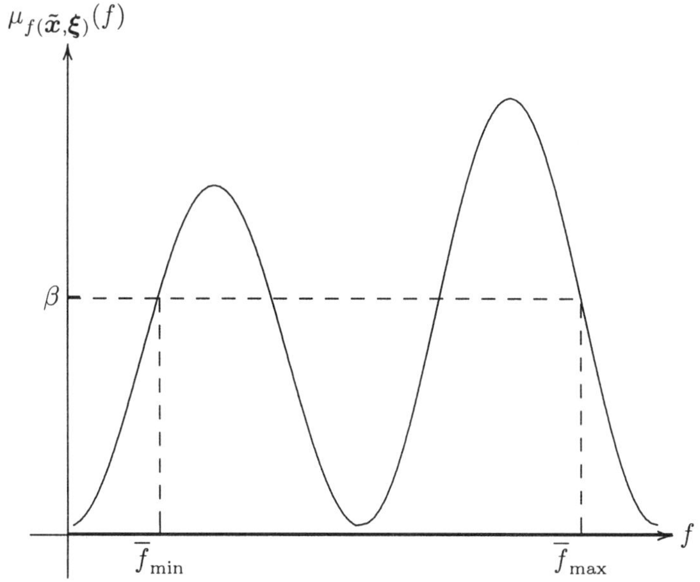

Figure 12.1: Minimization $\overline{f}_{\min}$ and Maximization $\overline{f}_{\max}$

Moreover, since for each fixed fuzzy decision $\tilde{\boldsymbol{x}}$ we have $\overline{f}_{\max} \geq \overline{f}_{\min}$, the maximax solution will be always larger than or equal to the minimax solution.

Now we conclude this section as follows.

Theorem 12.1 *For any fixed fuzzy decision* $\tilde{\boldsymbol{x}}$*, we have* $\overline{f}_{\max} \geq \overline{f}_{\min}$*, where* $\overline{f}_{\max}$ *and* $\overline{f}_{\min}$ *are determined by (12.16). Furthermore, for the maximax model (12.4) and minimax model (12.11), we have*

$$\max_{\tilde{\boldsymbol{x}}} \max_{\overline{f}} \overline{f} \geq \max_{\tilde{\boldsymbol{x}}} \min_{\overline{f}} \overline{f}. \tag{12.18}$$

Analogously, we can prove the following theorem.

Theorem 12.2 *For the minimax CCP model*

$$\begin{cases} \min\limits_{\tilde{\boldsymbol{x}}} \max\limits_{\overline{f}} \overline{f} \\ \text{subject to:} \\ \qquad \text{Pos}\left\{f(\tilde{\boldsymbol{x}}, \boldsymbol{\xi}) \geq \overline{f}\right\} \geq \beta \\ \qquad \text{Pos}\left\{g_j(\tilde{\boldsymbol{x}}, \boldsymbol{\xi}) \leq 0, j = 1, 2, \cdots, p\right\} \geq \alpha \end{cases} \tag{12.19}$$

and minimin model

$$\begin{cases} \min\limits_{\tilde{\boldsymbol{x}}} \min\limits_{\overline{f}} \overline{f} \\ \text{subject to:} \\ \qquad \text{Pos}\left\{f(\tilde{\boldsymbol{x}}, \boldsymbol{\xi}) \leq \overline{f}\right\} \geq \beta \\ \qquad \text{Pos}\left\{g_j(\tilde{\boldsymbol{x}}, \boldsymbol{\xi}) \leq 0, j = 1, 2, \cdots, p\right\} \geq \alpha, \end{cases} \tag{12.20}$$

we always have

$$\min_{\tilde{\boldsymbol{x}}} \max_{\overline{f}} \overline{f} \geq \min_{\tilde{\boldsymbol{x}}} \min_{\overline{f}} \overline{f}. \tag{12.21}$$

12.4 Fuzzy Simulations

We have introduced a computer technique of fuzzy simulations for checking fuzzy system constraints as well as for handling fuzzy objective and goal constraints.

In order to solve minimax CCP models, in this section we will present two additional types of fuzzy simulations for seeking the minimal value of $\overline{f}$ such that

$$\text{Pos}\left\{f(\tilde{\boldsymbol{x}}, \boldsymbol{\xi}) \leq \overline{f}\right\} \geq \beta$$

and for seeking maximal nonnegative positive and negative deviations for the fuzzy goal constraint

$$\text{Pos}\left\{f(\tilde{\boldsymbol{x}}, \boldsymbol{\xi}) + d^- - d^+ = \tilde{b}\right\} \geq \beta$$

where $\tilde{\boldsymbol{x}}$, $\boldsymbol{\xi}$, and $\tilde{b}$ are assumed to be fuzzy vectors with membership functions $\nu(\cdot)$, $\mu(\cdot)$ and $\mu_{\tilde{b}}(\cdot)$, respectively.

Handling Fuzzy Objective Constraints

Now we want to search for the minimum value of $\overline{f}$ for the following fuzzy objective constraint,

$$\text{Pos}\left\{f(\tilde{\boldsymbol{x}},\boldsymbol{\xi}) \le \overline{f}\right\} \ge \beta \tag{12.22}$$

for a given fuzzy decision vector $\tilde{\boldsymbol{x}}$. At first, we set $\overline{f} = +\infty$. Then we generate two crisp vectors $\boldsymbol{\xi}^0$ and $\tilde{\boldsymbol{x}}^0$ uniformly from the fuzzy vectors $\boldsymbol{\xi}$ and $\tilde{\boldsymbol{x}}$, respectively, such that $\mu(\boldsymbol{\xi}^0) \wedge \nu(\tilde{\boldsymbol{x}}^0) \ge \beta$ (i.e., the β-level sets of fuzzy vectors $\boldsymbol{\xi}$ and $\tilde{\boldsymbol{x}}$, respectively). If the β-level set of the fuzzy vector $\boldsymbol{\xi}$ is too complex to determine, we can sample a vector $\boldsymbol{\xi}^0$ from a hypercube Ω containing the β-level set and then accept or reject it, depending on whether $\mu(\boldsymbol{\xi}^0) \ge \beta$ or not. Certainly, in order to speed up the simulation process, the hypercube Ω should be designed as small as possible. For the fuzzy decision $\tilde{\boldsymbol{x}}$, the sampling process is analogous to the case of $\boldsymbol{\xi}$. We set $\overline{f} = f(\tilde{\boldsymbol{x}}^0,\boldsymbol{\xi}^0)$ provided that $\overline{f} > f(\tilde{\boldsymbol{x}}^0,\boldsymbol{\xi}^0)$. Repeating this process a given number N of times, the value $\overline{f}$ is regarded as the minimal value that the return function $f(\tilde{\boldsymbol{x}},\boldsymbol{\xi})$ achieves with at least possibility β. We now summarize the process as follows.

Step 1. Set $\overline{f} = +\infty$.

Step 2. Generate $\boldsymbol{\xi}^0$ and $\tilde{\boldsymbol{x}}^0$ uniformly from the β-level sets of fuzzy vectors $\boldsymbol{\xi}$ and $\tilde{\boldsymbol{x}}$, respectively.

Step 3. If $\overline{f} > f(\tilde{\boldsymbol{x}}^0,\boldsymbol{\xi}^0)$, then we set $\overline{f} = f(\tilde{\boldsymbol{x}}^0,\boldsymbol{\xi}^0)$.

Step 4. Repeat the second and third steps N times.

Step 5. Return $\overline{f}$.

Handling Fuzzy Goal Constraints

In minimax CCGP models there may be the following type of fuzzy goal constraint,

$$\text{Pos}\left\{f(\tilde{\boldsymbol{x}},\boldsymbol{\xi}) + d^- - d^+ = \tilde{b}\right\} \ge \beta, \tag{12.23}$$

for which we should find the maximal nonnegative values of d^- and d^+ for the given fuzzy decision $\tilde{\boldsymbol{x}}$ such that

$$\text{Pos}\{d^- \le \tilde{b} - f(\tilde{\boldsymbol{x}},\boldsymbol{\xi})\} \ge \beta, \quad \text{Pos}\{d^+ \le f(\tilde{\boldsymbol{x}},\boldsymbol{\xi}) - \tilde{b}\} \ge \beta.$$

First we set $d^- = d^+ = 0$. Then we generate three crisp vectors $\boldsymbol{\xi}^0$, $\tilde{\boldsymbol{x}}^0$, and $\tilde{b}^0$ from the β-level sets of fuzzy vectors $\boldsymbol{\xi}$, $\tilde{\boldsymbol{x}}$, and $\tilde{b}$, respectively. If $d^- < \tilde{b}^0 - f(\tilde{\boldsymbol{x}}^0,\boldsymbol{\xi}^0)$, then we set $d^- = \tilde{b}^0 - f(\tilde{\boldsymbol{x}}^0,\boldsymbol{\xi}^0)$. Analogously, if $d^+ < f(\tilde{\boldsymbol{x}}^0,\boldsymbol{\xi}^0) - \tilde{b}^0$, then we set $d^+ = f(\tilde{\boldsymbol{x}}^0,\boldsymbol{\xi}^0) - \tilde{b}^0$. Repeat the above process a given number N of times by generating new crisp vectors $\boldsymbol{\xi}^0$, $\tilde{\boldsymbol{x}}^0$, and $\tilde{b}^0$. The values of d^+ and d^- are regarded as the maximal nonnegative positive and negative deviations at the fuzzy decision $\tilde{\boldsymbol{x}}$, respectively. Notice that d^+ and d^- generated by this process are undoubtedly nonnegative. Now we summarize this process as follows.

Step 1. Set $d^+ = d^- = 0$.

Step 2. Generate $\boldsymbol{\xi}^0$, $\tilde{\boldsymbol{x}}^0$, and $\tilde{b}^0$ uniformly from the β-level sets of fuzzy vectors $\boldsymbol{\xi}$, $\tilde{\boldsymbol{x}}$, and $\tilde{b}$, respectively.

Step 3. If $d^+ < f(\tilde{\boldsymbol{x}}^0, \boldsymbol{\xi}^0) - \tilde{b}^0$, then we set $d^+ = f(\tilde{\boldsymbol{x}}^0, \boldsymbol{\xi}^0) - \tilde{b}^0$.

Step 4. If $d^- < \tilde{b}^0 - f(\tilde{\boldsymbol{x}}^0, \boldsymbol{\xi}^0)$, then we set $d^- = \tilde{b}^0 - f(\tilde{\boldsymbol{x}}^0, \boldsymbol{\xi}^0)$.

Step 5. Repeat the second and third and/or fourth steps N times.

Step 6. Return d^+ and d^-.

12.5 Numerical Examples

In fact, the fuzzy simulation-based genetic algorithm designed in Chapter 11 is also suitable for minimax CCP models for fuzzy decision systems. Traditionally, we can code a solution with either a binary vector or a floating number vector. However, for a fuzzy decision, we have to use fuzzy chromosomes in which each gene is a fuzzy set rather than a crisp digital. Here we use a fuzzy vector $V = (\tilde{x}_1, \tilde{x}_2, \cdots, \tilde{x}_n)$ as a fuzzy chromosome to represent a fuzzy solution to the minimax models, where n is the dimension and each component $\tilde{x}_i$ is sampled from the given reference collection of fuzzy sets X_i for $i = 1, 2, \cdots, n$. The procedure of fuzzy simulation-based genetic algorithm is presented as follows.

Genetic Algorithm Procedure

Step 0. *Input parameters pop_size, P_c and P_m.*

Step 1. *Initialize pop_size fuzzy chromosomes in which fuzzy simulations may be employed to check the feasibility.*

Step 2. *Update the fuzzy chromosomes by crossover and mutation operations in which the feasibility of offspring may be checked by fuzzy simulations.*

Step 3. *Calculate the objective values for all fuzzy chromosomes by fuzzy simulations.*

Step 4. *Compute the fitness of each fuzzy chromosome by rank-based evaluation function based on the objective values.*

Step 5. *Select the fuzzy chromosomes by spinning the roulette wheel.*

Step 6. *Repeat the second to fifth steps a given number of cycles.*

Step 7. *Report the best chromosome as the optimal fuzzy solution.*

Here we give two types of numerical examples performed on a personal computer with the following parameters: the population size is 30, the probability of crossover P_c is 0.3, the probability of mutation P_m is 0.2, and the parameter a in the rank-based evaluation function is 0.05. Each fuzzy simulation will be performed 2000 cycles.

Example 1: Suppose that a fuzzy decision $\tilde{\boldsymbol{x}} = (\tilde{x}_1, \tilde{x}_2, \tilde{x}_3)$ will be generated in the given Cartesian product $X_1 \otimes X_2 \otimes X_3$, where the reference collection X_1 is composed of all triangular fuzzy numbers $(t-1, t, t+1)$ with $t \in [1,5]$, X_2 all fuzzy numbers with membership functions $\mu_2(x) = 1/[1+(x-t)^2]$ with $t \in [3,6]$, and X_3 all fuzzy numbers with membership functions $\mu_3(x) = \exp(-|x-t|)$ with $t \in [2,4]$.

We also assume that the fuzzy decision $\tilde{\boldsymbol{x}} = (\tilde{x}_1, \tilde{x}_2, \tilde{x}_3)$ will be restricted by

$$\text{Pos}\left\{\tilde{a}_1\tilde{x}_1 + \tilde{a}_2\tilde{x}_2 + \tilde{a}_3\tilde{x}_3 \le 100\right\} \ge 0.80$$

where the technical coefficients $\tilde{a}_1$, $\tilde{a}_2$, and $\tilde{a}_3$ are triangular fuzzy numbers (8,9,10), (6,7,8), and (16,17,18), respectively.

The return function to be maximized will be assumed $\tilde{c}_1\tilde{x}_1 + \tilde{c}_2\tilde{x}_2^2 + \tilde{c}_3\tilde{x}_3^3$, where the coefficients $\tilde{c}_1$, $\tilde{c}_2$, and $\tilde{c}_3$ are fuzzy numbers with membership functions $\mu_{\tilde{c}_1}(x) = 1/[1+|x-3|]$, $\mu_{\tilde{c}_2}(x) = 1/[1+|x-2|]$, and $\mu_{\tilde{c}_3}(x) = 1/[1+|x-1|]$, respectively. We are concerned with maximizing the possible return with at least possibility 0.90.

Since there are multiple possible returns with at least the given possibility level, we have not only minimax but also maximax CCP models. The maximax model is written as

$$\text{(Maximax)} \begin{cases} \max\limits_{\tilde{\boldsymbol{x}}} \max\limits_{\overline{f}} \overline{f} \\ \text{subject to:} \\ \qquad \text{Pos}\left\{\tilde{c}_1\tilde{x}_1 + \tilde{c}_2\tilde{x}_2^2 + \tilde{c}_3\tilde{x}_3^3 \ge \overline{f}\right\} \ge 0.90 \\ \qquad \text{Pos}\left\{\tilde{a}_1\tilde{x}_1 + \tilde{a}_2\tilde{x}_2 + \tilde{a}_3\tilde{x}_3 \le 100\right\} \ge 0.80 \end{cases}$$

while the minimax model is given by

$$(\text{Minimax})\begin{cases}\max\limits_{\tilde{\boldsymbol{x}}}\min\limits_{\overline{f}}\overline{f}\\ \text{subject to:}\\ \qquad \text{Pos}\left\{\tilde{c}_1\tilde{x}_1+\tilde{c}_2\tilde{x}_2^2+\tilde{c}_3\tilde{x}_3^3\le\overline{f}\right\}\ge 0.90\\ \qquad \text{Pos}\left\{\tilde{a}_1\tilde{x}_1+\tilde{a}_2\tilde{x}_2+\tilde{a}_3\tilde{x}_3\le 100\right\}\ge 0.80.\end{cases}$$

A run of the fuzzy simulation-based genetic algorithm with 1000 generations shows that the optimal fuzzy solution $(\tilde{x}_1^*,\tilde{x}_2^*,\tilde{x}_3^*)$ for the maximax model is

$$\tilde{x}_1^*=(3.878,4.878,5.878),$$
$$\mu_{\tilde{x}_2^*}(x)=\frac{1}{1+(x-4.757)^2},$$
$$\mu_{\tilde{x}_3^*}(x)=\exp\left(-|x-2.002|\right)$$

whose maximal return with at least possibility 0.90 is $\overline{f}^*_{\max}=28.57$, while another run of the fuzzy simulation-based genetic algorithm with 1000 generations shows that the optimal fuzzy solution $(\tilde{x}_1^*,\tilde{x}_2^*,\tilde{x}_3^*)$ for the minimax model is

$$\tilde{x}_1^*=(3.852,4.852,5.852),$$
$$\mu_{\tilde{x}_2^*}(x)=\frac{1}{1+(x-4.615)^2},$$
$$\mu_{\tilde{x}_3^*}(x)=\exp\left(-|x-2.003|\right)$$

whose minimax return with at least possibility 0.90 is $\overline{f}^*_{\min}=23.87$. Notice that for this example we have $\overline{f}^*_{\max}>\overline{f}^*_{\min}$, which coincides with the result shown in Section 12.3.

Example 2: Now let us suppose that there are four fuzzy decision variables $\tilde{x}_1$, $\tilde{x}_2$, $\tilde{x}_3$, and $\tilde{x}_4$ that are taken from the reference collections of fuzzy sets X_1,X_2,X_3, and X_4, respectively, where X_1 is composed of all fuzzy numbers with membership functions $\mu_1(x)=1/[1+|x-t|]$ with $t\in[3,5]$, X_2 all fuzzy numbers with membership functions $\mu_2(x)=1/[1+(x-t)^2]$ with $t\in[2,4]$, X_3 all fuzzy numbers with membership functions $\mu_3(x)=\exp[-|x-t|]$ with $t\in[4,7]$, and X_4 all fuzzy numbers with membership functions $\mu_4(x)=\exp[-(x-t)^2]$ with $t\in[5,6]$. The system constraint on the fuzzy decision $\tilde{\boldsymbol{x}}=(\tilde{x}_1,\tilde{x}_2,\tilde{x}_3,\tilde{x}_4)$ is given by

$$\text{Pos}\left\{(\tilde{a}_1\tilde{x}_1+\tilde{a}_2\tilde{x}_2)\left(\tilde{a}_3\tilde{x}_3+\tilde{a}_4\tilde{x}_4\right)\le 300\right\}\ge 0.80$$

where the coefficients $\tilde{a}_1,\tilde{a}_2,\tilde{a}_3$, and $\tilde{a}_4$ are triangular fuzzy numbers (0,1,2), (1,2,3), (2,3,4), and (3,4,5), respectively.

At the first priority level, there is a fuzzy target level $\tilde{b}_1$ whose membership function is $\mu_{\tilde{b}_1}(x) = 1/[1 + |x - 30|]$. If we hope that the product $\tilde{x}_1\tilde{x}_3$ should achieve $\tilde{b}_1$ as far as possible with at least possibility 0.95, then we have a goal constraint

$$\text{Pos}\left\{\tilde{x}_1\tilde{x}_3 + d_1^- - d_1^+ = \tilde{b}_1\right\} \geq 0.95$$

where d_1^- will be minimized.

At the second priority level, we have a goal constraint

$$\text{Pos}\left\{\tilde{x}_2 + d_2^- - d_2^+ = \tilde{b}_2\right\} \geq 0.90$$

where $\tilde{b}_2$ is a fuzzy number with membership functions $\mu_{\tilde{b}_2}(x) = 1/[1 + |x - 3.5|]$, and d_2^- will be minimized.

At the third priority level, there is the following goal constraint

$$\text{Pos}\left\{\tilde{x}_4 + d_3^- - d_3^+ = \tilde{b}_3\right\} \geq 0.90$$

where $\tilde{b}_3$ is a fuzzy number with membership functions $\mu_{\tilde{b}_3}(x) = 1/[1 + |x - 7|]$, and d_3^- will be minimized.

Thus we have the following CCGP model,

$$\begin{cases} \text{lexmin}\left\{d_1^-, d_2^-, d_3^-\right\} \\ \text{subject to:} \\ \qquad \text{Pos}\left\{\tilde{x}_1\tilde{x}_3 + d_1^- - d_1^+ = \tilde{b}_1\right\} \geq 0.95 \\ \qquad \text{Pos}\left\{\tilde{x}_2 + d_2^- - d_2^+ = \tilde{b}_2\right\} \geq 0.90 \\ \qquad \text{Pos}\left\{\tilde{x}_4 + d_3^- - d_3^+ = \tilde{b}_3\right\} \geq 0.90 \\ \qquad \text{Pos}\left\{(\tilde{a}_1\tilde{x}_1 + \tilde{a}_2\tilde{x}_2)(\tilde{a}_3\tilde{x}_3 + \tilde{a}_4\tilde{x}_4) \leq 300\right\} \geq 0.80 \\ \qquad d_i^-, d_i^+ \geq 0, \quad i = 1, 2, 3. \end{cases}$$

When the positive and negative deviations are understood as the minimal nonnegative values of d_i^+ and d_i^-, respectively, the CCGP is a minimin model; when the positive and negative deviations are understood as the maximal nonnegative values of d_i^+ and d_i^-, respectively, the CCGP is a minimax model.

A run of the fuzzy simulation-based genetic algorithm with 1000 generations shows that the optimal fuzzy solution $(\tilde{x}_1^*, \tilde{x}_2^*, \tilde{x}_3^*, \tilde{x}_4^*)$ for the minimin model is

$$\mu_{\tilde{x}_1^*}(x) = \frac{1}{1 + |x - 4.8974|}, \qquad \mu_{\tilde{x}_2^*}(x) = \frac{1}{1 + (x - 3.0664)^2},$$

$$\mu_{\tilde{x}_3^*}(x) = \exp\left[-|x - 6.0061|\right], \quad \mu_{\tilde{x}_4^*}(x) = \exp\left[-(x - 5.6800)^2\right]$$

which can satisfy the first two goals, but the third objective is 0.8843, while another run of the fuzzy simulation-based genetic algorithm with 1000 generations shows that the optimal fuzzy solution $(\tilde{x}_1^*, \tilde{x}_2^*, \tilde{x}_3^*, \tilde{x}_4^*)$ for the minimax model is

$$\mu_{\tilde{x}_1^*}(x) = \frac{1}{1+|x-4.8883|}, \qquad \mu_{\tilde{x}_2^*}(x) = \frac{1}{1+(x-3.3181)^2},$$

$$\mu_{\tilde{x}_3^*}(x) = \exp\left[-|x-6.2672|\right], \quad \mu_{\tilde{x}_4^*}(x) = \exp\left[-(x-5.0072)^2\right]$$

which can satisfy only the first goal, but the second and third objectives are 0.6263 and 2.4285, respectively.

The time complexity of these numerical examples is the sum of the time spent for fuzzy simulation and the time spent for the genetic algorithm, where the computation time for fuzzy simulation is exactly proportional to the number of sampling points. We should mention that the computation time for fuzzy simulation has to be spent since we had assumed that there is no direct method to substitute for it. Certainly, if we had direct methods to estimate the possibility for some special constraints, we would employ them in order to speed up the process of evolution.

12.6 Notes

In addition to the maximax CCP models, this chapter introduced a series of minimax models. In the maximax models the function to be maximized is

$$\overline{f}_{\max} = \max\left\{\overline{f} \mid \text{Pos}\left\{f(\tilde{\boldsymbol{x}}, \boldsymbol{\xi}) \ge \overline{f}\right\} \ge \beta\right\},$$

while in the minimax models the function to be maximized is

$$\overline{f}_{\min} = \min\left\{\overline{f} \mid \text{Pos}\left\{f(\tilde{\boldsymbol{x}}, \boldsymbol{\xi}) \le \overline{f}\right\} \ge \beta\right\}.$$

It is clear that both minimax and maximax models are extreme cases. In fact, we can also define the CCP model in the following form,

$$\begin{cases} \max\ \lambda\overline{f}_{\min} + (1-\lambda)\overline{f}_{\max} \\ \text{subject to:} \\ \qquad \text{Pos}\left\{g_j(\tilde{\boldsymbol{x}}, \boldsymbol{\xi}) \le 0,\ j=1,2,\cdots,p\right\} \ge \alpha \end{cases} \tag{12.24}$$

where λ is a given number between 0 and 1. Notice that when $\lambda = 0$, it is a maximax model; when $\alpha = 1$, it is a minimax model.

Chapter 13

Outline of Uncertain Programming

Stochastic programming and fuzzy programming have already been separately considered. However, uncertain programming offers a unified treatment of them. More generally, uncertain programming, in contrast to deterministic mathematical programming where all parameters must be deterministic, is the optimization theory in uncertain (random, fuzzy, fuzzy random, gray, etc.) environments.

In this chapter, uncertain programming theory is sketched. Some further research problems appearing in this area are also posed.

13.1 Uncertainty

In order to make a satisfactory decision in practice, an important problem is to determine the type and accuracy of information. If complete information is required in the decision process, it will mean the expenditure of some extra time and money. If incomplete information is used to make a decision quickly, then it is possible to take a nonoptimal action. In fact, we cannot have complete accuracy in both information and decision. Since we have to balance the advantages of making better decisions against the disadvantages of getting more accurate information, incomplete information will almost surely be used in the real-life decision process.

The incomplete information may be described by stochastic variables, fuzzy sets, or other types of uncertain quantities. From the viewpoint of optimization theory, there is no difference among the uncertainties such as randomness, fuzziness, fuzzy randomness, and grayness except for the arithmetical operations on them.

Now let ξ be an uncertain quantity. Then the expected value of ξ is $E[\xi] = \int \xi\phi(\xi)d\xi$ when ξ is a random variable with probability density function $\phi(\xi)$. In addition, the chance of event $g(\xi) \le 0$ is defined by $\text{Ch}\{g(\xi) \le 0\}$, where the abbreviation Ch represents chance. When ξ is a random variable, then Ch is Pr; when ξ is a fuzzy set, then Ch is Pos.

13.2 Expected Value Models

Up to now, expected value models of uncertain programming have been developed only for the stochastic environment. The general form of expected value model is formulated as follows,

$$\begin{cases} \max\ E[f(\boldsymbol{x}, \boldsymbol{\xi})] \\ \text{subject to:} \\ \qquad E[g_j(\boldsymbol{x}, \boldsymbol{\xi})] \le 0, \quad j = 1, 2, \cdots, p \\ \qquad E[h_k(\boldsymbol{x}, \boldsymbol{\xi})] = 0, \quad k = 1, 2, \cdots, q \end{cases} \tag{13.1}$$

where $\boldsymbol{x}$ is a decision vector, $\boldsymbol{\xi}$ is an uncertain vector of parameters, $f(\boldsymbol{x}, \boldsymbol{\xi})$ is the return function, $g_j(\boldsymbol{x}, \boldsymbol{\xi})$ and $h_k(\boldsymbol{x}, \boldsymbol{\xi})$ are uncertain constraint functions for $j = 1, 2, \cdots, p$, $k = 1, 2, \cdots, q$, and E denotes the expectation operator.

The expected value model based on multiobjective programming has the following form,

$$\begin{cases} \max\ \left[E[f_1(\boldsymbol{x}, \boldsymbol{\xi})], E[f_2(\boldsymbol{x}, \boldsymbol{\xi})], \cdots, E[f_m(\boldsymbol{x}, \boldsymbol{\xi})]\right] \\ \text{subject to:} \\ \qquad E[g_j(\boldsymbol{x}, \boldsymbol{\xi})] \le 0, \quad j = 1, 2, \cdots, p \\ \qquad E[h_k(\boldsymbol{x}, \boldsymbol{\xi})] = 0, \quad k = 1, 2, \cdots, q \end{cases} \tag{13.2}$$

where $f_i(\boldsymbol{x}, \boldsymbol{\xi})$ are return functions for $i = 1, 2, \cdots, m$.

We can also formulate an uncertain decision system as an expected value goal programming model according to the priority structure and target levels set by the decision-maker,

$$\begin{cases} \min \sum\limits_{j=1}^{l} P_j \sum\limits_{i=1}^{m} (u_{ij} d_i^+ + v_{ij} d_i^-) \\ \text{subject to:} \\ \qquad E[f_i(\boldsymbol{x}, \boldsymbol{\xi})] + d_i^- - d_i^+ = b_i, \quad i = 1, 2, \cdots, m \\ \qquad E[g_j(\boldsymbol{x}, \boldsymbol{\xi})] \le 0, \qquad\qquad\quad j = 1, 2, \cdots, p \\ \qquad E[h_k(\boldsymbol{x}, \boldsymbol{\xi})] = 0, \qquad\qquad\quad k = 1, 2, \cdots, q \end{cases} \tag{13.3}$$

where P_j = the preemptive priority factor which expresses the relative importance of various goals, $P_j \gg P_{j+1}$, for all j, u_{ij} = weighting factor corresponding to positive deviation for goal i with priority j assigned, v_{ij} = weighting factor corresponding to negative deviation for goal i with priority j assigned, d_i^+ = positive deviation from the target of goal i, d_i^- = negative deviation from the target of goal i, f_i = a function in goal constraints, b_i = the target value according to goal i, l = number of priorities, m = number of goal constraints, and p = number of real constraints.

13.3 Chance-Constrained Programming

A chance-constrained programming (CCP) with uncertain coefficients may be written as follows,

$$\begin{cases} \max \overline{f} \\ \text{subject to:} \\ \qquad \text{Ch}\left\{f(\boldsymbol{x}, \boldsymbol{\xi}) \geq \overline{f}\right\} \geq \beta \\ \qquad \text{Ch}\left\{g_j(\boldsymbol{x}, \boldsymbol{\xi}) \leq 0, j = 1, 2, \cdots, p\right\} \geq \alpha \end{cases} \tag{13.4}$$

where α and β are predetermined confidence levels to constraints and objective, $\text{Ch}\{\cdot\}$ denotes the chance of the event in $\{\cdot\}$, especially, $\text{Ch}\{\cdot\}$ is $\Pr\{\cdot\}$ in a stochastic environment, $\text{Ch}\{\cdot\}$ is $\text{Pos}\{\cdot\}$ in a fuzzy environment, and $\overline{f}$ will be the maximum value that the objective function $f(\boldsymbol{x}, \boldsymbol{\xi})$ achieves with at least confidence level β.

Chance-constrained multiobjective programming (CCMOP) may be written as follows,

$$\begin{cases} \max \left[\overline{f}_1, \overline{f}_2, \cdots, \overline{f}_m\right] \\ \text{subject to:} \\ \qquad \text{Ch}\left\{f_i(\boldsymbol{x}, \boldsymbol{\xi}) \geq \overline{f}_i\right\} \geq \beta_i, \quad i = 1, 2, \cdots, m \\ \qquad \text{Ch}\left\{g_j(\boldsymbol{x}, \boldsymbol{\xi}) \leq 0\right\} \geq \alpha_j, \quad j = 1, 2, \cdots, p, \end{cases} \tag{13.5}$$

where α_j and β_i are predetermined confidence levels to the jth constraints and ith objectives, and $\overline{f}_i$ will be the maximum values that the objective functions $f_i(\boldsymbol{x}, \boldsymbol{\xi})$ achieve with at least confidence levels β_i, $j = 1, 2, \cdots, p$, $i = 1, 2, \cdots, m$, respectively.

We can also formulate an uncertain decision system as a chance-constrained goal programming (CCGP) according to the priority structure and target levels set by the decision-maker:

$$
\left\{
\begin{array}{ll}
\min \sum\limits_{j=1}^{l} P_j \sum\limits_{i=1}^{m} (u_{ij} d_i^+ + v_{ij} d_i^-) & \\
\text{subject to:} & \\
\qquad \mathrm{Ch}\left\{ f_i(\boldsymbol{x}, \boldsymbol{\xi}) + d_i^- - d_i^+ = b_i \right\} \ge \beta_i, & i = 1, 2, \cdots, m \\
\qquad \mathrm{Ch}\left\{ g_j(\boldsymbol{x}, \boldsymbol{\xi}) \le 0 \right\} \ge \alpha_j, & j = 1, 2, \cdots, p \\
\qquad d_i^-, d_i^+ \ge 0, & i = 1, 2, \cdots, m
\end{array}
\right. \tag{13.6}
$$

where P_j = the preemptive priority factor which expresses the relative importance of various goals, $P_j \gg P_{j+1}$, for all j, u_{ij} = weighting factor corresponding to positive deviation for goal i with priority j assigned, v_{ij} = weighting factor corresponding to negative deviation for goal i with priority j assigned, d_i^+ = positive deviation from the target of goal i, d_i^- = negative deviation from the target of goal i, f_i = a function in goal constraints, g_j = a function in real constraints, b_i = the target value according to goal i, l = number of priorities, m = number of goal constraints, and p = number of real constraints.

Note that in a CCGP, the positive and negative deviations are understood as the minimal nonnegative values of d_i^+ and d_i^- such that

$$
\mathrm{Ch}\left\{ d_i^+ \ge f_i(\boldsymbol{x}, \boldsymbol{\xi}) - b_i \right\} \ge \beta_i, \quad \mathrm{Ch}\left\{ d_i^- \ge b_i - f_i(\boldsymbol{x}, \boldsymbol{\xi}) \right\} \ge \beta_i \tag{13.7}
$$

for $i = 1, 2, \cdots, m$, respectively.

In fact, these CCP models are essentially types of maximax models (optimistic models) which maximize the maximum possible return. As opposed to maximax models, we can also construct a spectrum of minimax CCP models in which the underlying philosophy is based on selecting the alternative that provides the best of the worst possible return.

A single-objective minimax CCP model may be written as follows,

$$
\left\{
\begin{array}{l}
\max\limits_{\boldsymbol{x}} \min\limits_{\overline{f}} \overline{f} \\
\text{subject to:} \\
\qquad \mathrm{Ch}\left\{ f(\boldsymbol{x}, \boldsymbol{\xi}) \le \overline{f} \right\} \ge \beta \\
\qquad \mathrm{Ch}\left\{ g_j(\boldsymbol{x}, \boldsymbol{\xi}) \le 0, j = 1, 2, \cdots, p \right\} \ge \alpha
\end{array}
\right. \tag{13.8}
$$

where $\overline{f}$ will be the minimum value that the objective function $f(\boldsymbol{x}, \boldsymbol{\xi})$ achieves with at least confidence level β.

As an extension of single-objective case, the minimax CCMOP model is given by

$$\begin{cases} \max\limits_{\boldsymbol{x}} \left[\min\limits_{\overline{f}_1} \overline{f}_1, \min\limits_{\overline{f}_2} \overline{f}_2, \cdots, \min\limits_{\overline{f}_m} \overline{f}_m \right] \\ \text{subject to:} \\ \qquad \mathrm{Ch}\left\{ f_i(\boldsymbol{x}, \boldsymbol{\xi}) \le \overline{f}_i \right\} \ge \beta_i, \quad i = 1, 2, \cdots, m \\ \qquad \mathrm{Ch}\left\{ g_j(\boldsymbol{x}, \boldsymbol{\xi}) \le 0 \right\} \ge \alpha_j, \quad j = 1, 2, \cdots, p \end{cases} \tag{13.9}$$

where α_j and β_i are confidence levels for the constraints and objectives, and $\overline{f}_i$ should be the minimum values that the objective functions $f_i(\boldsymbol{x}, \boldsymbol{\xi})$ achieve with at least confidence levels β_i, $i = 1, 2, \cdots, m$, $j = 1, 2, \cdots, p$, respectively.

According to the priority structure and target levels set by the decision-maker, the CCGP model is written as follows,

$$\begin{cases} \min \sum\limits_{j=1}^{l} P_j \sum\limits_{i=1}^{m} (u_{ij} d_i^+ + v_{ij} d_i^-) \\ \text{subject to:} \\ \qquad \mathrm{Ch}\left\{ f_i(\boldsymbol{x}, \boldsymbol{\xi}) + d_i^- - d_i^+ = b_i \right\} \ge \beta_i, \quad i = 1, 2, \cdots, m \\ \qquad \mathrm{Ch}\left\{ g_j(\boldsymbol{x}, \boldsymbol{\xi}) \le 0 \right\} \ge \alpha_j, \quad j = 1, 2, \cdots, p \\ \qquad d_i^-, d_i^+ \ge 0, \quad i = 1, 2, \cdots, m. \end{cases} \tag{13.10}$$

Notice that the CCGP model is essentially a minimax model if the positive and negative deviations are understood as the *maximal* nonnegative values (rather than minimum in the minimin models) of d_i^+ and d_i^- such that

$$\mathrm{Ch}\left\{ d_i^+ \le f_i(\boldsymbol{x}, \boldsymbol{\xi}) - b_i \right\} \ge \beta_i, \quad \mathrm{Ch}\left\{ d_i^- \le b_i - f_i(\boldsymbol{x}, \boldsymbol{\xi}) \right\} \ge \beta_i \tag{13.11}$$

for $i = 1, 2, \cdots, m$, respectively, where the maximal nonnegative value means that if there are no positive d_i^+ and d_i^- satisfying the above inequalities, then we set $d_i^+ = 0$ and $d_i^- = 0$.

13.4 Dependent-Chance Programming

By *uncertain environment* we mean the solution set constrained by some uncertain conditions and generally represented by

$$g_j(\boldsymbol{x}, \boldsymbol{\xi}) \le 0, \quad j = 1, 2, \cdots, p \tag{13.12}$$

where $\boldsymbol{x}$ is a decision vector and $\boldsymbol{\xi}$ is a vector of uncertain parameters. Stochastic environment and fuzzy environment are two often-discussed uncertain environments.

A complex decision system usually undertakes multiple tasks and should satisfy some interior requirements. By *events* we mean these tasks and interior requirements.

The term *chance function* is the chance of satisfying an event and is represented by $f(\boldsymbol{x}) = \text{Ch}\{\text{the decision } \boldsymbol{x} \text{ satisfies the event}\}$.

A typical formulation of dependent-chance programming (DCP) with uncertain parameters is given as follows:

$$\begin{cases} \max\ f(\boldsymbol{x}) \\ \text{subject to:} \\ \qquad g_j(\boldsymbol{x}, \boldsymbol{\xi}) \leq 0, \quad j = 1, 2, \cdots, p \end{cases} \tag{13.13}$$

where $\boldsymbol{x}$ is a decision vector, $\boldsymbol{\xi}$ is an uncertain vector of parameters, $f(\boldsymbol{x})$ is a chance function of an event, and the uncertain environment is constrained as $g_j(\boldsymbol{x}, \boldsymbol{\xi}) \leq 0, j = 1, 2, \cdots, p$.

Since a complex decision system usually undertakes multiple tasks, there undoubtedly exist multiple potential objectives in the decision process. A dependent-chance multiobjective programming (DCMOP) with uncertain parameters has the following form,

$$\begin{cases} \max\ f(\boldsymbol{x}) = [f_1(\boldsymbol{x}), f_2(\boldsymbol{x}), \cdots, f_m(\boldsymbol{x})] \\ \text{subject to:} \\ \qquad g_j(\boldsymbol{x}, \boldsymbol{\xi}) \leq 0, \quad j = 1, 2, \cdots, p \end{cases} \tag{13.14}$$

where $f(\boldsymbol{x})$ is a vector of m functions $f_i(\boldsymbol{x})$, $i = 1, 2, \cdots, m$ in which some may be conventional rather than chance functions.

We can also formulate an uncertain decision system as a dependent-chance goal programming (DCGP) according to the priority structure and target levels set by the decision-maker,

$$\begin{cases} \min \sum\limits_{j=1}^{l} P_j \sum\limits_{i=1}^{m} (u_{ij} d_i^+ + v_{ij} d_i^-) \\ \text{subject to:} \\ \qquad f_i(\boldsymbol{x}) + d_i^- - d_i^+ = b_i, \quad i = 1, 2, \cdots, m \\ \qquad g_j(\boldsymbol{x}, \boldsymbol{\xi}) \leq 0, \qquad\qquad j = 1, 2, \cdots, p \\ \qquad d_i^-, d_i^+ \geq 0, \qquad\qquad\ \ i = 1, 2, \cdots, m \end{cases} \tag{13.15}$$

where P_j = the preemptive priority factor which expresses the relative importance of various goals, $P_j \gg P_{j+1}$, for all j, u_{ij} = weighting factor corresponding to positive deviation for goal i with priority j assigned, v_{ij} = weighting factor corresponding to negative deviation for goal i with priority j assigned, d_i^+ = positive deviation from the target of goal i, d_i^- = negative deviation from the target of goal i, f_i = a chance function or a conventional real-valued function in goal constraints, b_i = the target value according to goal i, l = number of priorities, m = number of goal constraints.

13.5 Further Research

From the theoretical viewpoint, different versions of uncertain programming will be created for different uncertain environments and more general mathematical analysis is needed. We have discussed single-objective programming, multiobjective programming, and goal programming in uncertain environments. We should also discuss multilevel programming, dynamic programming, and so forth in uncertain environments. For the mathematical properties of uncertain programming, we should consider sensitive analysis, upper/lower bound, dual theorems, optimality conditions, and so on.

From the computational viewpoint, we should design more effective computer algorithms. A series of simulation-based genetic algorithms has been presented in this book. However, these algorithms are only applicable to small-sized problems. In order to solve large-sized problems, we may try other intelligent computations such as neural networks and simulated annealing. Parallel computation is also worth mentioning. In addition, we may design some classical algorithms for special-structured uncertain programming in the light of mathematical properties.

From the applied viewpoint, the most useful lines of advance are likely to be generated in the different applied fields such as supply-allocation problem, production planning, scheduling, inventory network, queueing system, manufacturing system, finance, energy system, capital budgeting, system reliability, environmental protection, pattern recognition, vehicle routing, quality control, and risk analysis.

Appendix: The Laws of Large Numbers

The laws of large numbers are frequently used throughout this book. The purpose of this appendix is to provide some fundamental knowledge in this area.

First we introduce two concepts of convergence—convergence in probability and almost sure convergence.

Convergence in Probability. Suppose that $\{\xi_n\}$ is a sequence of random variables. The sequence $\{\xi_n\}$ is said to be convergent to a constant b in probability if for any given number $\epsilon > 0$,

$$\lim_{n\to\infty} \Pr\{|\xi_n - b| < \epsilon\} = 1.$$

Almost Sure Convergence. Suppose that $\{\xi_n\}$ is a sequence of random variables. The sequence $\{\xi_n\}$ is said to be convergent a. s. (almost surely) to a constant b if

$$\Pr\left\{\lim_{n\to\infty} \xi_n = b\right\} = 1.$$

We next provide the Chebyshev inequality, the weak law of large numbers and the strong law of large numbers without proofs. The interested reader may consult textbooks dealing with probability and statistics.

The Chebyshev Inequality. Let ξ be a random variable for which the variance $V(\xi)$ exists. Then for any given number $t > 0$,

$$\Pr\{|\xi - E(\xi)| > t\} \le \frac{V(\xi)}{t^2}.$$

The Weak Law of Large Numbers. Let $\{\xi_n\}$ be a sequence of independent random variables with $E(\xi_n^2) < \infty$ and $V(\xi_n) \le a$ for some number

a and all n. Let $S_n = \sum_{k=1}^{n} \xi_k$, $n = 1, 2, 3, \cdots$. Then $(S_n - E(S_n))/n$ converges to 0 in probability.

The Strong Law of Large Numbers. Let $\{\xi_n\}$ be a sequence of independent, identically distributed random variables with a common mean μ. Let $S_n = \sum_{k=1}^{n} \xi_k$, $n = 1, 2, 3, \cdots$ Then the sequence $\{S_n/n\}$ converges almost surely (a.s.) to μ.

Finally, we present some examples to illustrate the applications of the laws of large numbers. They are also the theoretical fundamentals of algorithms used in this book.

Example 1: Let f be an integrable function and $\Phi(\boldsymbol{\xi})$ be a probability distribution function. Our problem is to calculate the stochastic integral $\int f(\boldsymbol{\xi}) d\Phi(\boldsymbol{\xi})$. Now we suppose that $\{\boldsymbol{\xi}_n\}$ is a sequence of independent, identically distributed random variables with the common probability distribution function $\Phi(\boldsymbol{\xi})$. It is clear that the mean values

$$E(f(\boldsymbol{\xi}_n)) = \int f(\boldsymbol{\xi}) d\Phi(\boldsymbol{\xi})$$

for all n. It follows from the strong law of large numbers that

$$\frac{\sum_{n=1}^{N} f(\boldsymbol{\xi}_n)}{N} \longrightarrow \int f(\boldsymbol{\xi}) d\Phi(\boldsymbol{\xi}), \qquad \text{a. s.}$$

as $N \to \infty$. Therefore, by using a random number generator to generate $\boldsymbol{\xi}_n$, we can compute the integral numerically.

Example 2: Now we make N trials of tossing a coin with constant probability p of success (heads). Let N' be the number of successes, then N'/N is the relative frequency of success in N trials. Now for any $n = 1, 2, \cdots, N$, let $\xi_n = 1$ if a head is obtained on the nth toss and let $\xi_n = 0$ if a tail is obtained on the nth toss. Then $\{\xi_n\}$ is a sequence of random variables with a common mean p. Since $N' = \sum_{k=1}^{N} \xi_n$ always holds, by the strong law of large numbers, we know that

$$\frac{N'}{N} = \frac{\sum_{n=1}^{N} \xi_n}{N}$$

converges a.s. to p. Thus, for sufficiently large N it is reasonable to expect that N'/N will be close to p.

Example 3: Let $\boldsymbol{\xi}$ be a random vector, and g_i be real-valued functions, $i = 1, 2, \cdots, m$. Then $g_i(\boldsymbol{\xi})$ are also random variables for $i = 1, 2, \cdots, m$. Now we consider the system of inequalities, $g_i(\boldsymbol{\xi}) \le 0$, $i = 1, 2, \cdots, m$, which holds with the probability

$$p = \Pr\{g_i(\boldsymbol{\xi}) \le 0,\ i = 1, 2, \cdots, m\}.$$

Just as in the case of tossing a coin, we make N trials by producing N random vectors $\boldsymbol{\xi}_n$, $n = 1, 2, \cdots, N$, and N' is the number of occasions on which $g_i(\boldsymbol{\xi}_n) \le 0$, $i = 1, 2, \cdots, m$ for $n = 1, 2, \cdots, N$ (i.e., the number of random vectors satisfying the system of inequalities). Let us define

$$f(\boldsymbol{\xi}_n) = \begin{cases} 1, & \text{if } g_i(\boldsymbol{\xi}_n) \le 0, i = 1, 2, \cdots, m \\ 0, & \text{otherwise,} \end{cases}$$

then we have $E[f(\boldsymbol{\xi}_n)] = p$ for all n and $N' = \sum_{n=1}^{N} f(\boldsymbol{\xi}_n)$. It follows from the strong law of large numbers that

$$\frac{N'}{N} = \frac{\sum\limits_{n=1}^{N} f(\boldsymbol{\xi}_n)}{N}$$

converges a.s. to p. Thus the probability p can be estimated by N'/N provided that N is sufficiently large.

Example 4: Suppose that $\boldsymbol{\xi}$ is a random vector with probability distribution Φ and g is a real-valued function. The problem is to determine the maximal value $\overline{g}$ such that

$$\Pr\{g(\boldsymbol{\xi}) \ge \overline{g}\} \ge \alpha$$

where α is a predetermined confidence level with $0 < \alpha < 1$. Notice that the maximal value $\overline{g}$ must be achieved at the equality case

$$\Pr\{g(\boldsymbol{\xi}) \ge \overline{g}\} = \alpha.$$

Let $\{\boldsymbol{\xi}_1, \boldsymbol{\xi}_2, \cdots, \boldsymbol{\xi}_N\}$ be a sequence of random vectors sampled from the probability distribution function Φ. Now we define

$$f(\boldsymbol{\xi}_n) = \begin{cases} 1, & \text{if } g(\boldsymbol{\xi}_n) \ge \overline{g} \\ 0, & \text{otherwise} \end{cases} \qquad (n = 1, 2, \cdots, N)$$

which are a sequence of random variables, and $E[f(\boldsymbol{\xi}_n)] = \alpha$ for all n. By the strong law of large numbers, we obtain

$$\frac{\sum\limits_{n=1}^{N} f(\boldsymbol{\xi}_n)}{N} \longrightarrow \alpha, \quad \text{a. s.}$$

as $N \to \infty$. Notice that the sum $\sum_{n=1}^{N} f(\boldsymbol{\xi}_n)$ is just the number of $\boldsymbol{\xi}_n$ satisfying $g(\boldsymbol{\xi}_n) \geq \overline{g}$ for $n = 1, 2, \cdots, N$. Thus the value $\overline{g}$ can be taken as the N'th greatest element in the sequence $\{g(\boldsymbol{\xi}_1), g(\boldsymbol{\xi}_2), \cdots, g(\boldsymbol{\xi}_N)\}$, where N' is the integer part of αN.

Example 5: Several problems can be dealt with via the technique of sampling random variables. Now we try to determine the required number of samples. Suppose that the random variables $\xi_1, \xi_2, \cdots, \xi_N$ are sampled from some probability distribution with mean μ and variance σ^2. Let the arithmetic average of the N samples be

$$\overline{\xi} = \frac{1}{N}\left(\xi_1 + \xi_2 + \cdots + \xi_N\right).$$

Then the mean of $\overline{\xi}$ is

$$E(\overline{\xi}) = \frac{1}{N}\sum_{n=1}^{N} E(\xi_n) = \frac{1}{N} \cdot N\mu = \mu$$

and the variance of $\overline{\xi}$ is

$$V(\overline{\xi}) = \frac{1}{N^2} V\left(\sum_{n=1}^{N} \xi_n\right) = \frac{1}{N^2}\sum_{n=1}^{N} V(\xi_n) = \frac{1}{N^2} \cdot N \cdot \sigma^2 = \frac{\sigma^2}{N}$$

since the random variables ξ_n, $n = 1, 2, \cdots, N$ are independent. For any given number $t > 0$, the Chebyshev inequality implies that

$$\Pr\left\{|\overline{\xi} - \mu| \geq t\right\} \leq \frac{\sigma^2}{Nt^2}.$$

If we hope that the probability of $|\overline{\xi} - \mu| < t$ is at least α, then the sample size N must be such that $1 - \sigma^2/Nt^2 \leq \alpha$, that is

$$N \geq \frac{\sigma^2}{(1-\alpha)t^2}.$$

This means that $N = \sigma^2/(1-\alpha)t^2$ will be large enough to meet the specified confidence level α.

Bibliography

[1] Angelov, P., A generalized approach to fuzzy optimization, *International Journal of Intelligent Systems*, Vol. 9, 261–268, 1994.

[2] Bäck, T., *Evolutionary Algorithms in Theory and Practice*, Oxford University Press, New York, 1995.

[3] Balas, E., An additive algorithm for solving linear programs with zero-one variables, *Operations Research*, Vol. 13, 517–546, 1965.

[4] Bard, J.F., An algorithm for solving the general bilevel programming problem, *Mathematics of Operations Research*, Vol. 8, 260–272, 1983.

[5] Bard, J.F., and Moore, J.T., A branch and bound algorithm for the bilevel programming problem, *SIAM J. Sci. Statist. Comput.*, Vol. 11, 281–292, 1990.

[6] Bard, J.F., Optimality conditions for the bilevel programming problem, *Naval Research Logistics Quarterly*, Vol. 31, 13–26, 1984.

[7] Bazaraa, M.S., and Jarvis, J.J., *Linear Programming and Network Flows*, Wiley, New York, 1977.

[8] Bellman, R.E., *Dynamic Programming*, Princeton University Press, New Jersey, 1957.

[9] Bellman, R.E., and Zadeh, L.A., Decision making in a fuzzy environment, *Management Science*, Vol. 17, 141–164, 1970.

[10] Ben-Ayed, O., and Blair, C.E., Computational difficulties of bilevel linear programming, *Operations Research*, Vol. 38, 556–560, 1990.

[11] Ben-Ayed, O., Bilevel linear programming, *Computers and Operations Research*, Vol. 20, No. 5, 485–501, 1993.

[12] Bertsekas, D.P., and Tsitsiklis, J.N., *Parallel and Distributed Computation: Numerical Methods*, Prentice-Hall, Englewood Cliffs, NJ, 1989.

[13] Bialas, W.F., and Karwan, M.H., Two-level linear programming, *Management Science*, Vol. 30, 1004–1020, 1984.

[14] Bit, A.K., Biswal, M.P., and Alam, S.S., Fuzzy programming approach to multicriteria decision making transportation problem, *Fuzzy Sets and Systems*, Vol. 50, 135–141, 1992.

[15] Bouchon-Meunier, B., Kreinovich, V., Lokshin, A., and Nguyen, H.T., On the formulation of optimization under elastic constraints (with control in mind), *Fuzzy Sets and Systems*, Vol. 81, 5–29, 1996.

[16] Bratley, P., Fox, B.L., and Schrage, L.E., *A Guide to Simulation*, Springer-Verlag, New York, 1987.

[17] Buckley, J.J., and Hayashi, Y., Fuzzy genetic algorithm and applications, *Fuzzy Sets and Systems*, Vol. 61, 129–136, 1994.

[18] Candler, W. and Townsley, R., A linear two-level programming problem, *Computers and Operations Research*, Vol. 9, 59–76, 1982.

[19] Changchit, C. and Terrell, M.P., CCGP model for multiobjective reservoir systems, *Journal of Water Resources Planning and Management*, Vol. 115, No. 5, 658–670, 1989.

[20] Chankong, V. and Haims, Y.Y., *Multiobjective Decision Making: Theory and Methodology*, North-Holland, Amsterdam, 1983.

[21] Charnes, A. and Cooper, W.W., Chance-constrained programming, *Management Science*, Vol. 6, No. 1, 73–79, 1959.

[22] Charnes, A. and Cooper, W.W., *Management Models and Industrial Applications of Linear Programming*, Wiley, New York, 1961.

[23] Charnes, A. and Cooper, W.W., Chance constraints and normal deviates, *Journal of the American Statistical Association*, Vol. 57, 134–148, 1962.

[24] Charnes, A. and Cooper, W.W., Deterministic equivalents for optimizing and satisficing under chance-constraints, *Operations Research*, Vol. 11, No. 1, 18–39, 1963.

[25] Charnes, A. and Cooper, W.W., Goal programming and multiple objective optimizations: Part I, *European Journal of Operational Research*, Vol. 1, No. 1, 39–54, 1977.

[26] Chanas, S., Fuzzy programming in multiobjective linear programming—a parametric approach, *Fuzzy Sets and Systems*, Vol. 29, 303–313, 1989.

[27] Clayton, E., Weber, W., and Taylor III, B., A goal programming approach to the optimization of multiresponse simulation models, *IIE Trans.*, Vol. 14, 282–287, 1982.

[28] Dakin, R.J., A tree search algorithm for mixed integer programming problems, *Computer Journal*, Vol. 8, 250–255, 1965.

[29] Dantzig, G.B., *Linear Programming and Extensions*, Princeton University Press, 1963.

[30] De, P.K., Acharya, D., and Sahu, K.C., A chance-constrained goal programming model for capital budgeting, *Journal of the Operational Research Society*, Vol. 33, 635–638, 1982.

[31] Delgado, M., Verdegay, J.L., and Vila, M.A., A general model for fuzzy linear programming, *Fuzzy Sets and Systems*, Vol. 29, 21–29, 1989.

[32] Dempster, M.A.H.(ed), *Stochastic Programming*, Academic Press, London, 1980.

[33] Dharmadhikari, S. and Joag-dev, K., *Unimodality, Convexity, and Applications*, Academic Press, New York, 1988.

[34] Dubois, D. and Prade, H., *Fuzzy Sets and Systems, Theory and Applications*, Academic Press, New York, 1980.

[35] Dubois, D. and Prade, H., *Possibility Theory*, Plenum, New York, 1988.

[36] Dubois, D. and Prade, H., Fuzzy numbers: An overview, in *Analysis of Fuzzy Information*, Vol. 2, 3–39, Bezdek, J.C. (Ed.), CRC Press, Boca Raton, 1988.

[37] Dyer, J., Interactive goal programming, *Management Science,* Vol. 19, 62–70, 1972.

[38] Elmaghraby, S., *Activity Networks: Project Planning and Control by Network Models*, Wiley, New York, 1977.

[39] Ermoliev, Y. and Wets, R.J.-B.(eds), *Numerical Techniques for Stochastic Optimization*, Springer-Verlag, Berlin, 1988.

[40] Esogbue, A.O. and Bellman, R.E., Fuzzy dynamic programming and its extensions, *TIMS/Studies in the Management Sciences*, Vol. 20, 147–167, 1984.

[41] Filer, D., Fuzzy modeling of complex systems, *International Journal of Approximate Reasoning*, Vol. 5, 281–290, 1991.

[42] Fishman, G.S., *Monte Carlo: Concepts, Algorithms, and Applications*, Springer-Verlag, New York, 1996.

[43] Flachs, J. and Pollatschek, M.A., Further results on fuzzy mathematical programming, *Information and Control*, Vol. 38, 241–257, 1978.

[44] Fogel, D.B., An introduction to simulated evolutionary optimization, *IEEE Transactions on Neural Networks,* Vol. 5, 3–14, 1994.

[45] Fogel, D.B., *Evolution Computation: Toward a New Philosophy of Machine Intelligence*, IEEE Press, Piscataway, NJ, 1995.

[46] Foulds, L.R., *Optimization Techniques: An Introduction*, Springer-Verlag, New York, 1981.

[47] Garfinkel, R.S. and Nemhauser, G.L., *Integer Programming*, Wiley, New York, 1972.

[48] Gen, M. and Liu, B., Evolution program for production plan problem, *Engineering Design and Automation*, Vol. 1, No. 3, 199–204, 1995.

[49] Gen, M., Liu, B., and Ida K., Evolution program for deterministic and stochastic optimizations, *European Journal of Operational Research*, Vol. 94, No. 3, 618–625, 1996.

[50] Gen, M. and Liu, B., Evolution program for optimal capacity expansion, *Journal of Operations Research Society of Japan*, Vol. 40, No. 1, 1–9, 1997.

[51] Gen, M. and Liu, B., A genetic algorithm for nonlinear goal programming, *Evolutionary Optimization*, Vol.1, No.2, 1999.

[52] Goldberg, D.E., *Genetic Algorithms in Search, Optimization and Machine Learning,* Addison-Wesley, MA, 1989.

[53] Gomory, R.E, Outline of an algorithm for integer solutions to linear programs, *Bull. Amer. Math. Soc.*, Vol. 64, 275–278, 1958.

[54] Greenberg, N., *Integer Programming,* Academic Press, New York, 1971.

[55] Gu, J. and Tang, X., An application of MCDM in water resources problems, *Journal of Multi-Criteria Decision Analysis*, Vol. 5, 279–290, 1996.

[56] Hammersley, I.M. and Handscomb, D.C., *Monte Carlo Methods*, Wiley, New York, 1964.

[57] Hillier, F.S., Chance-constrained programming with 0-1 or bounded continuous decision variables, *Management Science*, Vol. 14, No. 1, 34–56, 1967.

[58] Holland, J.H., *Adaptation in Natural and Artificial Systems*, University of Michigan Press, Ann Arbor, 1975.

[59] Hwang, C. and Masud, A., *Multiple Objective Decision Making Methods and Applications,* Springer-Verlag, New York, 1979.

[60] Hwang, C.L., Paidy, S.R., Yoon, K., and Masud, A.S.M., Mathematical programming with multiple objectives: A tutorial, *Computers and Operations Research*, Vol. 7, 5–31, 1980.

[61] Hu, T.C., *Integer Programming and Network Flows*, Addison-Wesley, MA, 1969.

[62] Ignizio, J., *Goal Programming and Extensions,* Heath, Lexington, MA, 1976.

[63] Iwamura, K. and Liu, B., A genetic algorithm for chance constrained programming, *Journal of Information & Optimization Sciences*, Vol. 17, No. 2, 40–47, 1996.

[64] Iwamura, K. and Liu, B., Chance constrained integer programming models for capital budgeting in fuzzy environments, *Journal of the Operational Research Society*, Vol. 49, No. 8, 854–860, 1998.

[65] Iwamura, K. and Liu, B., Stochastic operation models for open inventory networks, *Journal of Information & Optimization Sciences*, Vol.20, No. 3, 1999.

[66] Iwamura, K. and Liu, B., Dependent-chance integer programming applied to capital budgeting, to appear in *Journal of the Operations Research Society of Japan.*

[67] Kall, P., *Stochastic Linear Programming*, Springer-Verlag, Berlin, 1976.

[68] Kall, P. and Wallace, S.W., *Stochastic Programming,* Wiley, Chichester, 1994.

[69] Kaufman, A., *Introduction to the Theory of Fuzzy Subsets*, Academic Press, New York, 1975.

[70] Kaufman, A. and Gupta, M.M., *Introduction to Fuzzy Arithmetic: Theory and Applications*, Van Nostrand Reinhold, New York, 1985.

[71] Kaufman, A. and Gupta, M.M., *Fuzzy Mathematical Models in Engineering and Management Science*, 2nd ed., North-Holland, Amsterdam, 1991.

[72] Keeney, R.L. and Raiffa, H., *Decisions with Multiple Objectives: Preferences and Value Tradeoffs*, Wiley, New York, 1976.

[73] Keown, A.J. and Martin, J.D., A chance constrained goal programming model for working capital management, *Engng Econ.*, Vol. 22, 153–174, 1977.

[74] Keown, A.J., A chance-constrained goal programming model for bank liquidity management, *Decision Sciences*, Vol. 9, 93–106, 1978.

[75] Keown, A.J. and Taylor, B.W., A chance-constrained integer goal programming model for capital budgeting in the production area, *Journal of the Operational Research Society*, Vol. 31, No. 7, 579–589, 1980.

[76] Klein G., Moskowitz, H. and Ravindran, A., Interactive multiobjective optimization under uncertainty, *Management Science*, Vol. 36, No. 1, 58–75, 1990.

[77] Klir, G.J. and Folger, T.A., *Fuzzy Sets, Uncertainty, and Information*, Prentice-Hall, Englewood Cliffs, NJ, 1980.

[78] Kolbin, V.V., *Stochastic Programming*, D.Reidel, Dordrecht, 1977.

[79] Koza, J.R., *Genetic Programming*, MIT Press, Cambridge, MA, 1992.

[80] Koza, J.R., *Genetic Programming, II*, MIT Press, Cambridge, MA, 1994.

[81] Lai, Y.-J. and Hwang, C.-L., *Fuzzy Multiple Objective Decision Making: Methods and Applications*, Springer-Verlag, New York, 1994.

[82] Law, A.M. and Kelton, W.D., *Simulation Modelling & Analysis*, 2nd edition, McGraw-Hill, New York, 1991.

[83] Lee, S.M., *Goal Programming for Decision Analysis*, Auerbach, Philadelphia, 1972.

[84] Lee, S.M. and Olson, D.L., A gradient algorithm for chance constrained nonlinear goal programming, *European Journal of Operational Research*, Vol. 22, 359–369, 1985.

[85] Liu, B. and Ku, C., Dependent-chance goal programming and an application, *Journal of Systems Engineering & Electronics*, Vol. 4, No. 2, 40–47, 1993.

[86] Liu, B., Dependent-chance goal programming and its genetic algorithm based approach, *Mathematical and Computer Modelling*, Vol. 24, No. 7, 43–52, 1996.

[87] Liu, B. and Esogbue, A.O., Fuzzy criterion set and fuzzy criterion dynamic programming, *Journal of Mathematical Analysis and Applications*, Vol. 199, No. 1, 293–311, 1996.

[88] Liu, B., Dependent-chance programming: A class of stochastic programming, *Computers & Mathematics with Applications*, Vol. 34, No. 12, 89–104, 1997.

[89] Liu, B. and Iwamura, K., Modelling stochastic decision systems using dependent-chance programming, *European Journal of Operational Research*, Vol. 101, No. 1, 193–203, 1997.

[90] Liu, B. and Iwamura, K., Chance constrained programming with fuzzy parameters, *Fuzzy Sets and Systems*, Vol. 94, No. 2, 227–237, 1998.

[91] Liu, B. and Iwamura, K., A note on chance constrained programming with fuzzy coefficients, *Fuzzy Sets and Systems*, Vol. 100, Nos. 1–3, 229–233, 1998.

[92] Liu, B., Outline of uncertain programming, *Proceedings of the Third International Symposium on Operations Research and Applications*, p. 480–489, Kunming, China, August 19–22, 1998.

[93] Liu, B., Stackelberg-Nash equilibrium for multilevel programming with multiple followers using genetic algorithms, *Computers & Mathematics with Applications*, Vol. 36, No. 7, 79–89, 1998.

[94] Liu, B., Uncertain programming: Modelling, evolutionary computation and applications, *Proceedings of Fourth Joint Conference on Information Sciences*, Vol. 3, p. 433–437, North Carolina, October 23–28, 1998,

[95] Liu, B., Minimax chance constrained programming models for fuzzy decision systems, *Information Sciences*, Vol. 112, Nos. 1–4, 25–38, 1998.

[96] Liu, B. and Zhao, R., *Stochastic Programming and Fuzzy Programming*, Tsinghua University Press, Beijing, 1998.

[97] Liu, B. and Esogbue, A.O., *Decision Criteria and Optimal Inventory Processes*, Kluwer Academic Publishers, Boston, 1999.

[98] Liu, B., Uncertain programming: A unifying optimization theory in various uncertain environments, *Proceedings of International Workshop on Computation, Optimization and Control, the 7th Bellman Continuum*, Santa Fe, New Mcxico, May 24–25, 1999.

[99] Liu, B., Dependent-chance programming in fuzzy environments, to appear in *Fuzzy Sets and Systems.*

[100] Liu, B., Dependent-chance programming with fuzzy decisions, *IEEE Transactions on Fuzzy Systems*, Vol. 7, No. 3, 1999.

[101] Liu, B. and Iwamura, K., Fuzzy programming with fuzzy decisions and fuzzy simulation based genetic algorithm, to appear in *Fuzzy Sets and Systems.*

[102] Liu, B., Uncertain programming: A tutorial, Technical Report, Tsinghua University, 1998.

[103] Luhandjula, M.K., Linear programming under randomness and fuzziness, *Fuzzy Sets and Systems*, Vol. 10, 45–55, 1983.

[104] Luhandjula, M.K., On possibilistic linear programming, *Fuzzy Sets and Systems*, Vol. 18, 15–30,1986.

[105] Luhandjula, M.K., Fuzzy optimization: An appraisal, *Fuzzy Sets and Systems*, Vol. 30, 257–282, 1989.

[106] Luhandjula, M.K., Fuzziness and randomness in an optimization framework, *Fuzzy Sets and Systems*, Vol. 77, 291–297, 1996.

[107] Mareš, M., *Computation Over Fuzzy Quantities*, CRC Press, Boca Raton, 1994.

[108] Mareschal, B., Stochastic multicriteria decision making and uncertainty, *European Journal of Operational Research,* Vol. 26, No. 1, 58–64, 1986.

[109] Martel, A. and Price, W., Stochastic programming applied to human resource planning, *Journal of the Operational Research Society*, Vol. 32, 187–196, 1981.

[110] Masud, A. and Hwang, C., Interactive sequential goal programming, *Journal of the Operational Research Society,* Vol. 32, 391–400, 1981.

[111] Michalewicz, Z., *Genetic Algorithms + Data Structures = Evolution Programs,* 3rd ed., Springer-Verlag, Berlin, 1996.

[112] Mital, K.V., *Optimization Methods*, Wiley, New York, 1976.

[113] Mitchell, M., *An Introduction to Genetic Algorithms*, MIT Press, Cambridge, MA, 1996.

[114] Morgan, B., *Elements of Simulation*, Chapamn & Hall, London, 1984.

[115] Morgan, D.R., Eheart, J.W., and Valocchi, A.J., Aquifer remediation design under uncertainty using a new chance constrained programming technique, *Water Resources Research*, Vol. 29, No. 3, 551–561, 1993.

[116] Mukherjee, S.P., Mixed strategies in chance-constrained programming, *Journal of the Operational Research Society*, Vol. 31, 1045–1047, 1980.

[117] Odanaka, T., *Dynamic Management Decision and Stochastic Control Processes*, World Scientific, Singapore, 1990.

[118] Ostasiewicz, W., A new approach to fuzzy programming, *Fuzzy Sets and Systems*, Vol. 7, 139–152, 1982.

[119] Negoita, C.V. and Ralescu, D., On fuzzy optimization, *Kybernetes*, Vol. 6, 193–195, 1977.

[120] Puri, M.L. and Ralescu, D., Fuzzy random variables, *Journal of Mathematical Analysis and Applications*, Vol. 114, 409–422, 1986.

[121] Ramer, A., Conditional possibility measures, *International Journal of Cybernetics and Systems*, Vol. 20, 233–247, 1989.

[122] Rockafellar, R.T., *Network Flows and Monotropic Optimization*, John Wiley & Sons, New York, 1984.

[123] Rubinstein, R.Y., *Simulation and the Monte Carlo Method*, Wiley, New York, 1981.

[124] Saade, J.J., Maximization of a function over a fuzzy domain, *Fuzzy Sets and Systems*, Vol. 62, 55–70, 1994.

[125] Saber, H.M. and Ravindran, A., Nonlinear goal programming theory and practice: A survey, *Computers and Operations Research*, Vol. 20, 275–291, 1993.

[126] Salkin, H.M., *Integer Programming*, Addison-Wesley, MA, 1974.

[127] Savard, G. and Gauvin, J., The steepest descent direction for nonlinear bilevel programming problem, *Operations Research Letters*, Vol. 15, 265–272, 1994.

[128] Schneider, M. and Kandel, A., Properties of the fuzzy expected value and the fuzzy expected interval in fuzzy environment, *Fuzzy Sets and Systems*, Vol. 26, 373–385, 1988.

[129] Sengupta, J.K., *Stochastic Programming: Methods and Applications*, North-Holland, Amsterdam, 1972.

[130] Shin, W.S. and Ravindran, A., Interactive multiple objective optimization: Survey I - continuous case, *Computers and Operations Research*, Vol. 18, No. 1, 97–114, 1991.

[131] Simmons, D.M., *Nonlinear Programming for Operations Research*, Prentice-Hall, Englewood Cliffs, NJ, 1975.

[132] Sivazlian, B.D. and Stanfel, L.E., *Optimization Techniques in Operations Research*, Prentice-Hall, Englewood Cliffs, NJ, 1975.

[133] Slowinski, R. and Teghem, Jr. J., Fuzzy versus stochastic approaches to multicriteria linear programming under uncertainty, *Naval Research Logistics*, Vol. 35, 673–695, 1988.

[134] Smith, J., *Computer Simulation Methods*, Hafner, New York, 1968.

[135] Sommer, G. and Pollatschek, M.A., A fuzzy programming approach to an air pollution regulation problem, *European Journal of Operational Research*, Vol. 10, 303–313, 1978.

[136] Steuer, R.E., *Multiple Criteria Optimization: Theory, Computation and Application*, Wiley, New York, 1986.

[137] Taha, H.A., *Integer Programming*, Macmillan, New York, 1978.

[138] Tanaka, H. and Asai, K., Fuzzy linear programming problems with fuzzy numbers, *Fuzzy Sets and Systems*, Vol. 13, 1–10, 1984.

[139] Teghem, Jr. J., DuFrane, D. and Kunsch, P., STRANGE: An interactive method for multiobjective linear programming under uncertainty, *European Journal Operational Research*, Vol. 26, No. 1, 65–82, 1986.

[140] Vajda, S., *Probabilistic Programming*, Academic Press, New York, 1972.

[141] Van de Panne, C. and Popp, W., Minimum cost cattle feed under probabilistic protein constraints, *Management Science,* Vol. 9, 405–430, 1963.

[142] Wagner, B.J. and Gorelick, S.M., Optimal ground water quality management under parameter uncertainty, *Water Resources Research,* Vol. 23, No. 7, 1162–1174, 1987.

[143] Weistroffer, H., An interactive goal programming method for nonlinear multiple-criteria decision-making problems, *Computers and Operations Research,* Vol. 10, No. 4, 311–320, 1983.

[144] Whalen, T., Decision making under uncertainty with various assumptions about available information, *IEEE Transactions on Systems, Man and Cybernetics*, Vol. 14, 888–900, 1984.

[145] Williams, H.P., *Model Building in Mathematical Programming*, Wiley, New York, 1978.

[146] Yager, R.R., Mathematical programming with fuzzy constraints and a preference on the objective, *Kybernetes*, Vol. 9, 285–291, 1979.

[147] Yager, R.R., On ordered weighted averaging aggregation operators in multicriteria decision making, *IEEE Transactions on Systems, Man and Cybernetics*, Vol. 18, 183–190, 1988.

[148] Yager, R.R., On the specificity of a possibility distribution, *Fuzzy Sets and Systems*, Vol. 50, 279–292, 1992.

[149] Yazenin, A.V., Fuzzy and stochastic programming, *Fuzzy Sets and Systems*, Vol. 22, 171–180, 1987.

[150] Yazenin, A.V., On the problem of possibilistic optimization, *Fuzzy Sets and Systems*, Vol. 81, 133–140, 1996.

[151] Zadeh, L.A., Fuzzy sets, *Information and Control*, Vol. 8, 338–353, 1965.

[152] Zadeh, L.A., Outline of a new approach to the analysis of complex systems and decision processes, *IEEE Transactions on Systems, Man and Cybernetics*, Vol. 3, 28–44, 1973.

[153] Zadeh, L.A., Fuzzy sets as a basis for a theory of possibility, *Fuzzy Sets and Systems*, Vol. 1, 3–28, 1978.

[154] Zangwill, W.I., *Nonlinear Programming*, Prentice-Hall, Englewood Cliffs, NJ, 1969.

[155] Zhao, R., Iwamura, K., and Liu, B., Chance constrained integer programming and stochastic simulation based genetic algorithms, *Journal of Systems Science and Systems Engineering*, Vol. 7, No. 1, 96–102, 1998.

[156] Zimmermann, H.-J., Description and optimization of fuzzy systems, *International Journal of General Systems*, Vol. 2, 209–215, 1976.

[157] Zimmermann, H.-J., Fuzzy programming and linear programming with several objective functions, *Fuzzy Sets and Systems*, Vol. 3, 45–55, 1978.

[158] Zimmermann, H.-J., Fuzzy mathematical programming, *Computers and Operations Research*, Vol. 10, 291–298, 1983.

[159] Zimmermann, H.-J., Zadeh, L.A., and Gaines, B.R. (eds.), *Fuzzy Sets and Decision Analysis*, North-Holland, Amsterdam, New York, Oxford, 1984.

[160] Zimmermann, H.-J., Applications of fuzzy set theory to mathematical programming, *Information Science*, Vol. 36, 29–58, 1985.

[161] Zimmermann, H.-J., *Fuzzy Set Theory and its Applications*, Kluwer Academic Publishers, Boston, 1985.

[162] Zimmermann, H.-J., Applications of fuzzy set theory to mathematical programming, *Information Sciences*, Vol. 36, 29–58, 1985.

List of Frequently Used Symbols

x, y	decision variables
$\tilde{x}$, $\tilde{y}$	fuzzy decision variables
$\boldsymbol{x}$, $\boldsymbol{y}$	decision vectors
$\tilde{\boldsymbol{x}}$, $\tilde{\boldsymbol{y}}$	fuzzy decision vectors
$\tilde{a}$, $\tilde{b}$, $\tilde{c}$	fuzzy parameters
ξ, η, τ	stochastic or fuzzy parameters
$\boldsymbol{\xi}$, $\boldsymbol{\eta}$, $\boldsymbol{\tau}$	stochastic or fuzzy vectors of parameters
μ	membership function
ϕ	probability density function
Φ	probability distribution function
f, f_i	objective functions
g, g_j	constraint functions
Pr	probability measure
Pos	possibility measure
Ch	chance measure
α, β	confidence levels
d_i^+, d_i^-	positive and negative deviations
S	feasible set
$\Re$	set of real numbers
$\Re^n$	n-dimensional Euclidean space
$\vee$	maximum operator
$\wedge$	minimum operator
lexmin	lexicographical minimization
eval	evaluation function in genetic algorithms

Index

Uncertain Programming

Baoding Liu, Tsinghua University, China

Stochastic programming and fuzzy programming are two widely used tools of mathematical programming dealing with stochastic and fuzzy optimization problems. *Uncertain Programming* provides a unifying principle of stochastic programming and fuzzy programming, and lays a foundation for optimization theory in uncertain environments.

Three broad classes of uncertain programming are expected value models, chance-constrained programming, and dependent-chance programming. In order to solve uncertain programming models, the book presents a series of stochastic/fuzzy simulation-based genetic algorithms. Some applications of uncertain programming are also documented.

The book reflects the most recent developments and emphasizes modeling ideas, evolutionary computations, as well as applications of uncertain programming, rather than mathematical theorems and proofs. This should be a valuable reference work for researchers, engineers, and students in the field of operations research, management science, information science, system science, computer science, and engineering.